THE HISTORY

OF

FRANCE

RELATED FOR THE RISING GENERATION.

AMS PRESS
NEW YORK

Reprinted from the edition of 1876, London
First AMS EDITION published 1969
Manufactured in the United States of America

Library of Congress Catalogue Card Number: 73-91786

AMS PRESS, INC.
NEW YORK, N. Y. 10003

THE

HISTORY OF FRANCE

RELATED FOR THE RISING GENERATION.

FRANÇOIS PIERRE GUILLAUME GUIZOT,
Born Oct. 4, 1787; died Sept. 12, 1874.
(*After a Photograph by Reutlinger.*)

THE HISTORY

OF

FRANCE

FROM

THE EARLIEST TIMES TO THE YEAR 1789.

RELATED FOR THE RISING GENERATION BY

M. GUIZOT,

AUTHOR OF "THE HISTORY OF CIVILIZATION IN EUROPE," ETC.

TRANSLATED FROM THE FRENCH BY

ROBERT BLACK, M.A.

IN FIVE VOLUMES.

VOLUME THE FIFTH.

LONDON

SAMPSON LOW, MARSTON, SEARLE, & RIVINGTON,

CROWN BUILDINGS, 188, FLEET STREET.

1876.

PUBLISHERS' ADVERTISEMENT.

THE death of M. Guizot at Val-Richer took place whilst he was dictating the last pages of Vol. IV. of his *History of France* to his daughter, Madame de Witt. The work to which he had consecrated the last years of his life was thus left incomplete. M. Guizot had planned his fifth and last volume, comprising the reign of Louis XV. and that of Louis XVI., down to the period of the meeting of the Constituent Assembly in 1789. The outlines of the chapters had already been traced. It is upon the plan thus laid down by M. Guizot, and with the aid of his directions and notes, that Madame de Witt has edited this Fifth Volume, the completion of which the author entrusted to her as being the one most intimately acquainted with his views. It will thus be seen that, though not coming complete from his hands, the material of this fifth volume is the work of the great historian himself, whose deeply lamented death alone prevented his putting the finishing strokes to the monument which he desired to raise for the honour and instruction of the country which was so dear to him, and which he served to his latest breath.

Crown Buildings, Fleet Street, September, 1876.

TABLE OF CONTENTS.

LIST OF ILLUSTRATIONS.

LOUIS XVI.

CHAPTER LI.

LOUIS XV., THE REGENCY AND CARDINAL DUBOIS (1715—1723).

AT the very moment when the master's hand is missed from his work the narrative makes a sudden bound out of the simple times of history. Under Henry IV., under Richelieu, under Louis XIV., events found quite naturally their guiding hand and their centre; men as well as circumstances formed a group around the head of the nation, whether king or minister, to thence unfold themselves quite clearly before the eyes of posterity. Starting from the reign of Louis XV. the nation has no longer a head, history no longer a centre; at the same time with a master of the higher order, great servants also fail the French monarchy; it all at once collapses, betraying thus the exhaustion of Louis XIV.'s latter years; decadence is no longer veiled by the remnants of the splendour which was still reflected from the great king and his great reign; the glory of olden France descends slowly to its grave. At the same time, and in a future as yet obscured, intellectual progress begins to dawn; new ideas of justice, of humanity, of generous equity towards the masses

germinate sparsely in certain minds; it is no longer Christianity
alone that inspires them, though the honour is reflected upon it in
a general way and as regards the principles with which it has
silently permeated modern society, but they who contribute to
spread them refuse with indignation to acknowledge the source
whence they have drawn them.   Intellectual movement no longer
appertains exclusively to the higher classes, to the ecclesiastics,
or to the members of the parliaments; vaguely as yet, and retarded
by apathy in the government as well as by disorder in affairs, it
propagates and extends itself imperceptibly pending that signal
and terrible explosion of good and evil which is to characterize the
close of the eighteenth century.   Decadence and progress are
going on confusedly in the minds as well as in the material condition of the nation.   They must be distinguished and traced
without any pretence of separating them.

There we have the reign of Louis XV. in its entirety.

The regency of the duke of Orleans and the ministry of Cardinal
Dubois showed certain traits of the general tendencies and to a
certain extent felt their influence; they formed, however, a distinct epoch, abounding in original efforts and bold attempts,
which remained without result but which testified to the lively
reaction in men's minds against the courses and fundamental
principles of the reign which had just ended.

Louis XIV. had made no mistake about the respect which his
last wishes were destined to meet with after his death.   In spite
of the most extreme precautions, the secret of the will had tran-
spired, giving occasion for some days past to secret intrigues.
Scarcely had the king breathed his last, when the duke of Orleans
was urged to get the regency conferred upon him by the dukes
and peers, simply making to Parliament an announcement of what
had been done.   The duke of Orleans was a better judge of the
moral authority belonging to that important body; and it was to
the Palace of Justice that he repaired on the morning of September 2, 1715.   The crowd there was immense; the young king
alone was not there, in spite of his great-grandfather's express
instructions.   The day was a decisive one; the legitimatized
princes were present, " the duke of Maine bursting with joy,"

says St. Simon: "a smiling, satisfied air overrippled that of audacity, of confidence, which nevertheless peeped through, and the politeness which seemed to struggle against it. He bowed right and left, piercing every one with his looks. Towards the peers, the earnestness, it is not too much to say the respectfulness, the slowness, the profoundness of his bow was eloquent. His head remained lowered even on recovering himself." The duke of Orleans had just begun to speak; his voice was not steady; he repeated the terms of which the king had made use, he said, for the purpose of confiding the dauphin to his care: "To you I commend him; serve him faithfully as you have served me, and labour to preserve to him his kingdom; I have made such dispositions as I thought wisest; but one cannot foresee everything: if there is anything that does not seem good, it will of course be altered."

The favour of the assembly was plainly with him, and the prince's accents became more firm: "I shall never," said he, " have any other purpose but to relieve the people, to re-establish good order in the finances, to maintain peace at home and abroad, and to restore unity and tranquillity to the church; therein I shall be aided by the wise representations of this august assembly, and I hereby ask for them in anticipation." The parliament was completely won; the right of representation (or remonstrance) was promised them; the will of Louis XIV. was as good as annulled; it was opened, it was read, and so were the two codicils. All the authority was entrusted to a council of regency of which the duke of Orleans was to be the head, but without preponderating voice and without power to supersede any of the members, all designated in advance by Louis XIV.   The person and the education of the young king, as well as the command of the household troops, were entrusted to the duke of Maine.

" It was listened to in dead silence and with a sort of indignation which expressed itself in all countenances," says St. Simon. "The king, no doubt, did not comprehend the force of what he had been made to do," said the duke of Orleans; " he assured me in the last days of his life that I should find in his dispositions nothing that I was not sure to be pleased with, and he

himself referred the ministers to me on business, with all the orders
to be given." He asked, therefore, to have his regency declared
such as it ought to be, "full and independent, with free formation
of the council of regency." The duke of Maine wished to say a
word. "You shall speak in your turn, sir," said the duke of
Orleans in a dry tone. The court immediately decided in his favour
by acclamation, and even without proceeding in the regular way
to vote. There remained the codicils, which annulled in fact the
Regent's authority. A discussion began between the duke of
Orleans and the duke of Maine; it was causing Philip of Orleans
to lose the advantage he had just won; his friends succeeded in
making him perceive this, and he put off the session until after
dinner. When they returned to the Palace of Justice the codicils
were puffed away like the will by the breath of popular favour.
The Duke of Maine, despoiled of the command of the king's household, declared that, under such conditions, it was impossible for
him to be answerable for the king's person, and that he demanded
to be relieved of that duty." "Most willingly, sir," replied the
Regent, "your services are no longer required;" and he forthwith explained to the Parliament his intention of governing affairs
according to the plan which had been found among the papers of
the duke of Burgundy. "Those gentry know little or nothing of
the French and of the way to govern them," had been the remark
of Louis XIV. on reading the schemes of Fénelon, the duke of
Beauvilliers and St. Simon. The Parliament applauded the
formation of the six councils of foreign affairs, of finance, of war,
of the marine, of *home* or the interior, of *conscience* or ecclesiastical
affairs; the Regent was entrusted with the free disposal of graces:
"I want to be free for good," said he, adroitly repeating a phrase
from *Télémaque*, "I consent to have my hands tied for evil."

The victory was complete. Not a shred remained of Louis
XIV.'s will. The duke of Maine, confounded and humiliated,
retired to his castle of Scéaux, there to endure the reproaches of
his wife. The king's affection and Madame de Maintenon's clever
tactics had not sufficed to found his power; the remaining
vestiges of his greatness were themselves about to vanish before
long in their turn.

THE REGENT ORLEANS.

On the 12th of September, the little king held a bed of justice; his governess, Madame de Ventadour, sat alone at the feet of the poor orphan, abandoned on the pinnacle of power. All the decisions of September 2 were ratified in the child's name. Louis XIV. had just descended to the tomb without pomp and without regret.. The joy of the people broke out indecently as the funeral train passed by; the nation had forgotten the glory of the great king, it remembered only the evils which had for so long oppressed it during his reign.

The new councils had already been constituted, when it was discovered that commerce had been forgotten; and to it was assigned a seventh body. "Three sorts of men, the choice of whom was dictated by propriety, weakness and necessity, filled the lists : in the first place, great lords, veterans in intrigue but novices in affairs, and less useful from their influence than embarrassing from their pride and their pettinesses; next, the Regent's friends, the cream of the *roués*, possessed with the spirit of opposition and corruption, ignorant and clever, bold and lazy, and far better calculated to harass than to conduct a government; lastly, below them, were pitch-forked in, pell-mell, councillors of State, masters of requests, members of parliament, well informed and industrious gentlemen, fated henceforth to crawl about at the bottom of the committees and, without the spur of glory or emulation, to repair the blunders which must be expected from the incapacity of the first and the recklessness of the second class amongst their colleagues " [Lemontey, *Histoire de la Régence*, t. i. p. 67]. "It is necessary," the young king was made to say in the preamble to the ordinance which established the councils, " that affairs should be regulated rather by unanimous consent than by way of authority."

How singular are the monstrosities of inexperience! At the head of the council of finance a place was found for the duke of Noailles, active in mind and restless in character, without any fixed principles, an adroit and a shameless courtier, strict in all religious observances under Louis XIV. and a notorious debauchee under the Regency, but intelligent, insolent, ambitious, hungering and thirsting to do good if he could, but evil if need were and in order to arrive at his ends. His uncle, Cardinal Noailles, who had been but lately threatened by the court of Rome with the loss of his hat and who had seen himself forbidden to approach the dying king, was now president of the council of conscience. Marshal d'Huxelles, one of the negotiators who had managed the treaty of Utrecht, was at the head of foreign affairs. The Regent had reserved to himself one single department, the Academy of sciences. "I quite intend," said he gaily, "to ask the king, on his majority, to let me still be secretary of State of the Academy."

The Regent's predilection, consolidating the work of Colbert, contributed to the development of scientific researches, for which the neatness and clearness of French thought rendered it thenceforth so singularly well adapted.

The gates of the prison were meanwhile being thrown open to many a poor creature; the Jansenists left the Bastille; others, who had been for a long time past in confinement, were still ignorant of the grounds for their captivity, which was by this time forgotten by everybody. A wretched Italian, who had been arrested the very day of his arrival in Paris thirty-five years before, begged to remain in prison; he had no longer any family, or relatives or resources. For a while the Protestants thought they saw their advantage in the clemency with which the new reign appeared to be inaugurated, and began to meet again in their assemblies; the Regent had some idea of doing them justice, re-establishing the edict of Nantes and reopening to the exiles the doors of their country, but his councillors dissuaded him, the more virtuous, like St. Simon, from catholic piety, the more depraved from policy and indifference. However, the lot of the Protestants remained under the Regency less hard than it had been under Louis XIV. and than it became under the duke of Bourbon.

The chancellor, Voysin, had just died. To this post the Regent summoned the attorney-general, D'Aguesseau, beloved and esteemed of all, learned, eloquent, virtuous, but too exclusively a man of parliament for the functions which had been confided to him. "He would have made a sublime premier president," said St. Simon, who did not like him. The magistrate was attending mass at St. André-des-Arts; he was not ignorant of the chancellor's death, when a valet came in great haste to inform him that the Regent wanted him at the Palais-Royal. D'Aguesseau piously heard out the remainder of the mass before obeying the prince's orders. The casket containing the seals was already upon the table. The duke of Orleans took the attorney-general by the arm and, going out with him into the gallery thronged with courtiers, said: " Gentlemen, here is your new and most worthy chancellor! " and he took him away with him to the Tuileries to pay his respects to the little king.

On returning home, still all in a whirl, D'Aguesseau went up to the room of his brother, " M. de Valjouan, a sort of Epicurean (*voluptueux*) philosopher, with plenty of wit and learning, but altogether one of the oddest creatures." He found him in his dressing-gown, smoking in front of the fire. " Brother," said he as he entered, " I have come to tell you that I am chancellor." " Chancellor! " said the other, turning round: " and what have you done with the other one?" " He died suddenly to-night." " Oh! very well, brother, I'm very glad; I would rather it were you than I :" and he resumed his pipe. Madame d'Aguesseau was better pleased. Her husband has eulogized her handsomely : " A wife like mine," he said, " is a good man's highest reward."

The new system of government, as yet untried and confided to men for the most part little accustomed to affairs, had to put up with the most formidable difficulties and to struggle against the most painful position. The treasury was empty and the country exhausted; the army was not paid, and the most honourable men, such as the duke of St. Simon, saw no other remedy for the evils of the State but a total bankruptcy and the convocation of the States-general. Both expedients were equally repugnant to the duke of Orleans. The duke of Noailles had entered upon a course of severe economy; the king's household was diminished, twenty-five thousand men were struck off the strength of the army, exemption from talliage for six years was promised to all such discharged soldiers as should restore a deserted house and should put into cultivation the fields lying waste. At the same time something was being taken off the crushing weight of the taxes and the State was assuming the charge of recovering them directly, without any regard for the real or supposed advances of the receivers-general; their accounts were submitted to the revision of the brothers Pâris, sons of an innkeeper in the Dauphinese Alps, who had made fortunes by military contracts and were all four reputed to be very able in matters of finance. They were likewise commissioned to *revise* the bills circulating in the name of the State, in other words, to suppress a great number without re-imbursement to the holder, a sort of bankruptcy in disguise, which did not help to raise the public credit. At the same time also a chamber of justice, instituted for that purpose, was prosecuting the tax-farmers (*traitants*), as Louis XIV. had done at the commencement of his reign, during the suit against Fouquet. All were obliged to account for their acquisitions and the state of their fortunes; the notaries were compelled to bring their books before the court. Several tax-farmers (*traitants*) killed themselves to escape the violence and severity of the procedure. The Parliament, anything but favourable to the speculators, but still less disposed to suffer its judicial privileges to be encroached upon, found fault with the decrees of the Chamber. The Regent's friends were eager to profit by the reaction which was manifesting itself in the public mind; partly from compassion, partly from shameful cupidity, all the courtiers set themselves to work to obtain grace for the prosecuted financiers. The finest ladies sold their protection with brazen faces; the Regent, who had sworn to show no favour to anybody, yielded to the solicitations of his friends, to the great disgust of M. Rouillé-Ducoudray, member of the council of finance, who directed the operations of the Chamber of Justice with the same stern frankness which had made him not long before say to a body of tax-farmers (*traitants*) who wanted to put at his disposal a certain number of shares in their enterprise, "And suppose I were to go shares with you, how could I have you hanged, in case you were rogues?" Nobody was really hanged, although torture and the penalty of death had been set down in the list of punishments to which the guilty were liable; out of four thousand five hundred amenable cases nearly three thousand had been exempted from the tax. "The corruption is so widespread," says the preamble to the edict of March, 1727, which suppressed the Chamber of Justice, "that nearly all conditions have been infected by it, in such sort that the most righteous severities could not be employed to punish so great a number of culprits without causing a dangerous interruption to commerce and a kind of general shock in the system of the State." The resources derived from the punishment of the tax-farmers (*traitants*), as well as from the revision of the State's debts, thus remaining very much below expectation, the deficit went on continually increasing. In order to re-establish the finances, the duke of Noailles demanded fifteen years' impracticable economy, as chimerical as the increment of the revenues on which he calculated; and the duke of Orleans finally suffered himself to be led away by the brilliant prospect which was flashed before his eyes by the Scotsman, Law, who had now for more than two years been settled in France.

Law, born at Edinburgh in 1671, son of a goldsmith, had for a long time been scouring Europe, seeking in a clever and systematic course of gambling a source of fortune for himself and the first foundation of the great enterprises he was revolving in his singularly inventive and daring mind. Passionately devoted to the financial theories he had conceived, Law had expounded them to all the princes of Europe in succession. "He says that of all the persons to whom he has spoken about his system he has found but two who apprehended it, to wit, the king of Sicily and my son," wrote Madame, the Regent's mother. Victor Amadeo, however, had rejected Law's proposals. "I am not powerful enough to ruin myself," he had said. Law had not been more successful with Louis XIV. The Regent had not the same repugnance for novelties of foreign origin; so soon as he was in power, he authorized the Scot to found a circulating and discount bank (*banque de circulation et d'escompte*), which at once had very great success and did real service. Encouraged by this first step, Law reiterated to the Regent that the credit of bankers and merchants decupled their capital; if the State became the universal banker and centralized all the values in circulation, the public fortune would naturally be decupled. A radically false system, fated to plunge the State and consequently the whole nation into the risks of speculation and trading without the guarantee of that activity, zeal and prompt resolution which able men of business can import into their private enterprises. The system was not as yet applied; the discreet routine of the French financiers was scared at such risky chances, the pride of the great lords sitting in the council was shocked at the idea of seeing the State turning banker, perhaps even trader. St. Simon maintained that what was well enough for a free State could not take place under an absolute government. Law went on, however; to his bank he had just added a great company. The king ceded to him Louisiana, which was said to be rich in gold and silver mines superior to those of Mexico and Peru. People vaunted the fertility of the soil, the facility offered for trade by the extensive and rapid stream of the Mississippi; it was by the name of that river that the new company was called at first, though it soon took the title of *Compagnie d'Occident*, when it had obtained the privilege of trading in Senegal and in Guinea; it became the *Compagnie des Indes*, on forming a fusion with the old enterprises which worked the trade of the East. For the generality, and in the current phraseology, it remained the *Mississippi;* and that is the name it has left in history. New Orleans was beginning to arise at the mouth of that river. Law had bought Belle-Isle-en-Mer and was constructing the port of Lorient.

The Regent's councillors were scared and disquieted; the chancellor proclaimed himself loudly against the deception or illusion which made of Louisiana a land of promise: he called to mind that Crozat had been ruined in searching for mines of the precious metals there. "The worst of him was his virtue," said Duclos. The Regent made a last effort to convert him as well as the duke of Noailles to the projects of Law. It was at a small house in the faubourg St. Antoine, called La Roquette, belonging to the last-named, that the four interlocutors discussed the new system thoroughly. "With the use of very sensible language Law had the gift of explaining himself so clearly and intelligibly that he left nothing to desire as concerned making himself apprehended and comprehended. The duke of Orleans liked him and relished him. He regarded him and all he did as

LA RUE QUINCAMPOIX.

work of his own creation. He liked, moreover, extraordinary and out-of-the-way methods, and he embraced them the more readily in that he saw the resources which had become so necessary for the State and all the ordinary operations of finance vanishing away. This liking of the Regent's wounded Noailles as being adopted at his expense. He wanted to be sole master in the matter of finance, and all the eloquence of Law could not succeed in convincing him." The chancellor stood firm; the Parliament, which ever remained identified in his mind with his country, was in the same way opposed to Law. The latter declared that the obstacles which arrested him at every step through the ill-will of the Council and of the magistrates were ruining all the fruits of his system. The representations addressed by the Parliament to the king, on the 20th of January, touching a re-coinage of all moneys, which had been suggested by Law, dealt the last blow at the chancellor's already tottering favour. On the morning of the 23rd M. de La Vrillière went to him on behalf of the Regent and demanded the return of the seals. D'Aguesseau was a little affected and surprised. " Monseigneur," he wrote to the duke of Orleans, " you gave me the seals without any merit on my part, you take them away without any demerit." He had received orders to withdraw to his estate at Fresnes: the Regent found his mere presence irksome. D'Aguesseau set out at once. " He had taken his elevation like a sage," says St. Simon, " and it was as a sage too that he fell." " The important point," wrote the disgraced magistrate to his son, " is to be well with oneself."

The duke of Noailles had resigned his presidency of the council of finance; but, ever adroit, even in disgrace, he had managed to secure himself a place in the council of regency. The seals were entrusted to M. d'Argenson, for some years past chief of police at Paris. " With a forbidding face, which reminded one of the three judges of Hades, he made fun out of everything with excellence of wit, and he had established such order amongst that innumerable multitude of Paris, that there was no single inhabitant of whose conduct and habits he was not cognizant from day to day, with exquisite discernment in bringing a heavy or light hand to bear on every matter that presented itself, ever leaning towards the gentler side, with the art of making the most innocent tremble before him" [*St. Simon*, t. xv. p. 387]. Courageous, bold, audacious in facing riots, and thereby master of the people, he was at the same time endowed with prodigious activity. "He was seen commencing his audiences at three in the morning, dictating to four secretaries at once on various subjects, and making his rounds at night whilst working in his carriage at a desk lighted with wax candles. For the rest, without any dread of parliament, which had often attacked him, he was in his nature royal and fiscal; he cut knots, he was a foe to lengthiness, to useless forms or such as might be skipped, to neutral or wavering conditions" [Lemontey, *Histoire de la Régence*, t. i. p. 77]. The Regent considered that he had secured to himself an effective instrument of his views: acceptance of the system had been the condition *sine quâ non* of M. d'Argenson's elevation.

He, however, like his predecessors, attempted before long to hamper the march of the audacious foreigner; but the die had been cast and the duke of Orleans outstripped Law himself in the application of his theories. A company, formed secretly and protected by the new keeper of the seals, had bought up the general farmings (*fermes générales*), that is to say, all the indirect taxes, for the sum of forty-eight million fifty-two thousand livres; the *Compagnie des Indes* re-purchased them for fifty-two millions; the general receipts were likewise conceded to it, and Law's bank was proclaimed a Royal Bank; the Company's shares already amounted to the supposed value of all the coin circulating in the kingdom, estimated at seven or eight hundred millions. Law thought he might risk everything in the intoxication which had seized all France, capital and province. He created some fifteen hundred millions of new shares, promising his shareholders a dividend of 12 per cent. From all parts silver and gold flowed into his hands; everywhere the paper of the bank was substituted for coin. The delirium had mastered all minds. The street called *Quincampoix*, for a long time past devoted to the operations of bankers, had become the usual meeting-place of the greatest lords as well as of discreet burgesses. It had been found necessary to close the two ends of the street with gates, open from six a.m. to nine p.m.; every house harboured business agents by the hundred; the smallest room was let for its weight in gold. The workmen who made the paper for the bank-notes could not keep up with the consumption. The most modest fortunes suddenly became colossal, lacqueys of yesterday were millionaires to-morrow; extravagance followed the progress of this outburst of riches, and the price of provisions followed the progress of extravagance.

JOHN LAW.

Enthusiasm was at its height in favour of the able author of so many benefits. Law became a convert to Catholicism and was made comptroller-general; all the court was at his feet: "My son was looking for a duchess to escort my granddaughter to Genoa," writes Madame, the Regent's mother: "'Send and choose one at Madame Law's,' said I; 'you will find them all sitting in her drawing-room.'" Law's triumph was complete; the hour of his fall was about to strike.

At the pinnacle of his power and success the new comptroller-general fell into no illusion as to the danger of the position. "He had been forced to raise seven stories on foundations which he had laid for only three," said a contemporary as clearsighted as impartial. Some large shareholders were already beginning to quietly realize their profits. The warrants of the *Compagnie des Indes* had been assimilated to the bank-notes; and the enormous quantity of paper tended to lower its value. First, there was a prohibition against making payments in silver above ten francs, and in gold above three hundred. Soon afterwards money was dislegalized as a tender, and orders were issued to take every kind to the Bank on pain of confiscation, half to go to the informer. Informing became a horrible trade; a son denounced his father. The Regent openly violated law and had this miscreant punished. The prince one day saw President Lambert de Vernon coming to visit him. "I am come," said the latter, "to denounce to your Royal Highness a man who has five hundred thousand livres in gold." The duke of Orleans drew back a step: "Ah! Mr. President," he cried: "what low vocation have you taken to?" "Monseigneur," rejoined the president, "I am obeying the law; but your Royal Highness may be quite easy, it is myself whom I have come to denounce, in hopes of retaining at least a part of this sum, which I prefer to all the bank-notes." "My money is at the king's service," was the proud remark of Nicolaï, premier president of the Exchequer-Chamber, "but it belongs to nobody." The great mass of the nation was of the same opinion as the two presidents; forty-five millions only found their way to the Bank; gold and silver were concealed everywhere. The crisis was becoming imminent; Law boldly announced that the value of the notes was reduced by a half. The public outcry was so violent that the Regent was obliged to withdraw the edict, as to which the council had not been consulted. "Since Law became comptroller-general, his head has been turned," said the prince. That same evening Law was arrested by the major of the Swiss; it was believed to be all over with him, but the admirable order in which were his books, kept by double entry after the Italian manner, as yet unknown in France, and the ingenious expedients he indicated for restoring credit, gave his partisans a moment's fresh confidence. He ceased to be comptroller-general, but he remained director of the Bank. The death-blow, however, had been dealt his system, for a panic terror had succeeded to the insensate enthusiasm of the early days. The prince of Conti had set the example of getting back the value of his notes; four waggons had been driven up to his house laden with money. It was suffocation at the doors of the Bank, changing small notes, the only ones now payable in specie. Three men were crushed to death on one day in the crowd. It was found necessary to close the entrances to Quincampoix Street, in order to put a stop to the feverish tumult arising from desperate speculation. The multitude moved to the Place Vendôme; shops and booths were thrown up; there was a share-fair; this ditty was everywhere sung in the streets :—

> " On Monday I bought share on share ;
> On Tuesday I was a millionaire ;
> On Wednesday took a grand abode ;
> On Thursday in my carriage rode ;
> On Friday drove to the Opera-ball ;
> On Saturday came to the paupers' hall."

To restore confidence, Law conceived the idea of giving the seals back to D'Aguesseau ; and the Regent authorized him to set out for Fresnes. In allusion to this step, so honourable for the magistrate who was the object of it, Law afterwards wrote from Venice to the Regent : " In my labours I desired to be useful to a great people, as the chancellor can bear me witness. . . . At his return I offered him my shares which were then worth more than a hundred millions, to be distributed by him amongst those who had need of them." The chancellor came back, though his influence could neither stop the evil nor even assuage the growing disagreement between the duke of Orleans and the Parliament. None could restore the public sense of security, none could prevent the edifice from crumbling to pieces. With ruin came crimes. Count Horn, belonging to the family of the celebrated Count Horn who was beheaded under Philip II. in company with Count Lamoral d'Egmont, murdered at an inn a poor jobber whom he had inveigled thither on purpose to steal his pocket-book. In spite of all his powerful family's entreaties, Count Horn died on the wheel together with one of his accomplices. It was represented to the Regent that the count's house had the honour of being connected with his : "Very well, gentlemen," said he, "then I will share the shame with you," and he remained inflexible.

The public wrath and indignation fastened henceforth upon Law, the author and director of a system which had given rise to so many hopes and had been the cause of so many woes. His carriage was knocked to pieces in the streets. President de Mesmes entered the Grand Chamber singing with quite a solemn air :—

> "Sirs, sirs, great news! What is it? It's—
> They've smash'd Law's carriage all to bits."

The whole body jumped up, more regardful of their hatred than of their dignity ; and "Is Law torn in pieces ?" was the cry. Law had taken refuge at the Palais-Royal. One day he appeared at the theatre in the Regent's box ; low murmurs recalled to the Regent's mind the necessity for prudence ; in the end he got Law away secretly in a carriage lent him by the duke of Bourbon.

Law had brought with him to France a considerable fortune ; he had scarcely enough to live upon when he retired to Venice where he died some years later (1729), convinced to the last of the utility of his system, at the same time that he acknowledged the errors he had committed in its application. "I do not pretend that I did not make mistakes," he wrote from his retreat, "I know I did and that if I had to begin again, I should do differently. I should go more slowly but more surely, and I should not expose the State and my own person to the dangers which may attend the derangement of a general system." "There was neither avarice nor rascality in what he did," says St Simon ; "he was a gentle, kind, respectful man, whom excess of credit and of fortune had not spoilt, and whose bearing, equipage, table and furniture could not offend any body. He bore with singular patience and evenness the obstructions that were raised against his operations, until at the last, finding himself short of means, and nevertheless seeking for them and wishing to present a front, he became crusty, gave way to temper, and his replies were frequently ill-considered. He was a man of system, calculation, comparison, well informed and profound in that sort of thing, who was the dupe of his Mississippi, and in good faith believed in forming great and wealthy establishments in America. He reasoned Englishwise, and did not know how opposed to those kinds of establishments are the levity of our nation and the inconveniences of a despotic government, which has a finger in everything, and under which what one minister does is always destroyed or changed by his successor." The disasters caused by Law's system have recoiled upon his memory. Forgotten are his honesty, his charity, his interest in useful works; remembered is nothing but the imprudence of his chimerical hopes and the fatal result of his enterprises, as deplorable in their effects upon the moral condition of France, as upon her wealth and her credit.

The Regent's rash infatuation for a system as novel as it was seductive had borne its fruits. The judgment which his mother had pronounced upon Philip of Orleans was justified to the last: "The fairies," said Madame, " were all invited to the birth of my son; and each endowed him with some happy quality. But one wicked fairy, who had been forgotten, came likewise, leaning upon her stick, and, not being able to annul her sisters' gifts, declared that the prince should never know how to make use of them."

Throughout the successive periods of intoxication and despair caused by the necessary and logical development of Law's system, the duke of Orleans had dealt other blows and directed other affairs of importance. Easy-going, indolent, often absorbed by his pleasures, the Regent found no great difficulty in putting up with the exaltation of the legitimatized princes; it had been for him sufficient to wrest authority from the duke of Maine, he let him enjoy the privileges of a prince of the blood. " I kept silence during the king's lifetime," he would say; " I will not be mean enough to break it now he is dead." But the duke of Bourbon, heir of the House of Condé, fierce in temper, violent in his hate, greedy of honours as well as of money, had just arrived at man's estate, and was wroth at sight of the bastards' greatness. He drew after him the count of Charolais his brother and the prince of Conti his cousin; on the 22nd of April, 1716, all three presented to the king a request for the revocation of Louis XIV.'s edict declaring his legitimatized sons princes of the blood and capable of succeeding to the throne. The duchess of Maine, generally speaking very indifferent about her husband, whom she treated haughtily, like a true daughter of the House of Condé, flew into a violent passion, this time, at her cousins' unexpected attack; she was for putting her own hand to the work of drawing up the memorial of her husband and of her brother-in-law, the count of Toulouse. "The greater part of the nights was employed at it," says Madame de Staal, at that time Mdlle. de Launay, a person of much wit, half lady's maid, half reader to the duchess. "The huge volumes, heaped-up on her bed like mountains overwhelming her, caused her," she used to say, "to look, making due allowances, like Enceladus, buried under Mount Etna. I was present at the work, and I also used to turn over the leaves of old chronicles and of ancient and modern jurisconsults, until excess of fatigue disposed the princess to take some repose."

All this toil ended in the following declaration on the part of the legitimatized princes : " The affair, being one of State, cannot be decided but by a king who is a major or indeed by the states-general." At the same time, and still at the instigation of the duchess of Maine, thirty-nine noblemen signed a petition, modestly addressed to " Our lords of the Parliament," demanding, in their turn, that the affair should be referred to the states-general, who alone were competent, when it was a question of the succession to the throne.

The Regent saw the necessity of firmness. " It is a maxim," he declared, " that the king is always a major as regards justice ; that which was done without the states-general has no need of their intervention to be undone." The decree of the council of regency, based on the same principles, suppressed the right of succession to the crown, and cut short all pretensions on the part of the legitimatized princes' issue to the rank of princes of the blood ; the rights thereto were maintained in the case of the duke of Maine and the count of Toulouse, for their lives, by the bounty of the Regent, " which did not prevent the duchess of Maine from uttering loud shrieks, like a maniac," says St. Simon, " or the duchess of Orleans from weeping night and day and refusing for two months to see anybody." Of the thirty-nine members of the nobility who had signed the petition to Parliament, six were detained in prison for a month, after which the duke of Orleans pardoned them. "You know me well enough to be aware that I am only nasty when I consider myself positively obliged to be," he said to them. The patrons, whose cause these noblemen had lightly embraced, were not yet at the end of their humiliations.

The duke of Bourbon was not satisfied with their exclusion from the succession to the throne: he claimed the king's education, which belonged of right, he said, to the first prince of the blood, being a major. In his hatred, then, towards the legitimatized, he accepted with alacrity the duke of St. Simon's proposal to simply reduce them to their rank by seniority in the peerage, with the proviso of afterwards restoring the privileges of a prince of the blood in favour of the count of Toulouse alone, as a reward for his services in the navy. The blow thus dealt gratified all the passions of the House of Condé and the wrath of Law, as well as that of the keeper of the seals, D'Argenson, against the Parliament, which for three months past had refused to enregister all edicts. On the 24th of August, 1718, at six in the morning, the Parliament received orders to repair to the Tuileries, where the king was to hold a bed of justice. The duke of Maine, who was returning from a party, was notified, as colonel of the Swiss, to have his regiment under arms; at eight o'clock the council of regency was already assembled; the duke of Maine and the count of Toulouse arrived in peer's robes. The Regent had flattered himself that they would not come to the bed of justice, and had not summoned them. He at once advanced towards the count of Toulouse, and said out loud that he was surprised to see him in his robes, and that he had not thought proper to notify him of the bed of justice, because he knew that, since the last edict, he did not like going to the Parliament. The count of Toulouse replied that that was quite true, but that, when it was a question of the welfare of the State, he put every other consideration aside. The Regent was disconcerted, he hesitated a moment, then, speaking low and very earnestly to the count of Toulouse, he returned to St. Simon:

"I have just told him all," said he, "I couldn't help it; he is
the best fellow in the world, and the one who touches my heart
the most. He was coming to me on behalf of his brother, who
had a shrewd notion that there was something in the wind and
that he did not stand quite well with me; he had begged
him to ask me whether I wished him to remain, or whether he
would not do well to go away. I confess to you that I thought
I did well to tell him that his brother would do just as well to go

THE DUKE OF MAINE.

away, since he asked me the question; that, as for himself, he
might safely remain, because he was to continue just as he is,
without alteration; but that something might take place rather
disagreeable for M. du Maine. Whereupon, he asked me how he
could remain, when there was to be an attack upon his brother,
seeing that they were but one, both in point of honour and as
brothers. I do believe, there they are just going out," added the
Regent, casting a glance towards the door, as the members of

the council were beginning to take their places : " they will be prudent ; the count of Toulouse promised me so." " But, if they were to do anything foolish, or were to leave Paris ? " " They shall be arrested, I give you my word," replied the duke of Orleans in a firmer tone than usual. They had just read the decree reducing the legitimatized to their degree in the peerage, and M. le duc had claimed the superintendence of the king's education, when it was announced that the Parliament in their scarlet robes were arriving

THE DUCHESS OF MAINE.

in the court of the palace. Marshal de Villeroi alone dared to protest. " Here, then," said he with a sigh, " are all the late king's dispositions upset ; I cannot see it without sorrow. M. du Maine is very unfortunate." " Sir," rejoined the Regent, with animation : " M. du Maine is my brother-in-law, but I prefer an open to a hidden enemy."

With the same air the duke of Orleans passed to the bed of justice, " with a gentle but resolute majesty, which was quite new to him ; eyes observant, but bearing grave and easy; M. le duc staid, circumspect, surrounded by a sort of radiance that adorned his whole person, and under perceptible restraint; the keeper of the seals, in his chair, motionless, gazing askance with that witful fire which flashed from his eyes and which seemed to pierce all bosoms, in presence of that Parliament which had so often given him orders standing at its bar as chief of police, in presence of that premier president, so superior to him, so haughty, so proud of his duke of Maine, so mightily in hopes of the seals." After his speech and the reading of the king's decree, the premier president was for attempting a remonstrance : D'Argenson mounted the step, approached the young king, and then, without taking any opinion, said in a very loud voice, " The king desires to be obeyed, and obeyed at once." There was nothing further for it but to enregister the edict; all the decrees of the Parliament were quashed.

Some old servants of Louis XIV., friends and confidants of the duke of Maine, alone appeared moved. The young king was laughing, and the crowd of spectators were amusing themselves with the scene, without any sensible interest in the court intrigues. The duchess of Maine made her husband pay for his humble behaviour at the council; " she was," says St. Simon, " at one time motionless with grief, at another boiling with rage, and her poor husband wept daily like a calf at the biting reproaches and strange insults which he had incessantly to pocket in her fits of anger against him."

In the excess of her indignation and wrath the duchess of Maine determined not to confine herself to reproaches. She had passed her life in elegant entertainments, in sprightly and frivolous intellectual amusements ; ever bent on diverting herself, she made up her mind to taste the pleasure of vengeance, and set on foot a conspiracy, as frivolous as her diversions. The object, however, was nothing less than to overthrow the duke of Orleans, and to confer the regency on the king of Spain, Philip V., with a council and a lieutenant, who was to be the duke of Maine. " When one has once acquired, no matter how, the rank of prince of the blood and the capability of succeeding to the throne," said the duchess, " one must turn the State upside down and set fire to the four

CARDINAL DUBOIS.

corners of the kingdom rather than let them be wrested from one."
The schemes for attaining this great result were various and
confused. Philip V. had never admitted that his renunciation of
the crown of France was seriously binding upon him; he had seen,
by the precedent of the war of devolution, how a powerful sovereign
may make sport of such acts; his Italian minister, Alberoni, an
able and crafty man, who had set the crown of Spain upon the
head of Elizabeth Farnese and had continued to rule her, cau-
tiously egged on his master into hostilities against France. They
counted upon the Parliaments, taking example from that of Paris,
on the whole of Brittany, in revolt at the prolongation of the tithe-
tax, on all the old court, accustomed to the yoke of the bastards
and of Madame de Maintenon, on Languedoc, of which the duke
of Maine was the governor; they talked of carrying off the duke
of Orleans and taking him to the castle of Toledo; Alberoni
promised the assistance of a Spanish army. The duchess of Maine
had fired the train, without the knowledge, she said, and probably
against the will, too, of her husband, more indolent than she in his
perfidy. Some scatter-brains of great houses were mixed up in
the affair: MM. de Richelieu, de Laval, and de Pompadour; there
was secret coming and going between the castle of Sceaux and the
house of the Spanish ambassador, the prince of Cellamare; M. de
Malézieux, the secretary and friend of the duchess, drew up a
form of appeal from the French nobility to Philip V., but nobody
had signed it or thought of doing so. They got pamphlets written
by Abbé Brigault, whom the duchess had sent to Spain; the
mystery was profound and all the conspirators were convinced of
the importance of their manœuvres; every day, however, the
Regent was informed of them by his most influential negotiator
with foreign countries, Abbé Dubois, his late tutor and the
most depraved of all those who were about him. Able and vigilant
as he was, he was not ignorant of any single detail of the plot and
was only giving the conspirators time to compromise themselves.
At last, just as a young abbé, Porto Carrero, was starting for Spain,
carrying important papers, he was arrested at Poitiers and his
papers were seized. Next day, Dec. 7, 1718, the prince of
Cellamare's house was visited and the streets were lined with

troops. Word was brought in all haste to the duchess of Maine. She had company, and dared not stir. M. de Châtillon came in; joking commenced. "He was a cold creature, who never thought of talking," says Madame de Staal in her memoirs. "All at once he said: 'Really there is some very amusing news: they have arrested and put in the Bastille, for this affair of the Spanish ambassador, a certain Abbé Bri ... Bri ....,' he could not remember the name, and those who knew it had no inclination to help him. At last he finished, and added, 'The most amusing part is, that he has told all, and so, you see, there are some folks in a great fix.' Thereupon he burst out laughing for the first time in his life. The duchess of Maine, who had not the least inclination thereto, said: 'Yes, that is very amusing.' 'Oh! it is enough to make you die of laughing,' he resumed: 'fancy those folks who thought their affair was quite a secret; here's one who tells more than he is asked and names everybody by name'!" The agony was prolonged for some days; jokes were beginning to be made about it at the duchess of Maine's; she kept friends with her to pass the night in her room, waiting for her arrest to come. Madame de Staal was reading Machiavelli's conspiracies: "Make haste and take away that piece of evidence against us," said Madame du Maine laughingly, "it would be one of the strongest."

The arrest came, however: it was six a.m., and everybody was asleep, when the king's men entered the duke of Maine's house. The Regent had for a long time delayed to act, as if he wanted to leave everybody time to get away; but the conspirators were too scatter-brained to take the trouble. The duchess was removed to Dijon, within the government and into the very house of the duke of Bourbon her nephew, which was a very bitter pill for her. The duke of Maine, who protested his innocence and his ignorance, was detained in the castle of Dourlans in Picardy. Cellamare received his passports and quitted France. The less illustrious conspirators were all put in the Bastille; the majority did not remain there long and purchased their liberty by confessions, which the duchess of Maine ended by confirming. "Do not leave Paris until you are driven thereto by force," Alberoni had written to the prince of Cellamare, "and do not start before you have fired all the mines."

Cellamare started, and the mines did not burst after his withdrawal; conspiracy and conspirators were covered with ridicule; the natural clemency of the Regent had been useful; the part of the duke and duchess of Maine was played out.

The only serious result of Cellamare's conspiracy was to render imminent a rupture with Spain. From the first days of the regency the old enmity of Philip V. towards the duke of Orleans and the secret pretensions of both of them to the crown of France, in case of little Louis XV.'s death, rendered the relations between the two courts thorny and strained at bottom, though still perfectly smooth in appearance. It was from England that Abbé Dubois urged the Regent to seek support. Dubois, born in the very lowest position, and endowed with a soul worthy of his origin, was " a little, lean man, wire-drawn, with a light-coloured wig, the look of a weasel, a clever expression," says St. Simon, who detested him : " all vices struggled within him for the mastery ; they kept up a constant hubbub and strife together. Avarice, debauchery, ambition were his gods; perfidy, flattery, slavishness his instruments; and complete unbelief his comfort. He excelled in low intrigues ; the boldest lie was second nature to him, with an air of simplicity, straightforwardness, sincerity, and often bashfulness." In spite of all these vices, and the depraving influence he had exercised over the duke of Orleans from his earliest youth, Dubois was able, often far-sighted, and sometimes bold ; he had a correct and tolerably practical mind. Madame, who was afraid of him, had said to her son on the day of his elevation to power : " I desire only the welfare of the State and your own glory ; I have but one request to make for your honour's sake, and I demand your word for it, that is, never to employ that scoundrel of an Abbé Dubois, the greatest rascal in the world, and one who would sacrifice the State and you to the slightest interest." The Regent promised ; yet a few months later and Dubois was Church-councillor of State, and his growing influence with the prince placed him, at first secretly and before long openly, at the head of foreign affairs.

James Stuart, King James II.'s son, whom his friends called James III. and his enemies Chevalier St. George, had just unsuccessfully attempted a descent upon Scotland. The jacobites had risen; they were crying aloud for their prince who remained concealed in Lorraine, when at last he resolved to set out and traverse France secretly. Agents, posted by the English ambassador, Lord Stair, were within an ace of arresting him, perhaps of murdering him. Saved by the intelligence and devotion of the post-mistress of Nonancourt, he embarked on the 26th of December at Dunkerque, too late to bring even moral support to the men who were fighting and dying for him. Six weeks after landing at Peterhead, in Scotland, he started back again without having struck a blow, without having set eyes upon the enemy, leaving to King George I. the easy task of avenging himself by sending to death upon the scaffold the noblest victims. The duke of Orleans had given him a little money, had known of and had encouraged his passage through France, but had accorded him no effectual aid: the wrath of both parties, nevertheless, fell on him.

Inspired by Dubois, weary of the weakness and dastardly incapacity of the Pretender, the Regent consented to make overtures to the king of England. The Spanish nation was favourable to France, but the king was hostile to the Regent; the English loved neither France nor the Regent, but their king had an interest in severing France from the Pretender for ever. Dubois availed himself ably of his former relations with Lord Stanhope, heretofore commander of the English troops in Spain, for commencing a secret negociation which soon extended to Holland, still closely knit to England. "The character of our Regent," wrote Dubois on the 10th of March, 1716, "leaves no ground for fearing lest he should pique himself upon perpetuating the prejudices and the procedure of our late court, and, as you yourself remark, he has too much wits not to see his true interest." Dubois was the bearer to the Hague of the Regent's proposals; King George was to cross over thither; the clever negotiator veiled his trip under the pretext of purchasing rare books; he was going, he said, to recover from the hands of the Jews Le Poussin's famous pictures of the Seven Sacraments, not long ago carried off from Paris. The order of succession to the crowns of France and England, conformably to the peace of Utrecht, was guaranteed in the scheme of treaty; that was the only important advantage to the Regent, who considered himself to be thus nailing the renunciation of Philip V.; in other respects all the concessions came from the side of France; her territory was forbidden ground to the Jacobites, and the Pretender, who had taken refuge at Avignon on papal soil, was to be called upon to cross the Alps. The English required the abandonment of the works upon the canal of Mardyck, intended to replace the harbour of Dunkerque; the Hollanders claimed commercial advantages. Dubois yielded on all the points, defending to the last with fruitless tenacity the title of king of France, which the English still disputed. The negotiations came to an end at length on the 6th of January, 1717, and Dubois wrote in triumph to the Regent: "I signed at midnight; so there are you quit of servitude (your own master), and here am I quit of fear." The treaty of the triple alliance brought the negotiator before long a more solid advantage; he was appointed secretary of state for foreign affairs; it was on this occasion that he wrote to Mr. Craggs, King George's minister, a letter which was worthy of his character, and which contributed a great deal towards gaining credit for the notion that he had sold himself to England: "If I were to follow only the impulse of my gratitude and were not restrained by respect, I should take the liberty of writing to H. B. Majesty to thank him for the place with which my lord the Regent has gratified me, inasmuch as I owe it to nothing but to the desire he felt not to employ in affairs common to France and England anybody who might not be agreeable to the King of Great Britain."

At the moment when the signature was being put to the treaty of the triple alliance, the sovereign of most distinction in Europe owing to the eccentric renown belonging to his personal merit, the czar Peter the Great, had just made flattering advances to France. He had some time before wished to take a trip to Paris, but Louis XIV. was old, melancholy and vanquished, and had declined the czar's visit. The Regent could not do the same thing, when, being at the Hague in 1717, Peter I. repeated the expression of his desire. Marshal Cossé was sent to meet him, and the honours due to the king himself were everywhere paid to him on the road. A singular mixture of military and barbaric roughness with the natural grandeur of a conqueror and creator of an empire, the czar mightily excited the curiosity of the Parisians. "Sometimes, feeling bored by the confluence of spectators," says Duclos, " but never disconcerted, he would dismiss them with a word, a gesture, or would go away without ceremony, to stroll whither his fancy impelled him. He was a mighty tall man, very well made, rather lean, face rather round in shape, a high forehead, fine eyebrows, complexion reddish and brown, fine black eyes, large, lively, piercing, well-opened; a glance majestic and gracious when he cared for it, otherwise stern and fierce, with a *tic* that did not recur often but that affected his eyes and his whole countenance, and struck terror. It lasted an instant, with a glance wild and terrible, and immediately passed away. His whole air indicated his intellect, his reflection, his grandeur, and did not lack a certain grace. In all his visits he combined a majesty the loftiest, the proudest, the most delicate, the most sustained, at the same time the least embarrassing when he had once established it, with a politeness which savoured of it, always and in all cases; masterlike everywhere, but with degrees according to persons. He had a sort of familiarity which came of frankness, but he was not exempt from a strong impress of that barbarism of his country which rendered all his ways prompt and sudden and his wishes uncertain, without bearing to be contradicted in any." Eating and drinking freely, getting drunk sometimes, rushing about the streets in hired coach, or cab, or the carriage of people who came to see him, of which he took possession unceremoniously, he testified towards the Regent a familiar good grace mingled with a certain superiority; at the play, to which they went together, the czar asked for beer; the Regent rose, took the goblet which was brought and handed it to Peter, who drank and, without moving, put the glass back on the tray which the Regent held all the while, with a slight inclination of the head which, however, surprised the public. At his first interview with the little king, he took up the child in his arms and kissed him over and over again, " with an air of tenderness and politeness which was full of nature and nevertheless intermixed with a something of grandeur, equality of rank and, slightly, superiority of age; for all that was distinctly perceptible." We know how he went to see Madame de Maintenon. One of his first visits was to the church of the Sorbonne; when he caught sight of Richelieu's monument, he ran up to it, embraced the statue, and "Ah! great man," said he, "if thou wert still alive, I would give thee one half of my kingdom to teach me to govern the other."

The czar was for seeing everything, studying everything; everything interested him, save the court and its frivolities; he did not go to visit the princesses of the blood, and confined himself to saluting them coldly, whilst passing along a terrace; but he was present at a sitting of the Parliament and of the academies, he examined the organization of all the public establishments, he visited the shops of the celebrated workmen, he handled the coining-die whilst there was being struck in his honour a medal bearing a Fame with these words: *Vires acquiret eundo* ('Twill gather strength as it goes). He received a visit from the doctors of the Sorbonne, who brought him a memorial touching the reunion of the Greek and Latin Churches: "I am a mere soldier," said he, "but I will gladly have an examination made of the memorial you present to me." Amidst all his chatting, studying, and information-hunting, Peter the Great did not forget the political object of his trip. He wanted to detach France from Sweden, her heretofore faithful ally, still receiving a subsidy which the czar would fain have appropriated to himself. Together with his own alliance he promised that of Poland and of Prussia. "France has nothing to fear from the emperor," he said: as for King George, whom he detested, "if any rupture should take place between him and the Regent, Russia would suffice to fill towards France the place of England as well as of Sweden."

Thanks to the ability of Dubois, the Regent felt himself infeoffed to England; he gave a cool reception to the overtures of the czar, who proposed a treaty of alliance and commerce. Prussia had already concluded secretly with France; Poland was distracted by intestine struggles; matters were confined to the establishment of amicable relations; France thenceforth maintained an ambassador in Russia, and the czar accepted the Regent's mediation between Sweden and himself. "France will be ruined by luxury and daintiness," said Peter the Great, at his departure, more im-

pressed with the danger run by the nation from a court which
was elegant even to effeminacy than by the irregularity of the
morals, to which elsewhere he was personally accustomed.

Dubois, however, went on negotiating, although he had displayed
no sort of alacrity towards the czar; he was struggling everywhere
throughout Europe against the influence of a broader, bolder,
more powerful mind than his own, less adroit perhaps in intrigue,
but equally destitute of scruples as to the employment of means.
Alberoni had restored the finances and reformed the administration of Spain; he was preparing an army and a fleet, meditating,
he said, to bring peace to the world, and beginning that great
enterprise by manœuvres which tended to nothing less than setting
fire to the four corners of Europe, in the name of an enfeebled
and heavy-going king, and of a queen ambitious, adroit, and
unpopular, "both of whom he had put under lock and key,
keeping the key in his pocket," says St. Simon. He dreamed of
reviving the ascendancy of Spain in Italy, of overthrowing the
protestant king of England, whilst restoring the Stuarts to the
throne, and of raising himself to the highest dignities in Church
and State. He had already obtained from Pope Clement XI. the
cardinal's hat, disguising under pretext of war against the Turks
the preparations he was making against Italy; he had formed an
alliance between Charles XII. and the czar, intending to sustain
by their united forces the attempts of the Jacobites in England.
His first enterprise, at sea, made him master of Sardinia within a
few days; the Spanish troops landed in Sicily. The emperor and
Victor Amadeo were in commotion; the pope, overwhelmed with
reproaches by those princes, wept, after his fashion, saying that
he had damned himself by raising Alberoni to the Roman purple;
Dubois profited by the disquietude excited in Europe by the bellicose attitude of the Spanish minister to finally draw the emperor
into the alliance between France and England. He was to renounce
his pretensions to Spain and the Indies, and give up Sardinia to
Savoy, which was to surrender Sicily to him. The succession to the
duchies of Parma and Tuscany was to be secured to the children of
the queen of Spain. "Every difficulty would be removed if there
were an appearance of more equality," wrote the Regent to Dubois

PETER THE GREAT AND LITTLE LOUIS XV.

on the 24th of January, 1718 : " I am quite aware that my personal interest does not suffer from this inequality, and that it is a species of touch-stone for discovering my friends as well at home as abroad. But I am Regent of France, and I ought to so behave myself that none may be able to reproach me with having thought of nothing but myself. I also owe some consideration to the Spaniards, whom I should completely disgust by making with the emperor an unequal arrangement, about which their glory and the honour of their monarchy would render them very sensitive. I should thereby drive them to union with Alberoni, whereas, if a war were necessary to carry our point, we ought to be able to say what Count Grammont said to the king : *At the time when we served your Majesty against Cardinal Mazarin.* Then the Spaniards themselves would help us." In the result, France and England left Holland and Savoy free to accede to the treaty ; but, if Spain refused to do so voluntarily within a specified time, the allies engaged to force her thereto by arms.

The Hollanders hesitated : the Spanish ambassador at the Hague had a medal struck representing the quadruple alliance as a coach on the point of falling, because it rested on only three wheels. Certain advantages secured to their commerce at last decided the States-general. Victor Amadeo regretfully acceded to the treaty which robbed him of Sicily : he was promised one of the Regent's daughters for his son.

Alberoni refused persistently to accede to the great coalition brought about by Dubois. Lord Stanhope proposed to go over to Spain in order to bring him round. " If my Lord comes as a lawgiver," said the cardinal, " he may spare himself the journey. If he comes as a mediator I will receive him ; but in any case I warn him that, at the first attack upon our vessels by an English squadron, Spain has not an inch of ground on which I would answer for his person." Lord Stanhope, nevertheless, set out for Spain, and had the good fortune to leave it in time, though without any diplomatic success. Admiral Byng, at the head of the English fleet, had destroyed the Spanish squadron before Messina ; the troops which occupied Palermo found themselves blockaded without hope of relief, and the nascent navy of Spain was strangled at the birth. Alberoni in his fury had the persons and goods seized of English residents settled in Spain, drove out the consuls, and orders were given at Madrid that no tongue should wag about the affairs of Sicily. The hope of a sudden surprise in England, on behalf of the Jacobites, had been destroyed by the death of the king of Sweden, Charles XII., killed on the 12th of December, 1718, at Freiderishalt, in Norway; the flotilla equipped by Alberoni for Chevalier St. George had been dispersed and beaten by the elements; the Pretender henceforth was considered to cost Spain too dear; he had just been sent away from her territory at the moment when the conspiracy of Cellamare failed in France; in spite of the feverish activity of his mind and the frequently chimerical extent of his machinations, Alberoni remained isolated in Europe, without ally and without support.

The treaty of the quadruple alliance had at last come to be definitively signed; Marshal d'Huxelles, head of the council of foreign affairs, an enemy to Dubois, and displeased at not having been invited to take part in the negotiations, at first refused his signature [*Mémoires de St. Simon*, t. xix. p. 365]. "At the first word the Regent spoke to him, he received nothing but bows, and the marshal went home to sulk; caresses, excuses, reasons, it was all of no use; Huxelles declared to the marquis of Effiat, who had been despatched to him, that he would have his hand cut off rather than sign. The duke of Orleans grew impatient and took a resolution very foreign to his usual weakness; he sent D'Antin to Marshal d'Huxelles bidding him to make choice of this: either to sign or lose his place, of which the Regent would immediately dispose in favour of somebody who would not be so intractable (*farouche*) as he. Oh! mighty power of *orviétan* (a counterpoison)! This man so independent, this great citizen, this courageous minister, had no sooner heard the threat and felt that it would be carried into effect than he bowed his head beneath his huge hat, which he always had on, and signed right off, without a word. He even read the treaty to the council of regency in a low and trembling voice, and when the Regent asked his opinion, 'the opinion of the treaty,' he answered between his teeth, with a bow." Some days later appeared, almost at the same time—the 17th of December, 1718, and the 9th of January, 1719—the manifestoes of England and France, proclaiming the resolution of making war upon Spain, whilst Philip V., by a declaration of December 25th, 1718, pronounced all renunciations illusory, and proclaimed his right to the throne of France in case of the death of Louis XV. At the same time he made an appeal to an assembly of the states-general against the tyranny of the Regent, " who was making alliances," he said, " with the enemies of the two crowns."

For once in a way Alberoni indulged the feelings of the king his master, and, in spite of the good will felt by a part of the grandees towards France, Spain was, on the whole, with him; he no longer felt himself to be threatened, as he had been a few months before, when the king's illness had made him tremble for his greatness and perhaps for his life. He kept the monarch shut up in his room, refusing entrance to even the superior officers of the palace [*Mémoires de St. Simon*, t. xv.]. " The marquis of Villena, major-domo major, having presented himself there one afternoon, one of the valets inside half opened the door and told him, with much embarrassment, that he was forbidden to let him in: ' You are insolent, sir,' replied the marquis; ' that cannot be.' He pushed the door against the valet and went in. The marquis, though covered with glory, being very weak on his legs, thus advances with short steps, leaning on his little stick. The queen and the cardinal see him and look at one another. The king was too ill to take notice of anything, and his curtains were drawn. The cardinal, seeing the marquis approach, went up to him and represented to him that the king wished to be alone and begged him to go away. ' That is not true,' said the marquis: ' I kept my eye upon you, and the king never said a word to you.' The cardinal, insisting, took him by the arm to make him go out; what with the heat of the moment and what with the push, the marquis, being feeble, fell into an arm-chair which happened to be by. Wroth at his fall, he raises his stick and brings it down with all his might, hammer and tongs, about the cardinal's ears, calling him a little rascal, a little hound, who deserved nothing short of the stirrup-leathers. When he did at last go out, the queen had looked on from her seat at this adventure all through, without moving or saying a word, and so had the few who were in the room, without daring to stir. The curious thing is that the cardinal mad as he was, but taken completely by surprise at the blows, did not defend himself and thought of nothing but getting clear. The same evening the marquis was exiled to his estates, without ever wanting to return from them, until the fall of Alberoni." Alberoni has sometimes been compared to the great cardinals who had governed France. To say nothing of the terror with which Richelieu inspired the grandees, who detested him, the prince of Condé would not have dared to touch Cardinal Mazarin with the tip of his cane, even when the latter "kissed his boots" in the courtyard of the castle at Havre.

Alberoni had persuaded his master that the French were merely awaiting the signal to rise in his favour; the most odious calumnies were everywhere circulating against the Regent; he did not generally show that he was at all disturbed or offended by them; however, when the poem of the *Philippics* by La Grange appeared, he desired to see it; the duke of St. Simon took it to him: "'Read it to me,' said the Regent. 'That I will never do, Monseigneur,' said I. He then took it and read it quite low, standing up, in the window of his little winter-closet, where we were. All at once, I saw him change countenance and turn towards me, tears in his eyes and very near fainting : 'Ah! said he to me, 'this is too bad, this horrid thing is too much for me.' He had lit upon the passage where the scoundrel had represented the duke of Orleans purposing to poison the king and all ready to commit his crime. I have never seen man so transfixed, so deeply moved, so overwhelmed by a calumny so enormous and so continuous. I had all the pains in the world to bring him round a little." King Louis XV., who had no love and scarcely any remembrance, preserved all his life some affection for the Regent and sincere gratitude for the care which the latter had lavished upon him. The duke of Orleans had never desired the crown for himself, and the attentions full of tender respect which he had shown the little king had made upon the child an impression which was never effaced.

The preparations for war with Spain meanwhile continued; the prince of Conti was nominally at the head of the army, Marshal Berwick was entrusted with the command. He accepted it, in spite of his old connexions with Spain, the benefits which Philip V. had heaped upon him, and the presence of his eldest son, the duke of Liria, in the Spanish ranks. There were others who attached more importance to gratitude: Berwick thought very highly of lieutenant-general Count d'Asfeldt and desired to have him in his army; the duke of Orleans spoke to him about it: " Monseigneur," answered D'Asfeldt, " I am a Frenchman, I owe you everything, I have nothing to expect save from you, but," taking the Fleece in his hand and showing it, " what would you have me do with this, which I hold, with the king's permission, from the king of Spain, if I were to serve against Spain, this being the greatest honour that I could have received ?" He phrased his repugnance so well and softened it down by so many expressions of attachment to the duke of Orleans that he was excused from serving against Spain, and he contented himself with superintending at Bordeaux the service of the commissariat. The French army, however, crossed the frontier in the month of March, 1719. " The Regent may send a French army whenever he pleases," wrote Alberoni on the 21st November, 1718: " proclaim publicly that there will not be a shot fired and that the king our master will have provisions ready to receive them." He had brought the king, the queen and the prince of the Asturias into the camp; Philip V. fully expected the desertion of the French army in a mass. Not a soul budged; some refugees made an attempt to tamper with certain officers of their acquaintance; their messenger was hanged in the middle of Marshal Berwick's camp. Fontarabia, St. Sebastian and the castle of Urgel fell before long into the power of the French; another division burnt, at the port of Los Pasages, six vessels which chanced to be on the stocks; an English squadron destroyed those at Centera and in the port of Vigo. Everywhere the depôts were committed to the flames: this cruel and destructive war against an enemy whose best troops were fighting far away and who was unable to offer more than a feeble resistance, gratified the passions and the interests of England rather than of France. " It was, of course, necessary," said Berwick, " that the English government should be able to convince the next parliament that nothing had been spared to diminish the navy of Spain." During this time the English fleet and the emperor's troops were keeping up an attack in Sicily upon the Spanish troops, who made a heroic defence, but were without resources or reinforcements and were diminishing consequently every day. The marquis of Leyden no longer held anything but Palermo and the region around Etna.

Alberoni had attempted to create a diversion by hurling into the midst of France the brand of civil war. Brittany, for a long time past discontented with its governor, the Marquis of Montesquiou, and lately worked upon by the agents of the duchess of Maine, was ripe for revolt; a few noblemen took up arms and called upon the peasants to *enter the forest* with them, that is, to take the field. Philip V. had promised the assistance of a fleet and had supplied some money. But the peasants did not rise, the Spanish ships were slow to arrive, the enterprise attempted against the Marquis of Montesquiou failed, the conspirators were surrounded in the forest of Noë, near Rennes; a great number were made prisoners and taken away to Nantes, where a special chamber inquired into the case against them. Three noblemen and one priest perished on the scaffold.

Insurrection, as well as desertion and political opposition, had been a failure; Philip V. was beaten at home as well as in Sicily. The Regent succeeded in introducing to the presence of the king of Spain an unknown agent, who managed to persuade the monarch that the cardinal was shirking his responsibility before Europe, asserting that the king and queen had desired the war and that he had confined himself to gratifying their passions. The duke of Orleans said, at the same time, quite openly, that he made war not against Philip V. or against Spain but against Alberoni only. Lord Stanhope declared, in the name of England, that no peace was possible, unless its preliminary were the dismissal of the pernicious minister.

The fall of Alberoni was almost as speedy as that which he had but lately contrived for his enemy the Princess des Ursins. On the 4th of December, 1719, he received orders to quit Madrid within eight days and Spain under three weeks. He did not see the king or queen again, and retired first to Genoa, going by France, and then finally to Rome. He took with him an immense fortune. It was discovered, after his departure, that he had placed amongst the number of his treasures the authentic will of Charles II., securing the throne of Spain to Philip V. He was pursued, his luggage ransacked and the precious document recovered. Alberoni had restored order in the internal administration of Spain, he had cleared away many abuses; Italian as he was he had resuscitated Spanish ambition. "I requickened a corpse," he used to say. His views were extensive and daring, but often chimerical; he had reduced to a nullity the sovereign whom he governed for so long, keeping him shut up far away from the world in a solitude which he was himself almost the only one to interrupt. "The queen has the devil in her," he used to say, "if she finds a man of the sword who has some mental resources and is a pretty good general, she will make a racket in France and in Europe." The queen did not find a general; and on the 17th of February, 1720, peace was signed at the Hague between Spain and the powers in coalition against her, to the common satisfaction of France and Spain, whom so many ties already united. The haughty Elizabeth Farnese looked no longer to anybody but the duke of Orleans for the elevation of her children.

So great success in negotiation, however servile had been his bearing, had little by little increased the influence of Dubois over his master. The Regent knew and despised him, but he submitted to his sway and yielded to his desires, sometimes to his fancies. Dubois had for a long while comprehended that the higher dignities of the Church could alone bring him to the grandeur of which he was ambitious; yet everything about him seemed to keep them out of his reach: his scandalous life, his perpetual intrigues, the baseness not of his origin but of his character and conduct; nevertheless, the see of Cambrai having become vacant by the death of Cardinal de la Trémoille, Dubois conceived the hope of obtaining it. "Impudent as he was," says St. Simon, "great as was the sway he had acquired over his master, he found himself very much embarrassed, and masked his effrontery by ruse: he told the duke of Orleans that he had dreamt a funny

dream that he was archbishop of Cambrai. The Regent, who saw
what he was driving at, answered him in a tone of contempt, ' Thou,
archbishop of Cambrai ! thou hast no thought of such a thing ?'
And the other persisting, he bade him think of all the scandal of
his life. Dubois had gone too far to stop on so fine a road, and
quoted to him precedents, of which there were, unfortunately,
only too many. The duke of Orleans, less moved by such bad
reasons than put to it how to resist the suit of a man whom he
was no longer wont to dare gainsay in anything, sought to get out
of the affair : ' Why! who would consecrate thee ?' ' Ah! if that's
all,' replied Dubois cheerfully, 'the thing is done, I know well
who will consecrate me; but is that all, once more ?' ' Well!
who ?' asked the Regent. ' Your premier almoner; there he is
outside, he will ask nothing better.' And he embraces the legs of
the duke of Orleans—who remains stuck and caught without
having the power to refuse—goes out, draws aside the bishop of
Nantes, tells him that he himself has got Cambrai, begs him to consecrate him—who promises immediately—comes in again, capers,
returns thanks, sings praises, expresses wonder, seals the matter
more and more surely by reckoning it done and persuading the
Regent that it is so, who never dared say no. That is how Dubois
made himself archbishop of Cambrai."

He was helped, it is said, by a strange patron. Destouches,
chargé d'affaires in London, who was kept well informed by
Dubois, went to see George I., requesting him to write to the
Regent recommending to him the negotiator of the treaties.
The king burst out laughing : " How can you ask a protestant
prince," said he, " to mix himself up with the making of an archbishop in France ? The Regent will laugh at the idea, as I do, and
will do nothing of the sort." " Pardon me, sir," rejoined Destouches,
" he will laugh, but he will do it, first out of regard for your
Majesty, and then because he will think it a good joke. I beseech
your Majesty to be pleased to sign the letter I have here all ready
written." King George signed, and the adroit Dubois became
archbishop of Cambrai. He even succeeded in being consecrated,
not only by the bishop of Nantes but also by Cardinal Rohan and
by Massillon, one of the glories of the French episcopate, a timid

man and a poor one, in despite of his pious eloquence. The Regent, as well as the whole court, was present at the ceremony, to the great scandal of the people attached to religion. Dubois received all the orders on the same day; and, when he was joked about it, he brazenfacedly called to mind the precedent of St. Ambrose. Dubois henceforth cast his eyes upon the cardinal's hat, and his negotiations at Rome were as brisk as those of Alberoni had but lately been with the same purpose.

Amidst so much defiance of decency and public morality, in the presence of such profound abuse of sacred things, God did not, nevertheless, remain without testimony, and his omnipotent justice had spoken. On the 21st of July, 1719, the duchess of Berry, eldest daughter of the Regent, had died at the Palais-Royal, at barely twenty-four years of age; her health, her beauty, and her wit were not proof against the irregular life she had led. Ere long a more terrible cry arose from one of the chief cities of the kingdom: "The plague," they said, "is at Marseilles, brought, none knows how, on board a ship from the East." The terrible malady had by this time been brooding for a month in the most populous quarters without anybody's daring to give it its real name. "The public welfare demands," said Chancellor d'Aguesseau, "that the people should be persuaded that the plague is not contagious, and that the ministry should behave as if it were persuaded of the contrary." Meanwhile emigration was commencing at Marseilles; the rich folks had all taken flight; the majority of the public functionaries, unfaithful to their duty, had imitated them, when, on the 31st of July, 1720, the Parliament of Aix, scared at the contagion, drew round Marseilles a sanitary line, proclaiming the penalty of death against all who should dare to pass it; the mayor (*viguier*) and the four sheriffs were left alone and without resources to confront a populace bewildered by fear, suffering and, ere long, famine. Then shone forth that grandeur of the human soul, which displays itself in the hour of terror, as if to testify of the divine image, still existing amidst the wreck of us. Whilst the Parliament was flying from threatened Aix and hurrying affrighted from town to town, accompanied or pursued in its rout by the commandant of the province, all that while the bishop of Marseilles, Monseigneur de Belzunce, the sheriffs Esteile and Moustier, and a simple officer of health, Chevalier Roze, sufficed in the depopulated town for all duties and all acts of devotion.

The plague showed a preference for attacking robust men, young people, and women in the flower of their age; it disdained the old and the sick: there was none to care for the dying, none to bury the dead. The doctors of Marseilles had fled, or dared not approach the dying without precautions which redoubled the terror. "The doctors ought to be abolished," wrote Dubois to the archbishop of Aix, " or ordered to show more ability and less cowardice, for it is a great calamity."

Some young doctors, arriving from Montpellier, raised the courage of their desponding brethren, and the sick no longer perished without help. Rallying round the bishop, the priests, assisted by the members of all the religious orders, flew from bedside to bedside, and from grave to grave, without being able to suffice for the duties of their ministry. "Look at Belzunce," writes M. Lemontey : "all he possessed, he has given; all who served him are dead; alone, in poverty, afoot, in the morning he penetrates into the most horrible dens of misery, and, in the evening, he is found again in the midst of places bescattered with the dying; he quenches their thirst, he comforts them as a friend, he exhorts them as an apostle, and on this field of death he gleans abandoned souls. The example of this prelate, who seems to be invulnerable, animates with courageous emulation—not the clergy of lazy and emasculated dignitaries, for they fled at the first approach of danger, but—the parish-priests, the vicars, and the religious orders ; not one deserts his colours, not one puts any bound to his fatigues save with his life. Thus perished twenty-six Recollects and eighteen Jesuits out of twenty-six. The Capucins summoned their brethren from the other provinces, and the latter rushed to martyrdom with the alacrity of the ancient Christians ; out of fifty-five the epidemic slew forty-three. The conduct of the priests of the Oratory was, if possible, more magnanimous. The functions of the sacred ministry were forbidden them by the bishop, a fanatical partisan of the bull *Unigenitus;* they refused to profit by their disqualification, and they devoted themselves to the service of the

BELZUNCE AMIDST THE PLAGUE-STRICKEN.

sick with heroic humility; nearly all succumbed, and there were still tears in the city for the Superior, a man of eminent piety."

During more than five months the heroic defenders of Marseilles struggled against the scourge. The bishop drew the populace on to follow in his steps, in processions or in the churches, invoking the mercy of God in aid of a city which terror and peril seemed to have the effect of plunging into the most awful corruption. Estelle, Moustier, and Chevalier Roze, heading the efforts attempted in all directions to protect the living and render the last offices to the dead, themselves put their hands to the work, aided by galley-men who had been summoned from the hulks. Courage was enough to establish equality between all ranks and all degrees of virtue. Monseigneur de Belzunce sat upon the seat of the tumbril laden with corpses, driven by a convict stained with every crime.

Marseilles had lost a third of its inhabitants; Aix, Toulon, Arles, the Cévennes, the Gévaudan were attacked by the contagion; fearful was the want in the decimated towns long deprived of every resource. The Regent had forwarded corn and money; the pope sent out three ships laden with provisions; one of the vessels was wrecked, the two others were seized by Barbary pirates, who released them as soon as they knew their destination. The cargo was deposited on a desert island in sight of Toulon. Thither it was that boats, putting off from Marseilles, went to fetch the alms of the pope, more charitable than many priests, accompanying his gifts with all the spiritual consolations and indulgences of his holy office. The time had not come for Marseilles and the towns of Provence to understand the terrible teaching of God. Scarcely had they escaped from the dreadful scourge which had laid them waste, when they plunged into excesses of pleasure and debauchery, as if to fly from the memories that haunted them. Scarcely was a thought given to those martyrs to devotion who had fallen during the epidemic; those who survived received no recompense; the Regent, alone, offered Monseigneur de Belzunce the bishopric of Laon, the premier ecclesiastical peerage in the kingdom; the saintly bishop preferred to remain in the midst of the flock for which he had battled against despair and death. It was only in 1802 that the city of Marseilles at last raised a monument to its bishop and its heroic magistrates.

Dubois, meanwhile, was nearing the goal of all his efforts. In order to obtain the cardinal's hat, he had embraced the cause of the Court of Rome, and was pushing forward the registration by Parliament of the Bull *Unigenitus*. The long opposition of the duke of Noailles at last yielded to the desire of restoring peace in the Church. In his wake the majority of the bishops and communities who had made *appeal* to the contemplated council renounced, in their turn, the protests so often renewed within the last few years. The Parliament was divided, but exiled to Pontoise, as a punishment for its opposition to the system of Law; it found itself threatened with removal to Blois. Chancellor d'Aguesseau had vainly sought to interpose his authority; a magistrate of the Grand Chamber, Perelle by name, was protesting eloquently against any derogation from the principles of liberty of the Gallican Church and of the parliaments: "Where did you find such maxims laid down?" asked the chancellor angrily. "In the pleadings of the late Chancellor d'Aguesseau," answered the councillor icily. D'Aguesseau gave in his resignation to the Regent, the Parliament did not leave for Blois; after sitting some weeks at Pontoise, it enregistered the formal declaration of the Bull, and at last returned to Paris on the 20th of December, 1720.

Dubois had reconciled France with the court of Rome; the latter owed him recompense for so much labour. Clement XI. had promised, but he could not make up his mind to bring down so low the dignity of the Sacred College; he died without having conferred the hat upon Dubois. During the conclave intrigues recommenced, conducted this time by Cardinal Rohan. The Jesuit Lafitteau, who had become bishop of Sisteron, and had for a long while been the secret agent of Dubois at Rome, kept him acquainted with all the steps taken to wrest a promise from Cardinal Conti, who was destined, it was believed, to unite the majority of the suffrages. "Do not be surprised," he adds, "to hear me say that I go by night to the conclave, for I have found out the secret of getting the key of it, and I constantly pass through five or six guard-posts, without their being able to guess who I am."

Cardinal Conti was old and feeble; all means were brought to bear upon him. Dubois had for a long time past engaged the services of Chevalier St. George; when the new pope was proclaimed under the name of Innocent XIII., he had signed a conditional promise in favour of Dubois. The Regent, who had but lately pressed his favourite's desires upon Clement XI., was not afraid to write to the new pontiff :—

"MOST HOLY FATHER,

"Your Holiness is informed of the favour which the late pope had granted me on behalf of the archbishop of Cambrai, of which his death alone prevented the fulfilment. I hope that Your Holiness will let it be seen, on your accession to the throne of St. Peter, that services rendered to the Church lose nothing by the death of the sovereign pontiffs, and that you will not think it unworthy of your earliest care to give me this public mark of the attention paid by the Holy See to the zeal which I profess for its interests. This kindness on the part of Your Holiness will crown the wishes I formed for your exaltation, will fill up the measure of the joy which it has caused me, will maintain our kindly relations to the advantage of the peace of the Church and the authority of the Holy See, and will fortify the zeal of the archbishop of Cambrai in the execution of my orders to the glory of the Pontificate and of Your Holiness."

On the 16th of July, 1721, Dubois was at last elected cardinal : it was stated that his elevation had cost eight millions of livres. The frivolous curiosity of the court was concerned with the countenance the new Eminence would make in his visits of ceremony, especially in that to *Madame*, his declared foe at all times. "He had nearly two months to prepare for it," says St. Simon, "and it must be admitted that he had made good use of them. He got himself up for his part and appeared before Madame with deep respect and embarrassment. He prostrated himself, as she advanced to greet him, sat down in the middle of the circle, covered his head for a moment with his red hat, which he removed immediately, and made his compliments; he began with

his own surprise at finding himself in such a position in presence
of Madame, spoke of the baseness of his birth and his first employ-
ments; employed them with much cleverness and in very choice
terms to extol so much the more the kindness, courage and power
of the duke of Orleans who from so low had raised him to where
he found himself; gave Madame some delicate incense; in fine,
dissolved in the most profound respect and gratitude, doing it so
well that Madame herself could not help, when he was gone,
praising his discourse and his countenance, at the same time adding
that she was mad to see him where he was.''

The bearing of the newly-elected was less modest at the council
of regency; he got himself accompanied thither by Cardinal
Rohan; their rank gave the two ecclesiastics precedence. The
duke of Noailles, d'Aguesseau and some other great lords refused
to sit with Dubois. "This day, sir, will be famous in history,"
said the duke of Noailles to the new cardinal: "it will not fail
to be remarked therein that your entrance into the council caused
it to be deserted by the grandees of the kingdom." Noailles was
exiled, as well as d'Aguesseau.

The great lords had made a decided failure in government.
Since 1718, the different councils had been abolished; defended
by Abbé St. Pierre, under the grotesque title of *Polysynodie*, they
had earned for the candid preacher of universal peace his exclusion
from the French Academy, which was insisted upon by the
remnants of the old court, whom he had mortally offended by
styling Louis XIV.'s governmental system a *viziership*. The
Regent had heaped favours upon the presidents and members of
the councils, but he had placed Dubois at the head of foreign
affairs and Le Blanc over the war-department. "I do not
inquire into the theory of councils," said the able Dubois to
the Regent by the mouth of his confidant Chavigny: "it was, as
you know, the object of worship to the shallow pates of the old
court. Humiliated by their nonentity at the end of the last reign,
they begot this system upon the reveries of M. de Cambrai. But
I think of you, I think of your interests. The king will reach his
majority, the grandees of the kingdom approach the monarque by
virtue of their birth; if to this privilege they unite that of being

then at the head of affairs, there is reason to fear that they may surpass you in complaisance, in flattery, may represent you as a useless phantom, and establish themselves upon the ruin of you. Suppress, then, these councils, if you mean to continue indispensable, and haste to supersede the great lords, who would become your rivals, by means of simple secretaries of State, who, without standing or family, will perforce remain your creatures."

The duke of Antin, son of Madame de Montespan, one of the most adroit courtiers of the old as well as of the new court, "honourless and passionless" (*sans honneur et sans humeur*), according to the Regent's own saying, took a severer view than Dubois of the arrangement to which he had contributed : " The councils are dissolved," he wrote in his memoirs ; " the nobility will never recover from it—to my great regret, I must confess. The kings who hereafter reign will see that Louis XIV., one of the greatest kings in the world, never would employ people of rank in any of his business ; that the Regent, a most enlightened prince, had begun by putting them at the head of all affairs, and was obliged to remove them at the end of three years. What can they and must they conclude therefrom ? That people of this condition are not fitted for business, and that they are good for nothing but to get killed in war. I hope I am wrong, but there is every appearance that the masters will think like that, and there will not be wanting folks who will confirm them in that opinion." A harsh criticism on the French nobility, too long absorbed by war or the court, living apart from the nation and from affairs, and thereby become incapable of governing, put down once for all by the iron hand of Richelieu, without·ever having been able to resume at the head of the country the rank and position which befitted them.

The special councils were dissolved, the council of regency diminished ; Dubois became premier minister in name, he had long been so in fact.

He had just concluded an important matter, one which the Regent had much at heart, the marriage of the king with the Infanta of Spain, and that of Mdlle. de Montpensier, daughter of the duke of Orleans, with the prince of the Asturias. The duke of St. Simon was entrusted with the official demand. Philip V.

was rejoiced to see his daughter's elevation to that throne which he still regarded as the first in the world; he purchased it by the concession made to the Regent.

The age of the Infanta was a serious obstacle; she was but three years old, the king was twelve. When the duke of Orleans went in state to announce to Louis XV. the negociation which tarried for nothing further but his consent, the young prince, taken by surprise, was tongue-tied, seemed to have his heart quite full, and his eyes grew moist. His preceptor, Fleury, bishop of Fréjus, who had just refused the archbishopric of Rheims, seeing that he must make up his mind to please the Regent or estrange him, supported what had just been said. " Marshal Villeroy, decided by the bishop's example, said to the king : ' Come, my dear master : the thing must be done with a good grace.' The Regent, very much embarrassed, the duke, mighty taciturn, and Dubois, with an air of composure, waited for the king to break a silence which lasted a quarter of an hour, whilst the bishop never ceased whispering to the king. As the silence continued, and the assembly of all the council, at which the king was about to appear, could not but augment his timidity, the bishop turned to the Regent and said to him : " His Majesty will go to the council, but he wants a little time to prepare himself for it." Thereupon the Regent replied that he was created to await the convenience of the king, saluted him with an air of respect and affection, went out and made signs to the rest to follow him. A quarter of an hour later the king entered the council, with his eyes still red, and replied with a very short and rather low *yes* to the Regent's question, whether he thought proper that the news of his marriage should be imparted to the council." " It was the assurance of peace with Spain, and the confirmation of the recent treaties; the Regent's enemies saw in it the climax of the policy, by the choice of an infant, which retarded the king's marriage " [*Mémoires secrets de Dubois*, t. ii. p. 163].

Accusations of greater gravity had been recently renewed against the duke of Orleans. The king had been ill; for just a moment the danger had appeared serious; the emotion in France was general, the cabal opposed to the Regent went beyond mere anxiety : "The consternation everywhere was great," says St. Simon : "I had the privileges of entry, and so I went into the king's chamber. I found it very empty ; the duke of Orleans seated at the chimney-corner, very forlorn and very sad. I went up to him for a moment, then I approached the king's bed. At that moment, Boulduc, one of his apothecaries, was giving him something to take. The duchess of la Ferté was at Boulduc's elbow, and, having turned round to see who was coming, she saw me and all at once said to me betwixt loud and soft : 'He is poisoned, he is poisoned.' 'Hold your tongue, do,' said I ; 'that is awful!' She went on again so much and so loud that I was afraid the king would hear her. Boulduc and I looked at one another and I immediately withdrew from the bed and from that madwoman, with whom I was on no sort of terms. The illness was not a long one, and the convalescence was speedy, which restored tranquillity and joy, and caused an outburst of *Te Deums* and rejoicings. On St. Louis' day, at the concert held every year on that evening at the Tuileries, the crowd was so dense that a pin would not have fallen to the ground in the garden. The windows of the Tuileries were decorated and crammed full, and all the roofs of the Carrousel filled with all that could hold on there, as well as the square. Marshal Villeroy revelled in this concourse, which bored the king, who kept hiding himself every moment in the corners ; the marshal pulled him out by the arm and led him up to the windows. Everybody shouted 'Hurrah ! for the king!' and the marshal, detaining the king, who would still have gone and hidden himself, said, "Pray look, my dear master, at all this company, all this people, it is all yours, it all belongs to you, you are their master, pray give them a look or two just to satisfy them !' A fine lesson for a governor, and one which he did not tire of impressing upon him, so fearful was he lest he should forget it ; accordingly he retained it very perfectly."

The duke of Beauvilliers and Fénelon taught the duke of Burgundy differently ; the duke of Montausier and Bossuet himself, in spite of the majestic errors of his political conceptions, had not forgotten in the education of the grand-dauphin the lesson of kings' duties towards their peoples.

Already, over the very infancy of Louis XV. was passing the breath of decay; little by little that people, as yet so attached to their young sovereign, was about to lose all respect and submission towards its masters, a trait long characteristic of the French nation.

The king's majority was approaching, the Regent's power seemed on the point of slipping from him; Marshal Villeroy, aged, witless and tactless, irritated at the elevation of Dubois, always suspicious of the Regent's intentions towards the young king, burst out violently against the minister and displayed towards the Regent an offensive distrust: " One morning," says Duclos, " when the latter came to give an account to the king of the nomination to certain benefices, he begged his Majesty to be pleased to walk into his closet, where he had a word to say to him in private. The governor objected, saying that he knew the duties of his place, that the king could have no secrets from his governor, protested that he would not lose sight of him for an instant, and that he was bound to answer for his person. The Regent, then taking a tone of superiority, said to the marshal, ' you forget yourself, sir; you do not see the force of your expressions; it is only the king's presence that restrains me from treating you as you deserve.' Having so said, he made a profound bow to the king and went out. The disconcerted marshal followed the Regent to the door, and would have entered upon a justification; all his talk all day long was a mixture of the Roman's haughtiness and the courtier's meanness " [*Mémoires de St. Simon*].

" Next day, at noon, Marshal Villeroy repaired to the duke of Orleans' to excuse himself, fancying he might attempt an explanation as equal with equal. He crosses with his grand airs, in the midst of the whole Court, the rooms which preceded the prince's closet; the crowd opens and makes way for him respectfully. He asks in a loud tone where the duke of Orleans is; the answer is that he is busy. ' I must see him, nevertheless,' says he: ' announce me!' The moment he advances towards the door, the marquis of La Fare, captain of the Regent's guards, shows himself between the door and the marshal, arrests him, and demands his sword; Le Blanc hands him the order from the king, and at the

THE BOY KING AND HIS PEOPLE.

same instant Count d'Artagnan, commandant of the musketeers, blocks him on the opposite side to La Fare. The marshal shouts, remonstrates; he is pitched into a chair, shut up in it, and passed out by one of the windows which opens door-wise on to the garden; at the bottom of the steps of the orangery behold a carriage with six horses, surrounded by twenty musketeers. The marshal, furious, storms, threatens; he is carried into the vehicle, the carriage starts, and in less than three hours the marshal is at Villeroi, eight or nine leagues from Versailles." The king wept a moment or two without saying a word; he was consoled by the return of the bishop of Fréjus, with whom it was supposed to be all over but who was simply at Bâville, at President Lamoignon's; his pupil was as much attached to him as he was capable of being; Fleury remained alone with him, and Marshal Villeroy was escorted to Lyons, of which he was governor; he received warning not to leave it, and was not even present at the king's coronation, which took place at Rheims on the 25th of October, 1722. Amidst the royal pomp and festivities, a significant formality was for the first time neglected: that was, admitting into the nave of the church the people, burgesses and artisans, who were wont to join their voices to those of the clergy and nobility when, before the anointment of the king, demand was made in a loud voice for the consent of the assembly, representing the nation. Even in external ceremonies, the kingship was becoming every day more and more severed from national sentiment and national movement.

The king's majority, declared on the 19th of February, 1723, had made no change in the course of the government; the young prince had left Paris and resumed possession of that Palace of Versailles, still full of mementoes of the great king. The Regent, more and more absorbed by his pleasures, passed a great deal of time at Paris; Dubois had the government to himself.

His reign was not long at this unparalleled pinnacle of his greatness; he had been summoned to preside at the assembly of the clergy, and had just been elected to the French Academy, where he was received by Fontenelle, when a sore from which he had long suffered reached all at once a serious crisis; an operation was indispensable, but he set himself obstinately against it; the duke of Orleans obliged him to submit to it, and it was his death-blow; the wretched cardinal expired, without having had time to receive the sacraments.

The elevation and power of Dubois had the fatal effect of lowering France in her own eyes; she had felt that she was governed by a man whom she despised and had a right to despise; this was a deep-seated and lasting evil, authority never recovered from the blow thus struck at its moral influence. Dubois, however, was more able and more far-sighted in his foreign policy than the majority of his predecessors and his contemporaries were; without definitively losing the alliance of Spain, reattached to the interests of France by the double treaty of marriage, he had managed to form a firm connexion with England, and to rally round France the European coalition but lately in arms against her. He maintained and made peace ingloriously; he obtained it some-times by meannesses in bearing and modes of acting; he enriched himself by his intrigues, abroad as well as at home; his policy none the less was steadfastly French, even in his relations with the court of Rome and in spite of his eager desire for the cardinal's hat. He died sadly, shamefully, without a friend and without regret, even on the part of the Regent, whom he had governed and kept in hand by active and adroit assiduity, by a hardihood and an effrontery to the influence of which that prince submitted, all the while despising it. Dubois had raised up again, to place himself upon it, that throne of premier minister on which none had found a seat since Richelieu and Mazarin; the duke of Orleans succeeded him without fuss, without parade, without even appearing to have any idea of the humiliation inflicted upon him by that valet, lying in his coffin, whom he had raised to power and whose place he was about to fill for a few days.

On the 2nd of December, 1723, three months and a half after the death of Dubois, the duke of Orleans succumbed in his turn. Struck down by a sudden attack of apoplexy, whilst he was chatting with his favourite for the time, the duchess of Falarie, he expired without having recovered consciousness. Lethargized by the excesses of the table and debauchery of all kinds, more and more incapable of application and work, the prince did not preserve sufficient energy to give up the sort of life which had ruined him. For a long while the physicians had been threatening him with a sudden death: "It is all I can desire," said he. Naturally brave, intelligent, amiable, endowed with a charm of manner which recalled Henry IV., kind and merciful like him, of a mind that was inquiring, fertile, capable of applying itself to the details of affairs, Philip of Orleans was dragged down by depravity of morals to the same in soul and mind; his judgment, naturally straight-forward and correct, could still discern between good and evil, but he was incapable of energetically willing the one and firmly resisting the other; he had governed equitably, without violence and without harshness, he had attempted new and daring courses and he had managed to abandon them without any excesses or severities; like Dubois, he had inspired France with a contempt which unfortunately did not protect her from contagion. When Madame died, an inscription had been put on the tomb of that honest, rude and haughty German: "Here lies Lazybones" (*Ci-gît l'oisiveté*). All the vices thus imputed to the Regent did not perish with him, when he succumbed at forty-nine years of age under their fatal effects. "The evil that men do lives after them, the good is oft interred with their bones;" the Regency was the signal for an irregularity of morals which went on increasing, like a filthy river, up to the end of the reign of Louis XV.; the fatal seed had been germinating for a long time past under the forced and frequently hypocritical decency of the old court; it burst out under the easy-going regency of an indolent and indul-gent prince, himself wholly given to the licentiousness which he excused and authorized by his own example. From the court the evil soon spread to the nation; religious faith still struggled with-in the soul, but it had for a long while been tossed about between contrary and violent opinions, it found itself disturbed, attacked, by the new and daring ideas which were beginning to dawn in politics as well as in philosophy. The break-up was already becoming manifest, though nobody could account for it, though no fixed plan was conceived in men's minds. People devoured the memoirs of Cardinal Retz and Madame de Motteville, which had just appeared; people formed from them their judgments upon

the great persons and great events which they had seen and
depicted.   The University of Paris, under the direction of Rollin,
was developing the intelligence and lively powers of burgessdom :
and Montesquieu, as yet full young, was shooting his missiles in
the *Lettres persanes* at the men and the things of his country with
an almost cynical freedom, which was as it were the alarum and
prelude of all the liberties which he scarcely dared to claim, but of
which he already let a glimpse be seen.   Evil and good were·grow-
ing up in confusion, like the tares and the wheat.   For more than
eighty years past France has been gathering the harvest of ages ;
she has not yet separated the good grain from the rubbish which
too often conceals it.

CHAPTER LII.

LOUIS XV., THE MINISTRY OF CARDINAL FLEURY (1723—1748).

THE riotous and frivolous splendour of the Regency had suffered eclipse; before their time, in all their vigour, through disgrace or by death, Law, Dubois and the Regent, had suddenly disappeared from the stage of the world. To these men, a striking group for different reasons, notwithstanding their faults and their vices, was about to succeed a discreet but dull and limp government, the reign of an old man and, moreover, a priest. The bishop of Fréjus, who had but lately been the modest preceptor of the king and was quietly ambitious and greedy of power, but without regard to his personal interests, was about to become Cardinal Fleury and to govern France for twenty years; in 1723, he was seventy years old.

Whether from adroitness or prudence, Fleury did not all at once aspire to all-powerfulness. Assured in his heart of his sway over the as yet dormant will of his pupil, he suffered the establishment of the duke of Bourbon's ministry, who was in a greater hurry to grasp the power he had so long coveted. When the king received his cousin, head of the House of Condé, who had but lately taken the place of the duke of Maine near his person, he sought in his preceptor's eyes the guidance he needed, and contented himself with sanctioning by an inclination of the head the elevation of the duke, presented by Fleury. The new duke of Orleans, as yet quite a youth, hovering between debauchery and devotion, obtained no portion of his father's heritage; he had taken away from him even the right of doing business with the king, a right secured to him by his office of colonel-general.

The bishop of Fréjus had nursed his power more skilfully; he kept the list of benefices, and he alone, it was said, knew how to unloosen the king's tongue; but he had not calculated upon the pernicious and all-powerful influence of the marchioness of Prie, favourite "by appointment" (*attitrée*) to the duke. Clever, adroit, depraved, she aspired to govern, and chose for her minister Pâris-Duverney, one of the four Dauphinese brothers who had been engaged under the regency in the business of the *visa*, and the enemies as well as rivals of the Scotsman Law. Whilst the king hunted, and Fleury exercised quietly the measure of power which as yet contented his desires, the duke, blinded by his passion for Madame de Prie, slavishly submissive to her slightest wishes, lavished, according to his favourite's orders, honours and graces in which she managed to traffic, enriching herself brazen-facedly. Under Louis XIV. Madame de Maintenon alone, exalted to the rank of wife, had taken part in State-affairs; amidst the irregularity of his life the Regent had never accorded women any political influence, and the confusion of the orgie had never surprised from his lips a single important secret; Madame de Prie was the first to become possessed of a power destined to frequently fall, after her, into hands as depraved as they were feeble.

The strictness of the views and of the character of Pâris-Duverney strove, nevertheless, in the home department, against the insensate lavishness of the duke, and the venal irregularities of his favourite; imbued with the maxims of order and regularity formerly impressed by Colbert upon the clerks of the Treasury, and not yet completely effaced by a long interregnum, he laboured zealously to cut down expenses and useless posts, to resuscitate and regulate commerce; his ardour, systematic and wise as it was, hurried him sometimes into strange violence and improvidence; in order to restore to their proper figure values and goods which still felt the prodigious rise brought about by the *System*, Pâris-Duverney depreciated the coinage and put a tariff on merchandize as well as wages. The commotion amongst the people was great; the workmen rioted, the tradesmen refused to accept the legal figure for their goods; several men were killed in the streets, and some shops put the shutters up. The misery, which the administration had meant to relieve, went on increasing; begging was prohibited; refuges and workshops were annexed to the poor-houses; attempts were made to collect there all the old, infirm and vagabond. The rigour of procedure, as well as the insufficiency of resources, caused the failure of the philanthropic project. Lightly conceived, imprudently carried out, the new law filled the refuges with an immense crowd, taken up in all quarters, in the villages, and on the high roads; the area of the relieving-houses became insufficient. "Bedded on straw, and fed on bread and water as they ought to be," wrote the comptroller-general Dodun, "they will take up less room and be less expense." Everywhere the poor wretches sought to fly; they were branded on the arm, like criminals. All this rigour was ineffectual; the useful object of Pâris-Duverney's decrees was not attained.

Other outrages, not to be justified by any public advantage, were being at the same time committed against other poor creatures, for a long while accustomed to severities of all kinds. Without freedom, without right of worship, without assemblies, the Protestants had, nevertheless, enjoyed a sort of truce from their woes during the easy-going regency of the duke of Orleans. Amongst the number of his vices Dubois did not include hypocrisy; he had not persecuted the remnants of French Protestantism, enfeebled, dumb, but still living and breathing. The religious enthusiasm of the Camisards had become little by little extinguished; their prophets and inspired ones, who were but lately the only ministers of the religion in the midst of a people forcibly deprived of its pastors, had given place to new servants of God, regularly consecrated to His work and ready to brave for

His sake all punishments. *The Church under the Cross*, as the
Protestants of France then called themselves, was reviving slowly,
secretly, in the desert, but it was reviving. The scattered
members of the flocks, habituated for so many years past to carefully conceal their faith in order to preserve it intact in their hearts,
were beginning to draw near to one another once more; discipline
and rule were once more entering within that Church, which had
been battered by so many storms and the total destruction of
which had been loudly proclaimed. In its origin, this immense
work, as yet silently and modestly progressing, had been owing to
one single man, Antony Court, born, in 1696, of a poor family, at
Villeneuve-de-Berg in the Vivarais. He was still almost a child
when he had perceived the awakening in his soul of an ardent desire
to rebuild the walls of holy Sion; without classical education,
nurtured only upon his reading of the Bible, guided by strong
common-sense and intrepid courage, combined with a piety as
sincere as it was enlightened, he had summoned to him the
preachers of the Cévennes, heirs of the enthusiastic Camisards.
From the depths of caverns, rocks and woods had come forth
these rude ministers, fanatics or visionaries as they may have
been, eagerly devoted to their work and imbued with their pious
illusions; Court had persuaded, touched, convinced them; some
of the faithful had gathered around him, and, since the 11th of
August, 1715, at the first of those synods in the desert, unknown
to the great king whose life was ebbing away at Versailles, the
Protestant Church of France had been reconstituting itself upon
bases as sound as they were strong; the functions of the *ancients*
were every where re-established; women were forbidden to hold
forth at assemblies; the Holy Scriptures were proclaimed as the
only law of faith; pastoral ordination was required of preachers
and ministers of the religion; Cortéis, a friend of Court's, went
to Switzerland to receive from the pastors of Zurich the imposition
of hands, which he transmitted afterwards to his brethren. Everywhere the new Evangelical ministry was being recruited. "I seek
them in all places," said Court, "at the plough or behind the
counter, everywhere where I find the call for martyrdom." Of
the six devoted men who signed the statutes of the first synod,

four were destined to a martyr's death. The restorer of French Protestantism had made no mistake about the *call* then required for the holy ministry. The synods of the desert became every year more numerous; deputies from the North, from the West, from the Centre, began to join those of the South. Persecution continued, but it was local, more often prompted by the fanatical zeal of the superintendents than by the sovereign impulse of government; the pastors died without having to sorrow for the Church, up-risen from its ruins, when a vague echo of this revival came striking upon the ears of the duke and Madame de Prie, amidst the galas of Chantilly. Their silence and their exhaustion had for some time protected the Protestants; fanaticism and indifference made common cause once more to crush them at their re-awakening.

The storm had now been brewing for some years; the bishop of Nantes, Lavergne de Tressan, grand almoner to the Regent, had attempted some time before to wrest from him a rigorous decree against the Protestants; the duke of Orleans, as well as Dubois, had rejected his overtures. Scarcely had the duke (of Bourbon) come into power, when the prelate presented his project anew; indifferent and debauched, a holder of seventy-six benefices, M. de Tressan dreamed of the cardinal's hat, and aspired to obtain it from the Court of Rome at the cost of a persecution. The government was at that time drifting about, without compass or steersman, from the hands of Madame de Prie to those of Pâris-Duverney: little cared they for the fate of the Reformers. "This cast-away of the Regency," says M. Lemontey, "was adopted without memorial, without examination, as an act of homage to the late king, and a simple executive formula. The ministers of Louis XVI. afterwards found the minute of the declaration of 1724, without any preliminary report, and simply bearing on the margin the date of the old edicts." For aiming the thunderbolts against the Protestants Tressan addressed himself to their most terrible executioner. Lamoignon de Bâville was still alive; old and almost at death's door as he was, he devoted the last days of his life to drawing up for the superintendents some private instructions, an able and a cruel monument of his past experience and his persistent animosity. He died with the pen still in his hand.

The new edict turned into an act of homage to Louis XIV. the rigours of Louis XV. "Of all the grand designs of our most honoured lord and great-grandfather, there is none that we have more at heart to execute than that which he conceived of entirely extinguishing heresy in his kingdom. Arrived at majority, our first care has been to have before us the edicts whereof execution has been delayed, especially in the provinces afflicted with the contagion. We have observed that the chief abuses which demand a speedy remedy relate to illicit assemblies, the education of children, the obligation of public functionaries to profess the catholic religion, the penalties against the relapsed, and the celebration of marriage, regarding which here are our intentions : Shall be condemned : preachers to the penalty of death, their accomplices to the galleys for life, and women to be shaved and imprisoned for life. Confiscation of property. Parents who shall not have baptism administered to their children within twenty-four hours and see that they attend regularly the catechism and the schools, to fines and such sums as they may amount to together ; even to greater penalties. Midwives, physicians, surgeons, apothecaries, domestics, relatives, who shall not notify the parish-priests of births or illnesses, to fines. Persons who shall exhort the sick, to the galleys or imprisonment for life, according to sex ; confiscation of property. The sick who shall refuse the sacraments, if they recover, to banishment for life,—if they die, to be dragged on a hurdle. Desert-marriages are illegal ; the children born of them are incompetent to inherit. Minors whose parents are expatriated may marry without their authority ; but parents whose children are on foreign soil shall not consent to their marriage, on pain of the galleys for the men and banishment for the women. Finally, of all fines and confiscations, half shall be employed in providing subsistence for the new converts."

Just as the last edicts of Louis XIV., the edict of 1724 rested upon an absolute contradiction : the legislators no longer admitted the existence of any reformers in the kingdom, and yet all the battery of the most formidable punishments was directed against that Protestant Church which was said to be defunct. The same contradiction was seen in the conduct of the ecclesiastics : Protestants could not be admitted to any position, or even accomplish the ordinary duties of civil life without externally conforming to Catholicism, and, to so conform, there was required of them not only an explicit abjuration, but even an anathema against their deceased parents. " It is necessary," said Chancellor d'Aguesseau, " either that the Church should relax her vigour by some modification, or, if she does not think she ought to do so, that she should cease requesting the king to employ his authority in reducing his subjects to the impossible by commanding them to fulfil a religious duty which the Church does not permit them to perform."

At this point is revealed a progress in ideas of humanity and justice : the edict of 1724 equalled in rigour the most severe proclamations of Louis XIV.; it placed the peace and often the life of reformers at the mercy not only of an enemy's denunciation, but of a priest's simple deposition ; it destroyed all the bonds of family and substituted for the natural duties a barbarous and depraving law, but general sentiment and public opinion were no longer in accord with the royal proclamations. The clergy had not solicited the edict, the work of an ambitious man backed up by certain fanatics ; they were at first embarrassed by it ; when the old hatreds revived and the dangerous intoxications of power had affected the souls of bishops and priests, the magistracy, who had formerly been more severe towards the reformers than even the superintendents of the provinces had been, pronounced on many points in favour of the persecuted ; the judges were timid, the legislation, becoming more and more oppressive, tied their hands, but the bias of their minds was modified, it tended to extenuate and not to aggravate the effects of the edict. The law was barbarous everywhere, the persecution became so only at certain spots, owing to the zeal of the superintendents or bishops ; as usual, the South of France was the first to undergo all the rigours of it. Emigration had ceased there for a long time past ; whilst the Norman or Dauphinese Reformers, on the revival of persecution, still sought refuge on foreign soil, whilst Sweden, wasted by the wars of Charles XII., invited the French Protestants into her midst, the peasants of the Cévennes or of the Vivarais, passionately attached to the soil they cultivated, bowed their heads, with a groan, to the storm, took refuge in their rocks and their caverns, leaving the cottages deserted and the harvests to be lost, returning to their houses and their fields as soon as the soldiery were gone, ever faithful to the proscribed assemblies in the desert and praying God for the king, to whose enemies they refused to give ear. Alberoni, and after him England, had sought to detach the persecuted Protestants from their allegiance; the Court was troubled at this; they had not forgotten the huguenot regiments at the battle of the Boyne. From the depths of their hiding-places the pastors answered for the fidelity of their flocks; the voice of the illustrious and learned Basnage, for a long while a refugee in Holland, encouraged his brethren in their heroic submission. As fast as the ministers died on the gallows, new servants of God came forward to replace them, brought up in the seminary which Antony Court had founded at Lausanne and managed to keep up by means of alms from protestant Europe. It was there that the most illustrious of the pastors of the desert, Paul Rabaut, already married and father of one child, went to seek the instruction necessary for the apostolic vocation which he was to exercise for so many years in the midst of so many and such formidable perils. "On determining to exercise the ministry in this kingdom," he wrote in 1746 to the superintendent of Languedoc, Lenain d'Asfeldt, "I was not ignorant of what I exposed myself to; so I regarded myself as a victim doomed to death. I thought I was doing the greatest good of which I was capable in devoting myself to the condition of a pastor. Protestants being deprived of the free exercise of their own religion, not seeing their way to taking part in the exercises of the Roman religion, not being able to get the books they would require for their instruction, consider, my lord, what might be their condition, if they were absolutely deprived of pastors. They would be ignorant of their most essential duties, and would fall either into fanaticism, the fruitful source of extravagances and irregularities, or into indifference and contempt for all religion." The firm moderation, the courageous and simple devotion breathed by this letter, were the distinctive traits of the career of Paul Rabaut, as well as of Antony Court; throughout a persecution which lasted nearly forty years, with alternations of severity and clemency, the chiefs of French Protestantism managed to control the often recurring desperation of their flocks. On the occasion of a temporary rising on the borders of the Gardon, Paul Rabaut wrote to the governor of Languedoc:—" When I desired to know whence this evil proceeded, it was reported to me that divers persons, finding themselves liable to lose their goods and their liberty, or to have to do acts contrary to their conscience, in respect of their marriages or the baptism of their children, and knowing no way of getting out of the kingdom and setting their conscience free, abandoned themselves to despair and attacked certain priests, because they regarded them as the primal and principal cause of the vexations done to them. Once more, I blame those people, but I thought it my duty to explain to you the cause of their despair. If it be thought that my ministry is necessary to calm the ruffled spirits, I shall comply with pleasure. Above all, if I might assure the Protestants of that district that they shall not be vexed in their conscience, I would pledge myself to bind over the greater number to stop those who would make a disturbance, supposing that there should be any." At a word from Paul Rabaut calmness returned to the most ruffled spirits; sometimes his audience was composed of ten or twelve thousand of the faithful; his voice was so resonant and so distinct, that in the open air it would reach the most remote. He prayed with a fervour and an unction which penetrated all hearts, and disposed them to hear, with fruits following, the word of God. Simple, grave, penetrating rather than eloquent, his preaching, like his life, bears the impress of his character. As moderate as fervent, as judicious as heroic in spirit, Paul Rabaut preached in the desert, at the peril of his life, sermons which he had composed in a cavern. "During more than thirty years," says one of his biographers, " he had no dwelling-place but grots, hovels and cabins, whither men went to draw him like a ferocious beast. He lived a long while in a hiding-place, which one of his faithful guides had contrived for him under a heap of stones and blackberry-bushes. It was discovered by a shepherd, and, such was the wretchedness of his condition, that, when forced to abandon it, he regretted that asylum more fitted for wild beasts than for men."

The hulks were still full of the audience of Paul Rabaut, and Protestant women were still languishing in the unwholesome dungeon of the tower of Constance, when the execution of the unhappy Calas, accused of having killed his son, and the generous indignation of Voltaire cast a momentary gleam of light within the sombre region of prisons and gibbets. For the first time public opinion, at white heat, was brought to bear upon the decision of the persecutors. Calas was dead, but the decree of the Parliament of Toulouse which had sentenced him, was quashed by act of the council: his memory was cleared, and the day of toleration for French Protestants began to glimmer, pending the full dawn of justice and liberty.

We have gone over in succession, and without break, the last cruel sufferings of the French Protestants; we now turn away our eyes with a feeling of relief mingled with respect and pride; we leave the free air of the desert to return to the rakes and effeminates of Louis XV.'s court. Great was the contrast between the government which persecuted without knowing why and the victims who suffered for a faith incessantly revived in their souls by suffering. For two centuries the French Reformation had not experienced for a single day the formidable dangers of indifference and luke-warmness.

The young king was growing up, still a stranger to affairs, solely occupied with the pleasures of the chase, handsome, elegant, with noble and regular features, a cold and listless expression. In the month of February 1725, he fell ill; for two days there was great danger. The duke thought himself to be threatened with the elevation of the House of Orleans to the throne. "I'll not be caught so again," he muttered between his teeth, when he came one night to inquire how the king was: "if he recovers, I'll have him married." The king did recover, but the Infanta was only seven years old. Philip V., who had for a short time abdicated, retiring with the queen to a remote castle in the heart of the forests, had just remounted the throne after the death of his eldest son,

LOUIS XV.

Louis I. Small-pox had carried off the young monarch, who had reigned but eight months. Elizabeth Farnese, aided by the pope's nuncio and some monks who were devoted to her, had triumphed over her husband's religious scruples and the superstitious counsels of his confessor; she was once more reigning over Spain, when she heard that the little Infanta-queen, whose betrothal to the king of France had but lately caused so much joy, was about to be sent away from the court of her royal spouse. " The Infanta must be started off and by coach too, to get it over sooner," exclaimed Count Morville, who had been ordered by Madame de Prie to draw up a list of the marriageable princesses in Europe. Their number amounted to ninety-nine; twenty-five Catholics, three Anglicans, thirteen Calvinists, fifty-five Lutherans, and three Greeks. The Infanta had already started for Madrid; the Regent's two daughters, the young widow of Louis I. and Mdlle. de Beaujolais, promised to Don Carlos, were on their way back to France; the advisers of Louis XV. were still looking out for a wife for him. Spain had been mortally offended, without the duke's having yet seen his way to forming a new alliance in place of that which he had just broken off. Some attempts at arrangement with George I. had failed; an English princess could not abjure Protestantism. Such scruples did not stop Catherine I., widow of Peter the Great, who had taken the power into her own hands to the detriment of the czar's grandson; she offered the duke her second daughter, the grand-duchess Elizabeth, for King Louis XV., with a promise of abjuration on the part of the princess, and of a treaty which should secure the support of all the Muscovite forces in the interest of France. At the same time the same negotiators proposed to the duke of Bourbon himself the hand of Mary Leckzinska, daughter of Stanislaus, the dispossessed king of Poland, guaranteeing to him, on the death of King Augustus, the crown of that kingdom.

The proposals of Russia were rejected. " The princess of Muscovy," M. de Morville had lately said, " is the daughter of a low-born mother and has been brought up amidst a still barbarous people." Every great alliance appeared impossible; the duke and Madame de Prie were looking out for a queen who would

belong to them and would secure them the king's heart. Their
choice fell upon Mary Leckzinska, a good, gentle, simple creature,
without wit or beauty, twenty-two years old and living upon the
alms of France with her parents, exiles and refugees at an old
commandery of the Templars at Weissenburg. Before this King
Stanislaus had conceived the idea of marrying his daughter to
Count d'Estrées; the marriage had failed through the Regent's
refusal to make the young lord a duke and peer. The distress of
Stanislaus, his constant begging-letters to the Court of France
were warrant for the modest submissiveness of the princess.
" Madame de Prie has engaged a queen, as I might engage a valet
to-morrow," writes Marquis d'Argenson; " it is a pity."

When the first overtures from the duke arrived at Weissenburg,
King Stanislaus entered the room where his wife and daughter
were at work, and, " Fall we on our knees, and thank God !" he
said. " My dear father," exclaimed the princess, " can you be
recalled to the throne of Poland ? " " God has done us a more
astounding grace," replied Stanislaus: " you are queen of
France ! "

" Never shall I forget the horror of the calamities we were
enduring in France, when Queen Mary Leckzinska arrived," says
M. d'Argenson. " A continuance of rain had caused famine, and
it was much aggravated by the bad government under the duke.
That government, whatever may be said of it, was even more
hurtful through bad judgment than from interested views, which
had not so much to do with it as was said. There were very
costly measures taken to import foreign corn; but that only
augmented the alarm, and, consequently, the dearness.

" Fancy the unparalleled misery of the country-places ! It was
just the time when everybody was thinking of harvests and ingather-
ings of all sorts of things, which it had not been possible to get in
for the continual rains; the poor farmer was watching for a dry
moment to get them in; meanwhile all the district was beaten with
many a scourge. The peasants had been sent off to prepare the
roads by which the queen was to pass, and they were only the
worse for it, insomuch that Her Majesty was often within a thought
of drowning; they pulled her from her carriage by the strong arm,

as best they might.   In several stopping-places she and her suite
were swimming in water which spread everywhere, and that in
spite of the unparalleled pains that had been taken by a tyrannical
ministry."

It was under such sad auspices that Mary Leckzinska arrived at
Versailles.   Fleury had made no objection to the marriage.
Louis XV. accepted it, just as he had allowed the breaking-off of
his union with the Infanta and that of France with Spain.   For a
while the duke had hopes of reaping all the fruit of the unequal
marriage he had just concluded for the king of France.   The queen
was devoted to him ; he enlisted her in an intrigue against Fleury.
The king was engaged with his old preceptor, the queen sent for
him, he did not return.   Fleury waited a long while.   The duke
and Pâris-Duverney had been found with the queen, they had papers
before them, the king had set to work with them.   When he went
back, at length, to his closet, Louis XV. found the bishop no longer
there ; search was made for him ; he was no longer in the palace.

The king was sorry and put out ; the duke of Mortemart, who
was his gentleman of the bedchamber, handed him a letter from
Fleury.   The latter had retired to Issy, to the country-house of the
Sulpicians ; he bade the king farewell, assuring him that he had
for a long while been resolved, according to the usage of his
youth, to put some space between the world and death.   Louis
began to shed tears ; Mortemart proposed to go and fetch Fleury,
and got the order given him to do so.   The duke had to write the
letter of recall.   Next morning the bishop was at Versailles, gentle
and modest as ever, and exhibiting neither resentment nor surprise.
Six months later, however, the king set out from Versailles to go
and visit the count and countess of Toulouse at Rambouillet.   The
duke was in attendance at his departure : " Do not make us wait
supper, cousin," said the young monarch graciously.   Scarcely had
his equipages disappeared, when a letter was brought : the duke
was ordered to quit the court and retire provisionally to Chantilly.
Madame de Prie was exiled to her estates in Normandy, where she
soon died of spite and anger.   The head of the House of Condé
came forth no more from the political obscurity which befitted his
talents.   At length Fleury remained sole master.

He took possession of it without fuss or any external manifesta-
tion ; caring only for real authority, he advised Louis XV. not to
create any premier minister and to govern by himself, like his
great-grandfather. The king took this advice, as every other, and
left Fleury to govern. This was just what the bishop intended ; a
sleepy calm succeeded the commotions which had been caused by
the inconsistent and spasmodic government of the duke ; galas and
silly expenses gave place to a wise economy, the real and important
blessing of Fleury's administration. Commerce and industry
recovered confidence ; business was developed ; the increase of the
revenues justified a diminution of taxation ; war, which was
imminent at the moment of the duke's fall, seemed to be escaped ;
the bishop of Fréjus became Cardinal Fleury ; the court of Rome
paid on the nail for the service rendered it by the new minister in
freeing the clergy from the tax of the fiftieth (*impot du cinquan-
tième*). " Consecrated to God and kept aloof from the commerce
of men," had been Fleury's expression, " the dues of the Church are
irrevocable and cannot be subject to any tax whether of ratification
or any other." The clergy responded to this pleasant exposition
of principles by a gratuitous gift of five millions. Strife ceased in
every quarter ; France found herself at rest, without lustre as
well as without prospect.

It was not, henceforth, at Versailles that the destinies of Europe
were discussed and decided. The dismissal of the Infanta had
struck a deadly blow at the frail edifice of the quadruple alliance,
fruit of the intrigues and diplomatic ability of Cardinal Dubois.
Philip V. and Elizabeth Farnese, deeply wounded by the affront
put upon them, had hasted to give the Infanta to the prince of
Brazil, heir to the throne of Portugal, at the same time that the
prince of the Asturias espoused a daughter of John V. Under
cover of this alliance, agreeable as it was to England, the faithful
patron of Portugal, the king of Spain was negotiating elsewhere,
with the emperor Charles VI., the most ancient and hitherto the
most implacable of his enemies. This prince had no son, and
wished to secure the succession to his eldest daughter, the archduchess Maria Theresa. The Pragmatic-Sanction which declared
this wish awaited the assent of Europe ; that of Spain was of

great value; she offered, besides, to open her ports to the Ostend Company, lately established by the emperor to compete against the Dutch trade.

The House of Austria divided the House of Bourbon, by opposing to one another the two branches of France and Spain; the treaty of Vienna was concluded on the 1st of May, 1725. The two sovereigns renounced all pretensions to each other's dominions respectively, and proclaimed, on both sides, full amnesty for the respective partisans. The emperor recognized the hereditary rights of Don Carlos to the duchies of Tuscany, Parma and Piacenza; he, at the same time, promised his good offices with England to obtain restitution of Gibraltar and Mahon. In spite of the negotiations already commenced with the duke of Lorraine, hopes were even held out to the two sons of Elizabeth Farnese, Don Carlos and Don Philip, of obtaining the hands of the archduchesses, daughters of the emperor.

When the official treaty was published and the secret articles began to transpire, Europe was in commotion at the new situation in which it was placed. George I. repaired to his German dominions, in order to have a closer view of the emperor's movements. There the count of Broglie soon joined him, in the name of France. The king of Prussia, Frederick William I., the king of England's son-in-law, was summoned to Hanover. Passionate and fantastic, tyrannical, addicted to the coarsest excesses, the king of Prussia had, nevertheless, managed to form an excellent army of sixty thousand men, at the same time amassing a military treasure amounting to twenty-eight millions; he joined, not without hesitation, the treaty of Hanover, concluded on the 3rd of September, 1725, between France and England. The Hollanders, in spite of their desire to ruin the Ostend Company, had not yet signed the convention; Frederick William was disturbed at their coming in: "Say, I declare against the emperor," said he in a letter which he communicated on the 5th of December to the ambassadors of France and England: "he will not fail to get the Muscovites and Poles to act against me. I ask whether their majesties will then keep my rear open? England, completely surrounded by sea, and France, happening to be covered by strong

places, consider themselves pretty safe, whilst the greater part of
my dominions are exposed to anything it shall seem good to
attempt.   By this last treaty, then, I engage in war for the benefit
of Mr. Hollander and Co., that they may be able to sell their tea,
coffee, cheese and crockery dearer; those gentlemen will not do
the least thing for me, and I am to do everything for them.
Gentlemen, tell me, is it fair? If you deprive the emperor of his
ships and ruin his Ostend trade, will he be a less emperor than he
is at this moment?   The pink of all (*le pot aux roses*) is to deprive
the emperor of provinces, but which? And to whose share will
they fall? Where are the troops? Where is the *needful*, wherewith to make war? Since it seems good to commence the dance,
it must of course be commenced. After war comes peace. Shall
I be forgotten? Shall I be the last of all? Shall I have to sign
perforce?"   The coarse common-sense of the Vandal soon prevailed over family alliances; Frederick William broke with France
and England in order to rally to the emperor's side. Russia, but
lately so attentive to France, was making advances to Spain:
" The Czar's envoy is the most taciturn Muscovite that ever came
from Siberia," wrote Marshal Tessé. " Goodman Don Miguel
Guerra is the minister with whom he treats, and the effect of
eight or ten apoplexies is that he has to hold his head with his
hands, else his mouth would infallibly twist round over his
shoulder. During their audience they seat themselves opposite
one another in arm-chairs, and, after a quarter of an hour's silence,
the Muscovite opens his mouth and says : ' Sir, I have orders from
the emperor, my master, to assure the Catholic king that he loves
him very much.' ' And I,' replies Guerra, ' do assure you that the
king my master loves your master the emperor very much.' After
this laconic conversation they stare at one another for a quarter of
an hour without saying anything, and the audience is over."

The tradition handed down by Peter the Great forbade any
alliance with England; M. de Campredon, French ambassador at
Petersburg, was seeking to destroy this prejudice. One of the
empress's ministers, Jokosinski, rushed abruptly from the conference ; he was half drunk, and he ran to the church where the
remains of the czar were lying. " O my dear master!" he cried

before all the people, " rise from the tomb, and see how thy memory is trampled under foot!" Antipathy towards England, nevertheless, kept Catherine I. aloof from the Hanoverian league; she made alliance with the emperor. France was not long before she

MARY LECZINSKA.

made overtures to Spain. Philip V. always found it painful to endure family dissensions; he became reconciled with his nephew, and accepted the intervention of Cardinal Fleury in his disagreements with England. The alliance, signed at Seville on the 29th

of November, 1729, secured to Spain, in return for certain commercial advantages, the co-operation of England in Italy.   The
duke of Parma had just died; the Infante Don Carlos, supported
by an English fleet, took possession of his dominions.   Elizabeth
Farnese had at last set foot in Italy.   She no longer encountered
there the able and ambitious monarch whose diplomacy had for so
long governed the affairs of the peninsula; Victor Amadeo had
just abdicated.   Scarcely a year had passed from the date of that
resolution, when, suddenly, from fear it was said of seeing his
father resume power, the young king, Charles Emmanuel, had him
arrested in his castle of Pontarlier.   "It will be a fine subject for
a tragedy, this that is just now happening to Victor, king of
Sardinia," writes M. d'Argenson.   "What a catastrophe without
a death!   A great king, who plagued Europe with his virtues and
his vices, with his courage, his artifices and his perfidies, who had
formed round him a court of slaves, who had rendered his dominion
formidable by his industry and his labours; indefatigable in his
designs, unresting in every branch of government, cherishing
none but great projects, credited in every matter with greater
designs than he had yet been known to execute, this king abdicates
unexpectedly, and, almost immediately, here he finds himself
arrested by his son, whose benefactor he had been so recently and
so extraordinarily!   This son is a young prince without merit,
without courage and without capacity, gentle and under control.
His ministers persuaded him to be ungrateful; he accomplishes
the height of crime, without having crime in his nature, and here
is his father shut up like a bear in a prison, guarded at sight like
a maniac, and separated from the wife whom he had chosen for
consolation in his retirement!"   Public indignation, however, soon
forced the hand of Charles Emmanuel's minister: Victor Amadeo
was released; his wife, detained in shameful captivity, was restored
to him; he died soon afterwards in that same castle of Pontarlier,
whence he had been carried off without a voice being raised in his
favour by the princes who were bound to him by the closest ties
of blood.

The efforts made in common by Fleury and Robert Walpole,
prime minister of the king of England, had for a long while been

successful in maintaining the general peace; the unforeseen death of Augustus of Saxony, king of Poland, suddenly came to trouble it. It was, thenceforth, the unhappy fate of Poland to be a constant source of commotion and discord in Europe. The elector of Saxony, son of Augustus II., was supported by Austria and Russia; the national party in Poland invited Stanislaus Leckzinski; he was elected at the Diet by sixty thousand men of family, and set out to take possession of the throne, reckoning upon the promises of his son-in-law, and on the military spirit which was reviving in France. The young men burned to win their spurs; the old generals of Louis XIV. were tired of idleness.

The ardour of Cardinal Fleury did not respond to that of the friends of King Stanislaus. Russia and Austria made an imposing display of force in favour of the elector of Saxony; France sent, tardily, a body of fifteen hundred men; this ridiculous reinforcement had not yet arrived when Stanislaus, obliged to withdraw from Warsaw, had already shut himself up in Dantzic. The Austrian general had invested the place.

News of the bombardment of Dantzic greeted the little French corps as they approached the fort of Wechselmunde. Their commander saw his impotence; instead of landing his troops, he made sail for Copenhagen. The French ambassador at that court, Count Plelo, was indignant to see his countrymen's retreat, and, hastily collecting a hundred volunteers, he summoned to him the chiefs of the expeditionary corps. "How could you resolve upon not fighting, at any price?" he asked. "That is easy to say," rejoined one of the officers roughly, "when you're safe in your closet." "I shall not be there long!" exclaims the count, and presses them to return with him to Dantzic. The officer in command of the detachment, M. de la Peyrouse Lamotte, yields to his entreaties. They set out both of them, persuaded at the same time of the uselessness of their enterprise and of the necessity they were under, for the honour of France, to attempt it. Before embarking Count Plelo wrote to M. de Chauvelin, the then keeper of the seals: "I am sure not to return; I commend to you my wife and children." Scarcely had the gallant little band touched land beneath the fort of Wechselmunde, when they marched up to the

Russian lines, opening a way through the pikes and muskets in hopes of joining the besieged, who at the same time effected a sally.　Already the enemy began to recoil at sight of such audacity, when M. de Plelo fell mortally wounded ; the enemy's battalions had hemmed in the French.　La Peyrouse succeeded, however, in effecting his retreat, and brought away his little band into the camp they had established under shelter of the fort.　For a month the French kept up a rivalry in courage with the defenders of Dantzic ; when at last they capitulated, on the 23rd of June, General Munich had conceived such esteem for their courage that he granted them leave to embark with arms and baggage.　A few days later King Stanislaus escaped alone from Dantzic, which was at length obliged to surrender on the 7th of July, and sought refuge in the dominions of the king of Prussia.　Some Polish lords went and joined him at Königsberg.　Partisan war continued still, but the arms and influence of Austria and Russia had carried the day ; the national party was beaten in Poland.　The pope released the Polish gentry from the oath they had made never to entrust the crown to a foreigner.　Augustus III., recognized by the mass of the nation, became the docile tool of Russia, whilst in Germany and in Italy the Austrians found themselves attacked simultaneously by France, Spain, and Sardinia.

Marshal Berwick had taken the fort of Kehl in the month of December, 1733 ; he had forced the lines of the Austrians at Erlingen at the commencement of the campaign of 1734, and he had just opened trenches against Philipsburg, when he pushed forward imprudently in a reconnoissance between the fires of the besiegers and besieged: a ball wounded him mortally, and he expired immediately, like Marshal Turenne ; he was sixty-three.　The duke of Noailles, who at once received the marshal's bâton, succeeded him in the command of the army by agreement with Marshal d'Asfeldt.　Philipsburg was taken after forty-eight days' open trenches, without Prince Eugene, all the while within hail, making any attempt to relieve the town.　He had not approved of the war : " Of three emperors that I have served," he would say, " the first, Leopold, was my father ; the emperor Joseph was my brother ; this one is my master."　Eugene was old and worn out ;

DEATH OF PLELO.

he preserved his ability, but his ardour was gone. Marshal Noailles and D'Asfeldt did not agree; France did not reap her advantages. The campaign of 1735 hung fire in Germany.

It was not more splendid in Italy, where the outset of the war had been brilliant. Presumptuous as ever, in spite of his eighty-two years, Villars had started for Italy, saying to Cardinal Fleury: " The king may dispose of Italy, I am going to conquer it for him." And, indeed, within three months, nearly the whole of Milaness was reduced. Cremona and Pizzighitone had surrendered; but already King Charles Emmanuel was relaxing his efforts with the prudent selfishness customary with his House. The Sardinian contingents did not arrive; the Austrians had seized a passage over the Po; Villars, however, was preparing to force it, when a large body of the enemy came down upon him. The king of Sardinia was urged to retire: " That is not the way to get out of this," cried the Marshal, and, sword in hand. he charged at the head of the body-guard; Charles Emmanuel followed his example; the Austrians were driven in. " Sir," said Villars to the king who was complimenting him, " these are the last sparks of my life; thus, at departing, I take my leave of it."

Death, in fact, had already seized his prey; the aged marshal had not time to return to France to yield up his last breath there; he was expiring at Turin, when he heard of Marshal Berwick's death before Philipsburg; " That fellow always was lucky," said he. On the 17th of June, 1734, Villars died, in his turn, by a strange coincidence in the very room in which he had been born when his father was French ambassador at the court of the duke of Savoy.

Some days later Marshals Broglie and Coigny defeated the Austrians before Parma; the general-in-chief, M. de Mercy, had been killed on the 19th of September; the prince of Wurtemberg, in his turn, succumbed at the battle of Guastalla, and yet these successes on the part of the French produced no serious result. The Spaniards had become masters of the kingdom of Naples and of nearly all Sicily; the Austrians had fallen back on the Tyrol, keeping a garrison at Mantua only. The duke of Noailles, then at the head of the army, was preparing for the siege of the place, in order to achieve that deliverance of Italy which was as early as then the dream of France, but the king of Sardinia and the queen of Spain were already disputing for Mantua; the Sardinian troops withdrew, and it was in the midst of his forced inactivity that the duke of Noailles heard of the armistice signed in Germany. Cardinal Fleury, weary of the war which he had entered upon with regret, disquieted too at the new complications which he foresaw in Europe, had already commenced negotiations; the preliminaries were signed at Vienna in the month of October, 1735.

The conditions of the treaty astonished Europe. Cardinal Fleury had renounced the ambitious idea suggested to him by Chauvelin; he no longer aspired to impose upon the emperor the complete emancipation of Italy, but he made such disposition as he pleased of the States there and reconstituted the territories according to his fancy. The kingdom of Naples and the Two Sicilies were secured to Don Carlos, who renounced Tuscany and the duchies of Parma and Piacenza. These three principalities were to form the appanage of Duke Francis of Lorraine, betrothed to the Archduchess Maria Theresa. There it was that France was to find her share of the spoil; in exchange for the dominions formed for him in Italy, Duke Francis ceded the duchies of Lorraine and Bar to King Stanislaus; the latter formally renounced the throne of Poland, at the same time preserving the title of king and resuming possession of his property; after him, Lorraine and the Barrois were to be united to the crown of France, as dower and heritage of that queen who had been but lately raised to the throne by a base intrigue and who thus secured to her new country a province so often taken and retaken, an object of so many treaties and negotiations, and thenceforth so tenderly cherished by France.

The negotiations had been protracted. England, stranger as she had been to the war, had taken part in the diplomatic proposals. The queen of Spain had wanted to keep the States in the north of Italy, as well as those in the south: " Shall I not have a new heir given me by and by?" said the duke of Tuscany, John Gaston de' Medici, last and unworthy scion of that illustrious family, who was dying without posterity: " which is the third child that

France and the Empire mean to father upon me ?" The king of Sardinia gained only Novara and Tortona, whilst the emperor recovered Milaness. France renounced all her conquests in Germany; she guaranteed the Pragmatic-Sanction. Russia evacuated Poland: peace seemed to be firmly established in Europe. Cardinal Fleury hasted to consolidate it, by removing from power the ambitious and daring politician whose influence he dreaded. " Chauvelin had juggled the war from Fleury," said the prince of Prussia, afterwards the great Frederick; " Fleury in turn juggles peace and the ministry from him."

"It must be admitted," wrote M. d'Argenson, "that the situation of Cardinal Fleury and the keeper of the seals towards one another is a singular one just now. The cardinal, disinterested, sympathetic, with upright views, doing nothing save from excess of importunity and measuring his compliance by the number and not the weight of the said importunities—the minister, I say, considers himself bound to fill his place as long as he is in this world. It is only as his own creature that he has given so much advancement to the keeper of the seals, considering him wholly his, good, amiable and of solid merit, without the aid of any intrigue ; and so his adjunction to the premier minister has made the keeper of the seals a butt for all the ministers. He has taken upon himself all refusals and left to the cardinal the honour of all benefits and graces ; he has transported himself in imagination to the time when he would be sole governor, and he would have had affairs set, in advance, upon the footing on which he calculated upon placing them. It must be admitted, as regards that, that he has ideas too lofty and grand for the State ; he would like to set Europe by the ears, as the great ministers did ; he is accused of resembling M. de Louvois, to whom he is related. Now the cardinal is of a character the very opposite to that of this adjunct of his. M. Chauvelin has embarked him upon many great enterprises, upon that of the late war amongst others ; but scarcely is His Eminence embarked by means of some passion that is worked upon, when the chill returns and the desire of getting out of the business becomes another passion with him. Altogether, I see no great harm in the keeper of the seals being no longer minister, for I do not like any but a homely (*bourgeoise*) policy, whereby one lives on good terms with one's neighbours and whereby one is merely their arbiter, for the sake of working a good long while and continuously at the task of perfecting the home-affairs of the kingdom and rendering Frenchmen happy."

M. d'Argenson made no mistake; the era of a great foreign policy had passed away for France. A king, who was frivolous and indifferent to his business as well as to his glory; a minister aged, economizing and timid; an ambitious few, with views more bold than discreet—such were henceforth the instruments at the disposal of France; the resources were insufficient for the internal government; the peace of Vienna and the annexation of Lorraine were the last important successes of external policy. Chauvelin had the honour of connecting his name therewith before disappearing for ever in his retreat at Grosbois, to expend his life in vain regrets for lost power and in vain attempts to recover it.

Peace reigned in Europe, and Cardinal Fleury governed France without rival and without opposition. He had but lately, like Richelieu, to whom, however, he did not care to be compared, triumphed over parliamentary revolt. Jealous of their ancient, traditional rights, the Parliament claimed to share with the government the care of watching over the conduct of the clergy. It was on that ground that they had rejected the introduction of the Legend of Gregory VII., recently canonized at Rome, and had sought to mix themselves up in the religious disputes excited just then by the pretended miracles wrought at the tomb of Deacon Pâris, a pious and modest Jansenist, who had lately died in the odour of sanctity in the parish of St. Médard. The cardinal had ordered the cemetery to be closed, in order to cut short the strange spectacles presented by the convulsionists; and, to break down the opposition of Parliament, the king had ordered, at a bed of justice, the registration of all the papal bulls succeeding the *Unigenitus*. In vain had D'Aguesseau, reappointed to the chancellorship, exhorted the Parliament to yield : he had fallen in public esteem. Abbé Pernelle, ecclesiastical councillor, as distinguished for his talent as for his courage, proposed a solemn declaration, analogous, at bottom, to the *maxims* of the Gallican Church, which had been drawn up by Bossuet, in the assembly of the clergy of France. The decision of the Parliament was quashed by the council. An order from the king, forbidding discussion, was brought to the court by Count Maurepas; its contents were divined, and Parliament refused to open it. The king iterated his injunctions. " If his Majesty were at the Louvre," cried Abbe Pernelle, " it would be the Court's duty to go and let him know how his orders are executed." " Marly is not so very far ! " shouted a young appeal-court councillor (aux enquêtes) eagerly. " To Marly ! To Marly !" at once repeated the whole Chamber. The old councillors themselves murmured between their teeth " To Marly ! " Fourteen cariages conveyed to Marly fifty magistrates, headed by the presidents. The king refused to receive them; in vain the premier president insisted upon it, to Cardinal Fleury ; the monarch and his Parliament remained equally obstinate. " What a sad position ! " exclaimed Abbé Pernelle, " not to be able to fulfil one's duties without falling into the crime of disobedience ! We speak, and we are forbidden a word; we deliberate, and we are threatened. What remains for us, then, in this deplorable position, but to represent to the king the impossibility of existing under form of Parliament, without having permission to speak; the impossibility, by consequence, of continuing our functions ? " Abbé Pernelle was carried off in the night and confined in the abbey of Corbigny, in Nivernais, of which he was titular head. Other councillors were arrested ; a hundred and fifty magistrates immediately gave in their resignation. Rising in the middle of the assembly, they went out two and two, dressed in their long scarlet robes, and threaded the crowd in silence. There was a shout as they went : " There go true Romans, and fathers of their country ! " " All those who saw this procession," says the advocate Barbier, " declare that it was something august and overpowering." The government did not accept the resignations ; the struggle continued. A hundred and thirty-nine members received letters under the king's seal (lettres de cachet), exiling them to the four quarters of France. The Grand Chamber had been spared ; the old councillors, alone remaining, enregistered purely and simply the declarations of the keeper of the seals. Once more the Parliament was subdued, it had testified its complete political impotence; the iron hand of Richelieu, the perfect address of Mazarin, were no longer necessary to silence it; the prudent moderation, the reserved frigidity of Cardinal Fleury had sufficed for the purpose. " The minister, victorious over the Parliament, had become the arbiter of Europe," said Frederick II., in his *History of my Time.* The standard of intelligences and of wills had everywhere sunk down to the level of the government of France; unhappily the day was coming when the thrones of Europe were about to be occupied by stronger and more expanded minds, whilst France was passing slowly from the hands of a more than octogenarian minister into those of a voluptuous monarch, governed by his courtiers and his favourites. Frederick II., Maria Theresa, Lord Chatham, Catherine II., were about to appear upon the scene; the French had none to oppose them but Cardinal Fleury with one foot in the grave, and, after him, King Louis XV. and Madame de Pompadour.

It was amidst this state of things that the death of the Emperor Charles VI. on the 20th of October, 1740, occurred to throw Europe into a new ferment of discord and war. Maria Theresa, the emperor's eldest daughter, was twenty-three years old, beautiful, virtuous, and of a lofty and resolute character; her rights to the paternal heritage had been guaranteed by all Europe. Europe, however, soon rose, almost in its entirety, to oppose them. The elector of Bavaria claimed the domains of the House of Austria, by virtue of a will of Ferdinand I., father of Charles V. The king of Poland urged the rights of his wife, daughter of the Emperor Joseph I. Spain put forth her claims to Hungary and Bohemia, apanage of the elder branch of the House of Austria. Sardinia desired her share in Italy. Prussia had a new sovereign, who spoke but little, but was the first to act.

Kept for a long while by his father in cruel captivity, always carefully held aloof from affairs, and, to pass the time, obliged to engage in literature and science, Frederick II. had ascended the throne in August, 1740, with the reputation of a mind cultivated, liberal and accessible to noble ideas. Voltaire, with whom he had become connected, had trumpeted his praises everywhere: the first act of the new king revealed qualities of which Voltaire had no conception. On the 23rd of December, after leaving a masked ball, he started post-haste for the frontier of Silesia, where he had collected thirty thousand men. Without preliminary notice, without declaration of war, he at once entered the Austrian territory, which was scantily defended by three thousand men and a few garrisons. Before the end of January, 1741, the Prussians were masters of Silesia. " I am going, I fancy, to play your game," Frederick had said, as he set off, to the French ambassador: " if the aces come to me we will share."

Meanwhile France, as well as the majority of the other nations, had recognized the young Queen of Hungary. She had been proclaimed at Vienna on the 7th of November, 1740; all her father's States had sworn alliance and homage to her. She had consented to take to the Hungarians the old oath of King Andreas II., which had been constantly refused by the House of Hapsburg: " If I, or any of my successors, at any time whatsoever, would infringe your privileges, be it permitted you, by virtue of this promise, you and your descendants, to defend yourselves, without being liable to be treated as rebels."

When Frederick II., encamped in the midst of the conquered provinces, made a proposal to Maria Theresa to cede him Lower Silesia, to which his ancestors had always raised pretensions, assuring her, in return, of his amity and support, the young queen, deeply offended, replied haughtily that she defended her subjects, she did not sell them. At the same time an Austrian army was advancing against the king of Prussia; it was commanded by Count Neipperg. The encounter took place at Molwitz, on the banks of the Neiss. For one instant Frederick, carried along by his routed cavalry, thought the battle was lost and his first step towards glory an unlucky business. The infantry, formed by the aged prince of Anhalt and commanded by Marshal Schwerin, late comrade of Charles XII., restored the fortune of battle; the Austrians had retired in disorder. Europe gave the king of Prussia credit for this first success, due especially to the excellent organization of his father's troops. " Each battalion," says Frederick, " was a walking battery, whose quickness in loading tripled their fire, which gave the Prussians the advantage of three to one."

Meanwhile, in addition to the heritage of the House of Austria, thus attacked and encroached upon, there was the question of the Empire. Two claimants appeared: Duke Francis of Lorraine, Maria Theresa's husband, whom she had appointed regent of her dominions, and the elector of Bavaria, grandson of Louis XIV.'s faithful ally, the only Catholic amongst the lay-electors of the Empire, who was only waiting for the signal from France to act, in his turn, against the queen of Hungary.

Cardinal Fleury's intentions remained as yet vague and secret. Naturally and stubbornly pacific as he was, he felt himself bound by the confirmation of the Pragmatic-Sanction, lately renewed, at the time of the treaty of Vienna. The king affected indifference. "Whom are you for making emperor, Souvré?" he asked one of his courtiers. "Faith, sir," answered the marquis, "I trouble myself very little about it; but, if your Majesty pleased, you might tell us more about it than anybody." "No," said the king: "I shall have nothing to do with it, I shall look on from Mont-Pagnotte" [a post of observation out of cannon-shot]. "Ah! sir," replied Souvré, "your Majesty will be very cold there and very ill lodged." "How so?" said the king. "Sir," replied Souvré, "because your ancestors never had any house built there." "A very pretty answer," adds the advocate Barbier, "and as regards the question, nothing can be made of it, because the king is mighty close."

A powerful intrigue was urging the king to war. Cardinal Fleury, prudent, economizing, timid as he was, had taken a liking for a man of adventurous and sometimes chimerical spirit. "Count Belle-Isle, grandson of Fouquet," says M. d'Argenson, "had more wit than judgment, and more fire than force, but he aimed very high." He dreamed of revising the map of Europe and of forming a zone of small States destined to protect France against the designs of Austria. Louis XV. pretended to nothing, demanded nothing for the price of his assistance; but France had been united from time immemorial to Bavaria: she was bound to raise the elector to the imperial throne. If it happened afterwards, in the dismemberment of the Austrian dominions, that the Low

MORIAMUR PRO REGE NOSTRO!

Countries fell to the share of France, it was the natural sequel of past conquests of Flanders, Lorraine and the Three Bishoprics. Count Belle-Isle did not disturb with his dreams the calm of the aged cardinal; he was modest in his military aspirations. The French navy was ruined, the king had hardly twenty vessels to send to sea; that mattered little, as England and Holland took no part in the contest; Austria was not a maritime power; Spain joined with France to support the elector. A body of forty thousand men was put under the orders of that prince, who received the title of lieutenant-general of the armies of the king of France. Louis XV. acted only in the capacity of Bavaria's ally and auxiliary. Meanwhile Marshal Belle-Isle, the king's ambassador and plenipotentiary in Germany, had just signed a treaty with Frederick II., guaranteeing to that monarch Lower Silesia. At the same time, a second French army under the orders of Marshal Maillebois entered Germany; Saxony and Poland came into the coalition. The king of England, George II., faithful to the Pragmatic-Sanction, hurrying over to Hanover to raise troops there, found himself threatened by Maillebois and signed a treaty of neutrality. The elector had been proclaimed, at Lintz, archduke of Austria: nowhere did the Franco-Bavarian army encounter any obstacle. The king of Prussia was occupying Moravia; Upper and Lower Austria had been conquered without a blow, and by this time the forces of the enemy were threatening Vienna. The success of the invasion was like a dream, but the elector had not the wit to profit by the good fortune which was offered him. On the point of entering the capital abandoned by Maria Theresa, he fell back and marched towards Bohemia; the gates of Prague did not open like those of Passau or of Lintz, it had to be besieged. The grand-duke of Tuscany was advancing to the relief of the town; it was determined to deliver the assault.

Count Maurice of Saxony, natural son of the late king of Poland, the most able and ere long the most illustrious of the generals in the service of France, had opposed the retrograde movement towards Bohemia. In front of Prague, he sent for Chevert, lieutenant-colonel of the regiment of Beauce, of humble origin, but destined to rise by his courage and merit to the highest rank in

the army; the two officers made a reconnoissance; the moment
and the point of attack were chosen. At the approach of night on
the 25th of November, 1741, Chevert called up a grenadier:
"Thou seest yonder sentry?" said he to the soldier. "Yes,
colonel." "He will shout to thee, 'Who goes there?'" "Yes,
colonel." "He will fire upon thee and miss thee." "Yes, colonel."
"Thou'lt kill him, and I shall be at thy heels." The grenadier
salutes and mounts up to the assault; the body of the sentry had
scarcely begun to roll over the rampart when Colonel Chevert
followed the soldier; the eldest son of Marshal Broglie was behind
him.

Fifty men had escaladed the wall before the alarm spread
through the town; a gate was soon burst to permit the entrance
of Count Maurice with a body of cavalry. Next day the elector
was crowned as king of Bohemia; on the 13th of January, 1742,
he was proclaimed emperor, under the name of Charles VII.

A few weeks had sufficed to crown the success; less time sufficed
to undo it. On flying from Vienna, Maria Theresa had sought
refuge in Hungary; the assembly of the Estates held a meeting
at Presburg; there she appeared, dressed in mourning, holding in
her arms her son, scarce six months old. Already she had known
how to attach the magnates to her by the confidence she had
shown them; she held out to them her child; "I am abandoned
of my friends," said she in Latin, a language still in use in Hungary amongst the upper classes; "I am pursued by my enemies,
attacked by my relatives; I have no hope but in your fidelity and
courage; we—my son and I—look to you for our safety."

The palatines scarcely gave the queen time to finish; already
the sabres were out of the sheaths and flashing above their heads.
Count Bathyany was the first to shout: "*Moriamur pro rege
nostro Mariâ Theresâ!*" The same shout was repeated everywhere; Maria Theresa, restraining her tears, thanked her defenders with gesture and voice; she was expecting a second child
before long: "I know not," she wrote to her mother-in-law the
duchess of Lorraine, "if I shall have a town left to be confined in."
Hungary rose, like one man, to protect her sovereign against the
excess of her misfortunes; the same spirit spread before long

through the Austrian provinces; bodies of irregulars, savage and cruel, formed at all points, attacking and massacring the French detachments they encountered, and giving to the war a character of ferocity which displayed itself with special excess against Bavaria. Count Ségur, besieged in Lintz, was obliged to capitulate on the 26th of January, and the day after the elector of Bavaria had received the imperial crown at Frankfurt—February 12, 1742—the Austrians, under the orders of General Khevenhuller, obtained possession of Munich, which was given up to pillage. Jokes then began to fly about in Paris at the expense of the emperor who had just been made after an interregnum of more than a year: "The thing in the world which it is perceived that one can most easily do without," said Voltaire, "is an emperor." "As Paris is always crammed with a number of Austrians in heart who are charmed at the sad events," writes the advocate Barbier, "they have put in the Bastille some indiscreet individuals who said in open *café* that the emperor was *John Lackland* and that a room would have to be fitted up for him at Vincennes. In point of fact, he remains at Frankfurt, and it would be very hard for him to go elsewhere in safety."

Meanwhile England had renounced her neutrality: the general feeling of the nation prevailed over the prudent and far-sighted ability of Robert Walpole; he succumbed, after his long ministry, full of honours and riches; the government had passed into warlike hands. The women of society, headed by the duchess of Marlborough, raised a subscription of 100,000*l.* which they offered unsuccessfully to the haughty Maria Theresa. Parliament voted more effectual aid, and English diplomacy adroitly detached the king of Sardinia from the allies whom success appeared to be abandoning. The king of Prussia had just gained at Czezlaw an important victory; next day, he was negotiating with the queen of Hungary. On the 11th of June the treaty which abandoned Silesia to Frederick II. was secretly concluded; when the signatures were exchanged at Berlin in the following month, the withdrawal of Prussia was everywhere known in Europe: "This is the method introduced and accepted amongst the allies: to separate and do a better stroke of business by being the first to make

terms," writes M. d'Argenson on 30th June: "it used not to be
so. The English were the first to separate from the great alliance
in 1711, and they derive great advantages from it; we followed
this terrible example in 1735 and got Lorraine by it; lastly, here
is the king of Prussia, but under much more odious circumstances,
since he leaves us in a terrible scrape, our armies, in the middle of
Germany, beaten and famine-stricken; the emperor, despoiled of
his hereditary dominions and his estates likewise in danger. All is
at the mercy of the maritime powers, who have pushed things to
the extremity we see; and we, France, who were alone capable of
resisting such a torrent at this date—here be we exhausted and
not in a condition to check these rogueries and this power, even
by uniting ourselves the most closely with Spain. Let be, let us
meddle no more; it is the greatest service we can render at this
date to our allies of Germany."

Cardinal Fleury had not waited for confirmation of the king
of Prussia's defection to seek likewise to negotiate; Marshal Belle-
Isle had been entrusted with this business and at the same time
with a letter addressed by the cardinal to Field-Marshal Königseck.
The minister was old, timid, displeased, disquieted at the war
which he had been surprised into; he made his excuses to the
Austrian negotiator and delivered his plenipotentiary into his
hands at the very outset: "Many people know," said he, "how
opposed I was to the resolutions we adopted, and that I was
in some sort compelled to agree to them. Your Excellency is
too well informed of all that passes not to divine who it was who
set everything in motion for deciding the king to enter into a
league which was so contrary to my inclinations and to my
principles."

For sole answer, Maria Theresa had the cardinal's letter published. At Utrecht, after the unparalleled disasters which were
overwhelming the kingdom and in spite of the concessions they
had been ordered to offer, the tone of Louis XIV.'s plenipoten-
tiaries was more dignified and prouder than that of the enfeebled
old man who had so long governed France by dint of moderation,
discretion and patient inertness. The allies of France were disquieted and her foes emboldened. Marshal Belle-Isle, shut up in

Prague, and Marshal Broglie, encamped near the town, remained isolated in a hostile country, hemmed in on all sides by a savage foe, maintaining order with difficulty within the fortress itself.

" Marshal Broglie is encamped under the guns of Prague," says Barbier's journal : " his camp is spoken of as a masterpiece. As there is reason to be shy of the inhabitants, who are for the queen of Hungary, a battery has been trained upon Prague, the garrison camps upon the ramparts, and Marshal Belle-Isle patrols every night.

Marshal Maillebois was at Dusseldorf, commissioned to observe the Hollanders and protect Westphalia ; he received orders to join Marshals Broglie and Belle-Isle. " It is the army of redemption for the captives," was the saying at Paris. At the same time that the marshal was setting out for Prague, Cardinal Fleury sent him the following instructions : " Engage in no battle of which the issue may be doubtful." All the defiles of Bohemia were carefully guarded ; Maillebois first retired on Egra, then he carried his arms into Bavaria, where Marshal Broglie came to relieve him of his command. Marshal Belle-Isle remained with the sole charge of the defence of Prague ; he was frequently harassed by the Austrians ; his troops were exhausted with cold and privation. During the night between the 16th and 17th of December, 1742, the marshal sallied from the town. " I stole a march of twenty-four hours good on Prince Lobkowitz, who was only five leagues from me," wrote Belle-Isle, on accomplishing his retreat ; " I pierced his quarters, and I traversed ten leagues of plain, having to plod along with eleven thousand foot and three thousand two hundred and fifty worn-out horses, M. de Lobkowitz having eight thousand good horses and twelve thousand infantry. I made such despatch that I arrived at the defiles before he could come up with me. I concealed from him the road I had resolved to take, for he had ordered the occupation of all the defiles and the destruction of all the bridges there are on the two main roads leading from Prague to Egra. I took one which pierces between the two others, where I found no obstacles but those of nature, and, at last, I arrived on the tenth day, without a check, though continually harassed by hussars in front, rear, and flank." The hospitals at Egra were choke full of sick soldiers ; twelve nights passed on the snow without blankets or cloaks had cost the lives of many men; a great number never recovered more than a lingering existence. Amongst them there was, in the king's regiment of infantry, a young officer, M. de Vauvenargues, who expired at thirty-two years of age, soon after his return to his country, leaving amongst those who had known him a feeling that a great loss had been suffered by France and human intellect.

Chevert still occupied Prague, with six thousand sick or wounded; the prince of Lorraine had invested the place and summoned it to surrender at discretion. "Tell your general," replied Chevert to the Austrian sent to parley, "that, if he will not grant me the honours of war, I will fire the four corners of Prague and bury myself under its ruins." He obtained what he asked for and went to rejoin Marshal Belle-Isle at Egra. People compared the retreat from Prague to the Retreat of the Ten Thousand; but the truth came out for all the fictions of flattery and national pride. A hundred thousand Frenchmen had entered Germany at the outset of the war; at the commencement of the year 1743 thirty-five thousand soldiers, mustered in Bavaria, were nearly all that remained to withstand the increasing efforts of the Austrians.

Marshal Belle-Isle was coldly received at Paris. "He is much inconvenienced by a sciatica," writes the advocate Barbier, "and cannot walk but with the assistance of two men. He comes back with grand decorations: prince of the empire, knight of the Golden Fleece, blue riband, marshal of France and duke. He is held accountable, however, for all the misfortunes that have happened to us; it was spread about at Paris that he was disgraced and even exiled to his estate at Vernon, near Gisors. It is true, nevertheless, that he has several times done business with the king, whether in M. Amelot's presence, on foreign affairs, or M. D'Aguesseau's, on military; but this restless and ambitious spirit is feared by the ministers."

Almost at the very moment when the Austrians were occupying Prague and Bohemia, Cardinal Fleury was expiring, at Versailles, at the age of ninety. "Madame Marshal Noailles, mother of the present marshal, who is at least eighty-seven but is all alive, runs about Paris and writes all day, sent to inquire after him. He sent

CARDINAL FLEURY.

answer to her, 'that she was cleverer than he—she managed to live; as for him, he was ceasing to exist.' In fact, it is the case of a candle going out, and being a long while about it. Many people are awaiting this result, and all the court will be starting at his very ghost, a week after he has been buried " [*Journal de Barbier*, t. ii. p. 348].

Cardinal Fleury had lived too long: the trials of the last years of his life had been beyond the bodily and mental strength of an old man elevated for the first time to power at an age when it is generally seen slipping from the hands of the most energetic. Naturally gentle, moderate, discreet, though stubborn and persevering in his views, he had not an idea of conceiving and practising a great policy. France was indebted to him for a long period of mediocre and dull prosperity, which was preferable to the evils that had for so long oppressed her, but as for which she was to cherish no remembrance and no gratitude, when new misfortunes came bursting upon her.

Both court and nation hurled the same reproach at Cardinal Fleury : he alone prevented the king from governing and turned his attention from affairs, partly from jealousy and partly from the old habit acquired as a preceptor, who can never see a man in one who has been his pupil. When the old man died *at last*, as M. d'Argenson cruelly puts it, France turned her eyes towards Louis XV. " The cardinal is dead : hurrah! for the king ! " was the cry amongst the people. The monarch himself felt as if he were emancipated. " Gentlemen, here am I—premier minister ! " said he to his most intimate courtiers. " When MM. de Maurepas and Amelot went to announce to him this death, it is said that he was at first overcome, and that when he had recovered himself, he told them that hitherto he had availed himself of Cardinal Fleury's counsels; but he relied upon it that they would so act that they would not need to place any one between them and him. If this answer is faithfully reported," adds the advocate Barbier, " it is sufficiently in the high style to let it be understood that there will be no more any premier minister, or at any rate any body exercising the functions thereof."

For some time previously, in view of the great age and rapid enfeeblement of Cardinal Fleury, Marshal Noailles, ever able and far-sighted, had been pressing Louis XV. to take into his own hands the direction of his affairs. Having the command on the frontier of the Low Countries, he had adopted the practice of writing directly to the king. "Until it may please Your Majesty to let me know your intentions and your will," said the marshal at the outset of his correspondence, "confining myself solely to what relates to the frontier on which you have given me the command, I shall speak with frankness and freedom about the object confided to my care, and shall hold my peace as regards the rest. If you, Sir, desire the silence to be broken, it is for you to order it." For the first time Louis XV. seemed to awake from the midst of that life of intellectual lethargy and physical activity which he allowed to glide along, without a thought, between the pleasures of the chase and the amusements invented by his favourite; a remembrance of Louis XIV. came across his mind, naturally acute and judicious as it was. "The late King, my great-grandfather," he writes to Marshal Noailles on the 26th of November, 1743, "whom I desire to imitate as much as I can, recommended me, on his death-bed, to take counsel in all things, and to seek out the best, so as always to follow it. I shall be charmed, then, if you will give me some; thus do I open your mouth, as the pope does the cardinals', and I permit you to say to me what your zeal and your affection for me and my kingdom prompt you." The first fruit of this correspondence was the entrance of Marshal Noailles into the Council. "One day as he was, in the capacity of simple courtier, escorting the king who was on his way to the Council, his Majesty said to him, "Marshal, come in; we are going to hold a council," and pointed to a place at his left, Cardinal Tencin being on his right. "This new minister does not please our secretaries of State. He is a troublesome inspector set over them, who meddles in everything though master of nothing." The renewal of active hostilities was about to deliver the ministers from Marshal Noailles.

The prudent hesitation and backwardness of Holland had at last yielded to the pressure of England. The States-general had sent twenty thousand men to join the army which George II. had just sent into Germany. It was only on the 15th of March, 1744, that Louis XV. formally declared war against the king of England and Maria Theresa, no longer as an auxiliary of the emperor, but in his own name and on behalf of France. Charles VII., a fugitive, driven from his hereditary dominions, which had been evacuated by Marshal Broglie, had transported to Frankfurt his ill fortune and his empty titles. France alone supported in Germany a quarrel the weight of which she had imprudently taken upon herself.

The effort was too much for the resources; the king's counsellors felt that it was; the battle of Dettingen, skilfully commenced on the 27th of June, 1743, by Marshal Noailles, and lost by the imprudence of his nephew, the duke of Gramont, had completely shaken the confidence of the armies; the emperor had treated with the Austrians for an armistice, establishing the neutrality of his troops, as belonging to the empire. Noailles wrote to the king on the 8th of July, "It is necessary to uphold this phantom, in order to restrain Germany, which would league against us, and furnish the English with all the troops therein, the moment the emperor was abandoned." It was necessary, at the same time, to look out elsewhere for more effectual support. The king of Prussia had been resting for the last two years, a curious and an interested spectator of the contests which were bathing Europe in blood, and which answered his purpose by enfeebling his rivals. He frankly and coolly flaunted his selfishness. "In a previous war with France," he says in his memoirs, "I abandoned the French at Prague, because I gained Silesia by that step. If I had escorted them to Vienna, they would never have given me so much." In turn, the successes of the queen of Hungary were beginning to disquiet him; on the 5th of June, 1744, he signed a new treaty with France; for the first time Louis XV. was about to quit Versailles and place himself at the head of an army. "If my country is to be devoured," said the king, with a levity far different from the solemn tone of Louis XIV., "it will be very hard on me to see it swallowed without personally doing my best to prevent it."

He had, however, hesitated a long while before he started.

There was a shortness of money. For all his having been head of the council of finance, Noailles had not been able to rid himself of ideas of arbitrary power. "When the late king, your great-grand-father, considered any outlay necessary," he wrote to Louis XV., "the funds had to be found, because it was his will. The case in question is one in which your Majesty ought to speak as master, and lay down the law to your ministers. Your comptroller-general ought, for the future, to be obliged to furnish the needful funds without daring to ask the reasons for which they are demanded of him, and still less to decide upon them. It was thus that the late king behaved towards M. Colbert and all who succeeded him in that office; he would never have done anything great in the whole course of his reign, if he had behaved otherwise." It was the king's common-sense which replied to this counsel: "We are still paying all those debts that the late king incurred for extraordinary occasions, fifty millions a year and more, which we must begin by paying off first of all." Later on, he adds gaily: "As for me, I can do without any equipage, and, if needful, the shoulder of mutton of the lieutenants of infantry will do perfectly well for me." "There is nothing talked of here but the doings of the king, who is in extraordinary spirits," writes the advocate Barbier; "he has visited the places near Valenciennes, the magazines, the hospitals; he has tasted the broth of the sick, and the soldiers' bread. The ambassador of Holland came, before his departure, to propose a truce in order to put us off yet longer. The king, when he was presented, merely said: 'I know what you are going to say to me, and what it is all about. I will give you my answer in Flanders.' This answer is a proud one, and fit for a king of France." The hopes of the nation were aroused: "Have we, then, a king?" said M. d'Argenson. Credit was given to the duchess of Châteauroux, Louis XV.'s new favourite, for having excited this warlike ardour in the king. Ypres and Menin had already surrendered after a few days' open trenches; siege had just been laid to Furnes. Marshal Noailles had proposed to move up the king's household troops in order to make an impression upon the enemy. "If they must needs be marched up," replied Louis XV., "I do not wish to separate from my household: *verbum sap.*"

LOUIS XV. AND THE AMBASSADOR OF HOLLAND.

The news which arrived from the army of Italy was equally encouraging; the prince of Condé, seconded by Chevert, had forced the passage of the Alps : " There will come some occasion when we shall do as well as the French have done," wrote Count Campo-Santo, who, under Don Philip, commanded the Spanish detachment; " it is impossible to do better."

Madame de Châteauroux had just arrived at Lille ; there were already complaints in the army of the frequent absence of the king on his visits to her, when alarming news came to cause forgetfulness of court intrigues and dissatisfaction : the Austrians had effected the passage of the Rhine by surprise near Philipsburg; Elsass was invaded. Marshal Coigny, who was under orders to defend it, had been enticed in the direction of Worms by false moves on the part of Prince Charles of Lorraine and had found great difficulty in recrossing the frontier. " Here we are on the eve of a great crisis," writes Louis XV. on the 7th of July. It was at once decided that the king must move on Elsass to defend his threatened provinces. The king of Prussia promised to enter Bohemia immediately with twenty thousand men, as the diversion was sure to be useful to France. Louis XV. had already arrived at Metz, and Marshal Noailles pushed forward in order to unite all the corps. On the 8th of August the king awoke in pain, prostrated by a violent head-ache; a few days later, all France was in consternation ; the king was said to have been given over.

" The king's danger was noised abroad throughout Paris in the middle of the night," writes Voltaire [*Siècle de Louis XV.*, p. 103] : " everybody gets up, runs about, in confusion, not knowing whither to go. The churches open at dead of night; nobody takes any more note of time, bed-time, or day-time or meal-time. Paris was beside itself; all the houses of officials were besieged by a continual crowd; knots collected at all the cross-roads. The people cried, 'If he should die, it will be for having marched to our aid.' People accosted one another, questioned one another in the churches, without being the least acquainted. There were many churches where the priest who pronounced the prayer for the king's health interrupted the intoning with his tears and the people responded with nothing but sobs and cries. The

courier who, on the 19th, brought to Paris the news of his convalescence was embraced and almost stifled by the people; they
kissed his horse, they escorted him in triumph. All the streets
resounded with a shout of joy: ' The king is well!' When the
monarch was told of the unparalleled transports of joy which had
succeeded those of despair, he was affected to tears, and, raising
himself up in a thrill of emotion which gave him strength, ' Ah!'
he exclaimed, ' how sweet it is to be so loved! What have I done
to deserve it ?' "

What had he done, indeed! And what was he destined to do ?
France had just experienced the last gush of that monarchical
passion and fidelity which had so long distinguished her and which
were at last used up and worn out through the faults of the
princes as well as through the blindness and errors of the nation
itself.

Confronted with death, the king had once more felt the religious
terrors which were constantly intermingled with the irregularity of
his life; he had sent for the queen, and had dismissed the duchess
of Châteauroux. On recovering his health, he found himself
threatened by new perils, aggravated by his illness and by the
troubled state into which it had thrown the public mind. After
having ravaged and wasted Elsass, without Marshals Coigny and
Noailles having been able to prevent it, Prince Charles had, without being harassed, struck again into the road towards Bohemia,
which was being threatened by the king of Prussia. "This
prince," wrote Marshal Belle-Isle on the 13th of September,
" has written a very strong letter to the king, complaining of the
quiet way in which Prince Charles was allowed to cross the Rhine:
he attributes it all to his Majesty's illness, and complains bitterly
of Marshal Noailles." And, on the 25th, to Count Clermont:
" Here we are, decided at last; the king is to start on Tuesday
the 27th for Lunéville and on the 5th of October will be at Stras-
bourg. Nobody knows as yet any further than that, and it is a
question whether he will go to Fribourg or not. The ministers
are off back to Paris. Marshal Noailles, who has sent for his
equipage hither, asked whether he should attend his Majesty, who
replied ' As you please,' rather curtly. Your Highness cannot

have a doubt about his doing so, after such a gracious permission."

Louis XV. went to the siege of Friburg, which was a long and a difficult one. He returned to Paris on the 13th of November to the great joy of the people. A few days later, Marshal Belle-Isle, whilst passing through Hanover in the character of negotiator, was arrested by order of George II. and carried to England a prisoner of war, in defiance of the law of nations and the protests of France. The moment was not propitious for obtaining the release of a marshal of France and an able general. The emperor Charles VII., who had but lately returned to his hereditary dominions and recovered possession of his capital, after fifteen months of Austrian occupation, died suddenly on the 20th of January, 1745, at forty-seven years of age. The face of affairs changed all at once; the honour of France was no longer concerned in the struggle; the grand-duke of Tuscany had no longer any competitor for the empire; the eldest son of Charles VII. was only seventeen; the queen of Hungary was disposed for peace. "The English ministry, which laid down the law for all, because it laid down the money, and which had in its pay, all at one time, the queen of Hungary, the king of Poland and the king of Sardinia, considered that there was everything to lose by a treaty with France and everything to gain by arms. War continued, because it had commenced" [Voltaire, *Siècle de Louis XV.*].

The king of France henceforth maintained it almost alone by himself. The young elector of Bavaria had already found himself driven out of Munich and forced by his exhausted subjects to demand peace of Maria Theresa. The election to the empire was imminent; Maximilian-Joseph promised his votes to the grand-duke of Tuscany; at that price he was re-established in his hereditary dominions. The king of Poland had rejected the advances of France, who offered him the title of emperor, beneath which Charles VII. had succumbed. Marshal Saxe bore all the brunt of the war. A foreigner and a protestant, for a long while under suspicion with Louis XV., and blackened in character by the French generals, Maurice of Saxony had won authority as well as glory by the splendour of his bravery and of his military genius.

Combining with quite a French vivacity the far-sightedness and the perseverance of the races of the North, he had been toiling for more than a year to bring about amongst his army a spirit of discipline, a powerful organization, a contempt for fatigue as well as for danger. "At Dettingen the success of the allies was due to their surprising order, for they were not seasoned to war," he used to say. Order did not as yet reign in the army of Marshal Saxe. In 1745, the situation was grave; the marshal was attacked with dropsy, his life appeared to be in danger. He nevertheless commanded his preparations to be made for the campaign, and, when Voltaire, who was one of his friends, was astounded at it, "It is no question of living, but of setting out," was his reply.

The king was preparing to set out, like Marshal Saxe; he had just married the dauphin to the eldest daughter of the king of Spain; the young prince accompanied his father to the front before Tournai, which the French army was besieging. On the 8th of May Louis XV. visited the outskirts; an attack from the enemy was expected, the field of battle was known beforehand. The village of Fontenoy had already been occupied by Marshal Noailles, who had asked to serve as aide-de-camp to Marshal Saxe, to whom he was attached by sincere friendship and whom he had very much contributed to advance in the king's good graces.

"Never did Louis XV. show more gaiety than on the eve of the fight," says Voltaire. "The conversation was of battles at which kings had been present in person. The king said that since the battle of Poitiers no king of France had fought with his son beside him, that since St. Louis none had gained any signal victory over the English, and that he hoped to be the first. He was the first up on the day of action; he himself at four o'clock awoke Count d'Argenson, minister of war, who on the instant sent to ask Marshal Saxe for his final orders. The marshal was found in a carriage of osier-work, which served him for a bed and in which he had himself drawn about when his exhausted powers no longer allowed him to sit his horse." The king and the dauphin had already taken up their positions of battle; the two villages of Fontenoy and Antoin, and the wood of Barri, were occupied by French troops. Two armies of fifty thousand men each were

BATTLE OF FONTENOY.

about to engage in the lists as at Dettingen. Austria had sent but eight thousand soldiers, under the orders of the old and famous general Königseck; the English and the Hollanders were about to bear all the burthen and heat of the day.

It was not five in the morning, and already there was a thunder of cannon. The Hollanders attacked the village of Antoin, the English that of Fontenoy. The two posts were covered by a redoubt which belched forth flames; the Hollanders refused to deliver the assault. An attack made by the English on the wood of Barri had been repulsed: "Forward, my lord, right to your front," said old Königseck to the duke of Cumberland, George II.'s son, who commanded the English; "the ravine in front of Fontenoy must be carried." The English advanced; they formed a deep and serried column, preceded and supported by artillery. The French batteries mowed them down right and left, whole ranks fell dead: they were at once filled up; the cannon which they dragged along by hand. pointed towards Fontenoy and the redoubts, replied to the French artillery. An attempt of some officers of the French guards to carry off the cannon of the English was unsuccessful. The two corps found themselves at last face to face.

The English officers took off their hats; Count Chabannes and the duke of Biron who had moved forward returned their salute: "Gentlemen of the French guard, fire!" exclaimed Lord Charles Hay. "Fire yourselves, gentlemen of England," immediately replied Count d'Auteroche, "we never fire first." [All fiction, it is said.] The volley of the English laid low the foremost ranks of the French guards. This regiment had been effeminated by a long residence in Paris and at Versailles; its colonel, the duke of Gramont, had been killed in the morning, at the commencement of the action; it gave way and the English cleared the ravine which defended Fontenoy. They advanced as if on parade; the majors [? sergeant-majors], small cane in hand, rested it lightly on the soldiers' muskets to direct their fire. Several regiments successively opposed to the English column found themselves repulsed and forced to beat a retreat; the English still advanced.

Marshal Saxe, carried about everywhere in his osier-litter, saw the danger with a calm eye; he sent the marquis of Meuse to the king: "I beg your Majesty," he told him to say, "to go back with the dauphin over the bridge of Calonne; I will do what I can to restore the battle." "Ah! I know well enough that he will do what is necessary," answered the king, "but I stay where I am." Marshal Saxe mounted his horse.

In its turn, the cavalry had been repulsed by the English; their fire swept away rank after rank of the regiment of Vaisseaux, which would not be denied. "How is it that such troops are not victorious?" cried Marshal Saxe, who was moving about at a foot's pace in the middle of the fire, without his cuirass, which his weakness did not admit of his wearing. He advanced towards Fontenoy; the batteries had just fallen short of ball. The English column had ceased marching; arrested by the successive efforts of the French regiments, it remained motionless, and seemed to receive no more orders, but it preserved a proud front, and appeared to be masters of the field of battle. Marshal Saxe was preparing for the retreat of the army; he had relinquished his proposal for that of the king, from the time that the English had come up and pressed him closely: "It was my advice, before the danger was so great," he said; "now there is no falling back."

A disorderly council was being held around Louis XV. With the fine judgment and sense which he often displayed when he took the trouble to have an opinion on his affairs, the king had been wise enough to encourage his troops by his presence without in any way interfering with the orders of Marshal Saxe. The duke of Richelieu vented an opinion more worthy of the name he bore than had been his wont in his life of courtiership and debauchery. "Throw forward the artillery against the column," he said, "and let the king's household with all the disposable regiments attack them at the same time; they must be fallen upon like so many foragers."

The retreat of the Hollanders admitted of the movement; the small field-pieces, as yet dragged by hand, were pointed against the English column. Marshal Saxe, with difficulty keeping his seat upon his horse, galloped hastily up to the Irish brigade, commanding all the troops he met on the way to make no more false attacks and to act in concert. All the forces of the French army burst simultaneously upon the English. The Irish regiments in the service of France, nearly all composed of Jacobite emigrants, fought with fury. Twice the brave enemy rallied, but the officers fell on all sides, the ranks were every where broken; at last they retired, without disorder, without enfeeblement, preserving even in defeat the honour of a vigorous resistance. The battle was gained at the moment when the most clear-sighted had considered it lost. Marshal Saxe had still strength left to make his way to the king. "I have lived long enough, Sir," he said, "now that I have seen your Majesty victorious. You now know on what the fortune of battles depends."

The victory of Fontenoy, like that of Denain, restored the courage and changed the situation of France. When the king of Prussia heard of his ally's success, he exclaimed with a grin: "This is about as useful to us as a battle gained on the banks of the Scamander." His selfish absorption in his personal and direct interests obscured the judgment of Frederick the Great. He, however, did justice to Marshal Saxe: "There was a discussion the other day as to what battle had reflected most honour on the general commanding," he wrote a long while after the battle of Fontenoy: "some suggested that of Almanza, others that of Turin: but I suggested—and everybody finally agreed—that it was undoubtedly, that in which the general had been at death's door when it was delivered."

The fortress of Tournai surrendered on the 22nd of May; the citadel capitulated on the 19th of June. Ghent, Bruges, Oudenarde, Dendermonde, Ostend, Nieuport, yielded one after another to the French armies. In the month of February, 1746, Marshal Saxe terminated the campaign by taking Brussels. By the 1st of the previous September Louis XV. had returned in triumph to Paris.

Henceforth he remained alone confronting Germany, which was neutral or had rallied round the restored empire. On the 13th of September, the grand duke of Tuscany had been proclaimed emperor at Frankfurt under the name of Francis I. The indomitable resolution of the queen his wife had triumphed; in spite of the checks she suffered in the Low Countries, Maria Theresa still withstood, at all points, the pacific advances of the belligerents.

On the 4th of June, the king of Prussia had gained a great victory at Freilberg. "I have honoured the bill of exchange your Majesty drew on me at Fontenoy," he wrote to Louis XV. A series of successful fights had opened the road to Saxony, Frederick headed thither rapidly; on the 18th of December he occupied Dresden.

This time, the king of Poland, elector of Saxony, forced the hand of the new empress: "The Austrians and the Saxons have just sent ministers hither to negotiate for peace," said a letter to France from the king of Prussia: "so I have no course open but to sign. Would that I might be fortunate enough to serve as the instrument of general pacification! After discharging my duty towards the State I govern and towards my family, no object will be nearer to my heart than that of being able to render myself of service to your Majesty's interests." Frederick the Great returned to Berlin covered with glory and definitively master of Silesia. "Learn once for all," he said at a later period in his instructions to his successor, "that, where a kingdom is concerned, you take when you can, and that you are never wrong when you are not obliged to hand over." An insolent and a cynical maxim of brute force, which conquerors have put in practice at all times without daring to set it up as a principle.

Whilst Berlin was in gala trim to celebrate the return of her monarch in triumph, Europe had her eyes fixed upon the unparalleled enterprise of a young man, winning, courageous and frivolous as he was, attempting to recover by himself alone the throne of his fathers. For nearly three years past, Charles Edward Stuart, son of Chevalier St. George, had been awaiting in France the fulfilment of the promises and hopes which had been flashed before his eyes. Weary of hope deferred, he had conceived the idea of a bold stroke. "Why not attempt to cross in a vessel to the north of Scotland?" had been the question put to him by Cardinal Tencin, who had some time before owed his cardinal's hat to the dethroned king of Great Britain. "Your presence will be enough to get you a party and an army, and France will be obliged to give you aid."

Charles Edward had followed this audacious counsel. Landing

MARSHAL SAXE.

in June, 1745, in the Highlands of Scotland, he had soon found the clans of the mountaineers hurrying to join his standard. At the head of this wild army, he had in a few months gained over the whole of Scotland. On the 20th of September he was proclaimed at Edinburgh regent of England, France, Scotland and Ireland for his father king James III. George II. had left Hanover; the duke of Cumberland, returning from Germany, took the command of the troops assembled to oppose the invader. Their success in the battle of Preston-Pans against General Cope had emboldened the Scots; at the end of December, 1745, Prince Charles Edward and his army had advanced as far as Derby.

It was the fate of the Stuarts, whether heroes or dastards, to see their hopes blasted all at once and to drag down in their fall their most zealous and devoted partisans. The aid, so often promised by France and Spain, had dwindled down to the private expeditions of certain brave adventurers. The duke of Richelieu, it was said, was to put himself at their head. "As to the embarkation at Dunkerque," writes the advocate Barbier at the close of the year 1745, "there is great anxiety about it, for we are at the end of December, and it is not yet done, which gives every one occasion to make up news according to his fancy. This uncertainty discourages the Frenchman, who gives out that our expedition will not take place or, at any rate, will not succeed." Charles Edward had already been forced to fall back upon Scotland. As in 1651, at the time of the attempt of Charles II., England remained quite cold in the presence of the Scottish invasion; the duke of Cumberland was closely pressing the army of the mountaineers. On the 23rd of April, 1746, the foes found themselves face to face at Culloden, in the environs of Inverness. Charles Edward was completely beaten and the army of the Highlanders destroyed; the prince only escaped either death or captivity by the determined devotion of his partisans, whether distinguished or obscure; a hundred persons had risked their lives for him, when he finally succeeded, on the 10th of October, in touching land, in Brittany, near St. Pol de Léon. His friends and his defenders were meanwhile dying for his cause on scaffold or gallows.

The anger and severity displayed by the English Government towards the Jacobites were aggravated by the checks encountered upon the Continent by the coalition. At the very moment when the duke of Cumberland was defeating Charles Edward at Culloden, Antwerp was surrendering to Louis XV. in person: Mons, Namur and Charleroi were not long before they fell. Prince Charles of Lorraine was advancing to the relief of the besieged places; Marshal Saxe left open to him the passage of the Meuse: the French camp seemed to be absorbed in pleasures; the most famous actors from Paris were ordered to amuse the general and the soldiers. On the 10th of October, in the evening, Madame Favart came forward on the stage: "To-morrow," said she, "there will be no performance, on account of the battle: the day after, we shall have the honour of giving you *Le Coq du Village*." At the same time, the marshal sent the following order to the columns which were already forming on the road from St. Tron to Liége, near the village of Raucoux: "Whether the attacks succeed or not, the troops will remain in the position in which night finds them, in order to recommence the assault upon the enemy."

The battle of October 11th left the battle-field in the hands of the victors, the sole result of a bloody and obstinate engagement. Marshal Saxe went to rest himself at Paris; the people's enthusiasm rivalled and endorsed the favours shown to him by the king. At the opera, the whole house rose at the entrance of the valiant foreigner who had dedicated his life to France; there was clapping of hands, and the actress who in the prologue took the character of Glory leaned over towards the marshal with a crown of laurel. " The marshal was surprised and refused it with profound bows. Glory insisted, and, as the marshal was too far off in the boxes for her to hand it to him, the duke of Biron took the crown from Glory's hands and passed it under Marshal Saxe's left arm. This striking action called forth fresh acclamations: 'Hurrah! for Marshal Saxe!' and great clapping of hands. The king has given the marshal Chambord for life, and has even ordered it to be furnished. Independently of all these honours, it is said that the marshal is extremely rich and powerful just now, solely as the result of his safe-conducts, which, being applicable to a considerable extent of country, have been worth immense sums to him." The second marriage of the dauphin, who had already lost the Infanta, with the princess of Saxony, daughter of the king of Poland, was about to raise, before long, the fortune and favour of Marshal Saxe to the highest pitch : he was proclaimed marshal-general of the king's armies.

So much luck and so much glory in the Low Countries covered, in the eyes of France and of Europe, the checks encountered by the king's armies in Italy. The campaign of 1745 had been very brilliant. Parma, Piacenza, Montferrat, nearly all Milaness, with the exception of a few fortresses, were in the hands of the Spanish and French forces. The king of Sardinia had recourse to nego- tiation ; he amused the marquis of Argenson, at that time Louis XV.'s foreign minister, a man of honest, expansive, but chimerical views. At the moment when the king and the marquis believed themselves to be remodelling the map of Europe at their pleasure, they heard that Charles Emmanuel had resumed the offensive. A French corps had been surprised at Asti, on the 5th of March ; thirty thousand Austrians marched down from the Tyrol, and the Spaniards evacuated Milan. A series of checks forced Marshal Maillebois to effect a retreat ; the enemy's armies crossed the Var and invaded French territory. Marshal Belle-Isle fell back to Puget, four leagues from Toulon.

The Austrians had occupied Genoa, the faithful ally of France : their vengefulness and their severe exactions caused them to lose the fruits of their victory. The grandees were ruined by war- requisitions ; the populace were beside themselves at the insolence of the conquerors ; senators and artisans made common cause. An Austrian captain having struck a workman, the passengers in the streets threw themselves upon him and upon his comrades who came to his assistance ; the insurrection spread rapidly in all quarters of Genoa ; there was a pillage of the weapons lying heaped in the palace of the Doges ; the senators put themselves at the head of the movement ; the peasants in the country flew to arms. The marquis of Botta, the Austrian commandant, being attacked on all sides and too weak to resist, sallied from the town with nine regiments. The allies, disquieted and dismayed, threatened

Provence and laid siege to Genoa.   Louis XV. felt the necessity
of not abandoning his ally; the duke of Boufflers and six thousand
French shut themselves up in the place.   " Show me the danger,"
the general had said on entering the town, " it is my duty to
ascertain it; I shall make all my glory depend upon securing you
from it."   The resistance of Genoa was effectual; but it cost the
life of the duke of Boufflers, who was wounded in an engagement
and died three days before the retreat of the Austrians, on the
6th of July, 1747.

On the 19th of July, *Common Sense* Belle-Isle (*Bon-Sens* de Belle-
Isle), as the Chevalier was called at court to distinguish him from
his brother the marshal, nicknamed *Imagination*, attacked with a
considerable body of troops the Piedmontese intrenchments at the
Assietta Pass, between the fortresses of Exilles and Fenestrelles; at
the same time, Marshal Belle-Isle was seeking a passage over the
Stura Pass, and the Spanish army was attacking Piedmont by way
of the Apennines.   The engagement at the heights of Assietta was
obstinate; Chevalier Belle-Isle, wounded in both arms, threw himself
bodily upon the palisades to tear them down with his teeth ; he was
killed, and the French sustained a terrible defeat; five thousand
men were left on the battle-field.   The campaign of Italy was
stopped.   The king of Spain, Philip V., enfeebled and exhausted
almost in infancy, had died on the 9th of July, 1746.   The fidelity
of his successor, Ferdinand VI., married to a Portuguese princess,
appeared doubtful; he had placed at the head of his forces in Italy
the marquis of Las Minas, with orders to preserve to Spain her
only army.   " The Spanish soldiers are of no more use to us than
if they were so much cardboard," said the French troops.   Europe
was tired of the war.   England avenged herself for her reverses
upon the Continent by her successes at sea; the French navy,
neglected systematically by Cardinal Fleury, did not even suffice
for the protection of commerce.   The Hollanders, who had for a
long while been undecided and had at last engaged in the struggle
against France without any declaration of war, bore, in 1747, the
burthen of the hostilities.   Count Lowendahl, a friend of Marshal
Saxe's, and, like him, in the service of France, had taken Sluys and
Sas-de-Gand; Bergen-op-Zoom was besieged; on the 1st of July,

Marshal Saxe had gained, under the king's own eye, the battle of Lawfeldt. As in 1672, the French invasion had been the signal for a political revolution in Holland; the aristocratical burgessdom, which had resumed power, succumbed once more beneath the efforts of the popular party, directed by the House of Nassau and supported by England. " The republic has need of a chief against an ambitious and perfidious neighbour who sports with the faith of treaties," said a deputy of the States-general on the day of the proclamation of the stadtholderate, re-established in favour of William IV., grand-nephew of the great William III., and son-in-law of the king of England, George II. Louis XV. did not let himself be put out by this outburst. " The Hollanders are good folks," he wrote to Marshal Noailles : " it is said, however, that they are going to declare war against us : they will lose quite as much as we shall."

Bergen-op-Zoom was taken and plundered on the 16th of September. Count Lowendahl was made a marshal of France. " Peace is in Maestricht, Sir," was Maurice of Saxony's constant remark to the king. On the 9th of April, 1748, the place was invested, before the thirty-five thousand Russians, promised to England by the Czarina Elizabeth, had found time to make their appearance on the Rhine. A congress was already assembled at Aix-la-Chapelle to treat for peace. The Hollanders, whom the marquis of Argenson before his disgrace used always to call " the ambassadors of England," took fright at the spectacle of Maestricht besieged; from parleys they proceeded to the most vehement urgency; and England yielded. The preliminaries of peace were signed on the 30th of April; it was not long before Austria and Spain gave in their adhesion. On the 18th of October the definitive treaty was concluded at Aix-la-Chapelle. France generously restored all her conquests, without claiming other advantages beyond the assurance of the duchies of Parma and Piacenza to the Infante Don Philip, son-in-law of Louis XV. England surrendered to France the island of Cape Breton and the colony of Louisbourg, the only territory she had preserved from her numerous expeditions against the French colonies and from the immense losses inflicted upon French commerce. The Great Frederic kept Silesia; the king of

Sardinia the territories already ceded by Austria. Only France had made great conquests; and only she retained no increment of territory. She recognized the Pragmatic Sanction in favour of Austria and the Protestant succession in favour of George II. Prince Charles Edward, a refugee in France, refused to quit the hospitable soil which had but lately offered so magnificent an asylum to the unfortunates of his house: he was, however, carried

ARREST OF CHARLES EDWARD.

off, whilst at the Opera, forced into a carriage, and conveyed far from the frontier. "As stupid as the peace!" was the bitter saying in the streets of Paris.

The peace of Aix-la-Chapelle had a graver defect than that of fruitlessness; it was not and could not be durable. England was excited, ambitious of that complete empire of the sea which she had begun to build up upon the ruins of the French navy and the decay of Holland, and greedy of distant conquests over colonies which the French could not manage to defend. In proportion as the old influence of Richelieu and of Louis XIV. over European policy became weaker and weaker, English influence, founded upon the growing power of a free country and a free government, went on increasing in strength. Without any other ally but Spain, herself wavering in her fidelity, the French remained exposed to the attempts of England, henceforth delivered from the phantom of the Stuarts. "The peace concluded between England and France in 1748 was, as regards Europe, nothing but a truce," says Lord Macaulay : "it was not even a truce in other quarters of the globe." The mutual rivalry and mistrust between the two nations began to show themselves everywhere, in the East as well as in the West, in India as well as in America.

CHAPTER LIII.

LOUIS XV., FRANCE IN THE COLONIES (1745—1763).

FRANCE was already beginning to perceive her sudden abasement in Europe; the defaults of her generals as well as of her government sometimes struck the king himself; he threw the blame of it on the barrenness of his times: "This age is not fruitful in great men," he wrote to Marshal Noailles: "you know that we miss subjects for all objects, and you have one before your eyes in the case of the army which certainly impresses me more than any other." Thus spoke Louis XV. on the eve of the battle of Fontenoy; Marshal Saxe was about to confer upon the French arms a transitory lustre; but the king, who loaded him with riches and honours, never forgot that he was not his born subject. "I allow that Count Saxe is the best officer to command that we have," he would say; "but he is a huguenot, he wants to be supreme, and he is always saying that, if he is thwarted, he will enter some other service. Is that zeal for France? I see, however, very few of ours who aim high like him."

The king possessed at a distance, in the colonies of the

Two Indies, as the expression then was, faithful servants of France, passionately zealous for her glory, "aiming high," ambitious or disinterested, able politicians or heroic pioneers, all ready to sacrifice both property and life for the honour and power of their country: it is time to show how La Bourdonnais, Dupleix, Bussy, Lally-Tolendal were treated in India; what assistance, what guidance, what encouragement the Canadians and their illustrious chiefs received from France, beginning with Champlain, one of the founders of the colony, and ending with Montcalm, its latest defender. It is a painful but a salutary spectacle to see to what meannesses a sovereign and a government may find themselves reduced through a weak complaisance towards the foreigner, in the feverish desire of putting an end to a war frivolously undertaken and feebly conducted.

French power in India threw out more lustre but was destined to speedier and perhaps more melancholy extinction than in Canada. Single-handed in the East the chiefs maintained the struggle against the incapacity of the French government and the dexterous tenacity of the enemy; in America the population of French extraction upheld to the bitter end the name, the honour and the flag of their country. "The fate of France," says Voltaire, "has nearly always been that her enterprises and even her successes beyond her own frontiers should become fatal to her." The defaults of the government and the jealous passions of the colonists themselves, in the eighteenth century, seriously aggravated the military reverses which were to cost the French nearly all their colonies.

More than a hundred years previously, at the outset of Louis XIV.'s personal reign and through the persevering efforts of Colbert marching in the footsteps of Cardinal Richelieu, an India Company had been founded for the purpose of developing French commerce in those distant regions, which had always been shrouded in a mysterious halo of fancied wealth and grandeur. Several times the Company had all but perished; it had revived under the vigorous impulse communicated by Law and had not succumbed at the collapse of his system. It gave no money to its shareholders, who derived their benefits only from a partial

concession of the tobacco revenues, granted by the king to the
Company, but its directors lived a life of magnificence in the East,
where they were authorized to trade on their own account.
Abler and bolder than all his colleagues, Joseph Dupleix,
member of a Gascon family and son of the comptroller-general
of Hainault, had dreamed of other destinies than the management
of a counting-house; he aspired to endow France with the empire
of India.   Placed at a very early age at the head of the French
establishments at Chandernuggur, he had improved the city and
constructed a fleet, all the while acquiring for himself an immense
fortune; he had just been sent to Pondicherry as governor-general
of the Company's agencies, when the war of succession to the
empire broke out in 1742.   For a long time past Dupleix and his
wife, who was called in India *Princess Jane*, had been silently
forming a vast network of communications and correspondence
which kept them acquainted with the innumerable intrigues of all
the petty native courts.   Madame Dupleix, a Creole, brought up in
India, understood all its dialects.   Her husband had been the first
to conceive the idea of that policy which was destined before long
to deliver India to the English, his imitators; mingling everywhere in the incessant revolutions which were hatching all about
him, he gave the support of France at one time to one pretender
and at another to another, relying upon the discipline of the
European troops and upon the force of his own genius for
securing the ascendancy to his protégé of the moment: thus increasing little by little French influence and dominion throughout
all the Hindoo territory.   Accustomed to dealing with the native
princes, he had partially adopted their ways of craft and violence;
more concerned for his object than about the means of obtaining
it, he had the misfortune, at the outset of the contest, to clash
with another who was ambitious for the glory of France, and as
courageous but less able a politician than he; their rivalry, their
love of power and their inflexible attachment to their own ideas,
under the direction of a feeble government, thenceforth stamped
upon the relations of the two great European nations in India a
regrettable character of duplicity: all the splendour and all the
efforts of Dupleix's genius could never efface it.

Concord as yet reigned between Dupleix and the governor of Bourbon and of Ile de France, Bertrand Francis Mahé de La Bourdonnais, when, in the month of September, 1746, the latter put in an appearance with a small squadron in front of Madras, already one of the principal English establishments. Commodore Peyton, who was cruising in Indian waters, after having been twice beaten by La Bourdonnais, had removed to a distance with his flotilla; the town was but feebly fortified; the English, who had for a while counted upon the protection of the Nabob of the Carnatic, did not receive the assistance they expected; they surrendered at the first shot, promising to pay a considerable sum for the ransom of Madras, which the French were to retain as security until the debt was completely paid. La Bourdonnais had received from France this express order: " You will not keep any of the conquests you may make in India." The chests containing the ransom of the place descended slowly from the *white town*, which was occupied solely by Europeans and by the English settlements, to the *black town*, inhabited by a mixed population of natives and foreigners of various races, traders or artisans. Already the vessels of La Bourdonnais, laden with these precious spoils, had made sail for Pondicherry; the governor of Bourbon was in a hurry to get back to his islands; autumn was coming on, tempests were threatening his squadron, but Dupleix was still disputing the terms of the treaty concluded with the English for the rendition of Madras; he had instructions, he said, to rase the city and place it thus dismantled in the hands of the Nabob of the Carnatic; the Hindoo prince had set himself in motion to seize his prey; the English burst out into insults and threats. La Bourdonnais, in a violent rage, on the point of finding himself arrested by order of Dupleix, himself put in prison the governor-general's envoys; the conflict of authority was aggravated by the feebleness and duplicity of the instructions from France. All at once a fearful tempest destroyed a part of the squadron in front of Madras; La Bourdonnais, flinging himself into a boat, had great difficulty in rejoining his ships; he departed, leaving his rival master of Madras and adroitly prolonging the negotiations, in order to ruin at least the black city, which alone was rich and prosperous, before giving over the place to the Nabob. Months rolled by and the French remained alone at Madras.

A jealous love of power and absorption in political schemes had induced Dupleix to violate a promise lightly given by La Bour- donnais in the name of France; he had arbitrarily quashed a capitulation of which he had not discussed the conditions. The report of this unhappy conflict, and the colour put upon it by the representations of Dupleix, were about to ruin at Paris the rival whom he had vanquished in India.

On arriving at Ile de France, amidst that colony which he had found exhausted, ruined, and had endowed with hospitals, arsenals, quays, and fortifications, La Bourdonnais learned that a new governor was already installed there. His dissensions with Dupleix had borne their fruits; he had been accused of having exacted too paltry a ransom from Madras, and of having accepted enormous presents; the Company had appointed a successor in his place. Driven to desperation, anxious to go and defend himself, La Bourdonnais set out for France with his wife and his four children; a prosecution had already been commenced against him. He was captured at sea by an English ship, and taken a prisoner to England. The good faith of the conqueror of Madras was known in London; one of the directors of the English Com- pany offered his fortune as security for M. de la Bourdonnais. Scarcely had he arrived in Paris when he was thrown into the Bastille, and for two years kept in solitary confinement. When his innocence was at last acknowledged and his liberty restored to him, his health was destroyed, his fortune exhausted by the expenses of the trial. La Bourdonnais died before long, employing the last remnants of his life and of his strength in pouring forth his anger against Dupleix, to whom he attributed all his woes. His indignation was excusable, and some of his grievances were well grounded; but the germs of suspicion thus sown by the un- fortunate prisoner released from the Bastille were destined before long to consign to perdition not only his enemy, but also, together with him, that French dominion in India to which M. de La Bourdonnais had dedicated his life.

Meanwhile Dupleix grew greater and greater, every day more

powerful and more daring.   The English had not forgotten the
affair of Madras.   On the 30th of August, 1748, Admiral Boscawen
went and laid siege to Pondicherry ; stopped at the outset by the
fort of Ariocapang, of the existence of which they were ignorant,
the disembarked troops could not push their trenches beyond an
impassable morass which protected the town.   The fire of the
siege-artillery scarcely reached the ramparts ; the sallies of the

LA BOURDONNAIS.

besieged intercepted the communications between the camp and
the squadron which, on its side, was bombarding the walls of
Pondicherry without any serious result.   Dupleix himself commanded the French batteries ; on the 6th of October he was
wounded, and his place on the ramparts was taken by Madame
Dupleix, seconded by her future son-in-law, M. de Bussy-Castelnau,
Dupleix's military lieutenant, animated by the same zeal for the

greatness of France.   The fire of the English redoubled; but
there was laughter in Pondicherry, for the balls did not carry so
far; and on the 20th of October, after forty days' siege, Admiral
Boscawen put to sea again, driven far away from the coasts by the
same tempests which two years before had compelled La Bourdonnais to quit Madras.   Twice had Dupleix been served in his
designs by the winds of autumn.   The peace of Aix-la-Chapelle
came to put an end to open war between the Europeans; at the
French establishments in the Indies the *Te Deum* was sung;
Dupleix alone was gloomy, despite the riband of St. Louis and the
title of marquis recently granted him by King Louis XV.: he had
been obliged to restore Madras to the English.

War soon recommenced in the name and apparently to the
profit of the Hindoo princes.   France and England had made
peace; the English and French Companies in India had not laid
down arms.   Their power, as well as the importance of their
establishments, was as yet in equipoise.   At Surat both Companies
had places of business; on the coast of Malabar, the English had
Bombay and the French Mahé; on the coast of Coromandel, the
former held Madras and Fort St. George, the latter Pondicherry
and Karikal.   The principal factories, as well as the numerous
little establishments which were dependencies of them, were
defended by a certain number of European soldiers and by
Sepoys, native soldiers in the pay of the Companies.

These small armies were costly and diminished to a considerable
extent the profits of trade.   Dupleix espied the possibility of a
new organization which should secure to the French in India the
preponderance, and ere long the empire even, in the two peninsulas.
He purposed to found manufactures, utilise native hand-labour and
develope the coasting-trade or *Ind to Ind* trade as the expression
then was; but he set his pretensions still higher and carried his
views still further.   He purposed to acquire for the Company and,
under its name, for France territories and subjects furnishing
revenues and amply sufficing for the expenses of the commercial
establishments.   The moment was propitious; the ancient empire
of the Great Mogul tottering to its base was distracted by revolutions, all the chops and changes whereof were attentively followed

by Madame Dupleix; two contested successions opened up at once, those of the vice-roy or soudhabar of the Deccan and of his vassal the nabob of the Carnatic. The Great Mogul, nominal sovereign of all the States of India, confined himself to selling to all the pretenders decrees of investiture without taking any other part in the contest. Dupleix, on the contrary, engaged in it ardently. He took sides in the Deccan for Murzapha Jung and in the Carnatic for Tchunda Sahib against their rivals supported by the English. Versed in all the resources of Hindoo policy, he had negotiated an alliance between his two protégés; both marched against the nabob of the Carnatic. He, though a hundred and seven years old, was at the head of his army, mounted on a magnificent elephant. He espied in the melley his enemy Tchunda Sahib and would have darted upon him; but, whilst his slaves were urging on the huge beast, the little French battalion sent by Dupleix to the aid of his allies marched upon the nabob, a ball struck him to the heart and he fell. The same evening Murzapha Jung was proclaimed soudhabar of the Deccan and he granted the principality of the Carnatic to Tchunda Sahib, at the same time reserving to the French Company a vast territory.

Some months rolled by, full of vicissitudes and sudden turns of fortune. Murzapha Jung, at first victorious and then vanquished by his uncle Nazir Jung, everywhere dragged at his heels as a hostage and a trophy of his triumph, had found himself delivered by an insurrection of the Patanian chiefs, Affghans by origin, settled in the south of India. The head of Nazir Jung had come rolling at his feet. For a while besieged in Pondicherry, but still negotiating and everywhere mingling in intrigues and conspiracies, Dupleix was now triumphant with his ally; the soudhabar of the Deccan made his entry in state upon French territory. Pondicherry was in holiday trim to receive him. Dupleix, dressed in the magnificent costume of the Hindoo princes, had gone with his troops to meet him. Both entered the town in the same palanquin to the sound of native cymbals and the military music of the French. A throne awaited the soudhabar, surrounded by the Affghan chiefs who were already claiming the reward of their services. The Hindoo prince needed the aid of France; he knew it, he proclaimed Dupleix nabob of all the provinces to the south of the river Krischna. Tchunda Sahib, but lately his ally, became his vassal—"the vassal of France," murmured Madame Dupleix, when she heard of this splendid recompense for so many public and private services. The ability and indomitable bravery of M. de Bussy soon extended the French conquests in the Deccan. Murzapha Jung had just been assassinated at the head of his army; Bussy proclaimed and supported a new soudhabar, who was friendly to the French and who ceded to them five provinces, of which the large town of Masulipatam, already in French hands, became the capital. A third of India was obedient to Dupleix; the Great Mogul sent him a decree of investiture and demanded of the Princess Jane the hand of her youngest daughter, promised to M. de Bussy. Dupleix well knew the frailty of human affairs and the dark intrigues of Hindoo courts; he breathed freely, however, for he was on his guard and the dream of his life seemed to be accomplished. "The empire of France is founded," he would say.

He reckoned without France, and without the incompetent or timid men who governed her. The successes of Dupleix scared King Louis XV. and his feeble ministers; they angered and discomfited England, which was as yet tottering in India, and whose affairs there had for a long while been ill managed, but which remained ever vigorous, active, animated by the indomitable ardour of a free people. At Versailles attempts were made to lessen the conquests of Dupleix, prudence was recommended to him, delay was shown in sending him the troops he demanded. In India England had at last found a man still young and unknown, but worthy of being opposed to Dupleix. Clive, who had almost in boyhood entered the Company's offices, turned out, after the turbulence of his early years, a heaven-born general; he was destined to continue Dupleix's work, when abandoned by France, and to found to the advantage of the English that European dominion in India which had been the governor of Pondicherry's dream. The war still continued in the Carnatic: Mahomet Ali, Tchunda Sahib's rival, had for the last six months been besieged in Trichinopoli; the English had several times, but

DEATH OF THE NABOB OF THE CARNATIC.

in vain, attempted to effect the raising of the siege; Clive, who had recently entered the Company's army, was for saving the last refuge of Mahomet Ali by a bold diversion against Arcot, the capital of the Carnatic. To him was given the command of the expedition he had suggested. In the month of September, 1751, he made himself master of Arcot by a surprise. The Hindoo populations left to themselves passed almost without resistance from one master to another; the Europeans did not signalize by the infliction of punishment the act of taking possession. Clive was before long attacked in Arcot by Tchunda Sahib, who was supported by a French detachment. He was not in a position to hold the town, so he took refuge in the fort, and there, for fifty days, withstood all the efforts of his enemies. Provisions fell short; every day the rations were becoming more insufficient; but Clive had managed to implant in his soldiers' hearts the heroic resolution which animated him. "Give the rice to the English," said the sepoys; "we will be content with the water in which it is boiled." A body of Mahrattas, allies of the English, came to raise the siege; Clive pursued the French on their retreat, twice defeated Tchunda Sahib, and, at last effecting a junction with the governor-general Lawrence, broke the investment of Trichinopoli, and released Mahomet Ali. Tchunda Sahib, in his turn shut up in Tcheringham, was delivered over to his rival by a Tanjore chieftain in whom he trusted; he was put to death; and the French commandant, a nephew of Law's, surrendered to the English. Two French corps had already been destroyed by Clive, who held the third army prisoners. Bussy was carrying on war in the Deccan, with great difficulty making head against overt hostilities and secret intrigues. The report of Dupleix's reverses arrived in France in the month of September, 1752. ·

The dismay at Versailles was great, and prevailed over the astonishment. There had never been any confidence in Dupleix's projects, there had been scarcely any belief in his conquests. The soft-hearted inertness of ministers and courtiers was almost as much disgusted at the successes as at the defeats of the bold adventurers who were attempting and risking all for the aggrandisement and puissance of France in the East. Dupleix secretly

received notice to demand his recall.   He replied by proposing to
have M. de Bussy nominated in his place.   " Never was so grand
a fellow as this Bussy !" he wrote.   The ministers and the Company cared little for the grandeur of Bussy or of Dupleix ; what
they sought was a dastardly security, incessantly troubled by the
enterprises of the politician and the soldier.   The tone of England
was more haughty than ever, in consequence of Clive's successes.
The recall of Dupleix was determined upon.

The governor of Pondicherry had received no troops, but he
had managed to reorganize an army, and had resumed the offensive in the Carnatic ; Bussy, set free at last as to his movements
in the Deccan, was preparing to rejoin Dupleix.   Clive was ill and
had just set out for England : fortune had once more changed
front.   The open conferences held with Saunders, English governor
of Madras, failed in the month of January, 1754 ; Dupleix wished
to preserve the advantages he had won, Saunders refused to listen
to that ; the approach of a French squadron was signalled.   The
ships appeared to be numerous.   Dupleix was already rejoicing at
the arrival of unexpected aid, when, instead of an officer commanding the twelve hundred soldiers from France, he saw the
apparition of M. Godeheu, one of the directors of the Company,
and but lately his friend and correspondent.   " I come to supersede you, sir," said the new arrival without any circumstance ;
" I have full powers from the Company to treat with the English."
The cabinet of London had not been deceived as to the importance
cf Dupleix in India ; his recall had been made the absolute condition of a cessation of hostilities.   Louis XV. and his ministers
had shown no opposition ; the treaty was soon concluded, restoring
the possessions of the two Companies within the limits they had
occupied before the war of the Carnatic, with the exception of the
district of Masulipatam, which became accessible to the English.
All the territories ceded by the Hindoo princes to Dupleix reverted
to their former masters ; the two Companies interdicted one
another from taking any part in the interior policy of India, and
at the same time forbade their agents to accept from the Hindoo
princes any charge, honour or dignity ; the most perfect equality
was re-established between the possessions and revenues of the

two great European nations, rivals in the East as well as in Europe; England gave up some petty forts, some towns of no importance, France ceded the empire of India.   When Godeheu signed the treaty, Trichinopoli was at last on the point of giving in.   Bussy was furious, and would have quitted the Deccan, which he still occupied, but Dupleix constrained him to remain there; he himself embarked for France with his wife and daughter,

DUPLEIX.

leaving in India, together with his life's work destroyed in a few days by the poltroonery of his country's government, the fortune he had acquired during his great enterprises, entirely sunk as it was in the service of France; the revenues destined to cover his advances were seized by Godeheu.

France seemed to comprehend what her ministers had not even an idea of; Dupleix's arrival in France was a veritable triumph. It was by this time known that the reverses which had caused so

much talk had been half repaired.   It was by this time guessed
how infinite were the resources of that empire of India, so lightly
and mean-spiritedly abandoned to the English.   " My wife and I
dare not appear in the streets of Lorient," wrote Dupleix, " because
of the crowd of people wanting to see us and bless us ;" the
comptroller-general, Hérault de Séchelles, as well as the king and
Madame de Pompadour, then and for a long while the reigning
favourite, gave so favourable a reception to the hero of India that
Dupleix, always an optimist, conceived fresh hopes.   " I shall
regain my property here," he would say, " and India will recover
in the hands of Bussy."

He was mistaken about the justice as he had been about the
discernment and the boldness of the French government ; not a
promise was accomplished ; not a hope was realized ; after delay upon
delay, excuse upon excuse, Dupleix saw his wife expire at the end of
two years, worn out with suffering and driven to despair : like her,
his daughter, affianced for a long time past to Bussy, succumbed
beneath the weight of sorrow ; in vain did Dupleix tire out the
ministers with his views and his projects for India, he saw even the
action he was about to bring against the Company vetoed by order
of the king.   Persecuted by his creditors, overwhelmed with regret
for the relatives and friends whom he had involved in his enterprises and in his ruin, he exclaimed a few months before his death :
" I have sacrificed youth, fortune, life in order to load with honour
and riches those of my own nation in Asia.   Unhappy friends, too
weakly credulous relatives, virtuous citizens have dedicated their
property to promoting the success of my projects ; they are now in
want. . . . I demand, like the humblest of creditors, that which
is my due ; my services are all stuff, my demand is ridiculous,
I am treated like the vilest of men.   The little I have left is
seized, I have been obliged to get execution stayed to prevent my
being dragged to prison !"   Dupleix died at last on the 11th of
November, 1763, the most striking, without being the last or the
most tragical, victim of the great French enterprises in India.

Despite the treaty of peace, hostilities had never really ceased
in India.   Clive had returned from England ; freed henceforth
from the influence, the intrigues and the indomitable energy of

Dupleix, he had soon made himself master of the whole of Bengal, he had even driven the French from Chandernuggur; Bussy had been unable to check his successes, he avenged himself by wresting away from the English all their agencies on the coast of Orissa, and closing against them the road between the Coromandel coast and Bengal.

Meanwhile the Seven Years' war had broken out; the whole of Europe had joined in the contest: the French navy, still feeble in spite of the efforts that had been made to restore it, underwent serious reverses on every sea. Count Lally-Tolendal, descended from an Irish family which took refuge in France with James II., went to Count d'Argenson, still minister of war, with a proposition to go and humble in India that English power which had been imprudently left to grow up without hindrance. M. de Lally had served with renown in the wars of Germany; he had seconded Prince Charles Edward in his brave and yet frivolous attempt upon England. The directors of the India Company went and asked M. d'Argenson to entrust to General Lally the king's troops promised for the expedition. "You are wrong," M. d'Argenson said to them: "I know M. de Lally, he is a friend of mine, but he is violent, passionate, inflexible as to discipline, he will not tolerate any disorder; you will be setting fire to your warehouses, if you send him thither." The directors, however, insisted, and M. de Lally set out on the 2nd of May, 1757, with four ships and a body of troops. Some young officers belonging to the greatest houses of France served on his staff.

M. de Lally's passage was a long one; the English reinforcements had preceded him by six weeks. On arriving in India, he found the arsenals and the magazines empty; the establishment of Pondicherry alone confessed to fourteen millions of debt. Meanwhile the enemy was pressing at all points upon the French possessions. Lally marched to Gondelour (Kaddalore), which he carried on the sixth day; he shortly afterwards invested Fort St. David, the most formidable of the English fortresses in India. The first assault was repulsed; the general had neither cannon nor beasts of burthen to draw them. He hurried off to Pondicherry and had the natives harnessed to the artillery-trains, taking pell-mell such

men as fell in his way without regard for rank or caste, imprudently wounding the prejudices most dear to the country he
had come to govern. Fort St David was taken and razed.
Devicotah, after scarcely the ghost of a siege, opened its gates.
Lally had been hardly a month in India, and he had already driven
the English from the southern coast of the Coromandel. "All
my policy is in these five words, but they are binding as an oath :
no English in the peninsula," wrote the general. He had sent
Bussy orders to come and join him in order to attack Madras.

The brilliant courage and heroic ardour of M. de Lally had
triumphed over the first obstacles ; his recklessness, his severity,
his passionateness were about to lose him the fruits of his
victories. "The commission I hold," he wrote to the directors of
the Company at Paris, "imports that I shall be held in horror by
all the people of the country." By his personal defaults he
aggravated his already critical position. The supineness of the
French government had made fatal progress amongst its servants ;
Count d'Aché, who commanded the fleet, had refused to second
the attempt upon Madras ; twice, whilst cruising in Indian waters,
the French admiral had been beaten by the English ; he took
the course back to Ile de France, where he reckoned upon
wintering. Pondicherry was threatened, and Lally found himself
in Tanjore where he had hoped to recover a considerable sum due
to the Company ; on his road he had attacked a pagoda, thinking
he would find there a great deal of treasure, but the idols were
hollow and of worthless material. The pagoda was in flames, the
disconsolate brahmins were still wandering round about their
temple ; the general took them for spies and had them tied to the
cannons' mouths. The danger of Pondicherry forced M. de Lally
to raise the siege of Tanjore ; the English fell back on Madras.

Disorder was at its height in the Company's affairs ; the vast
enterprises commenced by Dupleix required success and conquests,
but they had been abandoned since his recall, not without having
engulphed together with his private fortune a portion of the
Company's resources. Lally was angered at being every moment
shackled for want of money : he attributed it not only to the ill-
will but also to the dishonesty of the local authorities. He wrote,

in 1758, to M. de Leyrit, governor of Pondicherry : " Sir, this letter shall be an eternal secret between you and me, if you furnish me with the means of terminating my enterprise. I left you a hundred thousand livres of my own money to help you to meet the expenditure it requires. I have not found so much as a hundred sous in your purse and in that of all your council, you have both of you refused to let me employ your credit. I, however, consider you to be all of you under more obligation to the Company than I am, who have unfortunately the honour of no further acquaintance with it than to the extent of having lost half my property by it in 1720. If you continue to leave me in want of everything and exposed to the necessity of presenting a front to the general discontent, not only shall I inform the king and the Company of the fine zeal testified for their service by their employés here, but I shall take effectual measures for not being at the mercy, during the short stay I desire to make in this country, of the party-spirit and personal motives by which I see that every member appears to be actuated to the risk of the Company in general."

In the midst of this distress, and in spite of this ebullition, M. de Lally led his troops up in front of Madras ; he made himself master of the Black Town. " The immense plunder taken by the troops," says the journal of an officer who held a command under Count Lally, " had introduced abundance amongst them. Huge stores of strong liquors led to drunkenness and all the evils it generates. The situation must have been seen to be believed. The works, the guards in the trenches were all performed by drunken men. The regiment of Lorraine alone was exempt from this plague, but the other corps surpassed one another. Hence scenes of the most shameful kind and most destructive of subordination and discipline, the details of which confined within the limits of the most scrupulous truthfulness would appear a monstrous exaggeration." Lally in despair wrote to his friends in France : " Hell vomited me into this land of iniquities, and I am waiting like Jonah for the whale that shall receive me in its belly."

The attack on the White Town and on Fort St. George was repulsed ; and on the 18th of February, 1759, Lally was obliged to

raise the siege of Madras. The discord which reigned in the
army as well as amongst the civil functionaries was nowhere more
flagrant than between Lally and Bussy. The latter could not
console himself for having been forced to leave the Deccan in the
feeble hands of the marquis of Conflans. An expedition attempted
against the fortress of Wandiwash, of which the English had
obtained possession, was followed by a serious defeat; Colonel
Coote was master of Karikal. Little by little the French army
and French power in India found themselves cooped within the
immediate territory of Pondicherry. The English marched against
this town. Lally shut himself up there in the month of March,
1760. Bussy had been made prisoner, and Coote had sent him to
Europe. " At the head of the French army Bussy would be in a
position by himself alone to prolong the war for ten years," said
the Hindoos. On the 27th of November, the siege of Pondicherry
was transformed into an investment.

Lally had taken all the precautions of a good general, but he
had taken them with his usual harshness ; he had driven from the
city all the useless mouths ; 1400 Hindoos, old men, women and
children, wandered for a week between the English camp and the
ramparts of the town, dying of hunger and misery, without Lally's
consenting to receive them back into the place : the English at
last allowed them to pass. The most severe requisitions had been
ordered to be made on all the houses of Pondicherry, and the
irritation was extreme ; the heroic despair of M. de Lally was
continually wringing from him imprudent expressions : " I would
rather go and command a set of Caffres than remain in this
Sodom which the English fire, in default of Heaven's, must
sooner or later destroy," had for a long time past been a common
expression of the general's, whose fate was henceforth bound up
with that of Pondicherry.

He held out for six weeks, in spite of famine, want of money
and ever increasing dissensions. A tempest had caused great
havoc to the English squadron which was out at sea ; Lally was
waiting and waiting for the arrival of M. d'Aché with the fleet
which had but lately sought refuge at Ile de France after a fresh
reverse. From Paris, on the report of an attack projected by

LALLY AT PONDICHERRY.

the English against Bourbon and Ile de France, ministers had given orders to M. d'Aché not to quit those waters. Lally and Pondicherry waited in vain.

It became necessary to surrender, the council of the Company called upon the general to capitulate; Lally claimed the honours of war, but Coote would have the town at discretion : the distress was extreme as well as the irritation. Pondicherry was delivered up to the conquerors on the 16th of January, 1761; the fortifications and magazines were razed; French power in India, long supported by the courage or ability of a few men, was foundering, never to rise again. " Nobody can have a higher opinion than I of M. de Lally," wrote Colonel Coote : " he struggled against obstacles that I considered insurmountable and triumphed over them. There is not in India another man who could have so long kept an army standing without pay and without resources in any direction." " A convincing proof of his merits," said another English officer, " is his long and vigorous resistance in a place in which he was universally detested."

Hatred bears bitterer fruits than is imagined even by those who provoke it. The animosity which M. de Lally had excited in India was everywhere an obstacle to the defence; and it was destined to cost him his life and imperil his honour. Scarcely had he arrived in England, ill, exhausted by sufferings and fatigue, followed even in his captivity by the reproaches and anger of his comrades in misfortune, when he heard of the outbreak of public opinion against him in France; he was accused of treason; and he obtained from the English cabinet permission to repair to Paris. " I bring hither my head and my innocence," he wrote, on disembarking, to the minister of war, and he went voluntarily to imprisonment in the Bastille. There he remained nineteen months without being examined. When the trial commenced in December, 1764, the heads of accusation amounted to 160, the number of witnesses to nearly 200; the matter lasted a year and a half, conducted with violence on the part of M. de Lally's numerous enemies, with inveteracy on the part of the Parliament, still at strife with the government, with courage and firmness on the part of the accused. He claimed the jurisdiction of a court-martial, but his demand was rejected; when he saw himself confronted with the dock, the general suddenly uncovered his whitened head and his breast covered with scars, exclaiming, "So this is the reward for fifty years' service!" On the 6th of May, 1766, his sentence was at last pronounced. Lally was acquitted on the charges of high treason and malversation; he was found "guilty of violence, abuse of authority, vexations and exactions, as well as of having betrayed the interests of the king and of the Company." When the sentence was being read out to the condemned: "Cut it short, sir," said the count to the clerk, "come to the conclusions." At the words "betrayed the interests of the king," Lally drew himself up to his full height, exclaiming, "Never, never!" He was expending his wrath in insults heaped upon his enemies, when, suddenly drawing from his pocket a pair of mathematical compasses, he struck it violently against his heart: the wound did not go deep enough, M. de Lally was destined to drink to the dregs the cup of man's injustice.

On the 9th of May, at the close of the day, the valiant general whose heroic resistance had astounded all India mounted the scaffold on the Place de Grève, nor was permission granted to the few friends who remained faithful to him to accompany him to the place of execution; there was only the parish-priest of St. Louis en l'Ile at his side; as apprehensions were felt of violence and insult on the part of the condemned, he was gagged like the lowest criminal when he resolutely mounted the fatal ladder; he knelt without assistance and calmly awaited his death-blow. "Everybody," observed D'Alembert, expressing by that cruel saying the violence of public feeling against the condemned, "everybody, except the hangman, has a right to kill Lally." Voltaire's judgment, after the subsidence of passion and after the light thrown by subsequent events upon the state of French affairs in India before Lally's campaigns, is more just: "It was a murder committed with the sword of justice." King Louis XV. and his government had lost India; the rage and shame blindly excited amongst the nation by this disaster had been visited upon the head of the unhappy general who had been last vanquished in defending the remnants of French power. The English were masters for ever of India when the son of M. de Lally-Tollendal at last obtained, in 1780, the rehabilitation of his father's memory. Public opinion had not waited till then to decide the case between the condemned and his accusers.

Whilst the French power in India, after having for an instant had the dominion over nearly the whole peninsula, was dying out beneath the incapacity and feebleness of its government, at the moment when the heroic efforts of La Bourdonnais, Dupleix and Lally were passing into the domain of history, a people decimated by war and famine, exhausted by a twenty years' unequal struggle, was slowly expiring, preserving to the very last its hopes and its patriotic devotion. In the West Indies the whole Canadian people were still maintaining, for the honour of France, that flag which had just been allowed to slip from the desperate hands of Lally in the East. In this case, there were no enchanting prospects of power and riches easily acquired, of dominion over opulent princes and submissive slaves; nothing but a constant struggle against nature, still mistress of the vast solitudes, against vigilant rivals and a courageous and cruel race of natives. The history of the French colonists in Canada showed traits and presented characteristics rare in French annals; the ardour of the French nature and the suavity of French manners, seemed to be combined with the stronger virtues of the people of the North; everywhere, amongst the bold pioneers of civilization in the new world, the French marched in the first rank without ever permitting themselves to be surpassed by the intrepidity or perseverance of the Anglo-Saxons, down to the day when, cooped up within the first confines of their conquests, fighting for life and liberty, the Canadians defended foot to foot the honour of their mother-country, which had for a long while neglected them and at last abandoned them, under the pressure of a disastrous war conducted by a government as incapable as it was corrupt.

For a long time past the French had directed towards America their ardent spirit of enterprise; in the fifteenth century, on the morrow of the discovery of the new world, when the indomitable genius and religious faith of Christopher Columbus had just opened a new path to inquiring minds and daring spirits, the Basques, the

Bretons and the Normans were amongst the first to follow the road he had marked out; their light barques and their intrepid navigators were soon known among the fisheries of Newfoundland and the Canadian coast. As early as 1506 a chart of the St. Lawrence was drawn by John Denis, who came from Honfleur in Normandy. Before long the fishers began to approach the coasts, attracted by the fur-trade; they entered into relations with the native tribes, buying, very often for a mere song, the produce of their hunting, and introducing to them together with the first-fruits of civilization its corruptions and its dangers. Before long the savages of America became acquainted with the *fire-water.*

Policy was not slow to second the bold enterprises of the navigators. France was at that time agitated by various earnest and mighty passions : for a moment the Reformation, personified by the austere virtues and grand spirit of Coligny, had seemed to dispute the empire of the Catholic Church. The forecasts of the admiral became more and more sombre every day, he weighed the power and hatred of the Guises as well as of their partisans; in his anxiety for his countrymen and his religion he determined to secure for the persecuted Protestants a refuge, perhaps, a home in the new world, after that defeat of which he already saw a glimmer.

A first expedition had failed, after an attempt on the coasts of Brazil; in 1562, a new flotilla set out from Havre, commanded by John Ribaut of Dieppe. A landing was effected in a beautiful country, sparkling with flowers and verdure; the century-old trees, the vast forests, the unknown birds, the game, which appeared at the entrance of the glades and stood still fearlessly at the unwonted apparition of man—this spectacle, familiar and at the same time new, presented by nature at the commencement of May, caused great joy and profound gratitude amongst the French, who had come so far, through so many perils, to the borders of Florida ; they knelt down piously to thank God ; the savages, flocking together upon the shore, regarded them with astonishment mingled with respect. Ribaut and his companions took possession of the country in the name of France, and immediately began to construct a fort which they called Fort Charles, in honour of the young king, Charles IX. Detachments scoured the country and carried to a distance the name of France : during three years, through a course of continual suffering and intestine strife more dangerous than the hardships of nature and the ambushes of savages, the French maintained themselves in their new settlement, enlarged from time to time by new emigrants. Unhappily they had frequently been recruited from amongst men of no character, importing the contagion of their vices into the little colony which Coligny had intended to found the reformed church in the new world.   In 1565, a Spanish expedition landed in Florida.   Pedro Menendez de Avilès, who commanded it, had received from King Philip II. the title of adelantado (governor) of Florida; he had pledged himself, in return, to conquer for Spain this territory impudently filched from the jurisdiction which His Catholic Majesty claimed over the whole of America.   The struggle lasted but a few days, in spite of the despair and courage of the French colonists; a great number were massacred, others crowded on to the little vessels still at their disposal and carried to France the news of the disaster.   Menendez took possession of the ruined forts, of the scarcely cleared fields strewn with the corpses of the unhappy colonists.   " Are you Catholics or Lutherans ?" he demanded of his prisoners, bound two and two before him.   " We all belong to the reformed faith," replied John Ribaut, and he intoned in a loud voice a psalm : " Dust we are and to dust we shall return; twenty years more or less upon this earth are of small account ;" and, turning towards the adelantado, " do thy will," he said.   All were put to death, " As I judged expedient for the service of God and of your Majesty," wrote the Spanish commander to Philip II., " and I consider it a great piece of luck that this John Ribaut hath died in this place, for the king of France might have done more with him and five hundred ducats than with another man and five thousand, he having been the most able and experienced mariner of the day for knowing the navigation of the coasts of India and Florida."   Above the heap of corpses, before committing them to the flames, Menendez placed this inscription : " Not as Frenchmen, but as heretics."

Three years later, on the same spot on which the adelantado had heaped up the victims of his cruelty and his perfidy lay the bodies of the Spanish garrison. A Gascon gentleman, Dominic de Gourgues, had sworn to avenge the wrongs of France; he had sold his patrimony, borrowed money of his friends, and, trusting to his long experience in navigation, put to sea with three small vessels equipped at his expense. The Spaniards were living unsuspectingly as the French colonists had lately done; they had founded their principal settlement at some distance from the first landing-place, and had named it St. Augustin. De Gourgues attacked unexpectedly the little fort of San-Mateo; a detachment surrounded in the woods the Spaniards who had sought refuge there; all were killed or taken; they were hanged on the same trees which had but lately served for the execution of the French. " This I do not as to Spaniards, but as to traitors, thieves, and murderers," was the inscription placed by De Gourgues above their heads. When he again put to sea, there remained not one stone upon another of the fort of San-Mateo. France was avenged. " All that we have done was done for the service of the king and for the honour of the country," exclaimed the bold Gascon as he re-boarded his ship. Florida, nevertheless, remained in the hands of Spain; the French adventurers went carrying elsewhither their ardent hopes and their indomitable courage.

For a long while expeditions and attempts at French colonization had been directed towards Canada. James Cartier, in 1535, had taken possession of its coasts under the name of New France. M. de Roberval had taken thither colonists agricultural and mechanical; but the hard climate, famine and disease had stifled the little colony in the bud; religious and political disturbances in the mother-country were absorbing all thoughts; it was only in the reign of Henry IV., when panting France, distracted by civil discord, began to repose for the first time since more than a century, beneath a government just, able, and firm at the same time, that zeal for distant enterprises at last attracted to New France its real founder. Samuel de Champlain du Brouage, born in 1567, a faithful soldier of the king's so long as the war lasted, was unable to endure the indolence of peace. After long and perilous voyages, he enlisted in the company which M. de Monts, gentleman of the bedchamber in ordinary to Henry IV., had just formed for the trade in furs on the northern coast of America ; appointed vice-roy of Acadia, a new territory, of which the imaginary limits would extend in our times from Philadelphia to beyond Montreal, and furnished with a commercial monopoly, M. de Monts set sail on the 7th of April, 1604, taking with him, Calvinist though he was, Catholic priests as well as Protestant pastors. " I have seen our priest and the minister come to a fight over questions of faith," writes Champlain in his journal ; " I can't say which showed the more courage, or struck the harder, but I know that the minister sometimes complained to Sieur de Monts of having been beaten." This was the prelude to the conversion of the savages, which was soon to become the sole aim or the pious standard of all the attempts at colonization in New France.

M. de Monts and his comrades had been for many years struggling against the natural difficulties of their enterprise and against the ill-will or indifference which they encountered in the mother-country ; religious zeal was reviving in France ; the edict of Nantes had put a stop to violent strife ; missionary ardour animated the powerful society of Jesuits especially. At their instigation and under their direction a pious woman, rich and of high rank, the marchioness of Guercheville, profited by the distress amongst the first founders of the French colony; she purchased their rights, took possession of their territory, and, having got the king to cede to her the sovereignty of New France, from the St. Lawrence to Florida, she dedicated all her personal fortune to the holy enterprise of a mission amongst the Indians of America. Beside the adventurers, gentlemen or traders, attracted by the hope of gain or by zeal for discovery, there set out a large number of Jesuits, resolved to win a new empire for Jesus Christ. Champlain accompanied them. After long and painful explorations in the forests and amongst the Indian tribes, after frequent voyages to France on the service of the colony, he became at last, in 1606, the first governor of the nascent town of Quebec.

Never was colony founded under more pious auspices ; for some time past the Recollects had been zealously labouring for the conversion of unbelievers ; seconded by the Jesuits, who were before long to remain sole masters of the soil, they found themselves sufficiently powerful to forbid the protestant sailors certain favourite exercises of their worship: " At last it was agreed that they should not chant the psalms," says Champlain, "but that they should assemble to make their prayers." A hand more powerful than that of Madame de Guercheville or of the Jesuits was about to take the direction of the affairs of the colony as well as of France : Cardinal Richelieu had become premier minister.

The blind gropings and intestine struggles of the rival possessors of monopolies were soon succeeded by united action. Richelieu favoured commerce and did not disdain to apply thereto the resources of his great and fertile mind. In 1627, he put himself at the head of a company of a hundred associates on which the king conferred the possession as well as the government of New France, together with the commercial monopoly and freedom from all taxes for fifteen years. The colonists were to be French and Catholics ; huguenots were excluded : they alone had till then manifested any tendency towards emigration ; the attempts at colonization in America were due to their efforts : less liberal in New France than he had lately been in Europe, the cardinal thus enlisted in the service of the foreigner all the adventurous spirits and the bold explorers amongst the French Protestants, at the very moment when the English Puritans, driven from their country by the narrow and meddlesome policy of James I., were dropping anchor at the foot of Plymouth Rock, and were founding, in the name of religious liberty, a new protestant England, the rival ere long of that New France which was catholic and absolutist.

Champlain had died at Quebec on Christmas Day, 1635, after twenty-seven years' efforts and sufferings in the service of the nascent colony. Bold and enterprising, endowed with indomitable perseverance and rare practical faculties, an explorer of distant forests, an intrepid negotiator with the savage tribes, a wise and patient administrator, indulgent towards all, in spite of his ardent devotion, Samuel de Champlain had presented the rare intermixture of the heroic qualities of past times with the zeal for science and the practical talents of modern ages ; he was replaced in his government by a knight of Malta, M. de Montmagny. Quebec had a seminary, a hospital and a convent, before it possessed a population.

The foundation of Montreal was still more exclusively religious. The accounts of the Jesuits had inflamed pious souls with a noble emulation; a Montreal association was formed, under the direction of M. Olier, founder of St. Sulpice. The first expedition was placed under the command of a valiant gentleman, Paul de Maisonneuve, and of a certain Mademoiselle Mance, belonging to the middle-class of Nogent-le-Roi, who was not yet a nun, but who was destined to become the foundress of the hospital-sisters of Ville-Marie, the name which the religious zeal of the explorers intended for the new colony of Montreal.

It was not without jealousy that the governor of Quebec and the agents of the hundred associates looked upon the enterprise of M. de Maisonneuve; an attempt was made to persuade him to remain in the settlement already founded. " I am not come here to deliberate but to act," answered he : " it is my duty, as well as an honour to me, to found a colony at Montreal, and I shall go, though every tree were an Iroquois ! "

On the 16th of May, 1642, the new colonists had scarcely disembarked when they were mustered around Father Vimont, a Jesuit, clothed in his pontifical vestments. The priest, having first celebrated mass, turned to those present: " You are only a grain of mustard-seed," said he, " but you will grow until your branches cover the whole earth. You are few in number, but your work is that of God. His eye is upon you, and your children will replenish the earth." " You say that the enterprise of Montreal is of a cost more suitable for a king than for a few private persons too feeble to sustain it," wrote the associates of Montreal, in 1643, in reply to their adversaries, " and you further allege the perils of the navigation and the shipwrecks that may ruin it. You have made a better hit than you supposed in saying that it is a king's work, for the King of kings has a hand in it, He whom the winds and the sea obey. We, therefore, do not fear shipwrecks; He will not cause them save when it is good for us, and when it is for His glory, which is our only aim. If the finger of God be not in the affair of Montreal, if it be a human invention, do not trouble yourselves about it, it will never endure; but, if God have willed it, who are you that you should gainsay Him?"

The affair of Montreal stood, like that of Quebec; New France was founded, in spite of the sufferings of the early colonists, thanks to their courage, their fervent enthusiasm, and the support afforded them by the religious zeal of their friends in Europe. The jesuit missionaries every day extended their explorations, sharing with M. de la Salle the glory of the great discoveries of the West.   Champlain had before this dreamed of and sought for a passage across the continent, leading to the Southern seas and permitting of commerce with India and Japan.   La Salle, in his intrepid expeditions, discovered Ohio and Illinois, navigated the great lakes, crossed the Mississippi, which the Jesuits had been the first to reach, and pushed on as far as Texas.   Constructing forts in the midst of the savage districts, taking possession of Louisiana in the name of King Louis XIV., abandoned by the majority of his comrades and losing the most faithful of them by death, attacked by savages, betrayed by his own men, thwarted in his projects by his enemies and his rivals, this indefatigable explorer fell at last beneath the blows of a few mutineers, in 1687, just as he was trying to get back to New France; he left the field open after him to the innumerable travellers of every nation and every language who were one day to leave their mark on those measureless tracts. Everywhere, in the western regions of the American continent, the footsteps of the French, either travellers or missionaries, preceded the boldest adventurers.   It is the glory and the misfortune of France to always lead the van in the march of civilization, without having the wit to profit by the discoveries and the sagacious boldness of her children.   On the unknown roads which she has opened to the human mind and to human enterprise she has often left the fruits to be gathered by nations less inventive and less able than she, but more persevering and less perturbed by a confusion of desires and an incessant renewal of hopes.

The treaty of Utrecht had taken out of French hands the gates of Canada, Acadia and Newfoundland.   It was now in the neighbourhood of New France that the power of England was rising, growing rapidly through the development of her colonies, usurping little by little the empire of the seas. Canada was prospering, however; during the long wars which the condition of Europe had kept up in America, the Canadians had supplied the king's armies with their best soldiers. Returning to their homes and resuming without an effort the peaceful habits which characterized them, they skilfully cultivated their fields and saw their population increasing naturally without any help from the mother-country. The governors had succeeded in adroitly counterbalancing the

CHAMPLAIN.

influence of the English over the Indian tribes. The Iroquois, but lately implacable foes of France, had accepted a position of neutrality. Agricultural development secured to the country comparative prosperity, but money was scarce, the instinct of the population was not in the direction of commerce; it was every-where shackled by monopolies. The English were rich, free and bold; for them the transmission and the exchange of commodities were easy. The commercial rivalry which set in between the two nations was fatal to the French; when the hour of the final struggle came, the Canadians, though brave, resolute, passionately attached to France and ready for any sacrifice, were few in number compared with their enemies. Scattered over a vast territory, they possessed but poor pecuniary resources and could expect from the mother-country only irregular assistance, subject to variations of government and fortune as well as to the chances of maritime warfare and engagements at sea, always perilous for the French ships, which were inferior in build and in number, whatever might be the courage and skill of their commanders.

The capture of Louisbourg and of the island of Cape Breton by the English colonists, in 1745, profoundly disquieted the Canadians. They pressed the government to make an attempt upon Acadia: " The population has remained French," they said : " we are ready to fight for our relatives and friends who have passed under the yoke of the foreigner." The ministry sent the duke of Anville with a considerable fleet: storms and disease destroyed vessels and crews before it had been possible to attack. A fresh squadron, commanded by the marquis of La Jonquière, encountered the English off Cape Finisterre in Spain. Admiral Anson had seventeen ships, M. de La Jonquière had but six; he, however, fought desperately : " I never saw anybody behave better than the French commander," wrote the captain of the English ship *Windsor;* " and, to tell the truth, all the officers of that nation showed great courage; not one of them struck until it was absolutely impossible to manœuvre." The remnants of the French navy, neglected as it had been through the unreflecting economy of Cardinal Fleury, were almost completely destroyed, and England reckoned more than two hundred and fifty ships of war. Neither the successes in the Low Countries and in Germany nor the peace of Aix-la-Chapelle put a serious end to the maritime war : England used her strength to despoil the French for ever of the colonies which she envied them. The frontiers of Canada and Acadia had not been clearly defined by the treaties of peace. Distrust and disquiet reigned amongst the French colonists; the ardour of conquest fired the English, who had for a long while coveted the valley of the Ohio and its fertile territories. The covert hostility which often betrayed itself by acts of aggression was destined ere long to lead to open war.   An important emigration began amongst the Acadians; they had hitherto claimed the title of *neutrals*, in spite of the annexation of their territory by England, in order to escape the *test* oath and to remain faithful to the catholic faith; the priests and the French agents urged them to do more : more than 3000 Acadians left their fields and their cottages to settle on the French coasts, along the bay of Fundy. Every effort of the French governors who succeeded one another only too rapidly in Canada was directed towards maintaining the natural or factitious barriers between the two territories.   The savages, excited and flattered by both sides, loudly proclaimed their independence and their primitive rights over the country which the Europeans were disputing between themselves.   " We have not ceded our lands to anybody," they said : " and we have no mind to obey any king."   " Do you not know what is the difference between the king of France and the Englishman?" the Iroquois were asked by Marquis Duquesne, the then governor of Canada.   " Go and look at the forts which the king has set up and you will see that the land beneath his walls is still a hunting-ground, he having chosen the spots frequented by you simply to serve your need.   The Englishman, on the other hand, is no sooner in possession of land than the game is forced to quit, the woods are felled, the soil is uncovered and you can scarcely find the wherewithal to shelter yourselves at night."

The governor of Canada was not mistaken.   Where France established mere military posts and as it were landmarks of her political dominion, the English colonists, cultivators and traders, brought with them practical civilization, the natural and powerful enemy of savage life.   Already war was in preparation without regard to the claims of these humble allies, who were destined ere long to die out before might and the presence of a superior race. The French commander in the valley of the Ohio, M. de Contre-cœur, was occupied with preparations for defence, when he learned that a considerable body of English troops were marching against him under the orders of Colonel Washington.   He immediately despatched M. de Jumonville with thirty men to summon the

English to retire and to evacuate French territory. At break of day on the 18th of May, 1754, Washington's men surprised Jumonville's little encampment. The attack was unexpected; it is not known whether the French envoy had time to convey the summons with which he had been charged; he was killed together with nine men of his troops. The irritation caused by this event precipitated the commencement of hostilities. A corps of Canadians, reinforced by a few savages, marched at once against Washington; he was intrenched in the plain; he had to be attacked with artillery. The future hero of American independence was obliged to capitulate; the English retired with such precipitation that they abandoned even their flag.

Negotiations were still going on between London and Versailles, and meanwhile the governors of the English colonies had met together to form a sort of confederation against French power in the new world. They were raising militia everywhere. On the 20th of January, 1755, General Braddock with a corps of regulars landed at Williamsburg in Virginia. Two months later, or not until the end of April, in fact, Admiral Dubois de la Motte quitted Brest, with reinforcements and munitions of war for Canada. After him and almost in his wake went Admiral Boscawen from Plymouth, on the 27th of April, seeking to encounter him at sea. " Most certainly the English will not commence hostilities," said the English cabinet to calm the anxieties of France.

It was only off Newfoundland that Admiral Boscawen's squadron encountered some French vessels detached from the fleet in consequence of the bad weather. " Captain Hocquart, who commanded the *Alcide*," says the account of M. de Choiseul, " finding himself within hail of the *Dunkerque*, had this question put in English: ' Are we at peace or war?' The English captain appearing not to understand, the question was repeated in French. ' Peace! peace!' shouted the English. Almost at the same moment the *Dunkerque* poured in a broadside, riddling the *Alcide* with balls." The two French ships were taken; and a few days afterwards three hundred merchant vessels, peaceably pursuing their course, were seized by the English navy. The loss was immense as well as the disgrace.

France at last decided upon declaring war, which had already been commenced in fact for more than two years.

It was regretfully and as if compelled by a remnant of national honour that Louis XV. had just adopted the resolution of defending his colonies; he had, and the nation had as well, the feeling that the French were hopelessly weak at sea. " What use to us will be hosts of troops and plenty of money," wrote the advocate Barbier, " if we have only to fight the English at sea? They will take all our ships one after another, they will seize all our settlements in America and will get all the trade. We must hope for some division amongst the English nation itself, for the king personally does not desire war."

The English nation was not divided. The ministers and the parliament, as well as the American colonies, were for war. " There is no hope of repose for our thirteen colonies, as long as the French are masters of Canada," said Benjamin Franklin on his arrival in London in 1754. He was already labouring, without knowing it, at that great work of American independence which was to be his glory and that of his generation; the common efforts and the common interest of the thirteen American colonies in the war against France were the first step towards that great coalition which founded the United States of America.

The union with the mother country was as yet close and potent: at the instigation of Mr. Fox, soon afterwards Lord Holland, and at the time Prime Minister of England, parliament voted twenty-five millions for the American war. The bounty given to the soldiers and marines who enlisted was doubled by private subscription; 15,000 men were thus raised to invade the French colonies.

Canada and Louisiana together did not number 80,000 inhabitants, whilst the population of the English colonies already amounted to 1,200,000 souls; to the 2800 regular troops sent from France the Canadian militia added about 4000 men, less experienced but quite as determined as the most intrepid veterans of the campaigns in Europe. During more than twenty years the courage and devotion of the Canadians never faltered for a single day.

Then began an unequal but an obstinate struggle, of which the issue, easy to foresee, never cowed or appeased the actors in it. The able tactics of M. de Vaudreuil, governor of the colony, had forced the English to scatter their forces and their attacks over an immense territory, far away from the most important settlements; the forts which they besieged were scarcely defended. "A large enclosure, with a palisade round it, in which there were but one officer and nineteen soldiers," wrote the marquis of Montcalm at a later period, "could not be considered as a fort adapted to sustain a siege." In the first campaign, the settlements formed by the Acadian emigrants on the borders of the bay of Fundy were completely destroyed: the French garrisons were obliged to evacuate their positions.

This withdrawal left Acadia, or *neutral land*, at the mercy of the Anglo-Americans. Before Longfellow had immortalized, in the poem of *Evangeline*, the peaceful habits and the misfortunes of the Acadians, Raynal had already pleaded their cause before history; "A simple and a kindly people," he said, "who had no liking for blood, agriculture was their occupation; they had been settled in the low grounds, forcing back by dint of dikes the sea and rivers wherewith those plains were covered. The drained marshes produced wheat, rye, oats, barley and maize. Immense prairies were alive with numerous flocks; as many as sixty thousand horned cattle were counted there. The habitations, nearly all built of wood, were very commodious and furnished with the neatness sometimes found amongst our European farmers in the easiest circumstances. Their manners were extremely simple; the little differences which might from time to time arise between the colonists were always amicably settled by the elders. It was a band of brothers all equally ready to give or receive that which they considered common to all men."

War and its horrors broke in upon this peaceful idyl.

The Acadians had constantly refused to take the oath to England; they were declared guilty of having violated neutrality. For the most part the accusation was unjust, but all were involved in the same condemnation.

On the 5th of September, 1755, four hundred and eighteen

heads of families were summoned to meet in the church of Grand-Pré. The same order had been given throughout all the towns of Acadia. The anxious farmers had all obeyed. Colonel Winslow, commanding the Massachusetts militia, repaired thither with great array: "It is a painful duty which brings me here," he said: "I have orders to inform you that your lands, your houses and your crops are confiscated to the profit of the crown; you can carry off your money and your linen on your deportation from the province." The order was accompanied by no explanation; nor did it admit of any. All the heads of families were at once surrounded by the soldiers. By tens and under safe escort, they were permitted to visit once more the fields which they had cultivated, the houses in which they had seen their children grow up. On the 10th they embarked, passing on their way to the ships between two rows of women and children in tears. The young people had shown a disposition to resist, demanding leave to depart with their families: the soldiers crossed their bayonets. The vessels set sail for the English colonies, dispersing over the coast the poor creatures they had torn away from all that was theirs; many perished of want whilst seeking from town to town their families removed after them from Acadia; the charity of the American colonists relieved their first wants. Some French Protestants, who had settled in Philadelphia after the revocation of the edict of Nantes, welcomed them as brothers, notwithstanding the difference of their creed; for they knew all the heart-rending evils of exile.

Much emotion was excited in France by the woes of the Acadians. In spite of the declaration of war, Louis XV. made a request to the English cabinet for permission to send vessels along the coasts of America to pick up those unfortunates. "Our navigation act is against it," replied Mr. Grenville: "France cannot send ships amongst our colonies." A few Acadians, nevertheless, reached France: they settled in the outskirts of Bordeaux, where their descendants still form the population of two prosperous communes. Others founded in Louisiana settlements which bore the name of Acadia. The crime was consummated: the religious, pacific, inoffensive population, which but lately occupied the neutral land, had completely disappeared. The greedy colonists who envied them their farms and pasturage had taken possession of the spoil; Acadia was for ever in the power of the Anglo-Saxon race, which was at the same moment invading the valley of the Ohio.

General Braddock had mustered his troops at Wills Creek. in the neighbourhood of the Alleghany mountains. He meditated surprising Fort Duquesne, erected but a short time previously by the French on the banks of the Ohio. The little army was advancing slowly across the mountains and the forests; Braddock divided it into two corps, and, placing himself with Colonel Washington, who was at that time serving on his staff, at the head of twelve hundred men, he pushed forward rapidly : "Never," said Washington afterwards, "did I see a finer sight than the departure of the English troops on the 9th of July, 1755 ; all the men were in full uniform, marching in slow time and in perfect order; the sun was reflected from their glittering arms ; the river rolled its waves along on their right, and on their left the vast forest threw over them its mighty shadows. Officers and soldiers were equally joyous and confident of success."

Twice the attacking column had crossed the Monongahala by fording ; it was leaving the plain which extended to some distance from Fort Duquesne to enter the woodpath, when the advance-guard was all at once brought up by a tremendous discharge of artillery ; a second discharge came almost immediately from the right. The English could not see their enemy ; they were confused and fell back upon General Braddock and the main body of the detachment, who were coming up to their aid. The disorder soon became extreme. The regular troops, unaccustomed to this kind of warfare, refused to rally in spite of the efforts of their general, who would have had them manœuvre as in the plains of Flanders ; the Virginian militia alone, recurring to habits of forest-warfare, had dispersed, but without flying, hiding themselves behind the trees and replying to the French or Indian sharpshooters. Before long General Braddock received a mortal wound ; his staff had fallen almost to a man ; Colonel Washington alone, reserved by God for another destiny, still sought to rally

DEATH OF GENERAL BRADDOCK.

his men. " I have been protected by the almighty intervention of Providence beyond every human probability," he wrote to his brother after the action : " I received four balls in my clothes and I had two horses killed under me; nevertheless I came out of it safe and sound, whilst death was sweeping down my comrades around me." The small English corps was destroyed; the fugitives communicated their terror to the detachment of Colonel Dunbar, who was coming to join them. All the troops disbanded, spiking the guns and burning the munitions and baggage; in their panic the soldiers asked no question save whether the enemy were pursuing them. " We have been beaten, shamefully beaten," wrote Washington, " by a handful of French whose only idea was to hamper our march. A few moments before the action we thought our forces almost a match for all those of Canada, and yet, against every probability, we have been completely defeated and have lost everything." The small French corps, which sallied from Fort Duquesne under the orders of M. de Beaujeu, numbered only 200 Canadians and 600 Indians. It was not until three years later, in 1758, that Fort Duquesne, laid in ruins by the defenders themselves, at last fell into the hands of the English, who gave to it, in honour of the great English minister, the name of Pittsburg, which is borne to this day by a flourishing town.

The courage of the Canadians and the able use they had the wits to make of their savage allies still balanced the fortunes of war; but the continuance of hostilities betrayed more and more every day the inferiority of the forces and the insufficiency of the resources of the colony. " The colonists employed in the army, of which they form the greater part, no longer till the lands they had formerly cleared, far from clearing new ones," wrote the superintendent of Canada : " the levies about to be made will still further dispeople the country. What will become of the colony? There will be a deficiency of everything, especially of corn; up to the present the intention had been not to raise the levies until the work of spring was over. That indulgence can no longer be accorded, since the war will go on during the winter and the armies must be mustered as early as the month of April. Besides, the Canadians are decreasing fast; a great number have died of fatigue and disease. There is no relying," added the superintendent, " on the savages save so long as we have the superiority and so long as all their wants are supplied." The government determined to send reinforcements to Canada under the orders of the Marquis of Montcalm.

The new general had thirty-five years' service, though he was not yet fifty : he had distinguished himself in Germany and in Italy. He was brave, amiable, clever; by turns indolent and bold; skilful in dealing with the Indians, whom he inspired with feelings of great admiration; jealous of the Canadians, their officers and their governor, M. de Vaudreuil; convinced beforehand of the uselessness of all efforts and of the inevitable result of the struggle he maintained with indomitable courage. More intelligent than his predecessor, General Dieskau, who, like Braddock, had fallen through the error of conducting the war in the European fashion, he, nevertheless, had great difficulty in wrenching himself from the military traditions of his whole life. An expedition, in 1756, against Fort Oswego, on the right bank of Lake Ontario, was completely successful; General Webb had no time to relieve the garrison, which capitulated. Bands of Canadians and Indians laid waste Pennsylvania, Maryland and Virginia. Montcalm wrote to the minister of war, Rouillé : " It is the first time that, with 3000 men and less artillery, a siege has been maintained against 1800, who could be readily relieved by 2000, and who could oppose our landing, having the naval superiority on Lake Ontario. The success has been beyond all expectation. The conduct I adopted on this occasion and the arrangements I ordered are so contrary to the regular rules, that the boldness displayed in this enterprise must look like rashness in Europe. Therefore, I do beseech you, monseigneur, as the only favour I ask, to assure His Majesty that, if ever he should be pleased, as I hope, to employ me in his own armies, I will behave differently."

The same success everywhere attended the arms of the marquis of Montcalm. In 1757, he made himself master of Fort William Henry, which commanded the lake of Saint-Sacrement; in 1758, he repulsed with less than 4000 men the attack of General Abercrombie, at the head of 16,000 men, on Carillon, and forced the latter to relinquish the shores of Lake Champlain. This was cutting the enemy off once more from the road to Montreal; but Louisbourg, protected in 1757 by the fleet of Admiral Dubois de la Motte and now abandoned to its own resources, in vain supported an unequal siege; the fortifications were in ruins, the garrison was insufficient notwithstanding its courage and the heroism of the governor, M. de Drucourt. Seconded by his wife, who flitted about the ramparts, cheering and tending the wounded, he energetically opposed the landing of the English and maintained himself for two months in an almost open place. When he was at last obliged to surrender, on the 26th of July, Louisbourg was nothing but a heap of ruins; all the inhabitants of the islands of St. John and Cape Breton were transported by the victors to France.

Canada had by this time cost France dear; and she silently left it to its miserable fate. In vain did the governor, the general, the commissariat demand incessantly reinforcements, money, provisions: no help came from France. "We keep on fighting, nevertheless," wrote Montcalm to the minister of war, "and we will bury ourselves, if necessary, under the ruins of the colony." Famine, the natural result of neglecting the land, went on increasing; the Canadians, hunters and soldiers as they were, had only cleared and cultivated their fields in the strict ratio of their daily wants, there was a lack of hands, every man was under arms, destitution prevailed everywhere, the inhabitants of Quebec were reduced to siege-rations, the troops complained and threatened to mutiny, the enemy had renewed their efforts; in the campaign of 1758, the journals of the Anglo-American colonies put their land-forces at 60,000 men. "England has at the present moment more troops in motion on this continent than Canada contains inhabitants, including old men, women and children," said a letter to Paris from M. Doreil, war-commissioner. Mr. Pitt, afterwards Lord Chatham, who had lately come to the head of the English government, resolved to strike the last blow at the French power in America. Three armies simultaneously invaded Canada; on the 25th of June, 1759, a considerable fleet brought under the walls of Quebec General Wolfe, a young and hopeful officer who had attracted notice at the siege of Louisbourg: "If General Montcalm succeeds again this year in frustrating our hopes," said Wolfe, "he may be considered an able man; either the colony has resources that nobody knows of, or our generals are worse than usual."

Quebec was not fortified; the loss of it involved that of all Canada; it was determined to protect the place by an outlying camp; appeal was made to the Indian tribes, lately zealous in the service of France but now detached from it by ill fortune and diminution of the advantages offered them, and already for the most part won over by the English. The Canadian colonists, exhausted by war and famine, rose in mass to defend their capital. The different encampments which surrounded Quebec contained about thirteen thousand soldiers. "So strong a force had not been reckoned upon," says an eye-witness, "because nobody had expected to have so large a number of Canadians; but there prevailed so much emulation among this people that there were seen coming into the camp old men of eighty and children of from twelve to thirteen, who would not hear of profiting by the exemption accorded to their age." The poor cultivators, turned soldiers, brought to the camp their slender resources; the enemy was already devastating the surrounding country. "It will take them half a century to repair the damage," wrote an American officer in his journal of the expedition on the St. Lawrence. The bombardment of Quebec was commencing at the same moment.

For more than a month the town had stood the enemy's fire; all the buildings were reduced to ruins, and the French had not yet budged from their camp of Ange-Gardien. On the 31st of July, General Wolfe with 3000 men came and attacked them in front by the river St. Lawrence and in flank by the river Montmorency. He was repulsed by the firm bravery of the Canadians, whose French impetuosity seemed to have become modified by contact with the rough climates of the North. Immoveable in their trenches, they waited until the enemy was within range; and, when at length they fired, the skill of the practised hunters made fearful havoc in the English ranks. Everywhere repulsed, General Wolfe in despair was obliged to retreat. He all but died of vexation, overwhelmed with the weight of his responsibility. " I have only a choice of difficulties left," he wrote to the English cabinet.   Aid and encouragement did not fail him.

The forts of Carillon on Lake Champlain and of Niagara on Lake Ontario were both in the hands of the English.   A portion of the Canadians had left the camp to try and gather in the meagre crops which had been cultivated by the women and chil-

MONTCALM.

dren.   In the night between the 12th and 13th of September, General Wolfe made a sudden dash upon the banks of the St. Lawrence ; he landed at the creek of Foulon.   The officers had replied in French to the *Qui vive* (*Who goes there ?*) of the sentinels, who had supposed that what they saw passing was a long-expected convoy of provisions ; at daybreak the English army was ranged in order of battle on the plains of Abraham ; by evening, the French were routed, the marquis of Montcalm was dying and Quebec was lost.

General Wolfe had not been granted time to enjoy his victory. Mortally wounded in a bayonet-charge which he himself headed, he had been carried to the rear. The surgeons who attended to him kept watching the battle from a distance. "They fly," exclaimed one of them. "Who?" asked the general, raising himself painfully. "The French!" was the answer. "Then I am content to die," he murmured, and expired.

Montcalm had fought like a soldier in spite of his wounds; when he fell he still gave orders about the measures to be taken and the attempts to be made. "All is not lost," he kept repeating. He was buried in a hole pierced by a cannon-ball in the middle of the church of the Ursulines; and there he still rests. In 1827, when all bad feeling had subsided, Lord Dalhousie, the then English governor of Canada, ordered the erection at Quebec of an obelisk in marble bearing the names and busts of Wolfe and Montcalm with this inscription: *Mortem virtus communem, famam historia, monumentum posteritas dedit* [Valour, history, and posterity assigned fellowship in death, fame and memorial].

In 1759, the news of the death of the two generals was accepted as a sign of the coming of the end. Quebec capitulated on the 18th of September, notwithstanding the protests of the population. The government of Canada removed to Montreal.

The joy in England was great, as was the consternation in France. The government had for a long while been aware of the state to which the army and the brave Canadian people had been reduced, the nation knew nothing about it; the repeated victories of the marquis of Montcalm had caused illusion as to the gradual decay of resources. The English Parliament resolved to send three armies to America and the remains of General Wolfe were interred at Westminster with great ceremony. King Louis XV. and his ministers sent to Canada a handful of men and a vessel which suffered capture from the English; the governor's drafts were not paid at Paris. The financial condition of France did not permit her to any longer sustain the heroic devotion of her children.

M. de Lally-Tollendal was still struggling single-handed in

India, exposed to the hatred and the plots of his fellow-country-men as well as of the Hindoos, at the very moment when the Canadians, united in the same ideas of effort and sacrifice, were trying their last chance in the service of the distant mother-country which was deserting them. The command had passed from the hands of Montcalm into those of the general who was afterwards a marshal and duke of Lévis. He resolved, in the spring of 1760, to make an attempt to recover Quebec.

" All Europe," says Raynal, " supposed that the capture of the capital was an end to the great quarrel in North America. Nobody supposed that a handful of French who lacked everything, who seemed forbidden by fortune itself to harbour any hope, would dare to dream of retarding inevitable fate." On the 28th of April, the army of General de Lévis, with great difficulty main-tained during the winter, debouched before Quebec on those plains of Abraham but lately so fatal to Montcalm.

General Murray at once sallied from the place in order to engage before the French should have had time to pull themselves together. It was a long and obstinate struggle : the men fought hand to hand, with impassioned ardour, without the cavalry or the savages taking any part in the action; at nightfall General Murray had been obliged to re-enter the town and close the gates. The French, exhausted but triumphant, returned slowly from the pursuit; the unhappy fugitives fell into the hands of the Indians; General de Lévis had great difficulty in putting a stop to the carnage. In his turn he besieged Quebec.

One single idea possessed the minds of both armies : what flag would be carried by the vessels which were expected every day in the St. Lawrence ? " The circumstances were such on our side," says the English writer Knox, " that if the French fleet had been the first to enter the river, the place would have fallen again into the hands of its former masters." On the 9th of May, an English frigate entered the harbour. A week afterwards, it was followed by two other vessels. The English raised shouts of joy upon the ramparts, the cannon of the place saluted the arrivals. During the night between the 16th and 17th of May, the little French army raised the siege of Quebec. On the 6th of September, the united forces of Generals Murray, Amherst and Haviland invested Montreal.

A little wall and a ditch, intended to resist the attacks of Indians, a few pieces of cannon eaten up with rust, and 3500 troops—such were the means of defending Montreal. The rural population yielded at last to the good fortune of the English, who burnt on their march the recalcitrant villages. Despair was in every heart: M. de Vaudreuil assembled during the night a council of war. It was determined to capitulate in the name of the whole colony. The English generals granted all that was asked by the Canadian population; to its defenders they refused the honours of war. M. de Lévis retired to the island of Sainte-Hélène, resolved to hold out to the last extremity; it was only at the governor's express command that he laid down arms. No more than 3000 soldiers returned to France.

The capitulation of Montreal was signed on the 8th of September, 1760; on the 10th of February, 1763, the peace concluded between France, Spain, and England completed without hope of recovery the loss of all the French possessions in America; Louisiana had taken no part in the war, it was not conquered; France ceded it to Spain in exchange for Florida, which was abandoned to the English. Canada and all the islands of the St. Lawrence shared the same fate. Only the little islands of St. Pierre and Miquelon were preserved for the French fisheries. One single stipulation guaranteed to the Canadians the free exercise of the Catholic religion. The principal inhabitants of the colony went into exile on purpose to remain French. The weak hands of King Louis XV. and of his government had let slip the fairest colonies of France, Canada and Louisiana had ceased to belong to her; yet attachment to France subsisted there a long while and her influence left numerous traces there. It is an honour and a source of strength to France that she acts powerfully on men through the charm and suavity of her intercourse; they who have belonged to France can never forget her.

The struggle was over. King Louis XV. had lost his American colonies, the nascent empire of India and the settlements of Senegal. He recovered Guadaloupe and Martinique, but lately conquered by

the English, Chandernuggur and the ruins of Pondicherry. The
humiliation was deep and the losses were irreparable. All the
fruits of the courage, of the ability and of the passionate devotion
of the French in India and in America were falling into the hands
of England. Her government had committed many faults ; but
the strong action of a free people had always managed to repair
them. The day was coming when the haughty passions of the
mother-country and the proud independence of her colonies would
engage in that supreme struggle which has given to the world the
United States of America.

CHAPTER LIV.

LOUIS XV.—THE SEVEN YEARS' WAR—MINISTRY OF THE DUKE OF CHOISEUL (1748—1774).

IT was not only in the colonies and on the seas that the peace of Aix-la-Chapelle had seemed merely a truce destined to be soon broken: hostilities had never ceased in India or Canada; English vessels scoured the world, capturing, in spite of treaties, French merchant-ships; in Europe and on the continent, all the sovereigns were silently preparing for new efforts; only the government of King Louis XV., intrenched behind its disinterestedness in the negotiations and ignoring the fatal influences of weakness and vanity, believed itself henceforth beyond the reach of a fresh war. The nation, as oblivious as the government but less careless than it, because they had borne the burthen of the fault committed, were applying for the purpose of their material recovery that power of revival which, through a course of so many errors and reverses, has always saved France; in spite of the disorder in the finances and the crushing weight of the imposts, she was working and growing rich;

intellectual development was following the rise in material resources; the court was corrupt and inert, like the king, but a new life, dangerously free and bold, was beginning to course through men's minds: the wise, reforming instincts, the grave reflections of the dying Montesquieu no longer sufficed for them; Voltaire, who had but lately been still moderate and almost respectful, was about to commence with his friends of the *Encyclopédie* that campaign against the Christian faith which was to pave the way for the materialism of our own days. " Never was Europe more happy than during the years which rolled by between 1750 and 1758," he has said in his *Tableau du Siècle de Louis XV.* The evil, however, was hatching beneath the embers, and the last supports of the old French society were cracking-up noiselessly. The parliaments were about to disappear, the Catholic Church was becoming separated more and more widely every day from the people of whom it claimed to be the sole instructress and directress. The natural heads of the nation, the priests and the great lords, thought no longer and lived no longer as it. The public voice was raised simultaneously against the authority or insensate prodigality of Madame de Pompadour and against the refusal, ordered by the archbishop of Paris, of the sacraments. " The public, the public ! " wrote M. d'Argenson: " its animosity, its encouragements, its pasquinades, its insolence—that is what I fear above everything." The state of the royal treasury and the measures to which recourse was had to enable the State to make both ends meet aggravated the dissension and disseminated discontent amongst all classes of society. Comptrollers-general came one after another, all armed with new expedients; MM. de Machault, Moreau de Séchelles, de Moras, excited, successively, the wrath and the hatred of the people crushed by imposts in peace as well as war; the clergy refused to pay the twentieth, still claiming their right of giving only a free gift; the states-districts, Languedoc and Brittany at the head, resisted, in the name of their ancient privileges, the collection of taxes to which they had not consented; riots went on multiplying: they even extended to Paris, where the government was accused of kidnapping children for transportation to the colonies. The people rose, several police-agents were massacred; the king avoided passing through the capital on his way from Versailles to the camp at Compiègne : the path he took in the Bois de Boulogne received the name of Revolt Road. "I have seen in my days," says D'Argenson, "a decrease in the respect and love of the people for the kingship."

Decadence went on swiftly and no wonder. At forty years of age Louis XV., finding every pleasure pall, indifferent to or forgetful of business from indolence and disgust, bored by every thing and on every occasion, had come to depend solely on those who could still manage to amuse him. Madame de Pompadour had accepted this ungrateful and sometimes shameful task. Born in the ranks of the middle class, married young to a rich financier, M. Lenormant d'Étioles, Mdlle. Poisson, created marchioness of Pompadour, was careful to mix up more serious matters with the royal pleasures. The precarious lot of a favourite was not sufficient for her ambition. Pretty, clever, ingenious in devising for the king new amusements and objects of interest, she played comedy before him in her small apartments and travelled with him from castle to castle; she thus obtained from his easy prodigality enormous sums to build pleasaunces which she amused herself by embellishing : Bellevue, Babiole, the marchioness' house at Paris, cost millions out of the exhausted treasury. Madame de Pompadour was fond of porcelain ; she conceived the idea of imitating in France the china-work of Saxony, and founded first at Vincennes and then at Sèvres the manufacture of porcelain, which the king took under his protection, requiring the courtiers to purchase the proceeds of it at high prices. Everybody was anxious to please the favourite ; her incessantly renewed caprices contributed to develope certain branches of the trade in luxuries. The expenses of the royal household went on increasing daily ; the magnificent prodigalities of King Louis XIV. were surpassed by the fancies of Madame de Pompadour. Vigilant in attaching the courtiers to herself, she sowed broad-cast, all around her, favours, pensions, profitable offices, endowing the gentlemen to facilitate their marriage, turning a deaf ear to the complaints of the people as well as to the protests of the States or Parliaments. The greedy and frivolous crowd that thronged at her feet well deserved the severe judgment pronounced by Montesquieu on courtiers and courts : " Ambition amidst indolence, baseness amidst pride, the desire to grow rich without toil, aversion from truth, flattery, treason, perfidy, neglect of all engagements, contempt for the duties of a citizen, fear of virtue in the prince, hope in his weaknesses, and more than all that, the ridicule constantly thrown upon virtue, form, I trow, the characteristics of the greatest number of courtiers, distinctive in all places and at all times." The majesty of Louis XIV. and the long lustre of his reign had been potent enough to create illusions as to the dangers and the corruptions of the court ; the remnants of military glory were about to fade out round Louis XV. ; the court still swarmed with brave officers, ready to march to death at the head of the troops ; the command of armies henceforth depended on the favour of Madame the marchioness of Pompadour.

The day had come when the fortune of war was about to show itself fatal to France. Marshal Saxe had died at Chambord, still young and worn out by excesses rather than by fatigue ; this foreigner, this *huguenot*, as he was called by Louis XV., had been the last to maintain and continue the grand tradition of French generals. War, however, was inevitable ; five months of public or private negotiation, carried on by the ambassadors or personal agents of the king, could not obtain from England any reparation for her frequent violation of the law of nations : the maritime trade of France was destroyed ; the vessels of the royal navy were themselves no longer safe at sea. On the 21st of December, 1755, the minister of foreign affairs, Rouillé, notified to the English cabinet " that His Most Christian Majesty, before giving way to the effects of his resentment, once more de- manded from the king of England satisfaction for all the seizures made by the English navy, as well as restitution of all vessels, whether war-ships or merchant-ships, taken from the French, declaring that he should regard any refusal that might be made as an authentic declaration of war." England eluded the ques- tion of law, but refused restitution. On the 23rd of January, an embargo was laid on all English vessels in French ports,

and war was officially proclaimed. It had existed in fact for two
years past.

A striking incident signalized the commencement of hostilities.
Rather a man of pleasure and a courtier than an able soldier,
Marshal Richelieu had, nevertheless, the good fortune to connect
his name with the only successful event of the Seven Years' War
that was destined to remain impressed upon the mind of posterity.
Under his orders, a body of twelve thousand men, on board of a
squadron commanded by M. de la Galissonnière, left Toulon on
the 10th of April, 1756, at the moment when England was excited
by expectation of a coming descent upon her coasts. On the 17th,
the French attacked the island of Minorca, an important point
whence the English threatened Toulon and commanded the western
basin of the Mediterranean. Some few days later, the English
troops, driven out of Ciudadela and Mahon, had taken refuge in
Fort St. Philip, and the French cannon were battering the
ramparts of the vast citadel.

On the 10th of May an English fleet, commanded by Admiral
Byng, appeared in the waters of Port Mahon ; it at once attacked
M. de la Galissonnière. The latter succeeded in preventing the
English from approaching land. After an obstinate struggle,
Admiral Byng, afraid of losing his fleet, fell back on Gibraltar.
The garrison of Fort St. Philip waited in vain for the return of
the squadron : left to its own devices, it nevertheless held out ;
the fortifications seemed to be impregnable ; the siege-works
proceeded slowly ; the soldiers were disgusted and began to
indulge to excess in the wine of Spain. " No one who gets drunk
shall have the honour of mounting the breach," said Richelieu's
general order. Before long he resolved to attempt the assault.

Fort St. Philip towered up proudly on an enormous mass of
rock ; the French regiments flung themselves into the fosses,
setting against the ramparts ladders that were too short ; the
soldiers mounted upon one another's shoulders, digging their
bayonets into the interstices between the stones ; the boldest were
already at the top of the bastions. On the 28th of June, at daybreak, three of the forts were in possession of the French ; the
same day the English commandant decided upon capitulation.

The duke of Fronsac, Marshal Richelieu's son, hurried to Versailles to announce the good news. There was great joy at court and amongst the French nation: the French army and navy considered themselves avenged of England's insults. In London Admiral Byng was brought to trial: he was held responsible for the reverse, and was shot, notwithstanding the protests of Voltaire and of Richelieu himself. At the same time the king's troops were occupying Corsica in the name of the city of Genoa, the time-honoured ally of France. Mistress of half the Mediterranean and secure of the neutrality of Holland, France could have concentrated her efforts upon the sea and have maintained a glorious struggle with England, on the sole condition of keeping peace on the Continent. The policy was simple and the national interest palpable; King Louis XV. and some of his ministers understood this; but they allowed themselves to drift into forgetfulness of it.

For a long time past, under the influence of Count Kaunitz, a young diplomat equally bold and shrewd, "frivolous in his tastes and profound in his views," Maria Theresa was inclining to change the whole system of her alliances in Europe; she had made advances to France. Count Kaunitz had found means of pleasing Madame de Pompadour; the empress put the crowning touch to the conquest by writing herself to the favourite, whom she called "My cousin." The Great Frederick, on the contrary, all the time that he was seeking to renew with the king his former offensive and defensive relations, could not manage to restrain the flow of his bitter irony. Louis XV. had felt hurt, on his own account and on his favourite's; he still sought to hold the balance steady between the two great German sovereigns, but he was already beginning to lean towards the empress. A proposal was made to Maria Theresa for a treaty of guarantee between France, Austria and Prussia; the existing war between England and France was excepted from the defensive pact; France reserved to herself the right of invading Hanover. The same conditions had been offered to the king of Prussia; he was not contented with them. Whilst Maria Theresa was insisting at Paris upon obtaining an offensive as well as defensive alliance, Frederick II.

was signing with England an engagement not to permit the entrance into Germany of any foreign troops. " I only wish to preserve Germany from war," wrote the king of Prussia to Louis XV. On the 1st of May, 1756, at Versailles, Louis XV. replied to the Anglo-Prussian treaty by his alliance with the Empress Maria Theresa. The House of Bourbon was holding out the hand to the House of Austria; the work of Henry IV. and of Richelieu, already weakened by an inconsistent and capricious policy, was completely crumbling to pieces, involving in its ruin the military fortunes of France.

The prudent moderation of Abbé de Bernis, then in great favour with Madame de Pompadour and managing the negotiations with Austria, had removed from the treaty of Versailles the most alarming clauses. The empress and the king of France mutually guaranteed to one another their possessions in Europe, " each of the contracting parties promising the other, in case of need, the assistance of twenty-four thousand men." Russia and Saxony were soon enlisted in the same alliance; the king of Prussia's pleasantries, at one time coarse and at another biting, had offended the czarina Elizabeth and the elector of Saxony as well as Louis XV. and Madame de Pompadour. The weakest of the allies was the first to experience the miseries of that war so frivolously and gratuitously entered upon, from covetousness, rancour or weakness, those fertile sources of the bitterest sorrows to humanity.

" It is said that the king of Prussia's troops are on the march," wrote the duke of Luynes in his journal (September 3, 1756): " it is not said whither." Frederick II. was indeed on the march with his usual promptitude : a few days later, Saxony was invaded, Dresden occupied and the elector-king of Poland invested in the camp of Pirna. General Braun, hurrying up with the Austrians to the Saxons' aid, was attacked by Frederick on the 1st of October, near Lowositz; without being decisive, the battle was, nevertheless, sufficient to hinder the allies from effecting their junction. The Saxons attempted to cut their way through; they were hemmed in and obliged to lay down their arms; the king of Prussia established himself at Dresden, levying upon Saxony enormous military contributions and otherwise treating it as a conquered country. The unlucky elector had taken refuge in Poland.

The empress had not waited for this serious reverse to claim from France the promised aid. By this time it was understood how insufficient would be a body of twenty-four thousand men for a distant and hazardous war. Recently called to the council by King Louis XV., Marshal Belle-Isle, still full of daring in spite of his age, loudly declared that, " since war had come, it must be made on a large scale if it were to be made to any purpose and speedily." Some weeks later preparations were commenced for sending an army of a hundred thousand men to the Lower Rhine. The king undertook, besides, to pay four thousand Bavarians and six thousand Wurtemburgers who were to serve in the Austrian army. Marshal d'Estrées, grandson of Louvois, was placed at the head of the army already formed. He was not one of the favourite's particular friends. " Marshal d'Estrées," she wrote to Count Clermont, " is one of my acquaintances in society ; I have never been in a position to make him an intimate friend, but were he as much so as M. de Soubise, I should not take upon myself to procure his appointment, for fear of having to reproach myself with the results." Madame de Pompadour did not continue to be always so reserved, and M. de Soubise was destined before long to have his turn. M. de Belle-Isle had insisted strongly on the choice of Marshal d'Estrées : he was called " the Temporiser," and was equally brave and prudent. " I am accustomed," said the king, " to hear from him all he thinks." The army was already on the march.

Whilst hostilities were thus beginning throughout Europe, whilst negotiations were still going on with Vienna touching the second treaty of Versailles, King Louis XV., as he was descending the staircase of the marble court at Versailles on the 5th of January, 1757, received a stab in the side from a knife. Withdrawing full of blood the hand he had clapped to his wound, the king exclaimed : " There is the man who wounded me, with his hat on ; arrest him, but let no harm be done him ! " The guards were already upon the murderer and were torturing him pending the legal question. The king had been carried away, slightly wounded by a deep puncture from a penknife. In the soul of Louis XV. apprehension had succeeded to the first instinctive and kingly impulse of courage : he feared the weapon might be poisoned, and hastily sent for a confessor. The crowd of courtiers was already thronging to the dauphin's. To him the king had at once given up the direction of affairs.

Justice, meanwhile, had taken the wretched murderer in hand. Robert Damiens was a lacquey out of place, a native of Artois, of weak mind and sometimes appearing to be deranged. In his vague and frequently incoherent depositions, he appeared animated by a desire to avenge the wrongs of the Parliament; he burst out against the archbishop of Paris, Christopher de Beaumont, a virtuous prelate of narrow mind and austere character : "The archbishop of Paris," he said, "is the cause of all this trouble through ordering refusal of the sacraments." No investigation could discover any conspiracy or accomplices : with less coolness and fanatical resolution than Ravaillac, Damiens, like the assassin of Henry IV., was an isolated criminal, prompted to murder by the derangement of his own mind; he died, like Ravaillac, amidst fearful tortures which were no longer in accord with public sentiment and caused more horror than awe. France had ceased to tremble for the life of King Louis XV.

For one instant the power of Madame de Pompadour had appeared to be shaken : the king, in his terror, would not see her; M. de Machault, but lately her protégé, had even brought her orders to quit the palace. Together with the salutary terrors of death, Louis XV.'s repentance soon disappeared; the queen and the dauphin went back again to the modest and pious retirement in which they passed their life; the marchioness returned in triumph to Versailles. MM. de Machault and D'Argenson were exiled : the latter, who had always been hostile to the favourite, was dismissed with extreme harshness. The king had himself written the sealed letter : "Your services are no longer required. I command you to send me your resignation of the secretaryship of State for war and of all that appertains to the posts connected therewith, and to retire to your estate of Ormes." Madame de Pompadour was avenged.

LOUIS XV. AND DAMIENS.

The war, meanwhile, continued : the king of Prussia, who had at first won a splendid victory over the Austrians in front of Prague, had been beaten at Kolin and forced to fall back on Saxony. Marshal d'Estrées, slowly occupying Westphalia, had got the duke of Cumberland into a corner on the Weser.

On the morning of July 23, 1757, the marshal summoned all his lieutenant-generals. " Gentlemen," he said to them, " I do not assemble you to-day to ask whether we should attack M. de Cumberland and invest Hameln. The honour of the king's arms, his wishes, his express orders, the interest of the common cause, all call for the strongest measures. I only seek, therefore, to profit by your lights, and to combine with your assistance the means most proper for attacking with advantage." A day or two after, July 26th, the duke of Cumberland, who had fallen back on the village of Hastenbeck, had his intrenchments forced ; he succeeded in beating a retreat without being pursued ; an able movement of Prince Ferdinand of Brunswick, and a perhaps intentional mistake on the part of M. de Maillebois had caused a momentary confusion in the French army. Marshal d'Estrées, however, was not destined to enjoy for long the pleasure of his victory. Even before he had given battle the duke of Richelieu had set out from Versailles to supersede him in his command.

The conquest of Port Mahon had thrown around Richelieu a halo of glory ; in Germany, he reaped the fruits of Marshal d'Estrées' successes ; the electorate of Hanover was entirely occupied ; all the towns opened their gates ; Hesse Cassel, Brunswick, the duchies of Verden and of Bremen met with the same fate. The marshal levied on all the conquered countries heavy contributions, of which he pocketed a considerable portion. His soldiers called him " Father La Maraude." The pavilion of Hanover at Paris was built out of the spoils of Germany. Meanwhile, the duke of Cumberland, who had taken refuge in the marshes at the mouth of the Elbe, under the protection of English vessels, was demanding to capitulate ; his offers were lightly accepted. On the 8th of September, through the agency of Count Lynar, minister of the king of Denmark, the duke of Cumberland and the marshal signed at the advanced posts of the French army the famous convention of Closter-Severn. The king's troops kept all the conquered country; those of Hesse, Brunswick and Saxe-Gotha returned to their homes; the Hanoverians were to be cantoned in the neighbourhood of Stade. The marshal had not taken the precaution of disarming them.

Incomplete as the convention was, it nevertheless excited great emotion in Europe. The duke of Cumberland had lost the military reputation acquired at Fontenoy; the king of Prussia remained alone on the Continent, exposed to all the efforts of the allies; every day fresh reverses came down upon him: the Russian army had invaded the Prussian provinces and beaten marshal Schwald near Memel; twenty-five thousand Swedes had just landed in Pomerania. Desertion prevailed amongst the troops of Frederick, recruited as they often were from amongst the vanquished; it was in vain that the king, in his despair, shouted out on the battle-field of Kolin : " D'ye expect to live for ever, pray ? " Many Saxon or Silesian soldiers secretly left the army. One day Frederick himself kept his eye on a grenadier whom he had seen skulking to the rear of the camp : " Whither goest thou ? " he cried : " Faith, sir," was the answer, " I am deserting; I'm getting tired of being always beaten." " Stay once more," replied the king, without showing the slightest anger, " I promise that, if we are beaten, we will both desert together." In the ensuing battle the grenadier got himself killed.

For a moment, indeed, Frederick had conceived the idea of deserting simultaneously from the field of battle and from life. " My dear sister," he wrote to the margravine of Baireuth, " there is no port or asylum for me any more save in the arms of death." A letter in verse to the marquis of Argens pointed clearly to the notion of suicide. A firmer purpose, before long, animated that soul, that strange mixture of heroism and corruption. The king of Prussia wrote to Voltaire :

> Threaten'd with shipwreck tho' I be,
> I, facing storms that frown on me,
> Must kinglike think and live and die.

Fortune, moreover, seemed to be relaxing her severities. Under

FREDERICK II., KING OF PRUSSIA.

the influence of the hereditary grand-duke, a passionate admirer of Frederick II., the Russians had omitted to profit by their victories; they were by this time wintering in Poland, which was abandoned to all their exactions. The Swedes had been repulsed in the island of Rugen, Marshal Richelieu received from Versailles orders to remain at Halberstadt, and to send reinforcements to the army of the prince of Soubise; it was for this latter that Madame de Pompadour was reserving the honour of crushing the Great Frederick. More occupied in pillage than in vigorously pushing forward the war, the marshal tolerated a fatal licence amongst his troops. " Brigandage is more prevalent in the hearts of the superior officers than in the conduct of the private soldier, who is full of good will to go and get shot but not at all to submit to discipline. I'm afraid that they do not see at court the alarming state of things to their full extent," says a letter from Pâris-Duverney to the marquis of Crémille, " but I have heard so much of it and perhaps seen so much since I have been within eyeshot of this army, that I cannot give a glance at the future without being transfixed with grief and dread. I dare to say that I am not scared more than another at sight of abuses and disorder, but it is time to apply to an evil which is at its height other remedies than palliatives which, for the most part, merely aggravate it and render it incurable as long as war lasts. I have not seen and do not see here anything but what overwhelms me, and I feel still more wretched for having been the witness of it."

Whilst the plunder of Hanover was serving the purpose of feeding the insensate extravagance of Richelieu and of the army, Frederick II. had entered Saxony, hurling back into Thuringia the troops of Soubise and of the prince of Hildburghausen. By this time the allies had endured several reverses; the boldness of the king of Prussia's movements bewildered and disquieted officers as well as soldiers. " Might I ask your Highness what you think of his Prussian majesty's manœuvring ? " says a letter to Count Clermont from an officer serving in the army of Germany: " this prince, with eighteen or twenty thousand men at most, marches upon an army of fifty thousand men, forces it to recross a river, cuts off its rear-guard, crosses this same river before its very eyes, offers battle, retires, encamps leisurely and loses not a man. What calculation, what audacity in this fashion of covering a country !'' On the 3rd of November the Prussian army was all in order of battle on the left bank of the Saale, near Rosbach.

Soubise hesitated to attack : being a man of honesty and sense, he took into account the disposition of his army, as well as the bad composition of the allied forces, very superior in number to the French contingent. The command belonged to the duke of Saxe-Hildburghausen, who had no doubt of success. Orders were given to turn the little Prussian army, so as to cut off its retreat. All at once, as the allied troops were effecting their movement to scale the heights, the king of Prussia, suddenly changing front by one of those rapid evolutions to which he had accustomed his men, unexpectedly attacked the French in flank, without giving them time to form in order of battle. The batteries placed on the hills were at the same time unmasked and mowed down the infantry. The German troops at once broke up. Soubise sought to restore the battle by cavalry charges, but he was crushed in his turn. The rout became general, the French did not rally till they reached Erfurt ; they had left eight thousand prisoners and three thousand dead on the field.

The news of the defeat at Rosbach came bursting on France like a clap of thunder; the wrath, which first of all blazed out against Soubise, at whose expense all the rhymesters were busy, was reflected upon the king and Madame de Pompadour.

> With lamp in hand, Soubise is heard to say:
> " Why, where the devil can my army be ?
> I saw it hereabouts but yesterday :
> Has it been taken ? has it stray'd from me ?
> I'm always losing—head and all, I know :
> But wait till daylight, twelve o'clock or so !
> What do I see ? Oh! heav'ns, my heart's aglow :
> Prodigious luck ! Why, there it is, it is !
> Eh ! ventrebleu, what in the world is this ?
> I must have been mistaken—it's the foe.''

Frederick II. had renovated affairs and spirits in Germany; the day after Rosbach, he led his troops into Silesia against Prince Charles of Lorraine, who had just beaten the duke of Bevern ; the king of

Prussia's lieutenants were displeased and disquieted at such audacity. He assembled a council of war, and then, when he had expounded his plans, " Farewell, gentlemen," said he, " we shall soon have beaten the enemy or we shall have looked on one another for the last time." On the 3rd of December the Austrians were beaten at Lissa as the French had been at Rosbach, and Frederick II. became the national hero of Germany ; the protestant powers, but lately engaged, to their sorrow, against him, made up to the conqueror ; admiration for him permeated even the French army. " At Paris," wrote D'Alembert to Voltaire, " everybody's head is turned about the king of Prussia ; five months ago he was trailed in the mire."

"Cabinet-generals," says Duclos, " greedy of money, inex- perienced and presumptuous ; ignorant, jealous or ill-disposed ministers ; subalterns lavish of their blood on the battle-field and crawling at court before the distributors of favours—such are the instruments we employed. The small number of those who had not approved of the treaty of Versailles declared loudly against it ; after the campaign of 1757, those who had regarded it as a master-piece of policy forgot or disavowed their eulogies, and the bulk of the public, who cannot be decided by anything but the event, looked upon it as the source of all our woes." The counsels of Abbé de Bernis had for some time past been pacific ; from a court-abbé, elegant and glib, he had become, on the 25th of June, minister of foreign affairs. But Madame de Pompadour remained faithful to the empress. In the month of January, 1758, Count Clermont was appointed general-in-chief of the army of Germany. In disregard of the convention of Closter-Severn, the Hanoverian troops had just taken the field again under the orders of the grand-duke Ferdinand of Brunswick : he had already recovered possession of the districts of Luneberg, Zell, a part of Brunswick and of Bremen. In England, Mr. Pitt, afterwards Lord Chatham, had again come into office ; the king of Prussia could henceforth rely upon the firmest support from Great Britain.

He had need of it. A fresh invasion of Russians, aided by the savage hordes of the Zaporoguian Cossacks, was devastating

Prussia ; the sanguinary battle of Zorndorf, forcing them to fall
back on Poland, permitted Frederick to hurry into Saxony, which
was attacked by the Austrians. General Daun surprised and
defeated him at Hochkirch ; in spite of his inflexible resolution,
the king of Prussia was obliged to abandon Saxony. His ally
and rival, Ferdinand of Brunswick, had just beaten Count
Clermont at Crevelt.

The new commander-in-chief of the king's armies, prince of the
blood, brother of the late *Monsieur le Duc*, abbot commendatory of
St. Germain-des-Prés, "general of the Benedictines," as the
soldiers said, had brought into Germany, together with the
favour of Madame de Pompadour, upright intentions, a sincere
desire to restore discipline, and some great illusions about himself.
' I am very impatient, I do assure you, to be on the other side of
the Rhine," wrote Count Clermont to Marshal Belle-Isle : " all
the country about here is infested by runaway soldiers, con-
valescents, camp-followers, all sorts of understrappers, who
commit fearful crimes. Not a single officer does his duty, they
are the first to pillage ; all the army ought to be put under escort
and in detachments, and then there would have to be escorts for
those escorts. I hang, I imprison ; but, as we march by canton-
ments and the regimental (*particuliers*) officers are the first to show
a bad example, the punishments are neither sufficiently known nor
sufficiently seen. Everything smacks of indiscipline, of disgust at
the king's service and of asperity towards oneself. I see with pain
that it will be indispensable to put in practice the most violent and
the harshest measures." The king's army, meanwhile, was continuing to fall back ; a general outcry arose at Paris against the
general's supineness. On the 23rd of June he was surprised by
Duke Ferdinand of Brunswick in the strong position of Crevelt,
which he had occupied for two days past : the reserves did not
advance in time, orders to retreat were given too soon, the battle
was lost without disaster and without any rout ; the general was lost
as well as the battle. " It is certain," says the marquis of Vogel
in his narrative of the affair, " that Count Clermont was at table in
his head-quarters of Weschelen at one o'clock, that he had lost
the battle before six, arrived at Reuss at half-past ten, and went to

bed at midnight; that is doing a great deal in a short time." The count of Gisors, son of Marshal Belle-Isle, a young officer of the greatest promise, had been killed at Crevelt; Count Clermont was superseded by the marquis of Contades. The army murmured; they had no confidence in their leaders. At Versailles, Abbé de Bernis, who had lately become a cardinal, paid by his disgrace for the persistency he had shown in advising peace. He was chatting with M. de Stahrenberg, the Austrian ambassador, when he received a letter from the king, sending him off to his abbey of St. Médard de Soissons. He continued the conversation without changing countenance, and then, breaking off the conversation just as the ambassador was beginning to speak of business : " It is no longer to me, sir," he said, " that you must explain yourself on these great topics; I have just received my dismissal from his Majesty." With the same coolness he quitted the court and returned, pending his embassy to Rome, to those elegant intellectual pleasures which suited him better than the crushing weight of a ministry in disastrous times, under an indolent and vain-minded monarch, who was governed by a woman as headstrong as she was frivolous and depraved.

Madame de Pompadour had just procured for herself a support in her obstinate bellicosity : Cardinal Bernis was superseded in the ministry of foreign affairs by Count Stainville, who was created duke of Choiseul. After the death of Marshal Belle-Isle he exchanged the office for that of minister of war; with it he combined the ministry of the marine. The foreign affairs were entrusted to the duke of Praslin, his cousin. The power rested almost entirely in the hands of the duke of Choiseul. Of high birth, clever, bold, ambitious, he had but lately aspired to couple the splendour of successes in the fashionable world with the serious preoccupations of politics : his marriage with Mdlle. Crozat, a wealthy heiress, amiable and very much smitten with him, had strengthened his position. Elevated to the ministry by Madame de Pompadour and as yet promoting her views, he nevertheless gave signs of an independent spirit and a proud character capable of exercising authority firmly in the presence and the teeth of all obstacles. France hoped to find once more in M. de Choiseul a great minister; nor were her hopes destined to be completely deceived.

A new and secret treaty had just rivetted the alliance between France and Austria. M. de Choiseul was at the same time dreaming of attacking England in her own very home, thus dealing her the most formidable of blows. The preparations were considerable: M. de Soubise was recalled from Germany to direct the army of invasion. He was to be seconded in his command by the duke of Aiguillon, to whom, rightly or wrongly, was attributed the honour of having repulsed in the preceding year an attempt of the English at a descent upon the coasts of Brittany. The expedition was ready, there was nothing to wait for save the moment to go out of port, but Admiral Hawke was cruising before Brest; it was only in the month of November, 1759, that the marquis of Conflans, who commanded the fleet, could put to sea with twenty-one vessels. Finding himself at once pursued by the English squadron, he sought shelter in the difficult channels at the mouth of the Vilaine. The English dashed in after him. A partial engagement, which ensued, was unfavourable; and the commander of the French rear-guard, M. St. André du Verger, allowed himself to be knocked to pieces by the enemy's guns in order to cover the retreat. The admiral ran ashore in the bay of Le Croisic and burnt his own vessel; seven ships remained blockaded in the Vilaine. *M. de Conflans' job*, as the sailors called it at the time, was equivalent to a battle lost without the chances and the honour of the struggle. The English navy was triumphant on every sea and even in French waters.

The commencement of the campaign of 1759 had been brilliant in Germany: the duke of Broglie had successfully repulsed the attack made by Ferdinand of Brunswick on his positions at Bergen; the prince had been obliged to retire. The two armies, united under M. de Contades, invaded Hesse and moved upon the Weser; they were occupying Minden when Duke Ferdinand threw himself upon them on the 1st of August. The action of the two French generals was badly combined and the rout was complete. It was the moment of Canada's last efforts, and the echo of that

DEATH OF CHEVALIER D'ASSAS.

glorious death-rattle reached even to Versailles. The duke of Choiseul had, on the 19th of February, replied to a desperate appeal from Montcalm: " I am very sorry to have to send you word that you must not expect any reinforcements. To say nothing of their increasing the dearth of provisions of which you have had only too much experience hitherto, there would be great fear of their being intercepted by the English on the passage, and, as the king could never send you aid proportionate to the forces which the English are in a position to oppose to you, the efforts made here to procure it for you would have no other effect than to rouse the ministry in London to make still more considerable ones in order to preserve the superiority it has acquired in that part of the continent." The necessity for peace was beginning to be admitted even in Madame de Pompadour's little cabinets.

Maria Theresa, however, was in no hurry to enter into negotiations; her enemy seemed to be bending at last beneath the weight of the double Austrian and Russian attack. At one time Frederick had thought that he saw all Germany rallying round him; now, beaten and cantoned in Saxony, with the Austrians in front of him, during the winter of 1760, he was everywhere seeking alliances and finding himself everywhere rejected: " I have but two allies left," he would say, " valour and perseverance." Repeated victories, gained at the sword's point, by dint of boldness and in the extremity of peril, could not even protect Berlin. The capital of Prussia found itself constrained to open its gates to the enemy, on the sole condition that the regiments of Cossacks should not pass the line of enclosure. When the regular troops withdrew, the generals had not been able to prevent the city from being pillaged. The heroic efforts of the king of Prussia ended merely in preserving to him a foot-hold in Saxony. The Russians occupied Poland.

Marshal Broglie, on becoming general-in-chief of the French army, had succeeded in holding his own in Hesse; he frequently made Hanover anxious. To turn his attention elsewhither and in hopes of deciding the French to quit Germany, the hereditary prince of Brunswick attempted a diversion on the Lower Rhine;

he laid siege to Wesel whilst the English were preparing for a descent at Antwerp. Marshal Broglie detached M. de Castries to protect the city. The French corps had just arrived, it was bivouacking. On the night between the 15th and 16th of October, Chevalier d'Assas, captain in the regiment of Auvergne, was sent to reconnoitre. He had advanced some distance from his men and happened to stumble upon a large force of the enemy. The prince of Brunswick was preparing to attack. All the muskets covered the young captain : " Stir, and thou'rt a dead man," muttered threatening voices. Without replying, M. d'Assas collected all his strength and shouted : " Auvergne ! Here are the foe !" At the same instant he fell pierced by twenty balls. [Accounts differ : but this is the tradition of the Assas family.] The action thus begun was a glorious one. The hereditary prince was obliged to abandon the siege of Wesel and to re-cross the Rhine. The French divisions maintained their positions.

The war went on as bloodily as monotonously and fruitlessly, but the face of Europe had lately altered. The old king George II., who died on the 25th of September, 1760, had been succeeded on the throne of England by his grandson, George III., aged twenty-two, the first really native sovereign who had been called to reign over England since the fall of the Stuarts. George I. and George II. were Germans, in their feelings and their manners as well as their language; the politic wisdom of the English people had put up with them, but not without effort and ill-humour : the accession of the young king was greeted with transport. Pitt still reigned over Parliament and over England, governing a free country sovereign-masterlike. His haughty prejudice against France still ruled all the decisions of the English government, but Lord Bute, the young monarch's adviser, was already whispering pacific counsels destined ere long to bear fruit. Pitt's dominion was tottering when the first overtures of peace arrived in London. The duke of Choiseul proposed a congress. He at the same time negotiated directly with England. Whilst Pitt kept his answer waiting, an English squadron blockaded Belle-Isle, and the governor, M. de Sainte-Croix, left without relief, was forced to capitulate after a heroic resistance. When

the conditions demanded by England were at last transmitted to
Versailles, the English flag was floating over the citadel of Belle-
Isle, the mouth of the Loire and of the Vilaine was blockaded.
The arrogant pretensions of Mr. Pitt stopped at nothing short of
preserving the conquests of England in both hemispheres ; he
claimed, besides, the demolition of Dunkerque " as a memorial for
ever of the yoke imposed upon France." Completely separating
the interests of England from those of the German allies, he
did not even reply to the proposals of M. de Choiseul as to the
evacuation of Hesse and Hanover. Mistress of the sea, England
intended to enjoy alone the fruits of her victories.

The parleys were prolonged and M. de Choiseul seemed to be
resigned to the bitterest pill of concession, when a new actor
came upon the scene of negotiation ; France no longer stood
isolated face to face with triumphant England. The younger
branch of the House of Bourbon cast into the scale the weight of
its two crowns and the resources of its navy.

The king of Spain, Ferdinand VI., who died on the 10th of
August, 1759, had not left any children. His brother, Charles III.,
king of Naples, had succeeded him. He brought to the throne of
Spain a more lively intelligence than that of the deceased king, a
great aversion for England, of which he had but lately had cause
to complain, and the traditional attachment of his race to the
interests and the glory of France. The duke of Choiseul managed
to take skilful advantage of this disposition. At the moment
when Mr. Pitt was haughtily rejecting the modest ultimatum of
the French minister, the treaty between France and Spain, known
by the name of *Family Pact*, was signed at Paris (August 15,
1761).

Never had closer alliance been concluded between the two
courts, even at the time when Louis XIV. placed his grandson
upon the throne of Spain. It was that intimate union between all
the branches of the House of Bourbon which had but lately been
the great king's conception, and which had cost him so many
efforts and so much blood ; for the first time it was becoming
favourable to France ; the noble and patriotic idea of M. de
Choiseul found an echo in the soul of the king of Spain ; the

French navy, ruined and humiliated, the French colonies, threatened and all but lost, found faithful support in the forces of
Spain, recruited as they were by a long peace. The king of the
Two Sicilies and the Infante Duke of Parma entered into the
offensive and defensive alliance, but it was not open to any
other power in Europe to be admitted to this family-union,
cemented by common interests more potent and more durable
than the transitory combinations of policy. In all the ports of
Spain ships were preparing to put to sea. Charles III. had
undertaken to declare war against the English if peace were not
concluded before the 1st of May, 1762. France promised in that
case to cede to him the island of Minorca.

All negotiations with England were broken off; on the 20th of
September, Mr. Pitt recalled his ambassador; this was his last
act of power and animosity; he at the same time proposed to the
council of George III. to include Spain forthwith in the hostilities.
Lord Bute opposed this; he was supported by the young king as
well as by the majority of the ministers. Pitt at once sent in his
resignation, which was accepted. Lord Bute and the Tories came
into power. Though more moderate in their intentions, they were
as yet urged forward by popular violence and dared not suddenly
alter the line of conduct. The *family pact* had raised the hopes—
always an easy task—of France, the national impulse inclined
towards the amelioration of the navy; the estates of Languedoc
were the first in the field, offering the king a ship of war; their
example was everywhere followed; sixteen ships, first-rates, were
before long in course of construction, a donation from the great political or financial bodies; there were, besides, private subscriptions
amounting to thirteen millions; the duke of Choiseul sought out
commanders even amongst the mercantile marine, and everywhere
showed himself favourable to *blue* officers, as the appellation then
was of those whose birth excluded them from the navy-corps; the
knowledge of the nobly born often left a great deal to be desired,
whatever may have been their courage and devotion. This was a
last generous effort on behalf of the shreds of France's perishing
colonies. The English government did not give it time to bear
fruit: in the month of January, 1762, it declared war against

Spain.   Before the year had rolled by, Cuba was in the hands of
the English, the Philippines were ravaged and the galleons laden
with Spanish gold captured by British ships.   The unhappy
fate of France had involved her generous ally.   The campaign
attempted against Portugal, always hand in hand with England,
had not been attended with any result.   Martinique had shared
the lot of Guadaloupe, lately conquered by the English after a
heroic resistance.   Canada and India had at last succumbed.
War dragged its slow length along in Germany.   The brief

THE DUKE OF CHOISEUL.

elevation of the young czar Peter III., a passionate admirer of
the Great Frederick, had delivered the king of Prussia from a
dangerous enemy, and promised to give him an ally equally trusty
and potent.   France was exhausted, Spain discontented and
angry; negotiations recommenced, on what disastrous conditions
for the French colonies in both hemispheres has already been
remarked: in Germany the places and districts occupied by
France were to be restored; Lord Bute, like his great rival,
required the destruction of the port of Dunkerque.

This was not enough for the persistent animosity of Pitt. The preliminaries of peace had been already signed at Fontainebleau on the 3rd of November, 1762: when they were communicated to Parliament, the fallen minister, still the nation's idol and the real head of the people, had himself carried to the House of Commons. He was ill, suffering from a violent attack of gout; two of his friends led him with difficulty to his place and supported him during his long speech; being exhausted he sat down towards the end, contrary to all the usages of the House, without, however, having once faltered in his attacks upon a peace too easily made, of which it was due to him that England was able to dictate the conditions: "It is as a maritime power," he exclaimed, "that France is chiefly if not exclusively formidable to us," and the ardour of his spirit restored to his enfeebled voice the dread tones which Parliament and the nation had been wont to hear, " what we gain in this respect is doubly precious from the loss that results to her. America, sir, was conquered in Germany. Now you are leaving to France a possibility of restoring her navy."

The peace was signed, however, not without ill-humour on the part of England but with a secret feeling of relief; the burthens which weighed upon the country had been increasing every year. In 1762, Lord Bute had obtained from Parliament 450 millions (18,000,000l.) to keep up the war: "I wanted the peace to be a serious and a durable one," said the English minister in reply to Pitt's attacks; "if we had increased our demands, it would have been neither the one nor the other."

M. de Choiseul submitted in despair to the consequences of the long-continued errors committed by the Government of Louis XV. "Were I master," said he, " we would be to the English what Spain was to the Moors; if this course were taken, England would be destroyed in thirty years from now." The king was a better judge of his weakness and of the general exhaustion. "The peace we have just made is neither a good one nor a glorious one, nobody sees that better than I," he said in his private correspondence; "but, under such unhappy circumstances, it could not be better, and I answer for it that if we had continued the war, we should have made a still worse one next year." All the patriotic courage and zeal of the duke of Choiseul, all the tardy impulse springing from the nation's anxieties could not suffice even to palliate the consequences of so many years' ignorance, feebleness and incapacity in succession.

Prussia and Austria henceforth were left to confront one another, the only actors really interested in the original struggle, the last to quit the battle-field on to which they had dragged their allies. By an unexpected turn of luck, Frederick II. had for a moment seen Russia becoming his ally; a fresh blow came to wrest from him this powerful support. The czarina Catherine II., princess of Anhalt-Zerbst and wife of the czar Peter III., being on bad terms with her husband and in dread of his wrath, had managed to take advantage of the young czar's imprudence in order to excite a mutiny amongst the soldiers: he had been deposed, and died before long in prison. Catherine was proclaimed in his place. With her accession to the throne there commenced for Russia a new policy, equally bold and astute, having for its sole aim, unscrupulously and shamelessly pursued, the aggrandisement and consolidation of the imperial power: Russia became neutral in the strife between Prussia and Austria. The two sovereigns, left without allies and with their dominions drained of men and money, agreed to a mutual exchange of their conquests; the boundaries of their territories once more became as they had been before the Seven Years' war. Frederick calculated at more than eight hundred thousand men the losses caused to the belligerents by this obstinate and resultless struggle, the fruit of wicked ambition or culpable weaknesses on the part of governments. Thanks to the indomitable energy and the equally zealous and unscrupulous ability of the man who had directed her counsels during the greater part of the war, England alone came triumphant out of the strife. She had won India for ever; and, for some years at least, civilized America, almost in its entirety, obeyed her laws. She had won what France had lost, not by superiority of arms, or even of generals, but by the natural and proper force of a free people, ably and liberally governed.

The position of France abroad, at the end of the Seven Years' war, was as painful as it was humiliating; her position at home was still more serious and the deep-lying source of all the reverses which had come to overwhelm the French. Slowly lessened by the faults and misfortunes of King Louis XIV.'s later years, the kingly authority, which had fallen, under Louis XV., into hands as feeble as they were corrupt, was ceasing to inspire the nation with the respect necessary for the working of personal power; public opinion was no longer content to accuse the favourite and the ministers, it was beginning to make the king responsible for the evils suffered and apprehended. People waited in vain for a decision of the crown to put a stop to the incessantly renewed struggles between the Parliament and the clergy. Disquieted at one and the same time by the philosophical tendencies which were beginning to spread in men's minds and by the comptroller-general Machault's projects for exacting payment of the imposts upon ecclesiastical revenues, the archbishop of Paris, Christopher de Beaumont, and the bishop of Mirepoix, Boyer, who was in charge of the benefice-list, conceived the idea of stifling these dangerous symptoms by an imprudent recourse to the spiritual severities so much dreaded but lately by the people. Several times over, the last sacraments were denied to the dying who had declined to subscribe to the bull *Unigenitus*, a clumsy measure which was sure to excite public feeling and revive the pretensions of the parliaments to the surveillance, in the last resort, over the government of the Church; Jansenism, fallen and persecuted but still living in the depths of souls, numbered amongst the ranks of the magistracy, as well as in the university of Paris, many secret partisans; several parish-priests had writs of personal seizure issued against them, and their goods were confiscated. Decrees succeeded decrees; in spite of the king's feeble opposition the struggle was extending and reaching to the whole of France. On the 22nd of February, 1753, the Parliament of Paris received orders to suspend all the proceedings they had commenced on the ground of refusals of the sacraments; the king did not consent even to receive the representations. By the unanimous vote of the hundred and fifty-eight members sitting on the Court, Parliament determined to give up all service until the king should be pleased to listen. " We declare," said the representation, " that our zeal

THE MARCHIONESS OF POMPADOUR.

is boundless and that we feel sufficient courage to fall victims to our fidelity. The Court could not serve without being wanting to their duties and betraying their oaths."

Indolent and indifferent as he was, King Louis XV. acted as seldom and as slowly as he could; he did not like strife, and gladly saw the belligerents exhausting against one another their strength and their wrath; on principle, however, and from youthful tradition, he had never felt any liking for the parliaments. "The long robes and the clergy are always at daggers drawn," he would say to Madame de Pompadour: "they drive me distracted with their quarrels, but I detest the long robes by far the most. My clergy, at bottom, are attached to me and faithful to me; the others would like to put me in tutelage. . . . They will end by ruining the State; they are a pack of republicans. . . . . However, things will last my time at any rate." Severe measures against the Parliament were decided upon in council. Four magistrates were arrested and sent to fortresses; all the presidents, councillors of inquests and of requests were exiled; the grand chamber, which alone was spared, refused to administer justice. Being transferred to Pontoise, it persisted in its refusal. It was necessary to form a *King's Chamber*, installed at the Louvre; all the inferior jurisdictions refused to accept its decrees. After a year's strife, the Parliament returned in triumph to Paris in the month of August, 1754; the clergy received orders not to require from the dying any theological adhesion. Next year, the archbishop of Paris, who had paid no attention to the prohibition, was exiled in his turn.

Thus, by mutually weakening each other, the great powers and the great influences in the State were wasting away; the reverses of the French arms, the loss of their colonies and the humiliating peace of Paris aggravated the discontent. In default of good government the people are often satisfied with glory. This consolation, to which the French nation had but lately been accustomed, failed it all at once; mental irritation, for a long time silently brooding, cantoned in the writings of philosophers and in the quatrains of rhymesters, was beginning to spread and show itself amongst the nation; it sought throughout the State an object for its wrath : the powerful society of the Jesuits was the first to bear all the brunt of it.

A French Jesuit, Father Lavalette, had founded a commercial house at Martinique. Ruined by the war, he had become bankrupt to the extent of three millions ; the order having refused to pay, it was condemned by the Parliament to do so. The responsibility was declared to extend to all the members of the Institute, and public opinion triumphed over the condemnation with a " quasi-indecent" joy, says the advocate Barbier. Nor was it content with this legitimate satisfaction. One of the courts which had until lately been most devoted to the Society of Jesus had just set an example of severity. In 1759, the Jesuits had been driven from Portugal by the marquis of Pombal, King Joseph I.'s all-powerful minister; their goods had been confiscated, and their principal, Malagrida, handed over to the Inquisition, had just been burnt as a heretic (Sept. 20, 1761).

The Portuguese Jesuits had been feebly defended by the grandees ; the clergy were hostile to them. In France, their enemies showed themselves bolder than their defenders. Proudly convinced of the justice of their cause, the Fathers had declined the jurisdiction of the grand council, to which they had a right as all ecclesiastical bodies had, and they had consented to hand over to the Parliament the registers of their constitutions, up to that time carefully concealed from the eyes of the profane. The skilful and clear-sighted hostility of the magistrates was employed upon the articles of this code, so stringently framed of yore by enthusiastic souls and powerful minds, forgetful or disdainful of the sacred rights of human liberty. All the services rendered by the Jesuits to the cause of religion and civilization appeared effaced : forgotten were their great missionary enterprises, their founders and their martyrs, in order to set forth simply their insatiable ambition, their thirst after power, their easy compromises with evil passions condemned by the Christian faith. The assaults of the philosophers had borne their fruit in the public mind ; the olden rancour of the Jansenists imperceptibly promoted the severe inquiry openly conducted by the magistrates. Madame de Pompadour dreaded the influence of the Jesuits : religious fears might at any time be aroused again in the soul of Louis XV. The dauphin, who had been constantly faithful to them, sought in vain to plead their cause with the king. He had attacked the duke of Choiseul; the latter so far forgot himself, it is asserted, as to say to the prince: " Sir, I may have the misfortune to be your subject, but I will never be your servant." The minister had hitherto maintained a prudent reserve; he henceforth joined the favourite and the Parliament against the Jesuits.

On the 6th of August, 1761, the Parliament of Paris delivered a decree ordering the Jesuits to appear at the end of a year for the definite judgment upon their constitutions; pending the judicial decision, all their colleges were closed. King Louis XV. still hesitated, from natural indolence and from remembrance of Cardinal Fleury's maxims: "The Jesuits," the old minister would often say, " are bad masters, but you can make them useful tools." An ecclesiastical commission was convoked; with the exception of the bishop of Soissons, the prelates all showed themselves favourable to the Jesuits and careless of the old Gallican liberties. On their advice, the king sent a proposal to Rome for certain modifications in the constitutions of the order. Father Ricci, general of the Jesuits, answered haughtily: "Let them be as they are, or not be " (*Sint ut sunt, aut non sint*). Their enemies in France accepted the challenge. On the 6th of August, 1762, a decree of the Parliament of Paris, soon confirmed by the majority of the sovereign courts, declared that there was danger (*abus*) in the bulls, briefs and constitutions of the Society, pronounced its dissolution, forbade its members to wear the dress and to continue living in common under the sway of the general and other superiors. Orders were given to close all the jesuit houses. The principle of religious liberty, which had been so long ignored and was at last beginning to dawn on men's minds, was gaining its first serious victory by despoiling the Jesuits in their turn of that liberty for the long-continued wrongs whereof they were called to account. A strange and striking re-action in human affairs: the condemnation of the Jesuits was the precursory sign of the violence and injustice which was soon to be committed in the name of the most sacred rights and liberties, long violated with impunity by arbitrary power.

Vaguely and without taking the trouble to go to the bottom of his impression, Louis XV. felt that the Parliaments and the philosophers were dealing him a mortal blow whilst appearing to strike the Jesuits: he stood out a long while, leaving the quarrel to become embittered and public opinion to wax wroth at his indecision. "There is a hand to mouth administration," said an anonymous letter addressed to the king and Madame de Pompadour, "but there is no longer any hope of government. A time will come when the people's eyes will be opened, and peradventure that time is approaching."

The persistency of the duke of Choiseul carried the day at last: an edict of December, 1764, declared that the Society no longer existed in France, that it would merely be permitted to those who composed it "to live privately in the king's dominions, under the spiritual authority of the local ordinaries, whilst conforming to the laws of the realm." Four thousand Jesuits found themselves affected by this decree; some left France, others remained still in their families, assuming the secular dress. "It will be great fun to see Father Pérusseau turned abbé," said Louis XV. as he signed the fatal edict. "The Parliaments fancy they are serving religion by this measure," wrote D'Alembert to Voltaire, "but they are serving reason without any notion of it; they are the executioners on behalf of philosophy, whose orders they are executing without knowing it." The destruction of the jesuits served neither religion nor reason, for it was contrary to justice as well as to liberty; it was the wages and the bitter fruit of a long series of wrongs and iniquities committed but lately, in the name of religion, against justice and liberty.

Three years later, in 1767, the king of Spain, Charles III., less moderate than the government of Louis XV., expelled with violence all the members of the Society of Jesus from his territory, thus exciting the Parliament of Paris to fresh severities against the French Jesuits, and, on the 20th of July, 1773, the court of Rome itself, yielding at last to pressure from nearly all the sovereigns of Europe, solemnly pronounced the dissolution of the Order: "Recognizing that the members of this Society have not a little troubled the Christian commonwealth, and that for the welfare of

Christendom it were better that the Order should disappear." The last houses still offering shelter to the Jesuits were closed ; the general, Ricci, was imprisoned at the castle of St. Angelo, and the Society of Jesus, which had been so powerful for nearly three centuries, took refuge in certain distant lands, seeking in oblivion and silence fresh strength for the struggle which it was one day to renew.

The Parliaments were triumphant, but their authority, which seemed never to have risen so high or penetrated so far in the government of the State, was already tottering to its base.   Once more the strife was about to begin between the kingly power and the magistracy, whose last victory was destined to scarcely precede its downfall.   The financial embarrassments of the State were growing more serious every day : to the debts left by the Seven Years' war were added the new wants developed by the necessities of commerce and by the progress of civilization.   The Board of Works, a useful institution founded by Louis XV., was everywhere seeing to the construction of new roads, at the same time repairing the old ones ; the forced labour for these operations fell almost exclusively on the peasantry.   The Parliament of Normandy was one of the first to protest against " the impositions of forced labour, and the levies of money which took place in the district on pretext of repairs and maintenance of roads, without legal authority."   "France is a land which devours its inhabitants," cried the Parliament of Paris.   The Parliament of Pau refused to enregister the edicts; the Parliament of Brittany joined the Estates in protesting against the duke of Aiguillon, the then governor, "the which hath made upon the liberties of the province one of those assaults which are not possible save when the crown believes itself to be secure of impunity."   The noblesse having yielded in the States, the Parliament of Rennes gave in their resignation in a body.   Five of its members were arrested : at their head was the attorney-general, M. de la Chalotais, author of a very remarkable paper against the Jesuits.   It was necessary to form at St. Malo a *King's Chamber* to try the accused. M. de Calonne, an ambitious young man, the declared foe of M. de la Chalotais, was appointed attorney-general on the commission. He pretended to have discovered grave facts against the accused ;

he was suspected of having invented them.   Public feeling was at
its height : the magistrates loudly proclaimed the theory of *Classes*,
according to which all the Parliaments of France, responsible one
for another, formed in reality but one body, distributed by dele-
gation throughout the principal towns of the realm.   The king convoked a bed of justice, and, on the 2nd of March, 1766, he repaired
to the Parliament of Paris.   " What has passed in my Parliaments
of Pau and of Rennes has nothing to do with my other Parliaments,"
said Louis XV. in a firm tone to which the ears of the Parliament were no longer accustomed; " I have behaved in respect
of those two courts as comported with my authority, and I am not
bound to account to anybody.   I will not permit the formation in
my kingdom of an association which might reduce to a confederacy
of opposition the natural bond of identical duties and common
obligations, nor the introduction into the monarchy of an imaginary
body which could not but disturb its harmony.   The magistracy
does not form a body or order separate from the three orders of
the kingdom : the magistrates are my officers.   In my person alone
resides the sovereign power, of which the special characteristic is
the spirit of counsel, justice and reason : it is from me alone that
my courts have their existence and authority.   It is to me alone
that the legislative power belongs, without dependence and without
partition.   My people is but one with me, and the rights and
interests of the nation whereof men dare to make a body separate
from the monarch are necessarily united with my own and rest
only in my hands."

This haughty affirmation of absolute power, a faithful echo of
Cardinal Richelieu's grand doctrines, succeeded for a while in
silencing the representations of the Parliaments ; but it could not
modify the course of opinion, passionately excited in favour of
M. de La Chalotais.   On the 24th of December, 1766, after having
thrice changed the jurisdiction and the judges, the king annulled
the whole procedure by an act of his supreme authority.   " We
shall have the satisfaction," said the edict, " of finding nobody
guilty, and nothing will remain for us but to take such measures
as shall appear best adapted to completely restore and maintain
tranquillity in a province from which we have on so many

LOUIS XV. AND MADAME DUBARRY.

occasions had proofs of zeal for our service." M. de La Chalotais and his comrades were exiled to Saintes. They demanded a trial and a legal justification, which were refused. "It is enough for them to know that their honour is intact," the king declared. A Parliament was imperfectly re-constructed at Rennes; "It is D'Aiguillon's bailiff-court," was the contemptuous saying in Brittany. The governor had to be changed. Under the adminis-tration of the duke of Duras, the agitation subsided in the pro-vince; the magistrates who had resigned resumed their seats; M. de La Chalotais and his son, M. de Caradeuc, alone remained excluded by order of the king. The restored Parliament imme-diately made a claim on their behalf, accompanying the request with a formal accusation against the duke of Aiguillon. The states supported the Parliament. "What! sir," said the remon-strance; "they are innocent, and yet you punish them! It is a natural right that nobody should be punished without a trial; we have property in our honour, our lives, and our liberty, just as you have property in your crown. We would spill our blood to preserve your rights; but, on your side, preserve us ours. Sir, the province on its knees before you asks you for justice." A royal ordinance forbade any proceedings against the duke of Aiguillon and enjoined silence on the parties. Parliament having persisted, and declaring that the accusations against the duke of Aiguillon *attached* (*entachaient*) his honour, Louis XV., egged on by the chancellor, M. de Maupeou, an ambitious, bold, bad man, repaired in person to the office and had all the papers relating to the procedure removed before his eyes. The strife was becoming violent: the duke of Choiseul, still premier minister but sadly shaken in the royal favour, disapproved of the severities employed against the magistracy. All the blows dealt at the Parliaments recoiled upon him.

King Louis XV. had taken a fresh step in the shameful irregularity of his life; on the 15th of April, 1764, Madame de Pompadour had died, at the age of forty-two, of heart-disease. As frivolous as she was deeply depraved and base-minded in her calculating easiness of virtue, she had more ambition than com-ported with her mental calibre or her force of character; she had taken it into her head to govern, by turns promoting and over-throwing the ministers, herself proffering advice to the king, sometimes to good purpose, but more often still with a levity as fatal as her obstinacy. Less clever, less ambitious but more potent than Madame de Pompadour over the faded passions of a monarch aged before his time, the new favourite, Madame Dubarry, made the least scrupulous blush at the lowness of her origin and the irregularity of her life. It was, nevertheless, in her circle that the plot was formed against the duke of Choiseul. Bold, ambitious, restless, presumptuous sometimes in his views and his hopes, the minister had his heart too nearly in the right place and too proper a spirit to submit to either the yoke of Madame Dubarry or that of the shameless courtiers who made use of her influence. Chancellor Maupeou, the duke of Aiguillon and the new comptroller-general, Abbé Terray, a man of capacity, invention and no scruple at all, at last succeeded in triumphing over the force of habit, the only thing that had any real effect upon the king's listless mind. After twelve years' for a long while undisputed power, after having held in his hands the whole government of France and the peace of Europe, M. de Choiseul received from the king on the 24th of December, 1770, a letter in these terms :

" Cousin, the dissatisfaction caused me by your services forces me to banish you to Chanteloup, whither you will repair within twenty-four hours. I should have sent you much further off, but for the particular regard I have for Madame de Choiseul, in whose health I feel great interest. Take care your conduct does not force me to alter my mind. Whereupon I pray God, cousin, to have you in His holy and worthy keeping."

The thunderbolt which came striking the duke of Choiseul called forth a fresh sign of the times. The fallen minister was surrounded in his disgrace with marks of esteem and affection on the part of the whole court. The princes themselves and the greatest lords felt it an honour to pay him a visit at his castle of Chanteloup. He there displayed a magnificence which ended by swallowing up his wife's immense fortune, already much encroached upon during his term of power. Nothing was too much for the proud devotion and passionate affection of the duchess of Choiseul :

she declined the personal favours which the king offered her, setting all her husband's friends the example of a fidelity which was equally honourable to them and to him.   Acute observers read a tale of the growing weakness of absolute power in the crowd which still flocked to a minister in disgrace : the duke of Choiseul remained a power even during a banishment which was to last as long as his life.

With M. de Choiseul disappeared the sturdiest prop of the Parliaments.   In vain had the king ordered the magistrates to resume their functions and administer justice.   " There is nothing left for your Parliament," replied the premier president, " but to perish with the laws, since the fate of the magistrates should go with that of the State."   Madame Dubarry, on a hint from her able advisers, had caused to be placed in her apartments a fine portrait of Charles I. by Van Dyck.   " *France*," she was always reiterating to the king with vulgar familiarity, " France, thy Parliament will cut off *thy* head too ! "

A piece of ignorant confusion, due even more to analogy of name than to the generous but vain efforts often attempted by the French magistracy in favour of sound doctrines of government. The Parliament of Paris fell sitting upon curule chairs, like the old senators of Rome during the invasion of the Gauls ; the political spirit, the collected and combative ardour, the indomitable resolution of the English Parliament, freely elected representatives of a free people, were unknown to the French magistracy. Despite the courage and moral elevation it had so often shown, its strength had been wasted in a constantly useless strife ; it had withstood Richelieu and Mazarin ; already reduced to submission by Cardinal Fleury, it was about to fall beneath the equally bold and skilful blows of Chancellor Maupeou.   Notwithstanding the little natural liking and the usual distrust he felt for Parliaments, the king still hesitated.   Madame Dubarry managed to inspire him with fears for his person ; and he yielded.

During the night between the 19th and 20th of January, 1771, musketeers knocked at the doors of all the magistrates ; they were awakened in the king's name, at the same time being ordered to say whether they would consent to resume their service.   No equivocation possible! No margin for those developments of their ideas which are so dear to parliamentary minds! It was a matter of signing *yes* or *no*. Surprised in their slumbers, but still firm in their resolution of resistance, the majority of the magistrates signed *no*. They were immediately sent into banishment; their offices were confiscated. Those members of the Parliament from whom weakness or astonishment had surprised a *yes* retracted as soon as they were assembled, and underwent the same fate as their colleagues. On the 23rd of January, members delegated by the grand council, charged with the provisional administration of justice, were installed in the Palace by the chancellor himself. The registrar-in-chief, the ushers, the attorneys, declined or eluded the exercise of their functions; the advocates did not come forward to plead. The Court of Aids, headed by Lamoignon de Malesherbes, protested against the attack made on the great bodies of the State. "Ask the nation themselves, sir," said the president; "to mark your displeasure with the Parliament of Paris, it is proposed to rob them—themselves—of the essential rights of a free people." The Court of Aids was suppressed like the Parliament; six superior councils, in the towns of Arras, Blois, Châlons-sur-Marne, Lyon, Clermont and Poitiers, parcelled out amongst them the immense jurisdiction of Paris; the members of the grand council, assisted by certain magistrates of small esteem, definitively took the places of the banished, to whom compensation was made for their offices. The king appeared in person on the 13th of April, 1771, at the new Parliament; the chancellor read out the edicts. "You have just heard my intentions," said Louis XV.: "I desire that they may be conformed to. I order you to commence your duties. I forbid any deliberation contrary to my wishes and any representations in favour of my former Parliament, for I shall never change."

One single prince of the blood, the count of La Marche, son of the prince of Conti, had been present at the bed of justice. All had protested against the suppression of the Parliament. "It is one of the most useful boons for monarchs and of those most precious to Frenchmen," said the protest of the princes, "to have bodies of citizens, perpetual and irremoveable, avowed at all times by the kings and the nation, who, in whatever form and under whatever denomination they may have existed, concentrate in themselves the general right of all subjects to invoke the law." " Sir, by the law you are king, and you cannot reign but by it," said the Parliament of Dijon's declaration, drawn up by one of the mortar-cap presidents (*présidents à mortier*), the gifted president De Brosses. The princes were banished ; the provincial parliaments, mutilated like that of Paris or suppressed like that of Rouen, which was replaced by two superior councils, ceased to furnish a centre for critical and legal opposition. Amidst the rapid decay of absolute power, the transformation and abasement of the Parliaments by Chancellor Maupeou were a skilful and bold attempt to restore some sort of force and unity to the kingly authority. It was thus that certain legitimate claims had been satisfied, the extent of jurisdictions had been curtailed. the saleability of offices had been put down, the expenses of justice had been lessened. Voltaire had for a long time past been demanding these reforms, and he was satisfied with them. " Have not the Parliaments often been persecuting and barbarous ? " he wrote : " I wonder that the Welches (i. e. Barbarians, as Voltaire playfully called the French) should take the part of those insolent and intractable cits." He added, however : " Nearly all the kingdom is in a boil and consternation ; the ferment is as great in the provinces as in Paris itself."

The ferment subsided without having reached the mass of the nation ; the majority of the princes made it up with the court, the dispossessed magistrates returned one after another to Paris, astonished and mortified to see justice administered without them and advocates pleading before the *Maupeou* Parliament. The chancellor had triumphed and remained master : all the old jurisdictions were broken up, public opinion was already forgetting them ; it was occupied with a question more important still than the administration of justice. The ever increasing disorder in the finances was no longer checked by the enregistering of edicts ; the comptroller-general, Abbé Terray, had recourse shamelessly to every expedient of a bold imagination to fill the royal treasury ; it was necessary to satisfy the ruinous demands of Madame Dubarry and of the depraved courtiers who thronged about her. Successive bad harvests and the high price of bread still further aggravated the position. It was known that the king had a taste for private speculation; he was accused of trading in grain and of buying up the stores required for feeding the people. The odious rumour of this *famine-pact*, as the bitter saying was, soon spread amongst the mob. Before its fall, the Parliament of Rouen had audaciously given expression to these dark accusations: it had ordered proceedings to be taken against the *monopolists*. A royal injunction put a veto upon the prosecutions. "This prohibition from the crown changes our doubts to certainty," wrote the Parliament to the king himself: "when we said that the monopoly existed and was protected, God forbid, sir, that we should have had your Majesty in our eye, but possibly we had some of those to whom you distribute your authority." Silence was imposed upon the Parliaments, but without producing any serious effect upon public opinion, which attributed to the king the principal interest in a great private concern bound to keep up a certain parity in the price of grain. Contempt grew more and more profound: the king and Madame Dubarry by their shameful lives, Maupeou and Abbé Terray by destroying the last bulwarks of the public liberties, were digging with their own hands the abyss in which the old French monarchy was about to be soon engulfed.

For a long while pious souls had formed great hopes of the dauphin: honest, scrupulous, sincerely virtuous, without the austerity and extensive views of the duke of Burgundy, he had managed to live aloof, without intrigue and without open opposition, preserving towards the king an attitude of often sorrowful respect, and all the while remaining the support of the clergy and their partisans in their attempts and their aspirations. The queen, Mary Leczinska, a timid and proudly modest woman, resigned to her painful situation, lived in the closest intimacy with her son and still more with her daughter-in-law, Mary Josepha of Saxony, though the daughter of that elector who had but lately been elevated to the throne of Poland and had vanquished King Stanislaus. The sweetness, the tact, the rare faculties of the dauphiness had triumphed over all

obstacles. She had three sons. Much reliance was placed upon
the influence she had managed to preserve with the king, and on
the dominion she exercised over her husband's mind. In vain had
the dauphin, distracted at the woes of France, over and over again
solicited from the king the honour of serving him at the head of
the army ; the jealous anxiety of Madame de Pompadour was at one
with the cold indifference of Louis XV. as to leaving the heir to the
throne in the shade. The prince felt it deeply, in spite of his
pious resignation. "A dauphin," he would say, "must needs
appear a useless body, and a king strive to be everybody" (*un
homme universal*).

Whilst trying to beguile his tedium at the camp of Compiègne,
the dauphin, it is said, overtaxed his strength, and died at the age
of thirty-six on the 20th of December, 1765, profoundly regretted
by the bulk of the nation, who knew his virtues without troubling
themselves, like the court and the philosophers, about the stiffness
of his manners and his complete devotion to the cause of the clergy.
The new dauphin, who would one day be Louis XVI., was still a
child : the king had him brought into his closet. " Poor France !"
he said sadly, " a king of fifty-five and a dauphin of eleven !"
The dauphiness and Queen Mary Leczinska soon followed the
dauphin to the tomb (1767, 1768). The king, thus left alone and
scared by the repeated deaths around him, appeared for a while
to be drawn closer to his daughters, for whom he always retained
some sort of affection, a mixture of weakness and habit. One of
them, Madame Louise, who was deeply pious, left him to enter the
convent of the Carmelites ; he often went to see her, and granted her
all the favours she asked. But by this time Madame Dubarry had
become all-powerful ; to secure to her the honours of presentation
at court the king personally solicited the ladies with whom he was
intimate in order to get them to support his favourite on this new
stage ; when the youthful Marie Antoinette, archduchess of Austria
and daughter of Maria Theresa, whose marriage the duke of
Choiseul had negotiated, arrived in France, in 1770, to espouse the
dauphin, Madame Dubarry appeared alone with the royal family at
the banquet given at La Muette on the occasion of the marriage.
After each reaction of religious fright and transitory repentance,

after each warning from God that snatched him for an instant from the depravity of his life, the king plunged more deeply than before into shame. Madame Dubarry was to reign as much as Louis XV.

Before his fall the duke of Choiseul had made a last effort to revive abroad that fortune of France which he saw sinking at home without his being able to apply any effective remedy. He had vainly attempted to give colonies once more to France by founding in French Guiana settlements which had been unsuccessfully attempted by a Rouennese Company as early as 1634. The enterprise was badly managed; the numerous colonists, of very diverse origin and worth, were cast without resources upon a territory as unhealthy as fertile. No preparations had been made to receive them; the majority died of disease and want; *New France* henceforth belonged to the English, and the great hopes which had been raised of replacing it in *Equinoctial France*, as Guiana was named, soon vanished never to return. An attempt made about the same epoch at St. Lucie was attended with the same result. The great ardour and the rare aptitude for distant enterprises which had so often manifested themselves in France from the fifteenth to the seventeenth century seemed to be henceforth extinguished. Only the colonies of the Antilles, which had escaped from the misfortunes of war, and were by this time recovered from their disasters, offered any encouragement to the patriotic efforts of the duke of Choiseul. He had been more fortunate in Europe than in the colonies: henceforth Corsica belonged to France.

In spite of the French occupations, from 1708 to 1756, in spite of the refusals with which Cardinal Fleury had but lately met their appeals, the Corsicans, newly risen against the oppression of Genoa, had sent a deputation to Versailles to demand the recognition of their republic, offering to pay the tribute but lately paid annually to their tyrannical protectress. The hero of Corsican independence, Pascal Paoli, secretly supported by England, had succeeded for several years past not only in defending his country's liberty, but also in governing and at the same time civilizing it. This patriotic soul and powerful mind, who had managed to profit by the energetic passions of his compatriots whilst momentarily repressing their intestine quarrels, dreamed of an ideal constitution for his island ; he sent to ask for one of J. J. Rousseau, who was still in Switzerland and whom he invited to Corsica.   The philosophical chimeras of Paoli soon vanished before a piece of crushing news.   The Genoese, weary of struggling unsuccessfully against the obstinate determination of the Corsicans, and unable to clear off the debts which they had but lately incurred to Louis XV., had proposed to M. de Choiseul to cede to France their ancient rights over Corsica, as security for their liabilities.   A treaty, signed at Versailles on the 15th of May, 1768, authorized the king to perform all acts of sovereignty in the places and forts of Corsica ; a separate article accorded to Genoa an indemnity of two millions.

A cry arose in Corsica.   Paoli resolved to defend the independence of his country against France, as he had defended it against Genoa.   For several months now French garrisons had occupied the places still submitting to Genoa ; when they would have extended themselves into the interior, Paoli barred their passage ; he bravely attacked M. de Chauvelin, the king's lieutenant-general, who had just landed with a proclamation from Louis XV. to his new subjects.   "The Corsican nation does not let itself be bought and sold like a flock of sheep sent to market," said the protest of the republic's Supreme Council.   Fresh troops from France had to be asked for ; under the orders of Count Vaux they triumphed without difficulty over the Corsican patriots.   Mustering at the bridge of Golo for a last effort, they made a rampart of their dead ; the wounded had lain down amongst the corpses to give the survivors time to effect their retreat.   The town of Corte, the seat of the republican government, capitulated before long.   England had supplied Paoli with munitions and arms ; he had hoped more from the promises of the government and the national jealousy against France.   "The ministry is too weak and the nation too wise to make war on account of Corsica," said an illustrious judge, Lord Mansfield.   In vain did Burke exclaim: "Corsica, as a province of France, is for me an object of alarm!"   The House of Commons approved of the government's conduct, and England contented herself with offering to the vanquished Paoli a sympathetic hospitality; he left Corsica on an English frigate, accompanied by most of his friends, and it is in Westminster Abbey that he lies, after the numerous vicissitudes of his life, which fluctuated throughout the revolutions of his native land, from England to France and from France to England, to the day when Corsica, proud of having given a master to France and the Revolution, became definitively French with Napoleon.

Corsica was to be the last conquest of the old French monarchy. Great or little, magnificent or insignificant, from Richelieu to the duke of Choiseul, France had managed to preserve her territorial acquisitions; in America and in Asia, Louis XV. had shamefully lost Canada and the Indies; in Europe, the diplomacy of his ministers had given to the kingdom Lorraine and Corsica. The day of insensate conquests ending in a diminution of territory had not yet come. In the great and iniquitous dismemberment which was coming, France was to have no share.

Profound disquietude was beginning to agitate Europe: the king of Poland, Augustus III., had died in 1763, leaving the unhappy country over which he had reigned a prey to internal anarchy ever increasing and systematically fanned by the avidity or jealousy of the great powers, its neighbours. "As it is to the interest of the two monarchs of Russia and Prussia that the Polish commonwealth should preserve its right to free election of a king," said the secret treaty concluded in 1764 between Frederick II. and the Empress Catherine, "and that no family should possess itself of the elective throne of that country, the two undermentioned Majesties engage to prevent, by all means in their power, Poland from being despoiled of its right of election and transformed into an hereditary kingdom; they mutually promise to oppose in concert and, if necessary, by force of arms, all plans and designs which may tend thereto as soon as discovered."

A second article secured to the *dissidents*, as Protestants and Greeks were called in Poland, the protection of the king of Prussia and of the empress, "who will make every effort to persuade, by strong and friendly representations, the king and the commonwealth of Poland to restore to those persons the rights, privileges

DEFEAT OF THE CORSICANS AT GOLO.

and prerogatives they have acquired there, and which have been
accorded them in the past, as well in ecclesiastical as in civil
matters, but have since been, for the most part, circumscribed or
unjustly taken away. But, should it be impossible to attain that
end at once, the contracting parties will content themselves with
seeing that, whilst waiting for more favourable times and circumstances, the aforesaid persons are put beyond reach of the wrongs
and oppression under which they are at present groaning." In
order to remain masters of Poland and to prevent it from escaping
the dissolution with which it was threatened by its internal dissensions, Frederick and Catherine, who were secretly pursuing
different and often contrary courses, united to impose on the
Diet a native prince. "I and my ally the empress of Russia,"
said the king of Prussia, "have agreed to promote the selection
of a *Piast* (Pole), which would be useful and at the same time
glorious for the nation." In vain had Louis XV. by secret
policy, sought for a long while to pave the way for the
election of the prince of Conti to the throne of Poland, the
influence of Russia and of Prussia carried the day. Prince Ponia-
towski, late favourite of the Empress Catherine, was elected by
the Polish Diet; in discouragement and sadness, four thousand
nobles only had responded to the letters of convocation. The
new king, Stanislaus Augustus, handsome, intelligent, amiable,
cultivated, but feeble in character and fatally pledged to Russia,
sought to rally round him the different parties and to establish at
last, in the midst of general confusion, a regular and a strong
government. He was supported in this patriotic task by the
influence, ever potent in Poland, of the Czartoriskis. The far-
seeing vigilance of Frederick II. did not give them time to act.
"Poland must be left in her lethargy," he had said to the Russian
ambassador Saldern. "It is of importance," he wrote to Catherine,
"that Her Majesty the empress who knows perfectly well her own
interests and those of her friends and allies, should give orders of
the most precise kind to her ambassador at Warsaw, to oppose
any novelty in the form of government and, generally speaking,
the establishment of a permanent council, the preservation of the
commissions of war and of the treasury, the power of the king

and the unlimited concession on the prince's part of ability to distribute offices according to his sole will." The useful reforms being thus abandoned and the king's feeble power radically shaken, religious discord came to fill up the cup of disorder and to pave the way for the dismemberment as well as definitive ruin of unhappy Poland.

Subjected for a long time past to an increasing oppression, which was encouraged by a fanatical and unenlightened clergy, the Polish *dissidents* had conceived great hopes on the accession of Stanislaus Augustus; they claimed not only liberty of conscience and of worship, but also all the civil and political rights of which they were deprived. "It is no question of establishing the free exercise of different religions in Poland," wrote Frederick to Catherine; "it is necessary to reduce the question to its true issue, the demand of the dissident noblesse, and obtain for them the equality they demand together with participation in all acts of sovereignty." This was precisely what the clergy and the catholic noblesse were resolved never to grant. In spite of support from the empress and the king of Prussia, the demand of the dissidents was formally rejected by the Diet of 1766. At the Diet of 1767, Count Repnin, Catherine's ambassador and the real head of the government in Poland, had four of the most recalcitrant senators carried off and sent into exile in Russia. The Diet terrified, disorganized, immediately pronounced in favour of the dissidents. By the modifications recently introduced into the constitution of their country the Polish nobles had lost their *liberum veto;* unanimity of suffrages was no longer necessary in the Diet; the foreign powers were able to insolently impose their will upon it; the privileges of the noblesse as well as their traditional faith were attacked at the very foundations; religious fanaticism and national independence boiled up at the same time in every heart; the discontent, secretly fanned by the agents of Frederick, burst out, sooner than the skilful weavers of the plot could have desired, with sufficient intensity and violence to set fire to the four corners of Poland. By a bold surprise the confederates gained possession of Cracow and of the fortress of Barr, in Podolia; there it was that they swore to die for the sacred cause of catholic Poland.

For more than a century, in the face of many mistakes and many misfortunes, the Poles have faithfully kept that oath.

The bishop of Kaminck, Kraminski, had gone to Versailles to solicit the support of France. The duke of Choiseul, at first far from zealous in the cause of the Polish insurrection, had nevertheless sent a few troops, who were soon reinforced. The Empress Catherine had responded to the violence of the confederates of Barr by letting loose upon the Ukraine the hordes of Zaporoguian Cossacks, speedily followed by regular troops. The Poles, often beaten, badly led by chieftains divided amongst themselves, but ever ardent, ever skilful in seizing upon the smallest advantages, were sustained by the pious exhortations of the clergy, who regarded the war as a crusade; they were rejoiced to see a diversion preparing in their favour by the Sultan's armaments. " I will raise the Turks against Russia the moment you think proper," was the assurance given to the duke of Choiseul by the count of Vergennes, French ambassador at Constantinople, " but I warn you that they will be beaten." Hostilities broke out on the 30th of October, 1768; a Turkish army set out to aid the Polish insurrection. Absorbed by their patriotic passions, the catholic confederates summoned the Mussulmans to their assistance. Prince Galitzin, at the head of a Russian force very inferior to the Ottoman invaders, succeeded in barring their passage: the Turks fell back, invariably beaten by the Russian generals. Catherine at the same time summoned to liberty the oppressed and persecuted Greeks; she sent a squadron to support the rising which she had been fomenting for some months past. After a few brilliant successes, her arms were less fortunate at sea than on land. A French officer, of Hungarian origin, Baron Tott, sent by the duke of Choiseul to help the Sublime Porte, had fortified the straits of the Dardanelles: the Russians were repulsed; they withdrew, leaving the Greeks to the vengeance of their oppressors. The efforts which the Empress Catherine was making in Poland against the confederates of Barr had slackened her proceedings against Turkey; she was nevertheless becoming triumphant on the borders of the Vistula as well as on the banks of the Danube, when the far-sighted and bold policy of Frederick II. interfered in time to prevent Russia from taking possession of Poland as well as of the Ottoman empire.

Secretly favouring the confederates of Barr whom he had but lately encouraged in their uprising and whom he had suffered to make purchases of arms and ammunition in Prussia, Frederick II. had sought in Austria a natural ally, interested like himself in stopping the advances of Russia. The emperor, Maria Theresa's husband, had died in 1764; his son, Joseph II., who succeeded him, had conceived for the king of Prussia the spontaneous admiration of a young and ardent spirit for the most illustrious man of his times. In 1769, a conference which took place at Neisse brought the two sovereigns together. " The emperor is a man eaten up with ambition," wrote Frederick after the interview; " he is hatching some great design. At present, restrained as he is by his mother, he is beginning to chafe at the yoke he bears, and, as soon as he gets elbow-room, he will commence with some startling stroke; it was impossible for me to discover whether his views were directed towards the republic of Venice, towards Bavaria, towards Silesia or towards Lorraine : but we may rely upon it that Europe will be all on fire the moment he is master." A second interview, at Neustadt in 1770, clinched the relations already contracted at Neisse. Common danger brought together old enemies. " I am not going to have the Russians for neighbours," the Empress Maria Theresa was always repeating. The devastating flood had to be directed and at the same time stemmed. The feeble goodwill of France and the small body of troops commanded by Dumouriez were still supporting the Polish insurrection, but the duke of Choiseul had just succumbed to intrigue at home. There was no longer any foreign policy in France. It was without fear of intervention from her that the German powers began to discuss between them the partition of Poland.

She was at the same time suffering disseverment at her own hands through her intestine divisions and the mutual jealousy of her chiefs. In Warsaw the confederates had attempted to carry off King Stanislaus Augustus, whom they accused of betraying the cause of the fatherland; they had declared the throne vacant and took upon themselves to found an hereditary monarchy. To this supreme honour every great lord aspired, every small army-corps acted individually and without concert with the neighbouring leaders. Only a detachment of French, under the orders of Brigadier Choisi, still defended the fort of Cracow; General Suwarrow, who was investing it, forced them to capitulate : they obtained all the honours of war, but in vain was the Empress Catherine urged by D'Alembert and his friends the philosophers to restore their freedom to the glorious vanquished; she replied to them with pleasantries. Ere long the fate of Poland was about to be decided without the impotent efforts of France in her favour weighing for an instant in the balance. The political annihilation of Louis XV. in Europe had been completed by the dismissal of the duke of Choiseul.

The public conscience is lightened by lights which ability, even when triumphant, can never altogether obscure. The Great Frederick and the Empress Catherine have to answer before history for the crime of the partition of Poland, which they made acceptable to the timorous jealousy of Maria Theresa and to the youthful ambition of her son. As prudent as he was audacious, Frederick had been for a long time paving the way for the dismemberment of the country he had seemed to protect. Negotiations for peace with the Turks became the pretext for war-indemnities. Poland, vanquished, divided, had to pay the whole of them. " I shall not enter upon the portion that Russia marks out for herself," wrote Frederick to Count Solms, his ambassador at St. Petersburg : " I have expressly left all that blank in order that she may settle it according to her interests and her own good pleasure. When the negotiations for peace have advanced to a certain stage of consistency, it will no longer depend upon the Austrians to break them off if we declare our views unanimously as to Poland. She cannot rely any further upon France, which happens to be in such a fearful state of exhaustion that it could not give any help to Spain which was on the point of declaring war against England. If that war do not take place, it must be attributed simply to the smash in the finances of France. I guarantee, then, to the Russians all that may happen to suit them, they will do as much for me, and, supposing that the Austrians should consider their share of Poland too paltry in comparison with ours and it were desirable to satisfy them, one would only have to offer them that strip of the Venetian dominions which cuts them off from Trieste in order to keep them quiet; even if they were to turn nasty, I will answer for it with my head that our union with Russia, once clearly established, will tide them over all that we desire. They have to do with two powers and they have not a single ally to give them a shoulder."

Frederick said truly; his sound and powerful judgment took in the position of Europe : France, exhausted by the lingering decay of her government and in travail with new and confused elements which had as yet no strength but to shatter and destroy; Spain, lured on by France and then abandoned by her; England, disturbed at home by parliamentary agitation, favourably disposed to the court of Russia and for a long while allied to Frederick; Sweden and Denmark, in the throes of serious events; there was nothing to oppose the iniquity projected and prepared for with so much art and ability. It was in vain that the king of Prussia sought to turn into a joke the unscrupulous manœuvres of his diplomacy when he wrote to D'Alembert in January, 1772 : " I would rather undertake to put the whole history of the Jews into madrigals than to cause to be of one mind three sovereigns amongst whom must be numbered two women." The undertaking was already accomplished. Three months later, the first partition of Poland had been settled between Russia, Prussia, and Austria, and on the 2nd of September, 1772, the treaty was made known at Warsaw. The manifesto was short : " It is a general rule of policy," Frederick had said, " that, in default of unanswerable arguments, it is better to express oneself laconically and not go beating about the bush." The care of drawing it up had been entrusted to Prince Kaunitz. " It was of importance," said the document, " to establish the commonwealth of Poland on a solid basis whilst doing justice to the claims of the three powers for services rendered against the insurrection." The king and the senate protested. The troops of the allies surrounded Warsaw, and the Diet, being convoked, ratified by a majority of two voices the convention presented by the spoilers themselves. Catherine assigned to herself three thousand square leagues and 1,500,000

souls in Lithuania and Polish Livonia; Austria took possession
of two thousand five hundred square leagues and more than two
million souls in Red Russia and the Polish palatinates on the left
of the Vistula; the instigator and plotter of the whole business
had been the most modest of all : the treaty of partition brought
Prussia only nine hundred square leagues and 860,000 souls, but
he found himself master of Prussian Poland and of a henceforth
compact territory.   England had opposed, in Russia, the cession
of Dantzick to the Great Frederick.   " The ill-temper of France
and England at the dismemberment of Poland calls for serious
reflections," wrote the king of Prussia on the 5th of August, 1772 :
" these two courts are already moving heaven and earth to detach
the court of Vienna from our system; but as the three chief
points whence their support should come are altogether to seek in
France and there are neither system, nor stability, nor money
there, her projects will be given up with the same facility with
which they were conceived and broached.   They appear to me,
moreover, like the projects of the duke of Aiguillon, ebullitions of
French vivacity."

France did not do anything and could not do anything; the
king's secret negotiators, as well as the minister of foreign affairs,
had been tricked by the allied powers.   " Ah ! if Choiseul had
been here !" exclaimed King Louis XV., it is said, when he heard
of the partition of Poland.   The duke of Choiseul would no doubt
have been more clear-sighted and better informed than the duke of
Aiguillon, but his policy could have done no good.   Frederick II.
knew that.   " France plays so small a part in Europe," he wrote to
Count Solms, " that I merely tell you about the impotent efforts of
the French ministry's envy just to have a laugh at them and to let
you see in what visions the consciousness of its own weaknesses is
capable of leading that court to indulge."   " Oh, where *is* Poland ?"
Madame Dubarry had said to Count Wicholorsky, King Stanislaus
Augustus' chargé d'affaires, who was trying to interest her in the
misfortunes of his country.

The partition of Poland was barely accomplished, the confederates of Barr, overwhelmed by the Russian troops, were
still arriving in France to seek refuge there, and already King

Louis XV., for a moment roused by the audacious aggression
of the German courts, had sunk back into the shameful lethargy
of his life. When Madame Louise, the pious Carmelite of
St. Denis, succeeded in awakening in her father's soul a gleam of
religious terror, the courtiers in charge of the royal pleasures redoubled their efforts to distract the king from thoughts so perilous
for their own fortunes. Louis XV., fluctuating between remorse
and depravity, ruled by Madame Dubarry, bound hand and foot to
the triumvirate of Chancellor Maupeou, Abbé Terray and the duke
of Aiguillon, who were consuming between them in his name
the last remnants of absolute power, fell suddenly ill of small-pox.
The princesses, his daughters, had never had that terrible disease,
the scourge and terror of all classes of society, yet they bravely
shut themselves up with the king, lavishing their attentions upon
him to the last gasp. Death, triumphant, had vanquished the
favourite: Madame Dubarry was sent away as soon as the nature
of the malady had declared itself. The king charged his grand
almoner to ask pardon of the courtiers for the scandal he had
caused them. " Kings owe no account of their conduct save to
God only," he had often repeated to comfort himself for the shame
of his life. " It is just He whom I fear," said Maria Theresa,
pursued by remorse for the partition of Poland.

Louis XV. died on the 10th of May, 1774, in his sixty-fourth
year, after reigning fifty-nine years, despised by the people who had
not so long ago given him the name of Well-beloved, and whose
attachment he had worn out by his cold indifference about affairs
and the national interests as much as by the irregularities of his life.
With him died the old French monarchy, that proud power which
had sometimes ruled Europe whilst always holding a great position
therein. Henceforth France was marching towards the unknown,
tossed about as she was by divers movements, which were mostly
hostile to the old state of things, blindly and confusedly as yet, but,
under the direction of masters as inexperienced as they were
daring, full of frequently noble though nearly always extravagant
and reckless hopes, all founded on a thorough reconstruction of
the bases of society and of its ancient props. Far more even than
the monarchy, at the close of Louis XV.'s reign, did religion find

itself attacked and threatened ; the blows struck by the philosophers at fanaticism recoiled upon the Christian faith, transiently liable here below for human errors and faults over which it is destined to triumph in eternity.

CHAPTER LV.

LOUIS XV.—THE PHILOSOPHERS.

NOWHERE and at no epoch had literature shone with so vivid a lustre as in the reign of Louis XIV.; never has it been in a greater degree the occupation and charm of mankind, never has it left nobler and rarer models behind it for the admiration and imitation of the coming race: the writers of Louis XV.'s age, for all their brilliancy and all their fertility, themselves felt their inferiority in respect of their predecessors. Voltaire confessed as much with a modesty which was by no means familiar to him. Inimitable in their genius, Corneille, Bossuet, Pascal, Molière left their imprint upon the generation that came after them; it had judgment enough to set them by acclamation in the ranks of the classics; in their case, greatness displaced time. Voltaire took Racine for model; La Mothe imagined that he could imitate La Fontaine. The illustrious company of great minds which surrounded the throne of Louis XIV. and had so much to do with the lasting splendour of his reign had no reason to complain of ingratitude on the part of its successors; but, from the pedestal to which they raised it, it exercised no potent influence upon new thought and new passions. Enclosed in their glory as in a sanctuary, those noble spirits, discreet and orderly even in their audacities, might look forth on commotions and yearnings they had never known : they saw, with astonishment mingled with affright, their successors launching without fear or afterthought upon that boundless world of intellect, upon which the rules of conscience and the difficulties of practical life do not come in anywhere to impose limits. They saw the field everywhere open to human thought and they saw falling down on all sides the boundaries which they had considered sacred. They saw pioneers, as bold as they were thoughtless, marching through the mists of a glorious hope towards an unknown future, attacking errors and abuses, all the while that they were digging up the groundwork of society in order to lay new foundations, and they must have shuddered even in their everlasting rest to see ideas taking the place of creeds, doubt substituted for belief, generous aspirations after liberty, justice and humanity mingled, amongst the masses, with low passions and deep-seated rancour. They saw respect disappearing, the Church as well as the kingly power losing prestige every day, religious faith all darkened and dimmed in some corner of men's souls, and, amidst all this general instability, they asked themselves with awe, " Where are the guiding-reins of the society which is about to be ? What will be the props of the new fabric ? The foundations are overturned; what will the good man do ?"

Good men had themselves sometimes lent a hand to the work, beyond what they had intended or foreseen, perhaps ; Montesquieu, despite the wise moderation of his great and strong mind, had been the first to awaken that yearning for novelty and reforms which had been silently brooding at the bottom of men's hearts. Born in 1689 at the castle of La Brède, near Bordeaux, Montesquieu really belonged, in point of age, to the reign of Louis XIV., of which he bears the powerful imprint even amidst the boldness of his thoughts and expressions. Grandeur is the distinctive characteristic of Montesquieu's ideas as it is of the seventeenth century altogether. He was already councillor in the parliament of Bordeaux when

Louis XIV. died; next year (1716) he took possession of a mortar-cap-president's (*president à mortier*) office, which had been given up to him by one of his uncles. "On leaving college," he says, "there were put into my hands some law-books; I examined the spirit of them." Those profound researches, which were to last as long as his life, were more suited to his tastes than jurisprudence properly so called. "What has always given me rather a low opinion of myself," he would say, "is that there are very few positions in the commonwealth for which I should be really fit. As for my office of

MONTESQUIEU.

president, I have my heart in the right place, I comprehended sufficiently well the questions in themselves; but as to the procedure I did not understand anything about it. I paid attention to it, nevertheless; but what disgusted me most was to see fools with that very talent which, so to speak, shunned me." He resolved to deliver himself from the yoke which was intolerable to him and resigned his office; but by this time the world knew his name, in spite of the care ne had taken at first to conceal it. In 1721, when he still had his seat on the fleurs-de-lis, he had published his *Lettres persanes*, an imaginary trip of two exiled Parsees, freely criticizing Paris and France. The book appeared under the Regency, and bears the imprint of it in the licentiousness of the descriptions and the witty irreverence of the criticisms. Sometimes, however, the future gravity of Montesquieu's genius reveals itself amidst the shrewd or biting judgments. It is in the *Lettres persanes* that he seeks to set up the notion of justice above the idea of God himself. " Though there were no God," he says, " we should still be bound to love justice, that is to say, make every effort to be like that Being of whom we have so grand an idea and who, if He existed, would of necessity be just." Holy Scripture, before Montesquieu, had affirmed more simply and more powerfully the unchangeable idea of justice in every soul of man: " He who is judge of all the earth, shall not He do right?" Abraham had said when interceding with God for the righteous shut up in Sodom.

The success of the *Lettres persanes* was great; Montesquieu had said what many people thought without daring to express it; the doubt which was nascent in his mind, and which he could only withstand by an effort of will, the excessive freedom of the tone and of the style scared the authorities, however; when he wanted to get into the French Academy, in the place of M. de Sacy, Cardinal Fleury opposed it formally. It was only on the 24th of January, 1728, that Montesquieu, recently elected, delivered his reception speech. He at once set out on some long travels: he went through Germany, Hungary, Italy, Switzerland, Holland, and ended by settling in England for two years. The sight of political liberty had charmed him. " Ambassadors know no more about England than a six months' infant," he wrote in his journal: " when people see the devil to pay in the periodical publications, they believe that there is going to be a revolution next day; but all that is required is to remember that in England as elsewhere, the people are dissatisfied with the ministers and write what is only thought elsewhere. England is the freest country in the world, I do not except any republic." He returned to France so smitten with the parliamentary or *moderate* form of government, as he called it, that he seemed sometimes to forget the prudent maxim of the *Lettres persanes:* " It is true," said the Parsee Usbeck, " that, in consequence of a whimsicality (*bizarrerie*) which springs rather from the nature than from the mind of man, it is sometimes necessary to change certain laws; but the case is rare, and, when it occurs, it should not be touched save with a trembling hand."

On returning to his castle of La Brède after so many and such long travels, Montesquieu resolved to restore his tone by intercourse with the past. " I confess my liking for the ancients," he used to say; " this antiquity enchants me, and I am always ready to say with Pliny: You are going to Athens; revere the gods." It was not, however, on the Greeks that he concentrated the working of his mind; in 1734, he published his *Considérations sur les causes de la grandeur et de la décadence des Romains*. Montesquieu did not, as Bossuet did, seek to hit upon God's plan touching the destinies of mankind : he discovers in the virtues and vices of the Romans themselves the secret of their triumphs and of their reverses. The contemplation of antiquity inspires him with language often worthy of Tacitus, curt, nervous, powerful in its grave simplicity : " It seemed," he says, " that the Romans only conquered in order to give; but they remained so positively the masters that, when they made war on any prince, they crushed him, so to speak, with the weight of the whole universe."

Montesquieu thus performed the prelude to the great work of his life : he had been working for twenty years at the *Esprit des lois*, when he published it in 1748. " In the course of twenty years," he says, " I saw my work begin, grow, progress and end." He had placed as the motto to his book this Latin phrase, which at first excited the curiosity of readers : *Prolem sine matre creatam (Offspring begotten without a mother)*. " Young man," said Montesquieu, by this time advanced in years, to M. Suard (afterwards perpetual secretary to the French Academy), " young man, when a notable book is written, genius is its father and liberty its mother ; that is why I wrote upon the title-page of my work : *Prolem sine matre creatam*."

It was liberty at the same time as justice that Montesquieu sought and claimed in his profound researches into the laws which have from time immemorial governed mankind; that new instinctive idea of natural rights, those new yearnings which were beginning to dawn in all hearts, remained as yet, for the most part, upon the surface of their minds and of their lives; what was demanded at that time in France was liberty to speak and write rather than to act and govern. Montesquieu, on the contrary, went to the bottom of things, and, despite the natural moderation of his mind, he propounded theories so perilous for absolute power that he dared not have his book printed at Paris and brought it out in Geneva; its success was immense : before his death, Montesquieu saw twenty-one French editions published and translations in all the languages of Europe. " Mankind had lost its title-deeds," says Voltaire : " Montesquieu recovered and restored them."

The intense labour, the immense courses of reading, to which Montesquieu had devoted himself, had exhausted his strength. " I am overcome with weariness," he wrote in 1747 : " I propose to rest myself for the remainder of my days." " I have done," he said to M. Suard : " I have burnt all my powder, all my candles have gone out." " I had conceived the design of giving greater breadth and depth to certain parts of my *Esprit ;* I have become incapable of it : my reading has weakened my eyes, and it seems to me that what light I have left is but the dawn of the day when they will close for ever."

Montesquieu was at Paris, ill and sad at heart, in spite of his habitual serenity ; notwithstanding the scoffs he had admitted into his *Lettres persanes,* he had always preserved some respect for religion ; he considered it a necessary item in the order of societies ; in his soul and on his own private account he hoped and desired rather than believed. " Though the immortality of the soul were an error," he had said, " I should be sorry not to believe it ; I confess that I am not so humble as the atheists. I know not what they think, but as for me I would not truck the notion of my immortality for that of an ephemeral happiness. There is for me a charm in believing myself to be immortal like God himself. Independently of revealed ideas, metaphysical ideas give me, as regards my eternal happiness, strong hopes which I should not like to give up." As he approached the tomb, his views of religion appeared to become clearer. " What a wonderful thing ! " he would say, " the Christian religion, which seems to have no object but felicity in the next world, yet forms our happiness in this." He had never looked to life for any very keen delights ; his spirits were as even as his mind was powerful. " Study has been for me the sovereign remedy against the disagreeables of life," he wrote, " never having had any sorrow that an hour's reading did not dispel. I awake in the morning with a secret joy at beholding the light; I gaze upon the light with a sort of enchantment, and all the rest of the day I am content. I pass the night without awaking, and in the evening, when I go to bed, a sort of entrancement prevents me from giving way to reflections."

Montesquieu died as he had lived, without retracting any of his

E. RONJAT.

FONTENELLE.

ideas or of his writings. The priest of his parish brought him the sacraments, and, " Sir," said he, " you know how great God is ! " " Yes," replied the dying man, " and how little men are ! " He expired almost immediately on the 10th of February, 1755, at the age of sixty-six. He died at the beginning of the reign of the philosophers, whose way he had prepared before them without having ever belonged to their number. Diderot alone followed his bier. Fontenelle, nearly a hundred years old, was soon to follow him to the tomb.

Born at Rouen in February, 1657, and nephew of Corneille on

the mother's side, Fontenelle had not received from nature any of the unequal and sublime endowments which have fixed the dramatic crown for ever upon the forehead of Corneille; but he had inherited the wit, and indeed the brilliant wit (*bel esprit*), which the great tragedian hid beneath the splendours of his genius.   He began with those writings, superfine (*précieux*), dainty, tricked out in the fashion of the court and the drawing-room, which suggested La Bruyère's piquant portrait.

"Ascanius is a statuary, Hegio a metal-founder, Æschines a fuller, and Cydias a brilliant wit.   That is his trade; he has a sign, a workshop, articles made to order and apprentices who work under him.   Prose, verse, what d'ye lack?   He is equally successful in both.   Give him an order for letters of *consolation*, or on an absence; he will undertake them.   Take them ready made, if you like, and enter his shop, there is a choice assortment.   He has a friend whose only duty on earth is to puff him for a long while in certain society and then present him at their houses as a rare bird and a man of exquisite conversation, and thereupon, just as the musical man sings and the player on the lute touches his lute before the persons to whom he has been puffed, Cydias, after coughing, pulling up his wristband, extending his hand and opening his fingers, gravely spouts his quintessentiated ideas and his sophisticated arguments."

Fontenelle was not destined to stop here in his intellectual developments; when, at forty years of age, he became perpetual secretary to the Academy of Sciences, he had already written his book on the *Pluralité des Mondes*, the first attempt at that popularization of science which has spread so since then.   " I believe more and more," he said, " that there is a certain genius which has never yet been out of our Europe or, at least, has not gone far out of it."   This *genius*, clear, correct, precise, the genius of method and analysis, the genius of Descartes, which was at a later period that of Buffon and of Cuvier, was admirably expounded and developed by Fontenelle for the use of the ignorant.   He wrote for society and not for scholars, of whose labours and discoveries he gave an account to society.   His extracts from the labours of the Academy of Science and his eulogies of the Academicians are models of lucidness under an ingenious and subtle form, rendered simple and strong by dint of wit. "There is only truth that persuades," he used to say, "and even without requiring to appear with all its proofs. It makes its way so naturally into the mind, that, when it is heard for the first time, it seems as if one were merely remembering."

Equitable and moderate in mind, prudent and cold in temperament, Fontenelle passed his life in discussion without ever stumbling into disputes : "I am no theologian, or philosopher, or man of any denomination, of any sort whatever ; consequently I am not at all bound to be right, and I can with honour confess that I was mistaken, whenever I am made to see it." "How did you manage to keep so many friends without making one enemy ?" he was asked in his old age. "By means of two maxims," he answered : "Everything is possible ; everybody may be right" (*tout le monde a raison*). The friends of Fontenelle were moderate like himself ; impressed with his fine qualities, they pardoned his lack of warmth in his affections. "He never laughed," says Madame Geoffrin, his most intimate friend : " I said to him one day ; ' Did you ever laugh, M. de Fontenelle?' ' No,' he answered ; ' I never went *ha! ha! ha!*' That was his idea of laughing : he just smiled at smart things, but he was a stranger to any strong feeling. He had never shed tears, he had never been in a rage, he had never run, and, as he never did anything from sentiment, he did not catch impressions from others. He had never interrupted anybody, he listened to the end without losing anything ; he was in no hurry to speak, and, if you had been accusing against him, he would have listened all day without saying a syllable."

The very courage and trustiness of Fontenelle bore this stamp of discreet moderation. When Abbé St. Pierre was excluded from the French Academy under Louis XV. for having dared to criticize the government of Louis XIV., one single ball in the urn protested against the unjust pressure exercised by Cardinal Fleury upon the society. They all asked one another who the rebel was ; each defended himself against having voted against the minister's order ; Fontenelle alone kept silent ; when everybody had exculpated himself, "It must be myself, then," said Fontenelle half aloud.

So much cool serenity and so much taste for noble intellectual works prolonged the existence of Fontenelle beyond the ordinary limits; he was ninety-nine and not yet weary of life: " If I might but reach the strawberry-season once more!" he had said.   He died at Paris on the 9th of January, 1759; with him disappeared what remained of the spirit and traditions of Louis XIV.'s reign. Montesquieu and Fontenelle were the last links which united the seventeenth century to the new era.   In a degree as different as the scope of their minds they both felt respect for the past to which they were bound by numerous ties, and the boldness of their thoughts was frequently tempered by prudence.   Though naturally moderate and prudent, Voltaire was about to be hurried along by the ardour of strife, by the weaknesses of his character, by his vanity and his ambition far beyond his first intentions and his natural instincts.   The flood of free-thinking had spared Montesquieu and Fontenelle, it was about to carry away Voltaire almost as far as Diderot.

François Marie Arouet de Voltaire was born at Paris on the 21st of November, 1694.   " My dear father," said a letter from a relative to his family in Poitou, " our cousins have another son, born three days ago; Madame Arouet will give me some of the christening-sugarplums for you.   She has been very ill, but it is hoped that she is going on better; the infant is not much to look at, having suffered from a fall which his mother had."   M. Arouet, the father, of a good middle-class family, had been a notary at the Châtelet, and, in 1701 became paymaster of fees (*payeur d'épices*) to the court of exchequer, an honourable and a lucrative post, which added to the easy circumstances of the family.   Madame Arouet was dead when her youngest son was sent to the college of Louis-le-Grand, which at that time belonged to the Jesuits.   As early as then little Arouet, who was weak and in delicate health, but withal of a very lively intelligence, displayed a freedom of thought and a tendency to irreverence which already disquieted and angered his masters.   Father Lejay jumped from his chair and took the boy by the collar, exclaiming, " Wretch, thou wilt one of these days raise the standard of Deism in France!"   Father Pallou, his confessor, accustomed to read the heart, said as he shook his head, "This child is devoured with a thirst for celebrity."

Even at school and among the Jesuits, that passion for getting talked about, which was one of the weaknesses of Voltaire's character as well as one of the sources of his influence, was already to a certain extent gratified. The boy was so ready in making verses, that his masters themselves found amusement in practising upon his youthful talent. Little Arouet's snuff-box had been confiscated because he had passed it along from hand to hand in class; when he asked for it back from Father Porée, who was always indulgent towards him, the rector required an application in verse. A quarter of an hour later the boy returned with his treasure in his possession, having paid its ransom thus :—

> " Adieu, adieu, poor snuff-box mine,
> Adieu, we ne'er shall meet again :
> Nor pains, nor tears, nor pray'rs divine
> Will win thee back, my efforts are in vain !
> Adieu, adieu, poor box of mine,
> Adieu, my sweet crowns'-worth of bane ;
> Could I with money buy thee back once more,
> The treasury of Plutus I would drain.
> But ah ! not he the god I must implore ;
> To have thee back, I need Apollo's vein. . . .
> Twixt thee and me how hard a barrier-line,
> To ask for verse ! Ah, this is all my strain !
> Adieu, adieu, poor box of mine,
> Adieu, we ne'er shall meet again ! "

Arouet was still a child when a friend of his family took him to see Mdlle. Ninon de l'Enclos, as celebrated for her wit as for the irregularity of her life. " Abbé Châteauneuf took me to see her in my very tender youth," says Voltaire; " I had done some verses which were worth nothing, but which seemed very good for my age. She was then eighty-five. She was pleased to put me down in her will, she left me 2000 francs to buy books; her death followed close upon my visit and her will."

Young Arouet was finishing brilliantly his last year of rhetoric when John Baptist Rousseau, already famous, saw him at the distribution of prizes at the college. " Later on," wrote Rousseau, in the thick of his quarrels with Voltaire, " some ladies of my acquaintance had taken me to see a tragedy at the Jesuits' in

August, 1710, at the distribution of prizes which usually took place after those representations ; I observed that the same scholar was called up twice. I asked Father Tarteron, who did the honours of the room in which we were, who the young man was that was so distinguished amongst his comrades. He told me that it was a little lad who had a surprising turn for poetry, and proposed to introduce him to me ; to which I consented. He went to fetch him to me, and I saw him returning a moment afterwards with a young scholar who appeared to me to be about sixteen or seventeen, with an ill-favoured conntenance but with a bright and lively expression, and who came and shook hands with me with very good grace."

Scarcely had François Arouet left college when he was called upon to choose a career. " I do not care for any but that of a literary man," exclaimed the young fellow. " That," said his father, " is the condition of a man who means to be useless to society, to be a charge to his family and to die of starvation." The study of the law, to which he was obliged to devote himself, completely disgusted the poet, already courted by a few great lords who were amused at his satirical vein ; he led an indolent and disorderly life, which drove his father distracted ; the latter wanted to get him a place. " Tell my father," was the young man's reply to the relative commissioned to make the proposal, " that I do not care for a position which can be bought ; I shall find a way of getting myself one that costs nothing." " Having but little property when I began life," he wrote to M. d'Argenson, his sometime fellow-pupil, " I had the insolence to think that I should have got a place as well as another, if it were to be obtained by hard work and good will. I threw myself into the ranks of the fine arts, which always carry with them a certain air of vilification, seeing that they do not make a man king's counsellor in his councils. You may become a master of requests with money ; but you can't make a poem with money, and I made one."

This independent behaviour and the poem on the *Construction du chœur de Notre-Dame de Paris*, the subject submitted for competition by the French Academy, did not prevent young Arouet from being sent by his father to Holland in the train of the marquis of Châteauneuf, then French ambassador to the States-general; he committed so many follies that on his return to France M. Arouet forced him to enter a solicitor's office. It was there that the poet acquired that knowledge of business which was useful to him during the whole course of his long life; he, however, did not remain there long: a satire upon the French Academy which had refused him the prize for poetry and, later on, some verses as biting as they were disrespectful against the duke of Orleans, twice obliged their author to quit Paris. Sent into banishment at Sully-sur-Loire, he there found partisans and admirers; the merry life that was led at the Chevalier Sully's mitigated the hardships of absence from Paris. "Don't you go publishing abroad, I beg," wrote Arouet, nevertheless, to one of his friends, "the happiness of which I tell you in confidence : for they might perhaps leave me here long enough for me to become unhappy; I know my own capacity, I am not made to live long in the same place."

A beautiful letter addressed to the Regent and disavowing all the satirical writings which had been attributed to him, brought Arouet back to Paris at the commencement of the year 1717 ; he had been enjoying it for barely a few months when a new satire, entitled *J'ai vu* (*I have seen*) and bitterly criticizing the late reign, engaged the attention of society and displeased the Regent afresh. Arouet defended himself with just cause and with all his might against the charge of having written it. The duke of Orleans one day met him in the garden of the Palais-Royal : "Monsieur Arouet," said he, "I bet that I will make you see a thing you have never seen." "What, pray, monseigneur ?" "The Bastille." "Ah! monseigneur, I will consider it seen." Two days later, young Arouet was shut up in the Bastille.

> I needs must go ; I jog along in style,
> With close-shut carriage, to the royal pile
> Built in our fathers' days, hard by St. Paul,
> By Charles the Fifth. O brethren, good men all,
> In no such quarters may your lot be cast!
> Up to my room I find my way at last :
> A certain rascal with a smirking face
> Exalts the beauties of my new retreat,
> So comfortable, so compact, so neat.

Says he, " While Phœbus runs his daily race,
He never casts one ray within this place.
Look at the walls, some ten feet thick or so,
You'll find it all the cooler here, you know."
Then, bidding me admire the way they close
The triple doors and triple locks on those,
With gratings, bolts and bars on every side,
" It's all for your security," he cried.
At stroke of noon some skilly is brought in;
Such fare is not so delicate as thin.
I am not tempted by this splendid food,
But what they tell me is : " 'Twill do you good :
So eat in peace ; no one will hurry you."
Here in this doleful den I make ado,
Bastill'd, imprison'd, cabin'd, cribb'd, confined,
Nor sleeping, drinking, eating—to my mind ;
Betray'd by every one, my mistress too !
O Marc René ! [M. d'Argenson] whom Censor Cato's ghost
Might well have chosen for his vacant post,
O Marc René ! through whom 'tis brought about
That so much people murmur here below ;
To your kind word my durance vile I owe ;
May the good God some fine day pay you out !

Young Arouet passed eleven months in the Bastille ; he there wrote the first part of the poem called *La Henriade,* under the title of *La Ligue ;* when he at last obtained his release in April, 1718, he at the same time received orders to reside at Châtenay, where his father had a country house. It was on coming out of the Bastille that the poet took, from a small family-estate, that name of Voltaire which he was to render so famous. " I have been too unfortunate under my former name," he wrote to Mdlle. du Noyer, " I mean to see whether this will suit me better."

The players were at that time rehearsing the tragedy of *Œdipe,* which was played on the 18th of November, 1718, with great success. The daring flights of philosophy introduced by the poet into this profoundly and terribly religious subject excited the enthusiasm of the *roués ;* Voltaire was well received by the Regent, who granted him an honorarium. " Monseigneur," said Voltaire, " I should consider it very kind if his Majesty would be pleased to provide henceforth for my board, but I beseech your Highness to provide no more for my lodging." Voltaire's acts of imprudence were destined more than once to force him into leaving Paris; he all his life preserved such a horror of prison that it made him commit more than one platitude. "I have a mortal aversion for prison," he wrote in 1734; once more, however, he was to be an inmate of the Bastille.

Launched upon the most brilliant society, everywhere courted and flattered, Voltaire was constantly at work, displaying the marvellous suppleness of his mind by shifting from the tragedies of *Artémise* and *Marianne*, which failed, to the comedy of *L'Indiscret*, to numerous charming epistles, and lastly to the poem of *La Henriade*, which he went on carefully revising, reading fragments of it as he changed his quarters from castle to castle. One day, however, some criticisms to which he was not accustomed angered him so much that he threw into the fire the manuscript he held in his hand. "It is only worth burning, then," he exclaimed in a rage. President Hénault dashed at the papers. "I ran up and drew it out of the flames, saying that I had done more than they who did not burn the *Eneid* as Virgil had recommended; I had drawn out of the fire *La Henriade*, which Voltaire was going to burn with his own hands. If I liked, I might ennoble this action by calling to mind that picture of Raphael's at the Vatican which represents Augustus preventing Virgil from burning the *Eneid;* but I am not Augustus and Raphael is no more." Wholly indulgent and indifferent as might be the government of the Regent and of Dubois, it was a little scared at the liberties taken by Voltaire with the Catholic Church. He was required to make excisions in order to get permission to print the poem; the author was here, there and everywhere, in a great flutter and preoccupied with his literary, financial and fashionable affairs. In receipt of a pension from the queen and received as a visitor at La Source, near Orleans, by Lord Bolingbroke in his exile, every day becoming more brilliant and more courted, he was augmenting his fortune by profitable speculations and appeared on the point of finding himself well off, when an incident, which betrayed the remnant still remaining of barbarous manners, occurred to envenom for a long while the poet's existence. He had a quarrel at the Opera with Chevalier Rohan-Chabot, a court-libertine, of little

THE RESCUE OF "LA HENRIADE."

s 2

repute; the scene took place in the presence of Mdlle. Adrienne Lecouvreur; the great actress fainted: they were separated. Two days afterwards, when Voltaire was dining at the duke of Sully's, a servant came to tell him that he was wanted at the door of the hotel; the poet went out without any suspicion, though he had already been the victim of several ambuscades. A coach was standing in the street, and he was requested to get in; at that instant two men, throwing themselves upon him and holding him back by his clothes, showered upon him a hailstorm of blows with their sticks. The Chevalier de Rohan, prudently ensconced in a second vehicle and superintending the execution of his cowardly vengeance, shouted to his servants, "Don't hit him on the head, something good may come out of it." When Voltaire at last succeeded in escaping from these miscreants to take refuge in Sully's house, he was half dead.

Blows with a stick were not at that time an unheard-of procedure in social relations. "Whatever would become of us if poets had no shoulders!" was the brutal remark of the bishop of Blois, M. de Caumartin. But the customs of society did not admit a poet to the honour of obtaining satisfaction from whoever insulted him. The great lords, friends of Voltaire, who had accustomed him to attention and flattery, abandoned him pitilessly in his quarrel with Chevalier de Rohan. "Those blows were well gotten and ill given," said the prince of Conti. That was all the satisfaction Voltaire obtained. "The poor victim shows himself as much as possible at court, in the city," says the Marais news, "but nobody pities him, and those whom he considered his friends have turned their backs upon him."

Voltaire was not of a heroic nature, but excess of rage and indignation had given him courage; he had scarcely ever had a sword in his hand, he rushed to the fencers' and practised from morning till night in order to be in a position to demand satisfaction. So much ardour disquieted Chevalier de Rohan and his family; his uncle, the cardinal, took precautions. The lieutenant of police wrote to the officer of the watch: "Sir, his Highness is informed that Chevalier de Rohan is going away to-day, and, as he might have some fresh affair with Sieur de

Voltaire, or the latter might do something rash, his desire is for you to see that nothing comes of it."

Voltaire anticipated the intentions of the lieutenant of police: he succeeded in sending a challenge to Chevalier de Rohan; the latter accepted it for the next day, he even chose his ground: but before the hour fixed Voltaire was arrested and taken to the Bastille; he remained there a month. Public opinion was beginning to pity him. Marshal Villars writes in his memoirs:—

" The chevalier was very much inconvenienced by a fall which did not admit of his handling a sword. He took the course of having a caning administered in broad day to Voltaire, who, instead of adopting legal proceedings, thought vengeance by arms more noble. It is asserted that he sought it diligently, but too indiscreetly. Cardinal Rohan asked M. le Duc to have him put in the Bastille; orders to that effect were given and executed, and the poor poet, after being beaten, was imprisoned into the bargain. The public, whose inclination is to blame everybody and everything, justly considered, in this case, that everybody was in the wrong; Voltaire, for having offended Chevalier de Rohan; the latter, for having dared to commit a crime worthy of death in causing a citizen to be beaten; the government, for not having punished a notorious misdeed, and for having put the beatee in the Bastille to tranquillize the beater."

Voltaire left the Bastille on the 3rd of May, 1726, and was accompanied by an exon to Calais, having asked as a favour to be sent to England; but scarcely had he set foot on English territory, scarcely had he felt himself free, when the recurring sense of outraged honour made him take the road back to France. " I confess to you, my dear Thériot," he wrote to one of his friends, " that I made a little trip to Paris a short time ago. As I did not call upon you, you will easily conclude that I did not call upon anybody. I was in search of one man only, whom his dastardly instinct kept concealed from me, as if he guessed that I was on his track. At last the fear of being discovered made me depart more precipitately than I had come. That is the fact, my dear Thériot. There is every appearance of my never seeing you again. I have but two things to do with my life : to hazard it with honour, as soon as I can, and to end it in the obscurity of a retreat which suits my way of thinking, my misfortunes and the knowledge I have of men."

Voltaire passed three years in England, engaged in learning English and finishing *La Henriade*, which he published by subscription in 1727. Touched by the favour shown by English society to the author and the poem, he dedicated to the queen of England his new work, which was entirely consecrated to the glory of France ; three successive editions were disposed of in less than three weeks. Lord Bolingbroke, having returned to England and been restored to favour, did potent service to his old friend, who lived in the midst of that literary society in which Pope and Swift held sway, without, however, relaxing his reserve with its impress of melancholy. "I live the life of a *Rosicrucian*," he wrote to his friends, "always on the move and always in hiding." When, in the month of March, 1729, Voltaire at last obtained permission to revisit France, he had worked much without bringing out anything. The riches he had thus amassed appeared ere long : before the end of the year 1731 he put *Brutus* on the stage and began his publication of the *Histoire de Charles XII. ;* he was at the same time giving the finishing touch to *Ériphyle* and *La Mort de César.* *Zaïre*, written in a few weeks, was played for the first time on the 13th of August, 1732 ; he had dedicated it to Mr. Falkner, an English merchant who had overwhelmed him with attentions during his exile. " My satisfaction grows as I write to tell you of it," he writes to his friend Cideville in the fulness of joy : " never was a piece so well played as *Zaïre* at the fourth appearance. I very much wished you had been there ; you would have seen that the public does not hate your friend. I appeared in a box, and the whole pit clapped their hands at me. I blushed, I hid myself; but I should be a humbug, if I did not confess to you that I was sensibly affected. It is pleasant not to be dishonoured in one's own country."

Voltaire had just inaugurated the great national tragedy of his country, as he had likewise given it the only national epopee attempted in France since the *Chansons de geste ;* by one of those equally sudden and imprudent reactions to which he was always

subject, it was not long before he himself damaged his own success
by the publication of his *Lettres philosophiques sur les Anglais*.

The light and mocking tone of these letters, the constant comparison between the two peoples, with many a gibe at the English
but always turning to their advantage, the preference given to the
philosophical system of Newton over that of Descartes, lastly the
attacks upon religion concealed beneath the cloak of banter—
all this was more than enough to ruffle the tranquillity of
Cardinal Fleury. The book was brought before Parliament: Voltaire was disquieted. "There is but one letter about Mr. Locke,"
he wrote to M. de Cideville: "the only philosophical matter I
have treated of in it is the little trifle of the immortality of the soul,
but the thing is of too much consequence to be treated seriously.
It had to be mangled so as not to come into direct conflict with
our lords the theologians, gentry who so clearly see the spirituality
of the soul that, if they could, they would consign to the flames the
bodies of those who have a doubt about it." The theologians
confined themselves to burning the book; the decree of Parliament
delivered on the 10th of June, 1734, ordered at the same time the
arrest of the author; the bookseller was already in the Bastille.
Voltaire was in the country, attending the duke of Richelieu's
second marriage; hearing of the danger that threatened him, he
took fright and ran for refuge to Bâle. He soon left it to return
to the castle of Cirey, to the marchioness du Châtelet's, a woman
as learned as she was impassioned, devoted to literature, physics
and mathematics, and tenderly attached to Voltaire, whom she
enticed along with her into the paths of science. For fifteen years
Madame du Châtelet and Cirey ruled supreme over the poet's
life. There began a course of metaphysics, tales, tragedies;
Alzire, Mérope, Mahomet were composed at Cirey and played with
ever increasing success. Pope Benedict XIV. had accepted the
dedication of *Mahomet*, which Voltaire had addressed to him in order
to cover the freedoms of his piece. Every now and then, terrified
in consequence of some bit of antireligious rashness, he took flight,
going into hiding at one time to the court of Lorraine beneath the
wing of King Stanislaus, at another time in Holland, at a palace
belonging to the king of Prussia, the Great Frederick. Madame

du Châtelet, as unbelieving as he at bottom but more reserved in expression, often scolded him for his imprudence. "He requires every moment to be saved from himself," she would say : "I employ more policy in managing him than the whole Vatican employs to keep all Christendom in its fetters." On the appearance of danger, Voltaire ate his words without scruple ; his irreligious writings were usually launched under cover of the anonymous. At every step, however, he was advancing further and further into the lists, and at the very moment when he wrote to Father La Tour, "If ever anybody has printed in my name a single page which could scandalize even the parish-beadle, I am ready to tear it up before his eyes," all Europe regarded him as the leader of the open or secret attacks which were beginning to burst not only upon the catholic Church but upon the fundamental verities common to all Christians.

Madame du Châtelet died on the 4th of September, 1749, at Lunéville, where she then happened to be with Voltaire. Their intimacy had experienced many storms, yet the blow was a cruel one for the poet ; in losing Madame du Châtelet he was losing the centre and the guidance of his life. For a while he spoke of burying himself with Dom Calmet in the abbey of Senones ; then he would be off to England : he ended by returning to Paris, summoning to his side a widowed niece, Madame Denis, a woman of coarse wit and full of devotion to him, who was fond of the drama and played her uncle's pieces on the little theatre which he had fitted up in his rooms. At that time *Oreste* was being played at the Comédie-Française ; its success did not answer the author's expectations : "All that could possibly give a handle to criticism," says Marmontel, who was present, "was groaned at or turned into ridicule. The play was interrupted by it every instant. Voltaire came in, and, just as the pit were turning into ridicule a stroke of pathos, he jumped up and shouted, ' Oh ! you barbarians ; that is Sophocles ! ' *Rome Sauvée* was played on the stage of Sceaux, at the duchess of Maine's ; Voltaire himself took the part of Cicero. Lekain, as yet quite a youth and making his first appearance under the auspices of Voltaire, said of this representation : ' I do not think it possible to hear anything more pathetic and

real than M. de Voltaire: it was, in fact, Cicero himself thunder-
ing at the bar.' "

Despite the lustre of that fame which was attested by the
frequent attacks of his enemies as much as by the admiration of
his friends, Voltaire was displeased with his sojourn at Paris, and
weary of the Court and the men of letters. The king had always
exhibited towards him a coldness which the poet's adulation had
not been able to overcome ; he had offended Madame de Pompadour, who had but lately been well disposed towards him ; the
religious circle, ranged around the queen and the dauphin, was
of course hostile to him. " The place of historiographer to the
king was but an empty title," he says himself: " I wanted to make
it a reality by working at the history of the war of 1741 ; but, in
spite of my work, Moncrif had admittance to his Majesty and I
had not."

In tracing the tragic episodes of the war, Voltaire, set as his
mind was on the royal favour, had wanted in the first place to pay
homage to the friends he had lost. It was in the " eulogium of
the officers who fell in the campaign of 1741 " that he touchingly
called attention to the memory of Vauvenargues. He, born at Aix
on the 6th of August, 1715, died of his wounds, at Paris, in 1747.
Poor and proud, resigning himself with a sigh to idleness and
obscurity, the young officer had written merely to relieve his mind.
His friends had constrained him to publish a little book, one only, the
*Introduction à la connàissance de l'esprit humain, suivie de réflexions
et de maximes.* Its success justified their affectionate hopes :
delicate minds took keen delight in the first essays of Vauvenargues. Hesitating between religion and philosophy, with a
palpable leaning towards the latter, ill and yet bravely bearing
the disappointments and sufferings of his life, Vauvenargues was
already expiring at thirty years of age, when Provence was invaded by the enemy. The humiliation of his country and the peril
of his native province roused him from his tranquil melancholy: " All
Provence is in arms," he wrote to his friend Fauris de St Vincent,
" and here am I quite quietly in my chimney-corner ; the bad state
of my eyes and of my health is not sufficient excuse for me, and I
ought to be where all the gentlemen of the province are. Send

me word then, I beg, immediately whether there is still any employment to be had in our newly raised levies and whether I should be sure to be employed if I were to go to Provence." Before his friend's answer had reached Vauvenargues, the Austrians and the Piedmontese had been forced to evacuate Provence; the dying man remained in his chimney-corner, where he soon expired, leaving amongst the public and still more amongst those who had known him personally the impression of great promise sadly extinguished. "It was his fate," says his faithful biographer, M. Gilbert, "to be always opening his wings and to be unable to take flight."

Voltaire, quite on the contrary, was about to take a fresh flight. After several rebuffs and long opposition on the part of the eighteen ecclesiastics who at that time had seats in the French Academy, he had been elected to it in 1746. In 1750, he offered himself at one and the same time for the Academy of Sciences and the Academy of Inscriptions: he failed in both candidatures. This mishap filled the cup of his ill-humour. For a long time past Frederick II. had been offering the poet favours which he had long refused. The disgust he experienced at Paris through his insatiable vanity made him determine upon seeking another arena; after having accepted a pension and a place from the king of Prussia, Voltaire set out for Berlin.

But lately allied to France, to which he was ere long to deal such heavy blows, Frederick II. was French by inclination, in literature and in philosophy; he was a bad German scholar, he always wrote and spoke in French, and his court was the resort of the cultivated French wits too bold in their views to live in peace at Paris. Maupertuis, La Mettrie, and the marquis of Argens had preceded Voltaire to Berlin. He was received there with enthusiasm and as sovereign of the little court of philosophers. "A hundred and fifty thousand victorious soldiers," he wrote in a letter to Paris, "no attorneys, opera, plays, philosophy, poetry, a hero who is a philosopher and a poet, grandeur and graces, grenadiers and muses, trumpets and violins, Plato's symposium, society and freedom! Who would believe it? It is all true however!" Voltaire found his duties as chamberlain very light.

" It is Cæsar, it is Marcus Aurelius, it is Julian, it is sometimes Abbé Chaulieu, with whom I sup; there is the charm of retirement, there is the freedom of the country, with all those little delights of life which a lord of a castle who is a king can procure for his very obedient humble servants and guests. My own duties are to do nothing. I enjoy my leisure. I give an hour a day to the king of Prussia to touch up a bit his works in prose and verse : I am his grammarian, not his chamberlain. The rest of the day is my own and the evening ends with a pleasant supper. . . . . Never in any place in the world was there more freedom of speech touching the superstitions of men and never were they treated with more banter and contempt. God is respected, but all they who have cajoled men in His name are treated unsparingly." The coarseness of the Germans and the mocking infidelity of the French vied with each other in licence. Sometimes Voltaire felt that things were carried rather far. " Here be we, three or four foreigners, like monks in an abbey," he wrote : " please God the father abbot may content himself with making fun of us."

Literary or philosophical questions already gave rise sometimes to disagreements. " I am at present correcting the second edition which the king of Prussia is going to publish of the history of his country," wrote Voltaire; " fancy! in order to appear more impartial, he falls tooth and nail on his grandfather. I have lightened the blows as much as I could. I rather like this grandfather, because he displayed magnificence and has left some fine monuments. I had great trouble about softening down the terms in which the grandson reproaches his ancestor for his vanity in having got himself made a king; it is a vanity from which his descendants derive pretty solid advantages and the title is not at all a disagreeable one. At last I said to him : ' It is your grandfather, it is not mine; do what you please with him,' and I confined myself to weeding the expressions."

Whilst Voltaire was defending the Great Elector against his successor, a certain coldness was beginning to slide into his relations with Maupertuis, president of the Academy founded by the king at Berlin. " Maupertuis has not easy-going springs,' the poet wrote to his niece : " he takes my dimensions sternly with his quadrant. It is said that a little envy enters into his calculations." Already Voltaire's touchy vanity was shying at the rivals he encountered in the king's favour. " So it is known, then, by this time at Paris, my dear child," he writes to his niece, "that we have played the *Mort de César* at Potsdam, that Prince Henry is a good actor, has no accent, and is very amiable, and that this is the place for pleasure ? All that is true . . . but . . . The king's supper-parties are delightful ; at them people talk reason, wit, science ; freedom prevails thereat ; he is the soul of it all ; no ill temper, no clouds, at any rate no storms ; my life is free and well occupied . . . but . . . Opera, plays, carousals, suppers at Sans-Souci, military manœuvres, concerts, studies, readings . . . but . . . The city of Berlin, grand, better laid out than Paris ; palaces, play-houses, affable parish-priests, charming princesses, maids of honour beautiful and well made ; the mansion of Madame de Tyrconnel always full and sometimes too much so . . . but . . . but. . . . My dear child, the weather is beginning to settle down into a fine frost."

The " frost " not only affected Voltaire's relations with his brethren in philosophy, it reached even to the king himself. A far from creditable law-suit with a Jew completed Frederic's irritation. He forbade the poet to appear in his presence before the affair was over. " Brother Voltaire is doing penance here," wrote the latter to the margravine of Baireuth, the king of Prussia's amiable sister : " he has a beast of a lawsuit with a Jew, and, according to the law of the Old Testament, there will be something more to pay for having been robbed . . . ." Frederick, on his side, writes to his sister : " You ask me what the lawsuit is in which Voltaire is involved with a Jew. It is a case of a rogue wanting to cheat a thief. It is intolerable that a man of Voltaire's intellect should make so unworthy an abuse of it. The affair is in the hands of justice ; and, in a few days, we shall know from the sentence which is the greater rogue of the two. Voltaire lost his temper, flew in the Jew's face, and, in fact, behaved like a madman. I am waiting for this affair to be over to put his head under the pump (or reprimand him severely—*lui laver*

la tête) and see whether, at the age of fifty-six, one cannot make
him, if not reasonable, at any rate less of a rogue."

Voltaire settled matters with the Jew, at the same time asking
the king's pardon for what he called his giddiness. "This great
poet is always astride of Parnassus and Rue Quincampoix," said
the marquis of Argenson. Frederick had written him on the 24th
of February, 1751, a severe letter, the prelude and precursor of the
storms which were to break off before long the intimacy between the
king and the philosopher : " I was very glad to receive you," said the
king : " I esteemed your wit, your talents, your acquirements, and
I was bound to suppose that a man of your age, tired of wrangling
with authors and exposing himself to tempests, was coming hither
to take refuge as in a quiet harbour ; but you at the very first, in a
rather singular fashion, required of me that I should not engage
Fréron to write me news. D'Arnauld did you some injuries ; a
generous man would have pardoned them ; a vindictive man perse-
cutes those towards whom he feels hatred. In fine, though
D'Arnauld had done nothing so far as I was concerned, on your
account he had to leave. You went to the Russian minister's
to speak to him about matters you had no business to meddle with,
and it was supposed that I had given you instructions ; you meddled
in Madame de Bentinck's affairs, which was certainly not in your
province. Then you have the most ridiculous squabble in the
world with that Jew. You created a fearful uproar all through
the city. The matter of the Saxon bills is so well known in
Saxony that grave complaints have been made to me about them.
For my part, I kept peace in my household until your arrival,
and I warn you that, if you are fond of intrigue and cabal,
you have come to the wrong place. I like quiet and peaceable
folks who do not introduce into their behaviour the violent passions of tragedy ; in case you can make up your mind to live as a
philosopher, I shall be very glad to see you, but, if you give way to
the impetuosity of your feelings and quarrel with everybody, you
will do me no pleasure by coming hither, and you may just as well
remain at Berlin."

Voltaire was not proud, he readily heaped apology upon apology,
but he was irritable and vain; his ill-humour against Maupertuis

came out in a pamphlet, as bitter as it was witty, entitled, *La diatribe du docteur Akakia ;* copies were circulating in Berlin ; the satire was already printed anonymously, when the Great Frederick suddenly entered the lists.   He wrote to Voltaire : " Your effrontery astounds me after that which you have just done, and which is as clear as daylight. Do not suppose that you will make black appear white ; when one does not see, it is because one does not want to see everything ; but, if you carry matters to extremity, I will have everything printed, and it will then be seen that if your works deserve that statues should be raised to you, your conduct deserves handcuffs."

Voltaire, affrighted, still protesting his innocence, at last gave up the whole edition of the diatribe, which was burnt before his eyes in the king's own closet.   According to the poet's wily habit, some copy or other had doubtless escaped the flames.   Before long *Le docteur Akakia* appeared at Berlin, arriving modestly from Dresden by post ; people fought for the pamphlet, and everybody laughed ; the satire was spread over all Europe.   In vain did Frederick have it burnt on the Place d'Armes by the hands of the common hangman, he could not assuage the despair of Maupertuis.   " To speak to you frankly," the king at last wrote to the disconsolate president, " it seems to me that you take too much to heart both for an invalid and a philosopher an affair which you ought to despise.   How prevent a man from writing, and how prevent him from denying all the impertinences he has uttered ? I made investigations to find out whether any fresh satires had been sold at Berlin, but I heard of none ; as for what is sold in Paris, you are quite aware that I have not charge of the police of that city, and that I am not master of it. Voltaire treats you more gently than I am treated by the gazetteers of Cologne and Lubeck, and yet I don't trouble myself about it."

Voltaire could no longer live at Potsdam or at Sans-Souci, even Berlin seemed dangerous ; in a fit of that incurable perturbation which formed the basis of his character and made him commit so many errors, he had no longer any wish but to leave Prussia, only he wanted to go without embroiling himself with the king.   " I sent the Solomon of the North," he writes to Madame Denis on the

13th of January, 1753, " for his present, the cap and bells he gave
me, with which you reproached me so much. I wrote him a very
respectful letter, for I asked him for leave to go. What do you think
he did ? He sent me his great factotum Federshoff, who brought
me back my toys ; he wrote me a letter saying that he would rather
have me to live with than Maupertuis. What is quite certain is
that I would rather not live with either one or the other."

Frederick was vexed with Voltaire; he nevertheless found it
difficult to give up the dazzling charm of his conversation. Voltaire was hurt and disquieted, he wanted to get away ; the king,
however, exercised a strong attraction over him. But in spite of
mutual coquetting, making up, and protesting, the hour of separation was at hand; the poet was under pressure from his friends in
France ; in Berlin he had never completely neglected Paris. He
had just published his *Siècle de Louis XIV.*: he flattered himself
with the hope that he might again appear at court, though the
king had disposed of his place as historiographer in favour of
Duclos. Frederick at last yielded; he was on the parade, Voltaire
appeared there : " Ah ! Monsieur Voltaire," said the king, " so
you really intend to go away ? " " Sir, urgent private affairs and
especially my health leave me no alternative." " Monsieur, I wish
you a pleasant journey." Voltaire jumped into his carriage, and
hurried to Leipsic ; he thought himself free for ever from the
exactions and *tyrannies* of the king of Prussia.

The poet, according to his custom, had tarried on the way. He had
passed more than a month at Gotha, being overwhelmed with attentions by the duke, and by the duchess, for whom he wrote the dry
chronicle entitled *Les Annales de l'Empire.* He arrived at Frankfort
on the 31st of May only : the king's orders had arrived before him.

" Here is how this fine adventure came to pass," says Voltaire :
" There was at Frankfort one Freytag, who had been banished from
Dresden and had become an agent for the king of Prussia. . . . . .
He notified me on behalf of his Majesty that I was not to
leave Frankfort till I had restored the valuable effects I was
carrying away from his Majesty. ' Alack ! sir, I am carrying
away nothing from that country, if you please, not even the
smallest regret. What, pray, are those jewels of the Brandenburg

ARREST OF VOLTAIRE.

crown that you require?' 'It be, sir,' replied Freytag, 'the work of *poeshy* of the king, my gracious master.' 'Oh! I will give him back his prose and verse with all my heart,' replied I, 'though, after all, I have more than one right to the work. He made me a present of a beautiful copy printed at his expense. Unfortunately this copy is at Leipsic with my other luggage.' Then Freytag proposed to me to remain at Frankfort until the treasure which was at Leipsic should have arrived; and he signed an order for it."

The volume which Frederick claimed and which he considered it of so much importance to preserve from Voltaire's indiscretions contained amongst other things a burlesque and licentious poem, entitled the *Palladium*, wherein the king scoffed at everything and everybody in terms which he did not care to make public. He knew the reckless malignity of the poet who was leaving him, and he had a right to be suspicious of it; but nothing can excuse the severity of his express orders and still less the brutality of his agents. The package had arrived; Voltaire, agitated, anxious and ill, wanted to get away as soon as possible, accompanied by Madame Denis who had just joined him. Freytag had no orders, and refused to let him go; the prisoner loses his head, he makes up his mind to escape at any price, he slips from the hotel, he thinks he is free, but the police of Frankfort was well managed: " The moment I was off, I was arrested, I, my secretary and my people; my niece is arrested; four soldiers drag her through the mud to a cheesemonger's named Smith, who had some title or other of privy councillor to the king of Prussia; my niece had a passport from the king of France and, what is more, she had never corrected the king of Prussia's verses. They huddled us all into a sort of hostelry, at the door of which were posted a dozen soldiers; we were for twelve days prisoners of war, and we had to pay a hundred and forty crowns a day."

The wrath and disquietude of Voltaire no longer knew any bounds; Madame Denis was ill or feigned to be; she wrote letter upon letter to Voltaire's friends at the court of Prussia; she wrote to the king himself. The strife which had begun between the poet and the maladroit agents of the Great Frederick was becoming serious. " We would have risked our lives rather than let him get away," said Freytag; "and if I, holding a council of war with myself, had not found him at the barrier but in the open country, and he had refused to jog back, I don't know that I shouldn't have lodged a bullet in his head. To such a degree had I at heart the letters and writings of the king."

Freytag's zeal received a cruel rebuff: orders arrived to let the poet go. "I gave you no orders like that," wrote Frederick: "you should never make more noise than a thing deserves. I wanted Voltaire to give up to you the key, the cross and the volume of poems I had entrusted to him; as soon as all that was given up to you I can't see what earthly reason could have induced you to make this uproar." At last, on the 6th of July, "all this affair of Ostrogoths and Vandals being over," Voltaire left Frankfort precipitately. His niece had taken the road to Paris, whence she soon wrote to him: "There is nobody in France, I say nobody without exception, who has not condemned this violence mingled with so much that is ridiculous and cruel; it makes a deeper impression than you would believe. Everybody says that you could not do otherwise than you are doing, in resolving to meet with philosophy things so unphilosophical. We shall do very well to hold our tongues; the public speaks quite enough."

Voltaire held his tongue, according to his idea of holding his tongue, drawing in his poem of *La Loi naturelle,* dedicated at first to the margravine of Baireuth and afterwards to the duchess of Saxe-Gotha, a portrait of Frederick, which was truthful and at the same time bitter :—

> " Of incongruities a monstrous pile,
> Calling men brothers, crushing them the while ;
> With air humane, a misanthropic brute ;
> Ofttimes impulsive, sometimes over-'cute ;
> Weak 'midst his choler, modest in his pride ;
> Yearning for virtue, lust personified ;
> Statesman and author, of the slippery crew ;
> My patron, pupil, persecutor too."

Voltaire's intimacy with the Great Frederick was destroyed : it had for a while done honour to both of them, it had ended by betraying the pettinesses and the meannesses natural to the king as well as to the poet.   Frederick did not remain without anxiety on the score of Voltaire's rancour; Voltaire dreaded nasty diplomatic proceedings on the part of the king; he had been threatened with as much by Lord Keith, *Milord Maréchal*, as he was called on the Continent from the hereditary title he had lost in his own country through his attachment to the cause of the Stuarts :—

"Let us see in what countries M. de Voltaire has not had some squabble or made himself many enemies," said a letter to Madame Denis from the great Scotch lord when he had entered Frederick's service : "every country where the Inquisition prevails must be mistrusted by him; he would put his foot in it sooner or later. The Mussulmans must be as little pleased with his *Mahomet* as good Christians were.   He is too old to go to China and turn mandarin; in a word, if he is wise, there is no place but France for him.   He has friends there, and you will have him with you for the rest of his days; do not let him shut himself out from the pleasure of returning thither, for you are quite aware that, if he were to indulge in speech and epigrams offensive to the king my master, a word which the latter might order me to speak to the court of France would suffice to prevent M. de Voltaire from returning, and he would be sorry for it when it was too late."

Voltaire was already in France, but he dared not venture to Paris.   Mutilated, clumsy or treacherous issues of the *Abrégé de l'Histoire universelle* had already stirred the bile of the clergy; there were to be seen in circulation copies of *La Pucelle*, a disgusting poem which the author had been keeping back and bringing out alternately for several years past.   Voltaire fled from Colmar, where the Jesuits held sway, to Lyons, where he found Marshal Richelieu, but lately his protector and always his friend, who was repairing to his government of Languedoc.   Cardinal Tencin refused to receive the poet, who regarded this sudden severity as a sign of the feelings of the court towards him.   "The king told Madame de Pompadour that he did not want me to go to Paris; I am of his Majesty's opinion, I don't want to go to Paris," wrote Voltaire to the marquis of Paulmy.   He took fright and sought refuge in Switzerland, where he soon settled on the lake of Geneva, pending his purchase of the estate of Ferney in the district of Gex and that of Tourney in Burgundy. He was henceforth fixed, free to pass from France to Switzerland and from Switzerland to France. "I lean my left on Mount Jura," he used to say, "my right on the Alps, and I have the beautiful lake of Geneva in front of my camp, a beautiful castle on the borders of France, the hermitage of Délices in the territory of Geneva, a good house at Lausanne; crawling thus from one burrow to another, I escape from kings. Philosophers should always have two or three holes under ground against the hounds that run them down."

The perturbation of Voltaire's soul and mind was never stilled; the anxious and undignified perturbation of his outer life at last subsided: he left off trembling, and, in the comparative security which he thought he possessed, he gave scope to all his free-thinking, which had but lately been often cloaked according to circumstances. He had taken the communion at Colmar, to soften down the Jesuits; he had conformed to the rules of the convent of Senones, when he took refuge with Dom Calmet; at Délices he worked at the *Encyclopædia* which was then being commenced by D'Alembert and Diderot, taking upon himself in preference the religious articles and not sparing the creed of his neighbours, the pastors of Geneva, any more than that of the Catholic Church. "I assure you that my friends and I will lead them a fine dance; they shall drink the cup to the very lees," wrote Voltaire to D'Alembert. In the great campaign against Christianity undertaken by the philosophers, Voltaire, so long a wavering ally, will henceforth fight in the foremost ranks; it is he who shouts to Diderot, "Squelch the thing (*Écrasez l'infâme*)!" The masks are off, and the fight is bare-faced; the encyclopædists march out to the conquest of the world in the name of reason, humanity and free-thinking; even when he has ceased to work at the *Encyclopædia*, Voltaire marches with them.

The *Essai sur l'Histoire générale et les Mœurs* was one of the first broadsides of this new anti-religious crusade. "Voltaire will never write a good history," Montesquieu used to say: "he is like the monks, who do not write for the subject of which they treat, but for the glory of their order: Voltaire writes for his convent." The same intention betrayed itself in every sort of work that issued at that time from the hermitage of Délices, the poem on *Le Tremblement de terre de Lisbonne,* the drama of *Socrate,* the satire of the *Pauvre Diable,* the sad story of *Candide,* led the way to a series of publications every day more and more violent against the Christian faith. The tragedy of *l'Orphelin de la Chine* and that of *Tancrède,* the quarrels with Fréron, with Lefranc de Pompignan, and lastly with Jean Jacques Rousseau, did not satiate the devouring activity of the *Patriarch,* as he was called by the knot of philosophers. Definitively installed at Ferney, Voltaire took to building, planting, farming. He established round his castle a small industrial colony, for whose produce he strove to get a market everywhere. "Our design," he used to say, "is to ruin the trade of Geneva in a pious spirit." Ferney, moreover, held grand and numerously attended receptions; Madame Denis played her uncle's pieces on a stage which the latter had ordered to be built and which caused as much disquietude to the austere Genevese as to Jean Jacques Rousseau. It was on account of Voltaire's theatrical representations that Rousseau wrote his *Lettre contre les Spectacles.* "I love you not, sir," wrote Rousseau to Voltaire: "you have done me such wrongs as were calculated to touch me most deeply. You have ruined Geneva in requital of the asylum you have found there." Geneva was about to banish Rousseau before long, and Voltaire had his own share of responsibility in this act of severity so opposed to his general and avowed principles. Voltaire was angry with Rousseau, whom he accused of having betrayed the cause of philosophy; he was, as usual, hurried away by the passion of the moment, when he wrote, speaking of the exile: "I give you my word that if this blackguard (*polisson*) of a Jean Jacques should dream of coming (to Geneva), he would run great risk of mounting a ladder which would not be that of Fortune." At the very same time Rousseau was saying: "What have I done to bring upon myself the persecution of M. de Voltaire? And what worse have I to fear from him? Would M. de Buffon have me soften this tiger thirsting for my blood? He knows very well that nothing ever appeases or softens the fury of tigers; if I were to crawl upon the ground before Voltaire, he would triumph thereat, no doubt, but he would rend me none the less. Basenesses would dishonour me, but would not save me. Sir, I can suffer, I hope to learn how to die, and he who knows how to do that has never need to be a dastard."

Rousseau was high-flown and tragic ; Voltaire was cruel in his contemptuous levity ; but the contrast between the two philosophers was even greater in the depths of them than on the surface. Rousseau took his own words seriously, even when he was mad and his conduct was sure to belie them before long. He was the precursor of an impassioned and serious age, going to extremes in idea and placing deeds after words. In spite of occasional reticence dictated by sound sense, Voltaire had abandoned himself entirely in his old age to that school of philosophy, young, ardent, full of hope and illusions, which would fain pull down everything before it knew what it could set up, and the actions of which were not always in accordance with principles. " The men were inferior to their ideas." President De Brosses was justified in writing to Voltaire : " I only wish you had in your heart a half-quarter of the morality and philosophy contained in your works." Deprived of the counterpoise of political liberty, the emancipation of thought in the reign of Louis XV. had become at one and the same time a danger and a source of profound illusions ; people thought that they did what they said and that they meant what they wrote, but the time of actions and consequences had not yet come ; Voltaire applauded the severities against Rousseau, and still he was quite ready to offer him an asylum at Ferney ; he wrote to D'Alembert, " I am engaged in sending a priest to the galleys," at the very moment when he was bringing eternal honour to his name by the generous zeal which led him to protect the memory and the family of the unfortunate people named Calas.

The glorious and bloody annals of the French Reformation had passed through various phases ; liberty, always precarious, even under Henry IV. and whilst the Edict of Nantes was in force, and legally destroyed by its revocation, had been succeeded by periods of assuagement and comparative repose ; in the latter part of Louis XV.'s reign, about 1760, fresh severities had come to overwhelm the Protestants. Modestly going about their business, silent and timid, as inviolably attached to the king as to their hereditary creed, several of them had undergone capital punishment.　John Calas, accused of murdering his son, had been broken on the wheel at Toulouse; the reformers had been accustomed to these sombre dramas, but the spirit of the times had marched onward; ideas of justice, humanity and liberty, sown broad-cast by the philosophers, more imbued than they were themselves aware of with the holy influences of Christianity, had slowly and secretly acted upon men's minds; executions which had been so frequent in the sixteenth and seventeenth centuries caused trouble and dismay in the eighteenth; in vain did the fanatical passions of the populace of Toulouse find an echo in the magistracy of that city, it was no longer considered a matter of course that Protestants should be guilty of every crime, and that those who were accused should not be at liberty to clear themselves.　The philosophers had at first hesitated.　Voltaire wrote to Cardinal Bernis: " Might I venture to entreat your eminence to be kind enough to tell me what I am to think about the frightful case of this Calas, broken on the wheel at Toulouse on a charge of having hanged his own son ?　The fact is, they maintain here that he is quite innocent and that he called God to witness it. . . . . . This case touches me to the heart, it saddens my pleasures, it taints them.　Either the parliament of Toulouse or the Protestants must be regarded with eyes of horror." Being soon convinced that the parliament deserved all his indignation Voltaire did not grudge time, efforts or influence in order to be of service to the unfortunate remnant of the Calas family.　" I ought to look upon myself as in some sort a witness," he writes: " several months ago Peter Calas, who is accused of having assisted his father and mother in a murder, was in my neighbourhood with another of his brothers.　I have wavered a long while as to the innocence of this family; I could not believe that any judges would have condemned to a fearful death an innocent father of a family. There is nothing I have not done to enlighten myself as to the truth.　I dare to say that I am as sure of the innocence of this family as I am of my own existence."

For three years, with a constancy which he often managed to conceal beneath an appearance of levity, Voltaire prosecuted the work of clearing the Calas.　" It is Voltaire who is writing on behalf of this unfortunate family," said Diderot to Mdlle. Voland :

" O my friend, what a noble work for genius ! This man must needs have soul and sensibility; injustice must revolt him; he must feel the attraction of virtue. Why, what are the Calas to him ? What can awaken his interest in them ? What reason has he to suspend the labours he loves in order to take up their defence?" From the borders of the lake of Geneva, from his solitude at Genthod, Charles Bonnet, far from favourable generally to Voltaire, writes to Haller; "Voltaire has done a work on tolerance which is said to be good ; he will not publish it until after the affair of the unfortunate Calas has been decided by the king's council. Voltaire's zeal for these unfortunates might cover a multitude of sins ; that zeal does not relax, and, if they obtain satisfaction, it will be principally to his championship that they will owe it. He receives much commendation for this business, and he deserves it fully."

The sentence of the council cleared the accused and the memory of John Calas, ordering that their names should be erased and effaced from the registers, and the judgment transcribed upon the margin of the charge-sheet. The king at the same time granted Madame Calas and her children a gratuity of thirty-six thousand livres, a tacit and inadequate compensation for the expenses and losses caused them by the fanatical injustice of the parliament of Toulouse. Madame Calas asked no more. " To prosecute the judges and the ringleaders," said a letter to Voltaire from the generous advocate of the Calas, Elias de Beaumont, "requires the permission of the council, and there is great reason to fear that these petty plebeian kings appear powerful enough to cause the permission, through a weakness honoured by the name of policy, to be refused."

Voltaire, however, was triumphant. " You were at Paris," he writes to M. de Cideville, " when the last act of the tragedy finished so happily. The piece is according to the rules ; it is, to my think-ing, the finest fifth act there is on the stage." Henceforth he finds himself transformed into the defender of the oppressed. The Protestant Chaumont, at the galleys, owed to him his liberation ; he rushed to Ferney to thank Voltaire. The pastor, who had to introduce him, thus described the interview to Paul Rabaut : " I told him that I had brought him a little fellow who had come to throw himself at his feet to thank him for having, by his intercession, delivered him from the galleys, that it was Chaumont whom I had left in his antechamber, and whom I begged him to permit me to bring in. At the name of Chaumont M. de Voltaire showed a transport of joy and rang at once to have him brought in. Never did any scene appear to me more amusing and refreshing : ' What ! ' said he, ' my poor, little, good fellow, they sent you to the galleys ! What did they mean to do with you ? What a conscience they must have to put in fetters and chain to the oar a man who had committed no crime beyond praying to God in bad French ! ' He turned several times to me, denouncing persecution. He summoned into his room some persons who were staying with him, that they might share the joy he felt at seeing poor little Chaumont, who, though perfectly well attired for his condition, was quite astonished to find himself so well received. There was nobody, down to an ex-jesuit, Father Adam, who did not come forward to congratulate him."

Innate love of justice and horror of fanaticism had inspired Voltaire with his zeal on behalf of persecuted Protestants ; a more personal feeling, a more profound sympathy caused his grief and his dread when Chevalier de la Barre, accused of having mutilated a crucifix, was condemned, in 1766, to capital punishment ; the scepticism of the eighteenth century had sudden and terrible reactions towards fanatical violence, as a protest and a pitiable struggle against the doubt which was invading it on all sides ; the chevalier was executed ; he was not twenty years old. He was an infidel and a libertine, like the majority of the young men of his day and of his age ; the crime he expiated so cruelly was attributed to reading bad books, which had corrupted him. " I am told," writes Voltaire to D'Alembert, " that they said at their examination that they had been led on to the act of madness they committed by the works of the encyclopædists. I can scarcely believe it ; these madmen don't read ; and certainly no philosopher would have counselled profanation. The matter is important ; try to get to the bottom of so odious and dangerous a report." And, at another time, to Abbé Morellet : " You know that Councillor

Pasquier said in full parliament that the young men of Abbeville who were put to death had imbibed their impiety in the school and the works of the modern philosophers. . . . . They were mentioned by name, it is a formal denunciation. . . . . Wise men, under such terrible circumstances, should keep quiet and wait. . . . ."

Whilst keeping quiet, Voltaire soon grew frightened ; he fancied himself arrested even on the foreign soil on which he had sought refuge. "My heart is withered," he exclaims, "I am prostrated, I am tempted to go and die in some land where men are less unjust." He wrote to the Great Frederick, with whom he had resumed active correspondence, asking him for an asylum in the town of Clèves where he might find refuge together with the persecuted philosophers. His imagination was going wild. "I went to him," says the celebrated physician, Tronchin, an old friend of his ; "after I had pointed out to him the absurdity of his fearing that, for a mere piece of imprudence, France would come and seize an old man on foreign soil to shut him up in the Bastille, I ended by expressing my astonishment that a head like his should be deranged to the extent I saw it was. Covering his eyes with his clenched hands and bursting into tears: 'Yes, yes, my friend, I am mad!' was all he answered. A few days afterwards, when reflection had driven away fear, he would have defied all the powers of malevolence."

Voltaire did not find his brethren in philosophy so frightened and disquieted by ecclesiastical persecution as to fly to Clèves, far from "the home of society," as he had himself called Paris. In vain he wrote to Diderot: "A man like you cannot look save with horror upon the country in which you have the misfortune to live ; you really ought to come away into a country where you would have entire liberty not only to express what you pleased, but to preach openly against superstitions as disgraceful as they are sanguinary. You would not be solitary there ; you would have companions and disciples ; you might establish a chair there, the chair of truth. Your library might go by water, and there would not be four leagues' journey by land. In fine, you would leave slavery for freedom."

VOLTAIRE.

All these inducements having failed of effect, Voltaire gave up the foundation of a colony at Clèves, to devote all his energy to that at Ferney. There he exercised signorial rights with an active and restless guardianship which left him no illusions and but little sympathy in respect of that people whose sacred rights he had so often proclaimed. " The people will always be sottish and barbarous," he wrote to M. Bordes : " they are oxen needing a yoke, a goad, and a bit of hay." That was the sum and substance of what he thought; he was a stern judge of the French character, the genuine and deep-lying resources of which he sounded imperfectly, but the infinite varieties of which he recognized. " I always find it difficult to conceive," he wrote to M. de Constant, "how so agreeable a nation can at the same time be so ferocious, how it can so easily pass from the opera to the St. Bartholomew, be at one time made up of dancing apes and at another of howling bears, be so ingenious and so idiotic both together, at one time so brave and at another so dastardly." Voltaire fancied himself at a comedy still; the hour of tragedy was at hand. He and his friends were day by day weakening the foundations of the edifice; for eighty years past the greatest minds and the noblest souls have been toiling to restore it on new and strong bases; the work is not finished, revolution is still agitating the depths of French society, which has not yet recovered the only proper foundation-stones for greatness and order amongst a free people.

Henceforth Voltaire reigned peacefully over his little empire at Ferney, courted from afar by all the sovereigns of Europe who made any profession of philosophy. " I have a sequence of four kings" (*brelan de roi quatrième*), he would say with a laugh when he counted his letters from royal personages. The empress of Russia, Catherine II., had dethroned, in his mind, the Great Frederick. Voltaire had not lived in her dominions and at her court; he had no grievance against her; his vanity was flattered by the eagerness and the magnificent attentions of the *Semiramis of the North*, as he called her. He even forgave her the most odious features of resemblance to the Assyrian princess. " I am her knight in the sight and in the teeth of everybody," he wrote to

Madame du Deffand : " I am quite aware that people bring up
against her a few trifles on the score of her husband ; but these
are family matters with which I do not meddle, and besides it is
not a bad thing to have a fault to repair.   It is an inducement to
make great efforts in order to force the public to esteem and
admiration, and certainly her knave of a husband would never
have done any one of the great things my Catherine does every
day."   The portrait of the empress, worked in embroidery by
herself, hung in Voltaire's bedroom.   In vain had he but lately said
to Pastor Bertrand : " My dear philosopher, I have, thank God,
cut all connexion with kings ;" instinct and natural inclination
were   constantly re-asserting themselves.   Banished from the
court of Versailles by the disfavour of Louis XV., he turned in
despite towards the foreign sovereigns who courted him.   " Europe
is enough for me," he writes ; " I do not trouble myself much
about the Paris clique, seeing that that clique is frequently guided
by envy, cabal, bad taste, and a thousand petty interests which
are always opposed to the public interest."

Voltaire, however, returned to that Paris in which he was born,
in which he had lived but little since his early days, to which he
belonged by the merits as well as the defects of his mind, and in
which he was destined to die.   In spite of his protests about his
being a rustic and a republican, he had never allowed himself to
slacken the ties which united him to his Parisian friends ; the
letters of the patriarch of Ferney circulated amongst the philosophical fraternity ; they were repeated in the correspondence of
Grimm and Diderot with foreign princes ; from his splendid retreat
at Ferney he cheered and excited the literary zeal and often the
anti-religious ardour of the encyclopædists.   He had, however,
ceased all working connexion with that great work since it had
been suspended and afterwards resumed at the orders and with
the permission of Government.   The more and more avowed
materialistic theories revolted his shrewd and sensible mind ;
without caring to go to the bottom of his thought and contemplate
its consequences, he clung to the notion of Providence as to a waif
in the great shipwreck of positive creeds ; he could not imagine—

" This clock without a maker could exist."

it is his common sense, and not the religious yearnings of his soul, that makes him write in the poem of *La Loi naturelle :*

> O God, whom men ignore, whom everything reveals,
> Hear Thou the latest words of him who now appeals ;
> 'Tis searching out Thy law that hath bewilder'd me ;
> My heart may go astray, but it is full of Thee.

When he was old and suffering, he said to Madame Necker, in one of those fits of melancholy to which he was subject : " The thinking faculty is lost just like the eating, drinking and digesting faculties. The marionettes of Providence, in fact, are not made to last so long as It." In his dying hour Voltaire was seen showing more concern for terrestrial scandals than for the terrors of conscience, crying aloud for a priest and, with his mouth full of the blood he spat, still repeating in a half-whisper : " I don't want to be thrown into the kennel." A sad confession of the insufficiency of his convictions and of the inveterate levity of his thoughts ; he was afraid of the judgment of man without dreading the judgment of God. Thus was revealed the real depth of an infidelity of which Voltaire himself perhaps had not calculated the extent and the fatal influences.

Voltaire was destined to die at Paris ; there he found the last joys of his life and there he shed the last rays of his glory. For the twenty-seven years during which he had been away from it he had worked much, written much, done much. Whilst almost invariably disavowing his works, he had furnished philosophy with pointed and poisoned weapons against religion ; he had devoted to humanity much time and strength ; one of the last delights he had tasted was the news of the decree which cleared the memory of M. de Lally ; he had received into his house, educated and found a husband for the grand-niece of the great Corneille ; he had applied the inexhaustible resources of his mind at one time to good and at another to evil, with almost equal ardour ; he was old, he was ill, yet this same ardour still possessed him when he arrived at Paris on the 10th of February, 1778. The excitement caused by his return was extraordinary. " This new prodigy has stopped all other interest for some time," writes Grimm ; " it has put an end to rumours of war, intrigues in civil life, squabbles at court. Encyclopædic pride appeared diminished by half, the Sorbonne shook all over, the Parliament kept silence; all the literary world is moved, all Paris is ready to fly to the idol's feet." So much attention and so much glory had been too much for the old man. Voltaire was dying; in his fright he had sent for a priest and had confessed; when he rose from his bed by a last effort of the marvellous elasticity inherent in his body and his mind, he resumed for awhile the course of his triumphs. "M. de Voltaire has appeared for the first time at the Academy and at the play; he found all the doors, all the approaches to the Academy besieged by a multitude which only opened slowly to let him pass and then rushed in immediately upon his footsteps with repeated plaudits and acclamations. The Academy came out into the first room to meet him, an honour it had never yet paid to any of its members, not even to the foreign princes who had deigned to be present at its meetings. The homage he received at the Academy was merely the prelude to that which awaited him at the National theatre. As soon as his carriage was seen at a distance, there arose a universal shout of joy. All the kerb-stones, all the barriers, all the windows were crammed with spectators, and, scarcely was the carriage stopped, when people were already on the imperial and even on the wheels to get a nearer view of the divinity. Scarcely had he entered the house when Sieur Brizard came up with a crown of laurels which Madame de Villette placed upon the great man's head, but which he immediately took off, though the public urged him to keep it on by clapping of hands and by cheers which resounded from all corners of the house with such a din as never was heard.

"All the women stood up. I saw at one time that part of the pit which was under the boxes going down on their knees, in despair of getting a sight any other way. The whole house was darkened with the dust raised by the ebb and flow of the excited multitude. It was not without difficulty that the players managed at last to begin the piece. It was *Irène*, which was given for the sixth time. Never had this tragedy been better played, never less listened to, never more applauded. The illustrious old man rose to thank the public, and, the moment afterwards, there appeared on a pedestal in the middle of the stage a bust of this great man, and the actresses, garlands and crowns in hand, covered it with laurels; M. de Voltaire seemed to be sinking beneath the burden of age and of the homage with which he had just been overwhelmed. He appeared deeply affected, his eyes still sparkled amidst the pallor of his face, but it seemed as if he breathed no longer save with the consciousness of his glory. The people shouted: 'Lights! lights! that everybody may see him!' The coachman was entreated to go at a walk, and thus he was accompanied by cheering and the crowd as far as Pont Royal."

Thus is described in the words of an eye-witness the last triumph of an existence that had been one of ceaseless agitation, owing to Voltaire himself far more than to the national circumstances and events of the time at which he lived. His anxious vanity and the inexhaustible movement of his mind had kept him constantly fluctuating between alternations of intoxication and despair; he had the good fortune to die at the very pinnacle of success and renown, the only immortality he could comprehend or desire, at the outset of a new and hopeful reign; he did not see, he had never apprehended the terrible catastrophe to which he had been thoughtlessly contributing for sixty years. A rare piece of good fortune and one which might be considered too great, if the limits of eternal justice rested upon earth and were to be measured by our compass.

Voltaire's incessant activity bore many fruits which survived him; he contributed powerfully to the triumph of those notions of humanity, justice and freedom, which, superior to his own ideal, did honour to the eighteenth century; he became the model of a style, clear, neat, brilliant, the natural exponent of his own mind, far more than of the as yet confused hopes and aspirations of his age; he defended the rights of common sense and sometimes withstood the anti-religious passion of his friends, but he blasted both minds and souls with his sceptical gibes; his bitter and at the same time temperate banter disturbed consciences which would have been revolted by the materialistic doctrines of the Encyclopædists; the circle of infidelity widened under his hands; his disciples were able to go beyond him on the fatal path he had opened to them. Voltaire has remained the true representative of the mocking and stone-flinging phase of free-thinking, knowing nothing of the deep yearnings any more than of the supreme wretchlessness of the human soul, which it kept imprisoned within the narrow limits of earth and time. At the outcome from the bloody slough of the French Revolution and from the chaos it caused in men's souls, it was the infidelity of Voltaire which remained at the bottom of the scepticism and moral disorder of the France of our day. The demon which torments her is even more Voltairian than materialistic.

Other influences, more sincere and at the same time more dangerous, were simultaneously undermining men's minds. The group of Encyclopædists, less prudent and less temperate than Voltaire, flaunted openly the flag of revolt. At the head marched Diderot, the most daring of all, the most genuinely affected by his own ardour, without perhaps being the most sure of his ground in his negations. He was an original and exuberant nature, expansively open to all new impressions. " In my country," he says, " we pass within twenty-four hours from cold to hot, from calm to storm, and this changeability of climate extends to the persons. Thus, from earliest infancy they are wont to shift with every wind. The head of a Langrois stands on his shoulders like a weathercock on the top of a church-steeple; it is never steady at one point, and, if it comes round again to that which it had left, it is not to stop there. As for me, I am of my country; only residence at the capital and constant application have corrected me a little."

Narrow circumstances had their share in the versatility of Diderot's genius as well as in the variety of his labours. Son of a cutler at Langres, a strict and virtuous man, Denys Diderot, born in 1715, had at first been intended by his father for the church. He was educated at Harcourt College, and he entered an attorney's office. The young man worked incessantly, but not a law-book did he open. " What do you mean to be, pray ? " the lawyer asked him one day : " do you think of being an attorney ? " " No." " A barrister ? " " No." " A doctor ? " " No more than the rest." " What then ? " " Nothing at all. I like study, I am very happy, very contented, I ask no more." Diderot's father stopped the allowance he had been making his son, trusting thus to force him to choose a profession. But the young man gave lessons for a livelihood.

"I know a pretty good number of things," he wrote towards the end of his life, "but there is scarcely a man who doesn't know his own thing better than I do. This mediocrity in every sort is the consequence of insatiable curiosity and of means so small that they never permitted me to devote myself to one single branch of human knowledge. I have been forced all my life to

DIDEROT.

follow pursuits for which I was not adapted and to leave on one side those for which I had a call from inclination." Before he was thirty years old, and without any resource but his lessons and the work of every sort he did for third parties, Diderot married; he had not asked the consent of his parents, but this did not prevent him from saddling them before long with his wife and child. "She started yesterday," he writes quite simply to his father, "she will be with you in three days; you can say anything you like to her, and when you are tired of her you can send her back." Diderot intended to be free at any price, and he threw off, one after another, the fetters he had forged for himself, not without remorse, however, and not without acknowledging that he was thus wanting to all natural duties. "What can you expect," he would exclaim, "of a man who has neglected wife and daughter, got into debt, given up being husband and father?"

Diderot never neglected his friends; amidst his pecuniary embarrassments, when he was reduced to coin his brain for a livelihood, his labour and his marvellous facility were always at the service of all. It was to satisfy the requirements of a dangerous fair friend that he wrote his *Pensées philosophiques*, the sad tale of the *Bijoux indiscrets* and the *Lettre sur les Aveugles*, those early attacks upon religious faith which sent him to pass a few months in prison at the castle of Vincennes. It was to oblige Grimm that he for the first time gave his mind to painting and wrote his *Salons*, intended to amuse and instruct the foreign princes: "A pleasure which is only for myself affects me but slightly and lasts but a short time," he used to say: "it is for self and friends that I read, reflect, write, meditate, hear, look, feel. In their absence, my devotion towards them refers everything to them. I am always thinking of their happiness. Does a beautiful line strike me, they shall know it. Have I stumbled upon a beautiful trait, I make up my mind to communicate it to them. Have I before my eyes some enchanting scene; unconsciously, I meditate an account of it for them. To them I have dedicated the use of all my senses and of all my faculties, and that perhaps is the reason why everything is exaggerated, everything is embellished a little in my imagination and in my talk: and they sometimes reproach me with this, the ingrates!"

It was, further, in conjunction with his friends and in community of ideas that Diderot undertook the immense labour of the *Encyclopædia*. Having, in the first instance, received a commission from a publisher to translate the English collection of [Ephraim] Chambers, Diderot was impressed with a desire to unite in one and the same collection all the efforts and all the talents of his epoch, so as to render joint homage to the rapid progress of science. Won over by his enthusiasm, D'Alembert consented to share the task; and he wrote the beautiful exposition in the introduction. Voltaire sent his articles from *Délices*. The Jesuits had proposed to take upon

themselves a certain number of questions, but their co-operation
was declined : it was a monument to philosophy that the Encyclopædists aspired to raise : the clergy were in commotion at seeing
the hostile army, till then uncertain and unbanded, rally organized
and disciplined around this vast enterprise.   An early veto, soon,
however, taken off, compelled the philosophers to a certain
moderation : Voltaire ceased writing for the *Encyclopædia*, it was
not sufficiently free-going for him : " You admit articles worthy of
the Trévoux journal," he said to D'Alembert.   New severities
on the part of the Parliament and the grand council dealt a blow
to the philosophers before long : the editors' privilege was revoked.
Orders were given to seize Diderot's papers.   Lamoignon de
Malesherbes, who was at that time director of the press, and
favourable to freedom without ever having abused it in thought or
action, sent him secret warning.   Diderot ran home in consternation.   " What's to be done ? " he cried : " how move all my
manuscripts in twenty-four hours ?   I haven't time even to make
a selection.   And, above all, where find people who would and
can take charge of them safely ? "   " Send them all to me,"
replied M. de Malesherbes : " nobody will come thither to look
for them."

Feeble governments are ill served even by their worthiest
servants ; the severities ordered against the *Encyclopædia* did not
stop its publication ; D'Alembert, however, weary of the struggle,
had ceased to take part in the editorship.   Naturally cool and
moderate, when it was nothing to do with Mdlle. de Lespinasse,
the great affection of his life, the illustrious geometer was content
with a little : " Twelve hundred livres a year are enough for me,"
he wrote to the Great Frederick who was pressing him to settle in
his dominions : " I will not go and reap the succession to Maupertuis during his lifetime.   I am overlooked by government, just as
so many others by Providence : persecuted as much as anybody
can be, if some day I have to fly my country, I will simply ask Frederick's permission to go and die in his dominions, free and poor."

Frederick II. gave D'Alembert a pension ; it had but lately been
Louis XIV. who thus lavished kindnesses on foreign scholars : he
made an offer to the Encyclopædists to go and finish their vast

undertaking at Berlin. Catherine II. made the same offers, asking D'Alembert, besides, to take charge of the education of her son: " I know your honesty too well," she wrote, " to attribute your refusals to vanity, I know that the cause is merely love of repose in order to cultivate literature and friendship. But what is to prevent your coming with all your friends ? I promise you and them too all the comforts and every facility that may depend apon me : and perchance you will find more freedom and repose than you have at home. You do not yield to the entreaties of the king of Prussia and to the gratitude you owe him, it is true, but then he has no son. I confess that I have my son's education so much at heart and that you are so necessary to me that perhaps I press you too much. Pardon my indiscretion for the reason's sake, and rest assured that it is esteem which has made me so selfish."

D'Alembert declined the education of the hereditary Grand Duke, just as he had declined the presidency of the Academy at Berlin ; an infidel and almost a materialist by the geometer's rule, who knows no power but the laws of mathematics, he did not carry into anti-religious strife the bitterness of Voltaire, or the violence of Diderot. " Squelch the thing ! you are always repeating to me," he said to Voltaire on the 4th of May, 1762. " Ah ! my good friend, let it go to rack and ruin of itself, it is hurrying thereto faster than you suppose." More and more absorbed by pure science, which he never neglected save for the French Academy, whose perpetual secretary he had become, D'Alembert left to Diderot alone the care of continuing the *Encyclopædia.* When he died, in 1783, at fifty-six years of age, the work had been finished nearly twenty years. In spite of the bad faith of publishers, who mutilated articles to render them acceptable, in spite of the condemnation of the clergy and the severities of the council, the last volumes of the *Encyclopædia* had appeared in 1765.

This immense work, unequal and confused as it was, a medley of various and often ill-assorted elements, undertaken for and directed to the fixed end of an aggressive emancipation of thought, had not sufficed to absorb the energy and powers of Diderot. " I am awaiting with impatience the reflections of Pantophile Diderot on *Tancrède,*" wrote Voltaire: " everything is within the sphere of activity of his genius: he passes from the heights of metaphysics to the weaver's trade, and thence he comes to the stage."

The stage, indeed, occupied largely the attention of Diderot, who sought to introduce reforms, the fruit of his own thought as well as of imitation of the Germans, which he had not perhaps sufficiently considered. For the classic tragedies, the heritage of which Voltaire received from the hands of Racine, Diderot aspired to substitute the *natural drama*. His two attempts in that style, *Le Père de Famille* and *Le Fils naturel*, had but little success in

E.RONJAT.   J. LOSBALD

D'ALEMBERT.

France, and contributed to develope in Germany the school already founded by Lessing. An excess of false sensibility and an inflation of expression had caused certain true ideas to fall flat on the French stage. "You have the inverse of dramatic talent," said Abbé Arnauld to Diderot; "the proper thing is to transform oneself into all the characters, and you transform all the characters into yourself." The criticism did Diderot wrong: he had more wits than his characters, and he was worth more at bottom than those whom he described. Carried away by the richness as well as the unruliness of his mind, destitute as he was of definite and

fixed principles, he recognized no other moral law than the natural
impulse of the soul : " There is no virtue or vice," he used to say,
" but innate goodness or badness." Certain religious cravings,
nevertheless, sometimes asserted themselves in his conscience : he
had a glimmering perception of the necessity for a higher rule and
law : " O God, I know not whether Thou art," he wrote in
his *Interprétation de la Nature,* " but I will think as if Thou didst
see into my soul, I will act as if I were in Thy presence."

A strange illusion on the part of the philosopher about the
power of ideas as well as about the profundity of evil in the
human heart ! Diderot fancied he could regulate his life by a
perchance, and he was constantly hurried away by the torrent of
his passion into a violence of thought and language foreign to his
natural benevolence. It was around his name that the philosophic
strife had waxed most fierce : the active campaign undertaken by
his friends to open to him the doors of the French Academy
remained unsuccessful : " He has too many enemies," said Louis
XV., " his election shall not be sanctioned." Diderot did not offer
himself ; he set out for St. Petersburg ; the Empress Catherine
had loaded him with kindnesses. Hearing of the poverty of the
philosopher who was trying to sell his library to obtain a dower
for his daughter, she bought the books, leaving the enjoyment of
them to Diderot, whom she appointed her librarian, and, to secure
his maintenance in advance, she had a sum of fifty thousand livres
remitted to him. " So here I am obliged, in conscience, to live
fifty years," said Diderot.

He passed some months in Russia, admitted several hours
a day to the closet of the empress, chatting with a frankness
and a freedom which sometimes went to the extent of licence.
Catherine II. was not alarmed : " Go on," she would say :
" amongst men, anything is allowable." When the philosopher
went away, he shed hot tears, and " so did she, almost," he
declares. He refused to go to Berlin : absolute power appeared
to him more arbitrary and less indulgent in the hands of Frederick
than with Catherine. " It is said that at Petersburg Diderot is
considered a tiresome reasoner," wrote the king of Prussia to
D'Alembert in January, 1774 ; " he is incessantly harping on the

DIDEROT AND CATHERINE II.

same things. All I know is that I couldn't stand the reading of his books, intrepid reader as I am ; there is a self-sufficient tone and an arrogance in them which revolts my sense of freedom." The same sense of freedom which the king claimed for himself whilst refusing it to the philosopher, the philosopher, in his turn, refused to Christians, not less intolerant than he. The eighteenth century did not practise on its own account that respect for conscience which it, nevertheless, powerfully and to its glory promoted.

Diderot died on the 29th of July, 1784, still poor, an invalid for some time past, surrounded to the end by his friends, who rendered back to him that sincere and devoted affection which he made the pride of his life. Hearing of his sufferings from Grimm, the Empress Catherine had hired a furnished apartment for him ; he had just installed himself in it, when he expired ; without having retracted any one of his works, nearly all published under the veil of the anonymous, he was, nevertheless, almost reconciled with the Church, and was interred quietly in the chapel of the Virgin at St. Roch. The charm of his character had often caused people to forget his violence, which he himself no longer remembered the next day. " I should like to know this hot-headed metaphysician," was the remark made to Buffon by President De Brosses, who happened to be then at Paris ; and he afterwards added : " He is a nice fellow, very pleasant, very amiable, a great philosopher, a mighty arguer, but a maker of perpetual digressions. Yesterday he made quite five and twenty between nine o'clock and one, during which time he remained in my room. Oh ! how much more lucid is Buffon than all those gentry ! "

The magistrate's mind understood and appreciated the great naturalist's genius. Diderot felt in his own fashion the charm of nature, but, as was said by Chevalier Chastellux, " his ideas got drunk and set to work chasing one another." The ideas of Buffon, on the other hand, came out in the majestic order of a system under powerful organization and informed as it were with the very secrets of the Creator. " The general history of the world," he says, " ought to precede the special history of its productions ; and the details of singular facts touching the life

and habits of animals, or touching the culture and vegetation of
plants, belong perhaps less to natural history than do the general
results of the observations which have been made on the different
materials which compose the terrestrial globe, on the elevations,
the depressions and the unevennesses of its form, on the movement
of the seas, on the trending of mountains, on the position of
quarries, on the rapidity and effects of the currents of the sea—
this is nature on the grand scale."

M. Fleurens truly said : " Buffon aggrandises every subject he
touches."

Born at Montbard in Burgundy on the 7th of September, 1707,
Buffon belonged to a family of wealth and consideration in his
province.   In his youth he travelled over Europe with his friend
the duke of Kingston ; on returning home, he applied himself at
first to mathematics, with sufficient success to be appointed at
twenty-six years of age, in 1733, *adjunct* in the mechanical class
at the Academy of Sciences.   In 1739, he received the superintendence of the Jardin du Roi, not long since enlarged and
endowed by Richelieu, and lovingly looked after by the scholar
Dufay, who had just died, himself designating Buffon as his
successor.   He had shifted from mechanics to botany, " not," he
said, " that he was very fond of that science, which he had learnt
and forgotten three times," but he was aspiring just then to the
Jardin du Roi ; his genius was yet seeking its proper direction.
" There are some things for me," he wrote to President De Brosses,
" but there are some against, and especially my age ; however, if
people would but reflect, they would see that the superintendence
of the Jardin du Roi requires an active young man, who can stand
the sun, who is conversant with plants and knows the way to
make them multiply, who is a bit of a connoisseur in all the sorts
used in demonstration there, and above all who understands
buildings, in such sort that, in my own heart, it appears to me
that I should be exactly made for them ; but I have not as yet any
great hope."

In Buffon's hands the Jardin du Roi was transformed ; in proportion as his mind developed, the requirements of the study
appeared to him greater and greater ; he satisfied them fearlessly,

getting together collections at his own expense, opening new galleries, constructing hot-houses, being constantly seconded by the good-will of Louis XV., who never shrank from expenses demanded by Buffon's projects. The great naturalist died at eighty years of age, without having completed his work ; but he had imprinted upon it that indisputable stamp of greatness which was the distinctive feature of his genius. The Jardin du Roi, which became the Jardin des Plantes, has remained unique in Europe.

Fully engaged as he was in those useful labours, from the age of thirty, Buffon gave up living at Paris for the greater part of the year. He had bought the ruins of the castle of Montbard, the ancient residence of the dukes of Burgundy, overlooking his native town. He had built a house there which soon became dear to him, and which he scarcely ever left for eight months in the year. There it was, in a pavilion which overhung the garden planted in terraces, and from which he had a view of the rich plains of La Brenne, that the great naturalist, carefully dressed by five o'clock in the morning, meditated the vast plan of his works as he walked from end to end and side to side. " I passed delightful hours there," he used to say. When he summoned his secretary, the work of composition was completed. " M. de Buffon gives reasons for the preference he shows as to every word in his discourses, without excluding from the discussion even the smallest particles, the most insignificant conjunctions," says Madame Necker : " he never forgot that he had written ' the style is the man.' The language could not be allowed to derogate from the majesty of the subject. ' I made it a rule,' he used to say, ' to always fix upon the noblest expressions.' "

It was in this dignified and studious retirement that Buffon quietly passed his long life. " I dedicated," he says, " twelve, nay fourteen, hours to study ; it was my whole pleasure. In truth, I devoted myself to it far more than I troubled myself about fame ; fame comes afterwards, if it may, and it nearly always does."

Buffon did not lack fame ; on the appearance of the first three volumes of his *Histoire naturelle*, published in 1749, the breadth of his views, the beauty of his language and the strength of his mind excited general curiosity and admiration. The Sorbonne was in a flutter at certain bold propositions; Buffon, without being disconcerted, took pains to avoid condemnation. "I took the liberty," he says in a letter to M. Leblant, "of writing to the duke of Nivernais (then ambassador at Rome), who has replied to me in the most polite and most obliging way in the world; I hope, therefore, that my book will not be put in the Index, and, in truth, I have done all I could not to deserve it and to avoid theological squabbles, which I fear far more than I do the criticisms of physicists and geometricians." "Out of a hundred and twenty assembled doctors," he adds before long, "I had a hundred and fifteen, and their resolution even contains eulogies which I did not expect." Despite certain boldnesses which had caused anxiety, the Sorbonne had reason to compliment the great naturalist. The unity of the human race as well as its superior dignity were already vindicated in these first efforts of Buffon's genius, and his mind never lost sight of this great verity. "In the human species," he says, "the influence of climate shows itself only by slight varieties, because this species is one and is very distinctly separated from all other species; man, white in Europe, black in Africa, yellow in Asia and red in America, is only the same man tinged with the hue of climate; as he is made to reign over the earth, as the whole globe is his domain, it seems as if his nature were ready prepared for all situations; beneath the fires of the south, amidst the frosts of the north, he lives, he multiplies, he is found to be so spread about everywhere from time immemorial that he appears to affect no climate in particular. . . . . Whatever resemblance there may be between the Hottentot and the monkey, the interval which separates them is immense, since internally he is garnished with mind and externally with speech."

Buffon continued his work, adroitly availing himself of the talent and researches of the numerous co-operators whom he had managed to gather about him, directing them all with indefatigable vigilance in their labours and their observations. "Genius is but a greater aptitude for perseverance," he used to say, himself justifying his definition by the assiduity of his studies. "I had come to the sixteenth volume of my work on natural history," he writes with bitter regret, "when a serious and long illness interrupted for nearly two years the course of my labours.   This shortening of my life, already far advanced, caused one in my works.   I might, in the two years I have lost, have produced two or three volumes of the history of birds, without abandoning for that my plan of a history of minerals, on which I have been engaged for several years."

In 1753 Buffon had been nominated a member of the French Academy.   He had begged his friends to vote for his compatriot, Piron, author of the celebrated comedy *Métromanie*, at that time an old man and still poor.   " I can wait," said Buffon.   " Two days before that fixed for the election," writes Grimm, " the king sent for President Montesquieu, to whose lot it had fallen to be director of the Academy on that occasion, and told him that, understanding that the Academy had cast their eyes upon M. Piron and knowing that he was the author of several licentious works, he desired the Academy to choose some one else to fill the vacant place.   His Majesty at the same· time told him that he would not have any member belonging to the order of advocates."

Buffon was elected, and on the 25th of August, 1754, St. Louis' day, he was formally received by the Academy ; Grimm describes the session : " M. de Buffon did not confine himself to reminding us that Chancellor Séguier was a great man, that Cardinal Richelieu was a very great man, that Kings Louis XIV. and Louis XV. were very great men too, that the archbishop of Sens (whom he succeeds) was also a great man, and finally that all the forty were great men ; this celebrated man, disdaining the stale and heavy eulogies which are generally the substance of this sort of speech, thought proper to treat of a subject worthy of his pen and worthy of the Academy.   He gave us his ideas on style, and it was said, in consequence, that the Academy had engaged a writing-master."

" Well-written works are the only ones which will go down to posterity," said Buffon in his speech ; " quantity of knowledge, singularity of facts, even novelty in discoveries are not certain guarantees of immortality ; knowledge, facts, discoveries are easily abstracted and transferred.   Those things are outside the man ; the style is the man himself ; the style, then, cannot be abstracted or transferred or tampered with ; if it be elevated, noble, sublime, the author will be equally admired at all times, for it is only truth that is durable and even eternal."

Never did the great scholar who has been called " the painter of nature" relax his zeal for painstaking as a writer. "I am every day learning to write," he would still say at seventy years of age.

To the *Théorie de la Terre*, the *Idées générales sur les Animaux* and the *Histoire de l'Homme*, already published when Buffon was elected by the French Academy, succeeded the twelve volumes of the *Histoire des Quadrupèdes*, a masterpiece of luminous classifications and incomparable descriptions; eight volumes on *Oiseaux* appeared subsequently, a short time before the *Histoire des Minéraux;* lastly, a few years before his death, Buffon gave to the world the *Époques de la Nature.* " As in civil history one consults titles, hunts up medals, deciphers antique inscriptions to determine the epochs of revolutions amongst mankind, and to fix the date of events in the moral world, so, in natural history, we must ransack the archives of the universe, drag from the entrails of the earth the olden monuments, gather together their ruins and collect into a body of proofs all the indications of physical changes that can guide us back to the different ages of nature. It is the only way of fixing certain points in the immensity of space and of placing a certain number of memorial-stones on the endless road of time."

" This is what I perceive with my mind's eye," Buffon would say, " thus forming a chain which, from the summit of Time's ladder, descends right down to us." " This man," exclaimed Hume, with an admiration which surprised him out of his scepticism, "this man gives to things which no human eye has seen a probability almost equal to evidence."

Some of Buffon's theories have been disputed by his successors' science ; as D'Alembert said of Descartes : " If he was mistaken about the laws of motion, he was the first to divine that there must be some." Buffon divined the epochs of nature, and by the intuition of his genius, absolutely unshackled by any religious prejudice, he involuntarily reverted to the account given in Genesis : " We are persuaded," he says, "independently of the authority of the sacred books, that man was created last and that he only came to wield the sceptre of the earth when that earth was found worthy of his sway."

It has often been repeated, on the strength of some expressions let fall by Buffon amongst intimates, that the panorama of nature had shut out from his eyes the omnipotent God, creator and preserver of the physical world as well as of the moral law. Wrong has been done the great naturalist; he had answered beforehand these incorrect opinions as to his fundamental ideas. "Nature is not a being," he said; "for that being would be God;" and he adds: "Nature is the system of the laws established by the Creator." The supreme notion of Providence appears to his eyes in all its grandeur, when he writes: "The verities of nature were destined to appear only in course of time, and the Supreme Being kept them to Himself as the surest means of recalling man to Him when his faith, declining in the lapse of ages, should become weak; when, remote from his origin, he might begin to forget it; when, in fine, having become too familiar with the spectacle of nature, he would no longer be moved by it and would come to ignore the Author. It was necessary to confirm from time to time and even to enlarge the idea of God in the mind and heart of man. Now every new discovery produces this grand effect, every new step that we make in nature brings us nearer to the Creator. A new verity is a species of miracle; its effect is the same and it only differs from the real miracle in that the latter is a startling stroke which God strikes instantaneously and rarely instead of making use of man to discover and exhibit the marvels which He has hidden in the womb of Nature, and in that, as these marvels are operating every instant, as they are open at all times and for all time to his contemplation, God is constantly recalling him to Himself, not only by the spectacle of the moment but, further, by the successive development of His works."

Buffon was still working at eighty years of age; he had undertaken a dissertation on style, a development of his reception-speech at the French Academy. Great sorrows had crossed his life; married late to a young wife whom he loved, he lost her early; she left him a son, brought up under his wing and the object of his constant solicitude.   Just at the time of sending him to school, he wrote to Madame Daubenton, wife of his able and learned co-operator : " I expect Buffonet on Sunday ; I have arranged all his little matters : he will have a private room, with a closet for his man-servant ; I have got him a tutor in the school-house itself, and a little companion of his own age ; I do not think that he will be at all unhappy."   And, at a later date, when he is expecting this son who has reached man's estate and has been travelling in Europe : " My son has just arrived ; the empress and the grand duke have treated him very well and we shall have some fine minerals, the collection of which is being at this moment completed.   I confess that anxiety about his return has taken away my sleep and the power of thinking."

When the young Count de Buffon, an officer in the artillery and at first warmly favourable to the noble professions of the French Revolution, had, like his peers, to mount the scaffold of the Terror, he damned with one word the judges who profaned in his person his father's glory.   " Citizens," he exclaimed from the fatal car, " my name is Buffon."   With less respect for the rights of genius than was shown by the Algerian pirates who let pass, without opening them, the chests directed to the great naturalist, the executioner of the Committee of public safety cut off his son's head.

This last drop of bitterness and the cruel spectacle of social disorder Buffon had been spared ; he had died at the Jardin du Roi on the 14th of April, 1788, preserving at eighty years of age and even in the feebleness of ill health all the powers of his intelligence and the calm serenity of his soul ; his last lines dictated to his son were addressed to Madame Necker, who had been for a long time past on the most intimate terms with him.   Faithful in death to the instincts of order and regularity which had always controlled his mind even in his boldest flight, he requested that all the ceremonies of religion should be fulfilled around his body. His son had it removed to Montbard, where it lies between his father and his wife.

Buffon had lived long, he had accomplished in peace his great work, he had reaped the fruits of it ; on the eve of the terrible

BUFFON.

shocks whereof no presage disturbed his spirit, "directed for fifty years towards the great objects of nature," the illustrious scholar had been permitted to see his statue placed during his lifetime in the Jardin du Roi.   On sending to the Empress Catherine his bust which she had asked him for, he wrote to his son who had charge of it : " I forgot to remark to you whilst talking of bust and effigy that, by the king's order, they have put at the bottom of my statue the following inscription : *Majestati naturæ par ingenium* (*Genius to match the majesty of nature*).   It is not from pride that I send you this, but perhaps Her Majesty will have it put at the bottom of the bust."

" How many great men do you reckon ?" Buffon was asked one day.   " Five," answered he at once : " Newton, Bacon, Leibnitz, Montesquieu and myself."

This self-appreciation, fostered by the homage of his contemporaries, which showed itself in Buffon undisguisedly with an air of ingenuous satisfaction, had poisoned a life already extinguished ten years before amidst the bitterest agonies.   Taking up arms against a society in which he had not found his proper place, Jean Jacques Rousseau had attacked the present as well as the past, the Encyclopædists as well as the old social organization.   It was from the first his distinctive trait to voluntarily create a desert around him. The eighteenth century was in its nature easily seduced; liberal, generous and open to allurements, it delighted in intellectual contentions, even the most dangerous and the most daring; it welcomed with alacrity all those who thus contributed to its pleasures.   The charming drawing-rooms of Madame Geoffrin, of Madame du Deffand, of Madlle. Lespinasse, belonged of right to philosophy.   " Being men of the world as well as of letters, the philosophers of the eighteenth century had passed their lives in the pleasantest and most brilliant regions of that society which was so much attacked by them.   It had welcomed them, made them famous; they had mingled in all the pleasures of its elegant and agreeable existence ; they shared in all its tastes, its manners, all the refinements, all the susceptibilities of a civilization at the same time old and rejuvenated, aristocratic and literary; they were of that old regimen which was demolished by their hands.

The philosophical circle was everywhere, amongst the people of the court, of the church, of the long robe, of finance; haughty here, complaisant there, at one time indoctrinating, at another amusing its hosts, but everywhere young, active, confident, recruiting and battling everywhere, penetrating and fascinating the whole of society" [M. Guizot, *Madame la comtesse de Rumford*]. Rousseau never took his place in this circle; in this society, he marched in front like a pioneer of new times, attacking tentatively all that he encountered on his way. "Nobody was ever at one and the same time more factious and more dictatorial," is the clever dictum of M. Saint Marc Girardin.

Rousseau was not a Frenchman: French society always felt that, in consequence of certain impressions of his early youth which were never to be effaced. Born at Geneva on the 28th of June, 1712, in a family of the lower middle class, and brought up in the first instance by an intelligent and a pious mother, he was placed, like Voltaire and Diderot, in an attorney's office. Dismissed with disgrace "as good for nothing but to ply the file," the young man was bound apprentice to an engraver, "a clownish and violent fellow," says Rousseau, "who succeeded very shortly in dulling all the brightness of my boyhood, brutalizing my lively and loving character and reducing me in spirit, as I was in fortune, to my real position of an apprentice."

Rousseau was barely sixteen when he began that roving existence, which is so attractive to young people, so hateful in ripe age, and which lasted as long as his life. Flying from his master whose brutality he dreaded, and taking refuge at Charmettes in Savoy with a woman whom he at first loved passionately, only to leave her subsequently with disgust, he had reached the age of one and twenty and had already gone through many adventures when he set out, heart-sore and depraved, to seek at Paris a means of subsistence. He had invented a new system of musical notation; the Academy of sciences, which had lent him a favourable ear, did not consider the discovery useful. Some persons had taken an interest in him, but Rousseau could never keep his friends; and he had many, zealous and devoted. He was sent to Venice as secretary to the French ambassador

M. de Montaigu. He soon quarrelled with the ambassador and returned to Paris. He found his way into the house of Madame Dupin, wife of a rich farmer-general (of taxes). He was considered clever; he wrote little plays, which he set to music. Enthusiastically welcomed by the friends of Madame Dupin, he contributed to their amusements. "We began with the *Engagement téméraire*," says Madame d'Épinay in her *Mémoires :* "it is a new play by M. Rousseau, a friend of M. de Francueil's, who introduced him to us. The author played a part in his piece. Though it is only a society-play, it was a great success. I doubt, however, whether it would be successful at the theatre, but it is the work of a clever man and no ordinary man. I do not quite know, though, whether it is what I saw of the author or of the piece that made me think so. He is complimentary without being polite or at least without having the air of it. He seems to be ignorant of the usages of society, but it is easy to see that he has infinite wit. He has a brown complexion, and eyes full of fire light up his face. When he has been speaking and you watch him, you think him good-looking; but, when you recall him to memory, it is always as a plain man. He is said to be in bad health; it is probably that which gives him from time to time a wild look."

It was amidst this brilliant intimacy, humiliating and pleasant at the same time, that Rousseau published his *Discours sur les Sciences et les Arts*. It has been disputed whether the inspiration was such as he claimed for this production, the first great work which he had ever undertaken and which was to determine the direction of his thoughts. "I was going to see Diderot at Vincennes," he says, "and, as I walked, I was turning over the leaves of the *Mercure de France*, when I stumbled upon this question proposed by the Academy of Dijon: *Whether the advance of sciences and arts has contributed to the corruption or purification of morals*. All at once I felt my mind dazzled by a thousand lights, crowds of ideas presented themselves at once with a force and a confusion which threw me into indescribable bewilderment; I felt my head seized with a giddiness like intoxication, a violent palpitation came over me, my bosom began to heave. Unable to breathe any longer as I walked, I flung myself down under one of

the trees in the avenue and there spent half an hour in such
agitation that, on rising up, I found all the front of my waistcoat
wet with tears without my having had an idea that I had shed
any." Whether it were by natural intuition or the advice of
Diderot, Jean Jacques had found his weapons; poor and obscure
as he was, he attacked openly the brilliant and corrupt society
which had welcomed him for its amusement. Spiritualistic at
heart and nurtured upon Holy Scripture in his pious childhood, he
felt a sincere repugnance for the elegant or cynical materialism
which was every day more and more creeping over the eighteenth
century. "Sciences and arts have corrupted the world," he said,
and he put forward, as proof of it, the falsity of the social code,
the immorality of private life, the frivolity of the drawing-rooms
into which he had been admitted. "Suspicions, heartburnings,
apprehensions, coldness, reserve, hatred, treason lurk incessantly
beneath that uniform and perfidious veil of politeness, under that
so much vaunted urbanity which we owe to the enlightenment of
our age."

Rousseau had launched his paradox; the frivolous and polite
society which he attacked was amused at it without being troubled
by it: it was a new field of battle opened for brilliant jousts of
wit; he had his partisans and his admirers. In the discussion
which ensued, Jean Jacques showed himself more sensible and
moderate than he had been in the first exposition of his idea; he
had wanted to strike, to astonish: he soon modified the violence
of his assertions. "Let us guard against concluding that we
must now burn all libraries and pull down the universities and
academies," he wrote to King Stanislaus: "we should only
plunge Europe once more into barbarism, and morals would gain
nothing by it. The vices would remain with us and we should
have ignorance besides. In vain would you aspire to destroy the
sources of the evil, in vain would you remove the elements of vanity,
indolence and luxury, in vain would you even bring men back to
that primal equality, the preserver of innocence and the source of
all virtue: their hearts once spoilt will be so for ever. There is
no remedy now, save some great revolution, almost as much to be
feared as the evil which it might cure, and one which it were

blamcable to desire and impossible to forecast.   Let us, then, leave
the sciences and arts to assuage, in some degree, the ferocity of
the men they have corrupted . . . . The enlightenment of the
wicked is at any rate less to be feared than his brutal stupidity."

Rousseau here showed the characteristic which invariably
distinguished him from the philosophers, and which ended by
establishing deep enmity between them and him ; the eighteenth
century espied certain evils, certain sores in the social and political
condition, believed in a cure and blindly relied on the power of its
own theories.   Rousseau, more earnest, often more sincere, made
a better diagnosis of the complaint, he described its horrible
character and the dangerousness of it, he saw no remedy and he
pointed none out.   Profound and grievous impotence, whose
utmost hope is an impossible recurrence to the primitive state of
savagery !   " In the private opinion of our adversaries," says M.
Royer-Collard eloquently, " it was a thoughtless thing, on the great
day of creation, to let man loose, a free and intelligent agent, into
the midst of the universe; thence the mischief and the mistake.
A higher wisdom comes forward to repair the error of Providence,
to restrain His thoughtless liberality and to render to prudently
mutilated mankind the service of elevating it to the happy
innocence of the brute."

Before Rousseau and better than he, Christianity had recognized
and proclaimed the evil; but it had, at the same time, announced
to the world a remedy and a Saviour.

Henceforth Rousseau had chosen his own road : giving up the
drawing-rooms and the habits of that elegant society for which he
was not born and the admiration of which had developed his pride,
he made up his mind to live independent, copying music to get his
bread, now and then smitten with the women of the world who
sought him out in his retirement, in love with Madame d'Epinay
and Madame d'Houdetot, anon returning to the coarse servant-
wench whom he had but lately made his wife and whose children
he had put in the foundling-hospital.   Music at that time absorbed
all minds : Rousseau brought out a little opera entitled *Le Devin de
village* (*The Village Wizard*), which had a great success.   It was
played at Fontainebleau before the king.   " I was there that day,"

writes Rousseau, "in the same untidy array which was usual with me ; a great deal of beard and wig rather badly trimmed. Taking this want of decency for an act of courage, I entered in this state the very room into which would come, a short time afterwards, the king, the queen, the royal family and all the court . . . . When the lights were lit, seeing myself in this array in the midst of people all extensively got up, I began to be ill at ease ; I asked myself if I were in my proper place, if I were properly dressed, and, after a few moments' disquietude, I answered *yes*, with an intrepidity which arose perhaps more from the impossibility of getting out of it than from the force of my arguments. After this little dialogue, I plucked up so much, that I should have been quite intrepid if there had been any need of it. But, whether it were the effect of the master's presence or natural kindness of heart, I observed nothing but what was obliging and civil in the curiosity of which I was the object. I was steeled against all their gibes, but their caressing air, which I had not expected, overcame me so completely that I trembled like a child when things began. I heard all about me a whispering of women who seemed to me as beautiful as angels and who said to one another below their breath : ' This is charming, this is enchanting : there is not a note that does not appeal to the heart.' The pleasure of causing emotion in so many loveable persons moved me myself to tears."

The emotions of the eighteenth century were vivid and easily roused ; fastening upon everything without any earnest purpose and without any great sense of responsibility it grew as hot over a musical dispute as over the gravest questions of morality or philosophy. Grimm had attacked French music, Rousseau supported his thesis by a *Lettre sur la Musique*. It was the moment of the great quarrel between the Parliament and the Clergy. "When my letter appeared, there was no more excitement save against me," says Rousseau : " it was such that the nation has never recovered from it. When people read that this pamphlet probably prevented a revolution in the State, they will fancy they must be dreaming." And Grimm adds in his correspondence : " The Italian actors who have been playing for the last ten months

ROUSSEAU AND MADAME D'ÉPINAY.

on the stage of the Opéra de Paris and who are called here *bouffons*, have so absorbed the attention of Paris that the Parliament, in spite of all its measures and proceedings which should have earned it celebrity, could not but fall into complete oblivion.   A wit has said that the arrival of Manelli saved us from a civil war, and Jean Jacques Rousseau of Geneva, whom his friends have dubbed the citizen of citizens (*le citoyen par excellence*), that eloquent and bilious foe of the sciences, has just set fire to the four corners of Paris with a *Lettre sur la Musique*, in which he proves that it is impossible to set French words to music. . . . What is not easy to believe, and is none the less true for all that, is that M. Rousseau was afraid of being banished for this pamphlet.   It would have been odd to see Rousseau banished for having spoken ill of French music, after having with impunity dealt with the most delicate political matter."

Rousseau had just printed his *Discours sur l'Inegalité des conditions*, a new and violent picture of the corruptions of human society.   "Inequality being almost *nil* in a state of nature," he says, " it derives its force and increment from the development of our faculties and from the progress of the human mind . . . . according to the poet it is gold and silver, but according to the philosopher it is iron and corn which have civilized men and. ruined the human race."

The singularity of his paradox had worn off; Rousseau no longer astounded, he shocked the good sense as well as the aspirations, superficial or generous, of the eighteenth century : the *Discours sur l'Inegalité des conditions* was not a success.   " I have received, sir, your new book against the human race," wrote Voltaire ; " I thank you for it.   You will please men to whom you tell truths about them and you will not make them any better.   Never was so much good wit expended in the desire to make beasts of us ; one feels disposed to walk on all fours when one reads your work.   However, as it is more than sixty years since I lost the knack, I unfortunately find it impossible to recover it, and I leave that natural gait to those who are better fitted for it than you or I.   No more can I embark upon a visit to the savages of Canada, first, because the illnesses to which I am subject

render a European doctor necessary to me, secondly, because war
has been introduced into that country, and because the examples
of our nations have rendered the savages almost as wicked as
ourselves. I shall confine myself to being a peaceable savage in
the solitude I have selected hard by your own country, where you
ought to be."

Rousseau had, indeed, thought of returning and settling at
Geneva. In 1754, during a trip he made thither, he renounced
the Catholic faith which he had embraced at sixteen under the
influence of Madame de Warens without any more conviction than
he carried with him in his fresh abjuration. "Ashamed," says he,
" at being excluded from my rights of citizenship by the profession
of a cult other than that of my fathers, I resolved to resume
the latter openly. I considered that the Gospel was the same
for all Christians, and that, as the fundamental difference of dogma
arose from meddling with explanations of what could not be
understood, it appertained in every country to the sovereign
alone to fix both the cult and the unintelligible dogma, and that,
consequently, it was the duty of the citizen to accept the dogma
and follow the cult prescribed by law." Strange eccentricity of
the human mind ! The shackles of civilization are oppressive to
Rousseau, and yet he would impose the yoke of the State upon
consciences. The natural man does not reflect, and does not
discuss his religion; whilst seeking to recover the obliterated
ideal of nature, the philosopher halts on the road at the principles
of Louis XIV. touching religious liberties.

Madame d'Épinay had offered Rousseau a retreat in her little
house, the Hermitage. There it was that he began the tale of
La Nouvelle Héloise, which was finished at Marshal de Montmorency's, when the susceptible and cranky temper of the philosopher had justified the malevolent predictions of Grimm. The
latter had but lately said to Madame d'Épinay : " I see in
Rousseau nothing but pride concealed everywhere about him;
you will do him a very sorry service in giving him a home at the
Hermitage, but you will do yourself a still more sorry one. Solitude will complete the blackening of his imagination; he will fancy
all his friends unjust, ungrateful, and you first of all, if you once

refuse to be at his beck and call; he will accuse you of having bothered him to live under your roof and of having prevented him from yielding to the wishes of his country. I already see the germ of these accusations in the turn of the letters you have shown me."

Rousseau quarrelled with Madame d'Épinay, and shortly afterwards with all the philosophical circle: Grimm, Helvétius, D'Holbach, Diderot; his quarrels with the last were already of old date, they had made some noise. "Good God!" said the duke of Castries in astonishment, "wherever I go I hear of nothing but this Rousseau and this Diderot! Did anybody ever? Fellows who are nobody, fellows who have no house, who lodge on a third floor! Positively, one can't stand that sort of thing!" The rupture was at last complete, it extended to Grimm as well as to Diderot. "Nobody can put himself in my place," wrote Rousseau, "and nobody will see that I am a being apart, who has not the character, the maxims, the resources of the rest of them, and who must not be judged by their rules."

Rousseau was right; he was a being apart; and the philosophers could not forgive him for his independence. His merits as well as his defects annoyed them equally: his *Lettre contre les Spectacles* had exasperated Voltaire, the stage at *Délices* was in danger: "It is against that Jean Jacques of yours that I am most enraged," he writes in his correspondence with D'Alembert: "he has written several letters against the scandal to deacons of the Church of Geneva, to my ironmonger, to my cobbler. This archmaniac, who might have been something if he had left himself in your hands, has some notion of standing aloof; he writes against theatricals after having done a bad play; he writes against France which is a mother to him; he picks up four or five rotten old hoops off Diogenes' tub and gets inside them to bay; he cuts his friends; he writes to me myself the most impertinent letter that ever fanatic scrawled. He writes to me in so many words: 'You have corrupted Geneva in requital of the asylum she gave you;' as if I cared to soften the manners of Geneva, as if I wanted an asylum, as if I had taken any in that city of Socinian preachers, as if I were under any obligation to that city!"

More moderate and more equitable than Voltaire, D'Alembert felt the danger of discord amongst the philosophical party. In vain he wrote to the irritated poet : " I come to Jean Jacques, not Jean Jacques Lefranc de Pompignan, who thinks he is somebody, but to Jean Jacques Rousseau, who thinks he is a cynic and who is only inconsistent and ridiculous. I grant that he has written you an impertinent letter, I grant that you and your friends have reason to complain of that ; in spite of all this, however, I do not approve of your declaring openly against him, as you are doing, and, thereanent, I need only quote to you your own words : ' What will become of the little flock, if it is divided and scattered ?' We do not find that Plato, or Aristotle, or Sophocles, or Euripides wrote against Diogenes, although Diogenes said something insulting to them all. Jean Jacques is a sick man with a good deal of wit, and one who only has wit when he has fever ; he must neither be cured nor have his feelings hurt." Voltaire replied with haughty temper to these wise counsels, and the philosophers remained for ever embroiled with Rousseau.

Isolated henceforth by the good as well as by the evil tendencies of his nature, Jean Jacques stood alone against the philosophical circle which he had dropped as well as against the protestant or catholic clergy whose creeds he often offended. He had just published *Le Contrat Social*, " The Gospel," says M. Saint-Marc Girardin, " of the theory as to the sovereignty of the State representing the sovereignty of the people." The governing powers of the time had some presentiment of its danger ; they had vaguely comprehended what weapons might be sought therein by revolutionary instincts and interests ; their anxiety and their anger as yet brooded silently ; the director of publications (*de la librairie*), M. de Malesherbes, was one of the friends and almost one of the disciples of Rousseau whom he shielded ; he himself corrected the proofs of the *Émile* which Rousseau had just finished. The book had barely begun to appear, when, on the 8th of June, 1762, Rousseau was awakened by a message from la Maréchale de Luxembourg : the Parliament had ordered *Émile* to be burned and its author arrested. Rousseau took flight, reckoning upon finding refuge at Geneva. The influence of the French government pursued him thither; the grand council condemned *Émile*. One single copy had arrived at Geneva: it was this which was burned by the hand of the common hangman, nine days after the burning at Paris in the Place de Grève. "The *Contrat Social* has received its whipping on the back of *Émile*," was the saying at Geneva. "At the instigation of M. de Voltaire they have avenged upon me the cause of God," Jean Jacques declared.

Rousseau rashly put his name to his books; Voltaire was more prudent. One day, having been imprisoned for some verses which were not his, he had taken the resolution to impudently repudiate the paternity of his own works: "You must never publish anything under your own name," he wrote to Helvetius; "*La Pucelle* was none of my doing, of course. Master Joly de Fleury will make a fine thing of his requisition, I shall tell him that he is a calumniator, that *La Pucelle* is his own doing, which he wants to put down to me out of spite."

Geneva refused asylum to the proscribed philosopher; he was warned of hostile intentions on the part of the *magnific signiors* of Berne. Neuchâtel and the king of Prussia's protection alone were left: thither he went for refuge. Received with open arms by the governor, my lord Marshal (Keith), he wrote thence to the premier syndic Favre a letter abdicating his rights of burghership and citizenship in the town of Geneva: "I have neglected nothing," he said, "to gain the love of my compatriots; nobody could have had worse success. I desire to indulge them even in their hate; the last sacrifice remaining for me to make is that of a name which was dear to me."

Some excitement, nevertheless, prevailed at Geneva; Rousseau had partisans there. The success of *Émile* had been immense at Paris and was destined to exercise a serious influence upon the education of a whole generation. "It is good," wrote Voltaire, "that the brethren should know that yesterday six hundred persons came, for the third time, to protest on behalf of Jean Jacques against the Council of Geneva, which had dared to condemn the *Vicaire savoyard*." The Genevese magistrates thought it worth while to defend their acts; the *Lettres écrites de la Campagne*, published to that end, were the work of the attorney-general Robert

Tronchin. Rousseau replied to them in the *Lettres de la Montagne*, with a glowing eloquence having a spice of irony. He hurled his missiles at Voltaire, whom, with weakly exaggeration, he accused of being the author of all his misfortunes : " Those gentlemen of the Grand Council," he said, " see M. de Voltaire so often, how is it that he did not inspire them with a little of that tolerance which he is incessantly preaching, and of which he sometimes has need ? If they had consulted him a little on this matter, it appears to me that he might have addressed them pretty nearly thus : Gentlemen, it is not the arguers who do harm ; philosophy can gang its ain gait without risk ; the people either do not hear it at all or let it babble on, and pay it back all the disdain it feels for them. I do not argue myself, but others argue, and what harm comes of it ? We have arranged that my great influence in the court and my pre- tended omnipotence should serve you as a pretext for allowing a free, peaceful course to the sportive jests of my advanced years ; that is a good thing, but do not, for all that, burn graver writings, for that would be too shocking. I have so often preached tolerance ! It must not be always required of others and never displayed towards them. This poor creature believes in God, let us pass over that ; he will not make a sect. He is a bore, all arguers are. If all bores of books were to be burnt, the whole country would have to be made into one great fire-place. Come, come, let us leave those to argue who leave us to joke ; let us burn neither people nor books and remain at peace, that is my advice.—That, in my opinion, is what might have been said, only in better style, by M. de Voltaire, and it would not have been, as it seems to me, the worst advice he could have given."

My lord Marshal had left Neuchâtel ; Rousseau no longer felt safe there ; he made up his mind to settle in the island of St. Pierre, in the middle of the lake of Bienne. Before long an order from the Bernese Senate obliged him to quit it " within four and twenty hours, and with a prohibition against ever returning, under the heaviest penalties." Rousseau went through Paris and took refuge in England, whither he was invited by the friendliness of the his- torian Hume. There it was that he began writing his *Confessions*.

Already the reason of the unhappy philosopher, clouded as it had sometimes been by the violence of his emotions, was beginning to be shaken at the foundations; he believed himself to be the victim of an immense conspiracy, at the head of which was his friend Hume. The latter flew into a rage, he wrote to Baron d'Holbach : " My dear Baron, Rousseau is a scoundrel." Rousseau was by this time mad.

He returned to France. The prince of Conti, faithful to his philosophical affections, quartered him at the castle of Trye, near Gisors. Thence he returned to Paris, still persecuted, he said, by invisible enemies. Retiring, finally, to the pavilion of Ermenonville, which had been offered to him by M. de Girardin, he died there at the age of sixty-six, sinking even more beneath imaginary woes than under the real sorrows and bitter deceptions of his life. The disproportion between his intellect and his character, between the boundless pride and the impassioned weakness of his spirit, had little by little estranged his friends and worn out the admiration of his contemporaries. By his writings Rousseau acted more powerfully upon posterity than upon his own times : his personality had ceased to do his genius injustice.

He belonged moreover and by anticipation to a new era; from the restless working of his mind, as well as from his moral and political tendencies, he was no longer of the eighteenth century properly speaking, though the majority of the philosophers out-lived him ; his work was not their work, their world was never his. He had attempted a noble reaction, but one which was fundamentally and in reality impossible. The impress of his early education had never been thoroughly effaced : he believed in God, he had been nurtured upon the Gospel in childhood, he admired the morality and the life of Jesus Christ; but he stopped at the boundaries of adoration and submission. " The spirit of Jean Jacques Rousseau inhabits the moral world, but not that other which is above," M. Joubert has said in his *Pensées*. The weapons were insufficient and the champion was too feeble for the contest; the spirit of the moral world was vanquished as a foregone conclusion. Against the systematic infidelity which was more and more creeping over the eighteenth century, the Christian faith alone, with all its forces, could fight and triumph. But the Christian faith was obscured and enfeebled, it clung to the vessel's rigging instead of defending its powerful hull; the flood was rising meanwhile, and the dikes were breaking one after another. The religious belief of the Savoyard vicar, imperfect and inconsistent, such as it is set forth in *Émile*, and that sincere love of nature which was recovered by Rousseau in his solitude remained powerless to guide the soul and regulate life.

"What the eighteenth century lacked" [M. Guizot, *Mélanges biographiques* (*Madame la Comtesse de Rumford*)], "what there was of superficiality in its ideas and of decay in its morals, of senselessness in its pretensions and of futility in its creative power, has been strikingly revealed to us by experience; we have learnt it to our cost. We know, we feel the evil bequeathed to us by that memorable epoch. It preached doubt, egotism, materialism. It laid for some time an impure and blasting hand upon noble and beautiful phases of human life. But if the eighteenth century had done only that, if such had been merely its chief characteristic, can any one suppose that it would have carried in its wake so many and such important matters, that it would have so moved the world? It was far superior to all its sceptics, to all its cynics. What do I say? Superior? Nay it was essentially opposed to them and continually gave them the lie. Despite the weakness of its morals, the frivolity of its forms, the mere dry bones of such and such of its doctrines, despite its critical and destructive tendency, it was an ardent and a sincere century, a century of faith and disinterestedness. It had faith in the truth, for it claimed the right thereof to reign in this world. It had faith in humanity, for it recognized the right thereof to perfect itself and would have had that right exercised without obstruction. It erred, it lost itself amidst this twofold confidence, it attempted what was far beyond its right and power; it misjudged the moral nature of man and the conditions of the social state. Its ideas as well as its works contracted the blemish of its views. But, granted so much, the original idea, dominant in the eighteenth century, the belief that man, truth and society are made for one another, worthy of one another and called upon to form a union, this correct and salutary belief rises up and overtops all its history. That belief it was the first to proclaim and would fain have realized. Hence its power and

its popularity over the whole face of the earth.   Hence also, to
descend from great things to small, and from the destiny of man
to that of the drawing-room, hence the seductiveness of that epoch
and the charm it scattered over social life.   Never before were
seen all the conditions, all the classes that form the flower of a
great people, however diverse they might have been in their
history and still were in their interests, thus forgetting their past,
their personality, in order to draw near to one another, to unite in
a communion of the sweetest manners, and solely occupied in
pleasing one another, in rejoicing and hoping together during fifty
years which were to end in the most terrible conflicts between
them."

At the death of King Louis XV., in 1774, the easy-mannered
joyance, the peaceful and brilliant charm of fashionable and
philosophical society were reaching their end : the time of stern
realities was approaching with long strides.

CHAPTER LVI.

LOUIS XVI.—MINISTRY OF M. TURGOT. 1774—1776.

OUIS XV. was dead; France breathed once more; she was weary of the weakness as well as of the irregularities of the king who had untaught her her respect for him, and she turned with joyous hope towards his successor, barely twenty years of age, but already loved and impatiently awaited by his people. "He must be called Louis le Désiré," was the saying in the streets before the death-rattle of Louis XV. had summoned his grandson to the throne. The feeling of dread which had seized the young king was more prophetic than the nation's joy. At the news that Louis XV. had just heaved his last sigh in the arms of his pious daughters, Louis XVI. and Marie Antoinette both flung themselves upon their knees, exclaiming, "O God, protect us, direct us, we are too young."

The monarch's youth did not scare the country, itself everywhere animated and excited by a breath of youth. There were congratulations on escaping from the well-known troubles of a regency; the king's ingenuous inexperience, moreover, opened a vast field for the most contradictory hopes. The philosophers counted upon taking possession of the mind of a good young sovereign, who was said to have his heart set upon his people's happiness; the clergy and the Jesuits themselves expected every thing from the young prince's pious education; the old parliaments, mutilated, crushed down, began to raise up their heads again, whilst the economists were already preparing their most daring projects. Like literature, the arts had got the start, in the new path, of the politicians and the magistrates. M. Turgot and M. de Malesherbes had not yet laid their enterprising hands upon the old fabric of French administration, and already painting, sculpture, architecture, and music had shaken off the shackles of the past. The conventional graces of Vanloo, of Watteau, of Boucher, of Fragonard, had given place to a severer school. Greuze was putting upon canvas the characters and ideas of Diderot's *Drame naturel;* but Vien, in France, was seconding the efforts of Winkelman and of Raphaël Mengs in Italy; he led his pupils back to the study of ancient art; he had trained Regnault, Vincent, Ménageot, and lastly Louis David, destined to become the chief of the modern school; Julien, Houdon, the last of the Coustous, were following the same road in sculpture: Soufflot, an old man by this time, was superintending the completion of the church of St. Geneviève, dedicated by Louis XV. to the commemoration of his recovery at Metz, and destined, from the majestic simplicity of its lines, to the doubtful honour of becoming the Pantheon of the revolution; Servandoni had died a short time since, leaving to the church of St. Sulpice the care of preserving his memory; everywhere were rising charming mansions imitated from the palaces of Rome. The painters, the sculptors and the architects of France were sufficient for her glory; only Grétry and Monsigny upheld the honour of that French music which was attacked by Grimm and by Jean Jacques Rousseau; but it was at Paris that the great quarrel went on between the Italians and the Germans: Piccini and Glück divided society, wherein their rivalry excited violent passions. Everywhere and on all questions, intellectual movement was becoming animated with fresh ardour; France was marching towards the region of storms, in the blindness of her confidence and joyance; the atmosphere seemed purer since Madame Dubarry had been sent to a convent by one of the first orders of young Louis XVI.

Already, however, farseeing spirits were disquieted; scarcely had he mounted the throne. when the king summoned to his side, as his minister, M. de Maurepas, but lately banished by Louis XV., in 1749, on a charge of having tolerated, if not himself written, songs disrespectful towards Madame de Pompadour. "The first day," said the disgraced minister, "I was nettled; the second, I was comforted."

M. de Maurepas, grandson of Chancellor Pontchartrain, had been provided for, at fourteen years of age, by Louis XIV. with the reversion of the ministry of marine, which had been held by his father, and had led a frivolous and pleasant life; through good fortune and evil fortune he clung to the court; when he was recalled thither, at the age of sixty-three, on the suggestion of Madame Adelaide, the queen's aunt, and of the dukes of Aiguillon and La Vrillière, both of them ministers and relations of his, he made up his mind that he would never leave it again. On arriving at Versailles, he used the expression, "premier minister;" "Not at all," said the king abruptly. "Oh! very well," replied M. de Maurepas, "then to teach your Majesty to do without one." Nobody, however, did any business with Louis XVI. without his being present, and his address was sufficient to keep at a distance or diminish the influence of the princesses as well as of the queen. Marie Antoinette had insisted upon the recall of M. de Choiseul, who had arranged her marriage and who had remained faithful to the Austrian alliance. The king had refused angrily. The sinister accusations which had but lately been current as to the causes of the dauphin's death had never been forgotten by his son.

An able man, in spite of his incurable levity, M. de Maurepas soon sacrificed the duke of Aiguillon to the queen's resentment; the people attached to the old court accused her of despising etiquette; it was said that she had laughed when she received the respectful condolence of aged dames looking like beguines in

THE CHURCH OF ST. GENEVILVE.

their coifs; already there circulated amongst the public bitter ditties, such as,—

> My little queen, not twenty-one,
> Maltreat the folks, as you've begun,
> And o'er the border you shall run . . . .

The duke of Aiguillon, always hostile to the Choiseuls and the house of Austria, had lent his countenance to the murmurs; Marie Antoinette was annoyed, and, in her turn, fostered the distrust felt by the people towards the late ministers of Louis XV.; in the place of the duke of Aiguillon, who had the ministry of war and that of foreign affairs both together, the count of Muy and the count of Vergennes were called to power. Some weeks later, the obscure minister of marine, M. de Boynes, made way for the superintendent of the district (*généralité*) of Limoges, M. Turgot.

Anne Robert Jacques Turgot, born at Paris on the 10th of May, 1727, was already known and everywhere esteemed, when M. de Maurepas, at the instance, it is said, of his wife whom he consulted on all occasions, summoned him to the ministry. He belonged to an ancient and important family by whom he had been intended for the Church. When a pupil at Louis-le-Grand college, he spent his allowance so quickly that his parents became alarmed; they learned before long that the young man shared all he received amongst out-of-college pupils too poor to buy books.

This noble concern for the wants of others, as well as his rare gifts of intellect, had gained young Turgot devoted friends. He was already leaning towards philosophy, and he announced to his fellow-pupils his intention of giving up his ecclesiastical status; he was a prior of Sorbonne; the majority disapproved of it. "Thou'rt but a younger son of a Norman family," they said, "and, consequently, poor. Thou'rt certain to get excellent abbotries and to be a bishop early. Then thou'lt be able to realize thy fine dreams of administration and to become a states-man at thy leisure, whilst doing all manner of good in thy diocese. It depends on thyself alone to make thyself useful to thy country, to acquire a high reputation, perhaps to carve thy way to the ministry; if thou enter the magistracy, as thou desirest, thou breakest the plank which is under thy feet, thou'lt be confined to hearing causes, and thou'lt waste thy genius, which is fitted for the most important public affairs." "I am very fond of you, my dear friends," replied M. Turgot, "but I don't quite understand what you are made of. As for me, it would be impossible for me to devote myself to wearing a mask all my life." He became councillor-substitute to the attorney-general, and before long councillor in the Parliament, on the 30th of December, 1752. Master of requests in 1753, he consented to sit in the King's Chamber, when the Parliament suspended the administration of justice. "The Court," he said, "is exceeding its powers." A sense of equity thus enlisted him in the service of absolute government. He dreaded, moreover, the corporate spirit, which he considered narrow and intolerant. "When you say, *We*," he would often repeat, "do not be surprised that the public should answer, *You*."

Intimately connected with the most esteemed magistrates and economists, such as MM. Trudaine, Quesnay, and Gournay, at the same time that he was writing in the *Encyclopædia*, and constantly occupied in useful work, Turgot was not yet five and thirty when he was appointed superintendent of the district of Limoges. There, the rare faculties of his mind and his sincere love of good found their natural field; the country was poor, crushed under imposts, badly intersected by roads badly kept, inhabited by an ignorant populace, violently hostile to the recruitment of the militia. He encouraged agriculture, distributed the talliages more equitably, amended the old roads and constructed new ones, abolished forced labour (*corvées*), provided for the wants of the the poor and wretched during the dearth of 1770 and 1771, and declined, successively, the superintendentship of Rouen, of Lyons, and of Bordeaux, in order that he might be able to complete the useful tasks he had begun at Limoges. It was in that district, which had become dear to him, that he was sought out by the kindly remembrance of Abbé de Véry, his boyhood's friend, who was intimate with Madame de Maurepas. Scarcely had he been installed in the department of marine and begun to conceive vast plans, when the late ministers of Louis XV. succumbed at last beneath the popular hatred; in the place of Abbé Terray, M. Turgot became comptroller-general.

The old parliamentarians were triumphant; at the same time as Abbé Terray, Chancellor Maupeou was disgraced, and the judicial system he had founded fell with him. Unpopular from the first, the Maupeou Parliament had remained in the nation's eyes the image of absolute power corrupted and corrupting. The suit between Beaumarchais and Councillor Goëzman had contributed to decry it, thanks to the uproar the able pamphleteer had managed to cause; the families of the former magistrates were powerful, numerous, esteemed, and they put pressure upon public opinion; M. de Maurepas determined to retract the last absolutist attempt of Louis XV.'s reign; his first care was to send and demand of Chancellor Maupeou the surrender of the seals. "I know what you have come to tell me," said the latter to the Duke of La Vrillière, who was usually charged with this painful mission, "but I am and shall continue to be chancellor of France," and he kept his seat whilst addressing the minister, in accordance with his official privilege. He handed to the duke the casket of seals, which the latter was to take straight to M. de Miromesnil. "I had gained the king a great cause," said Maupeou; "he is pleased to re-open a question which was decided; as to that, he is master." Imperturbable and haughty as ever, he retired to his estate at Thuit, near the Andelys, where he drew up a justificatory memorandum of his ministry, which he had put into the king's hands, without ever attempting to enter the court or Paris again; he died in the country, at the outset of the revolutionary storms, on the 29th of July, 1792, just as he had made the State a patriotic present of 800,000 livres. At the moment when the populace were burning him in effigy in the streets of Paris together with Abbé Terray, when he saw the recall of the parliamentarians, and the work of his whole life destroyed, he repeated with his usual coolness: "If the king is pleased to lose his kingdom—well, he is master."

Abbé Terray had been less proud, and was more harshly treated. It was in vain that he sought to dazzle the young king

with ably prepared memorials. " I can do no more," he said,
" to add to the receipts, which I have increased by sixty millions;
I can do no more to keep down the debts, which I have reduced
by twenty millions. . . . It is for you, Sir, to relieve your people
by reducing the expenses. This work, which is worthy of your
kind heart, was reserved for you." Abbé Terray had to refund
nearly 900,000 livres to the public treasury. Being recognized
by the mob as he was passing over the Seine in a ferry boat, he
had some difficulty in escaping from the hands of those who
would have hurled him into the river.

The contrast was great between the crafty and unscrupulous
ability of the disgraced comptroller-general and the complete
disinterestedness, large views, and noble desire of good which
animated his successor. After his first interview with the king,
at Compiègne, M. Turgot wrote to Louis XVI. :—" Your Majesty
has been graciously pleased to permit me to place before your eyes
the engagement you took upon yourself, to support me in the
execution of plans of economy which are at all times, and now
more than ever, indispensable. I confine myself for the moment,
sir, to reminding you of these three expressions :—1° No bankruptcies; 2° No augmentation of imposts; 3° No loans. No
bankruptcy, either avowed or masked by forced reductions. No
augmentation of imposts: the reason for that lies in the condition
of your people, and still more in your Majesty's own heart   No
loans; because every loan always diminishes the disposable
revenue: it necessitates, at the end of a certain time, either
bankruptcy or augmentation of imposts. . . . Your Majesty will
not forget that, when I accepted the office of comptroller-general,
I perceived all the preciousness of the confidence with which you
honour me . . . but, at the same time I perceived all the danger
to which I was exposing myself. I foresaw that I should have to
fight single-handed against abuses of every sort, against the efforts
of such as gain by those abuses, against the host of the prejudiced
who oppose every reform and who, in the hands of interested persons, are so powerful a means of perpetuating disorder. I shall be
feared, shall be even hated by the greater part of the court, by all
that solicit favours. . . . This people to whom I shall have sacrificed

myself is so easy to deceive, that I shall perhaps incur its hatred through the very measures I shall take to defend it against harassment. I shall be calumniated, and perhaps with sufficient plausibility to rob me of your Majesty's confidence. . . . You will remember that it is on the strength of your promises that I undertake a burthen perhaps beyond my strength; that it is to you personally, to the honest man, to the just and good man, rather than to the king, that I commit myself."

It is to the honour of Louis XVI. that the virtuous men who served him, often with sorrow and without hoping anything from their efforts, always preserved their confidence in his intentions: "It is quite encouraging," wrote M. Turgot to one of his friends, "to have to serve a king who is really an honest and a well-meaning man." The burthen of the necessary reforms was beyond the strength of the minister as well as of the sovereign; the violence of opposing currents was soon about to paralyze their genuine efforts and their generous hopes.

M. Turgot set to work at once. Whilst governing his district of Limoges, he had matured numerous plans and shaped extensive theories. He belonged to his times and to the school of the philosophers as regarded his contempt for tradition and history; it was to natural rights alone, to the innate and primitive requirements of mankind, that he traced back his principles and referred as the basis for all his attempts. "The rights of associated men are not founded upon their history but upon their nature," says the *Mémoire au Roi sur les Municipalités*, drawn up under the eye of Turgot. By this time he desired no more to reform old France; he wanted a new France. Before ten years are over," he would say, "the nation will not be recognizable, thanks to enlightenment. This chaos will have assumed a distinct form. Your Majesty will have quite a new people, and the first of peoples." A profound error, which was that of the whole Revolution, and the consequences of which would have been immediately fatal, if the powerful instinct of conservatism and of natural respect for the past had not maintained between the regimen which was crumbling away and the new fabric connexions more powerful and more numerous than their friends as well as their enemies were aware of.

Two fundamental principles regulated the financial system of M. Turgot, economy in expenditure and freedom in trade; everywhere he ferreted out abuses, abolishing useless offices and payments, exacting from the entire administration that strict probity of which he set the example. Louis XVI. supported him conscientiously at that time in all his reforms; the public made fun of it: "The king," it was said, "when he considers himself an abuse, will be one no longer." At the same time, a decree of September 13th, 1774, re-established at home that freedom of trade in grain which had been suspended by Abbé Terray, and the edict of April, 1776, founded freedom of trade in wine. "It is by trade alone, and by free trade, that the inequality of harvests can be corrected," said the minister in the preamble of his decree. "I have just read M. Turgot's master-piece," wrote Voltaire to D'Alembert: "it seems to reveal to us new heavens and a new earth." It was on account of his financial innovations that the comptroller-general particularly dreaded the return of the old Parliament, with which he saw himself threatened every day. "I fear opposition from the Parliament," he said to the king. "Fear nothing," replied the king warmly, "I will stand by you;" and, passing over the objections of the best politician amongst his ministers, he yielded to M. de Maurepas, who yielded to public opinion. On the 12th of November, 1774, the old Parliament was formally restored.

The king appeared at the bed of justice, the princes, the dukes and the peers were present; the magistrates were introduced: "The king my grandfather," said Louis XVI., "compelled by your resistance to his repeated orders, did what the maintenance of his authority and the obligation of rendering justice to his people required of his wisdom. To-day I recall you to functions which you never ought to have given up. Appreciate all the value of my bounties, and do not forget them." At the same time the keeper of the seals read out an edict which subjected the restored Parliament to the same jurisdiction which had controlled the Maupeou Parliament. The latter had been sent to Versailles to form a grand council there.

Stern words are but a sorry cloak for feeble actions: the restored magistrates grumbled at the narrow limits imposed upon their authority; the duke of Orleans, the duke of Chartres, the prince of Conti supported their complaints; it was in vain that the king for some time met them with refusals; threats soon gave place to concessions; and the parliaments everywhere reconstituted, enfeebled in the eyes of public opinion, but more than ever obstinate and Fronde-like, found themselves free to harass, without doing any good, the march of an administration becoming every day more difficult. " Your Parliament may make barricades," Lord Chesterfield had remarked contemptuously to Montesquieu, " it will never raise barriers."

M. Turgot, meanwhile, was continuing his labours, preparing a project for equitable redistribution of the talliage and his grand system of a graduated scale (*hiérarchie*) of municipal assemblies, commencing with the parish, to culminate in a general meeting of delegates from each province; he threatened, in the course of his reforms, the privileges of the noblesse and of the clergy, and gave his mind anxiously to the instruction of the people, whose condition and welfare he wanted to simultaneously elevate and augment; already there was a buzz of murmurs against him, confined as yet to the courtiers, when the dearness of bread and the distress which ensued in the spring of 1775 furnished his adversaries with a convenient pretext. Up to that time the attacks had been cautious and purely theoretical. M. Necker, an able banker from Geneva, for a long while settled in Paris, hand and glove with the philosophers, and keeping up, moreover, a great establishment, had brought to the comptroller-general a work which he had just finished on the trade in grain; on many points he did not share M. Turgot's opinions. " Be kind enough to ascertain for yourself," said the banker to the minister, " whether the book can be published without incon-venience to the government." M. Turgot was proud and some-times rude : " Publish, sir, publish," said he, without offering his hand to take the manuscript, " the public shall decide." M. Necker, out of pique, published his book; it had an immense sale; other pamphlets, more violent and less solid, had already appeared; at

the same moment a riot, which seemed to have been planned and
to be under certain guidance, broke out in several parts of France.
Drunken men shouted about the public thoroughfares, "Bread!
cheap bread!"

Burgundy had always been restless and easily excited. It was
at Dijon that the insurrection began; on the 20th of April, the
peasantry moved upon the town and smashed the furniture of a
councillor in the Maupeou Parliament, who was accused of
monopoly; they were already overflowing the streets, exasperated
by the cruel answer of the governor, M. de la Tour du Pin:
"You want something to eat? Go and graze; the grass is just
coming up." The burgesses trembled in their houses; the bishop
threw himself in the madmen's way and succeeded in calming
them with his exhortations. The disturbance had spread to
Pontoise; there the riot broke out on the 1st of May, the market
was pillaged; on the 2nd, at Versailles, a mob collected under the
balcony of the castle. Everywhere ruffians of sinister appearance
mingled with the mob, exciting its passions and urging it to
acts of violence: the same men, such as are only seen in troublous
days, were at the same time scouring Brie, Soissonnais, Vexin and
Upper Normandy; already barns had been burnt and wheat
thrown into the river; sacks of flour were ripped to pieces before
the king's eyes, at Versailles. In his excitement and dismay he
promised the mob that the bread-rate should for the future be
fixed at two sous; the rioters rushed to Paris.

M. Turgot had been confined to his bed for some months by an
attack of gout; the Paris bakers' shops had already been pillaged; the rioters had entered simultaneously by several gates,
badly guarded; only one bakery, the owner of which had taken
the precaution of putting over the door a notice with *shop to let*
on it, had escaped the madmen. The comptroller-general had
himself put into his carriage and driven to Versailles: at his
advice the king withdrew his rash concession; the current
price of bread was maintained: "No firing upon them," Louis
XVI. insisted. The lieutenant of police, Lenoir, had shown
weakness and inefficiency; Marshal Biron was entrusted with the
repression of the riot. He occupied all the main thoroughfares

and cross-roads; sentries were placed at the bakers' doors; those
who had hidden themselves were compelled to bake. The octroi-
dues on grain were at the same time suspended at all the markets;
wheat was already going down; when the Parisians went out
of doors to see the riot, they couldn't find any. " Well done,
general in command of the flour (*général des farines*)," said the
tremblers, admiring the military arrangements of Marshal Biron.

The Parliament had caused to be placarded a decree against
street-assemblies, at the same time requesting the king to lower
the price of bread. The result was deplorable; the severe resolution of the council was placarded beside the proclamation of the
Parliament; the magistrates were summoned to Versailles. The
prosecution of offenders was forbidden them; it was entrusted
to the provost's department. " The proceedings of the brigands
appear to be combined," said the keeper of the seals; " their
approach is announced; public rumours indicate the day, the
hour, the places at which they are to commit their outrages. It
would seem as if there were a plan formed to lay waste the
country-places, intercept navigation, prevent the carriage of wheat
on the high roads, in order to starve out the large towns, and
especially the city of Paris." The king at the same time forbade
any " remonstrance." " I rely," said he on dismissing the court,
" upon your placing no obstacle or hindrance in the way of the
measures I have taken, in order that no similar event may occur
during the period of my reign."

The troubles were everywhere subsiding, the merchants were
recovering their spirits; M. Turgot had at once sent fifty
thousand francs to a trader whom the rioters had robbed of a
boat full of wheat which they had flung in to the river; two of
the insurgents were at the same time hanged at Paris on a gallows
forty feet high and a notice was sent to the parish-priests,
which they were to read from the pulpit in order to enlighten
the people as to the folly of such outbreaks and as to the
conditions of the trade in grain: " My people, when they know
the authors of the trouble, will regard them with horror," said
the royal circular. The authors of the trouble have remained
unknown; to his last day, M. Turgot believed in the existence

of a plot concocted by the prince of Conti, with the design of overthrowing him.

Severities were hateful to the king; he had misjudged his own character, when, at the outset of his reign, he had desired the appellation of *Louis le Sévère.* "Have we nothing to reproach ourselves with in these measures?" he was incessantly asking M. Turgot, who was as conscientious but more resolute than his master. An amnesty preceded the coronation, which was to take place at Rheims on the 11th of June, 1775.

A grave question presented itself as regarded the king's oath: should he swear, as the majority of his predecessors had sworn, to exterminate heretics? M. Turgot had aroused Louis XVI.'s scruples upon this subject; "Tolerance ought to appear expedient in point of policy for even an infidel prince," he said: "but it ought to be regarded as a sacred duty for a religious prince." His opinion had been warmly supported by M. de Malesherbes, premier president of the Court of Aids. The king in his perplexity consulted M. de Maurepas. "M. Turgot is right," said the minister, "but he is too bold. What he proposes could hardly be attempted by a prince who came to the throne at a ripe age and in tranquil times. That is not your position. The fanatics are more to be dreaded than the heretics. The latter are accustomed to their present condition. It will always be easy for you not to employ persecution. Those old formulas, of which nobody takes any notice, are no longer considered to be binding." The king yielded; he made no change in the form of the oath, and confined himself to stammering out a few incoherent words. At the coronation of Louis XV. the people, heretofore admitted freely to the cathedral, had been excluded; at the coronation of Louis XVI. the officiator, who was the coadjutor of Rheims, omitted the usual formula, addressed to the whole assembly, "Will you have this king for your king?" This insolent neglect was soon to be replied to by the sinister echo of the sovereignty of the people. The clergy, scared by M. Turgot's liberal tendencies, reiterated their appeals to the king against the liberties tacitly accorded to Protestants. "Finish," they said to Louis XVI., "the work which Louis the Great began and which Louis the Well-beloved continued." The king answered with vague assurances; already MM. Turgot and de Malesherbes were entertaining him with a project which conceded to Protestants the civil status.

M. de Malesherbes, indeed, had been for some months past seconding his friend in the weighty task which the latter had undertaken. Born at Paris on the 6th of December, 1721, son of the chancellor William de Lamoignon, and for the last twenty-three years premier president in the Court of Aids, Malesherbes had invariably fought on behalf of honest right and sound liberty; popularity had followed him in exile; it had increased continually since the accession of Louis XVI., who lost no time in recalling him; he had just presented to the king a remarkable memorandum touching the reform of the fiscal regimen, when M. Turgot proposed to the king to call him to the ministry in the place of the duke of La Vrillière. M. de Maurepas made no objection: "He will be the link of the ministry," he said, "because he has the eloquence of tongue and of heart." "Rest assured," wrote Mdlle. de Lespinasse, "that what is well will be done and will be done well. Never, no never, were two more enlightened, more disinterested, more virtuous men more powerfully knit together in a greater and a higher cause." The first care of M. de Malesherbes was to protest against the sealed letters (*lettres de cachet*—summary arrest), the application whereof he was for putting in the hands of a special tribunal; he visited the Bastille, releasing the prisoners confined on simple suspicion. He had already dared to advise the king to a convocation of the states-general. "In France," he had written to Louis XVI., "the nation has always had a deep sense of its rights and its liberty. Our maxims have been more than once recognized by our kings; they have even gloried in being the sovereigns of a free people. Meanwhile, the articles of this liberty have never been reduced to writing, and the real power, the power of arms, which, under a feudal government, was in the hands of the grandees, has been completely centred in the kingly power . . . We ought not to hide from you, sir, that the way which would be most simple, most natural, and most in conformity with the constitution of this monarchy, would be to hear the nation itself in full assembly, and nobody should have the poltroonery to use any other language to you; nobody should leave you in ignorance that the unanimous wish of the nation is to obtain-states-general or at the least states-provincial. . . . Deign to consider, Sir, that on the day you grant this precious liberty to your people it may be said that a treaty has been concluded between king and nation against ministers and magistrates: against the ministers, if there be any perverted enough to wish to conceal from you the truth; against the magistrates, if there ever be any ambitious enough to pretend to have the exclusive right of telling you it."

Almost the whole ministry was in the hands of reformers; a sincere desire to do good impelled the king towards those who promised him the happiness of his people. Marshal Muy had succumbed to a painful operation: " Sir," he had said to Louis XVI., before placing himself in the surgeons' hands, "in a fortnight I shall be at your Majesty's feet or with your august father." He had succumbed. M. Turgot spoke to M. de Maurepas of the duke of St. Germain. "Propose him to the king," said the minister, adding his favourite phrase: "one can but try."

In the case of government, trials are often a dangerous thing. M. de St. Germain, born in the Jura in 1707 and entered first of all amongst the Jesuits, had afterwards devoted himself to the career of arms: he had served the Elector Palatine, Maria Theresa, and the Elector of Bavaria; enrolled finally by Marshal Saxe, he had distinguished himself under his orders; as lieut.-general during the Seven Years' War, he had brought up his division at Rosbach more quickly than his colleagues had theirs, he had fled less far than the others before the enemy; but his character was difficult, suspicious, exacting; he was always seeing everywhere plots concocted to ruin him: " I am persecuted to the death," he would say. He entered the service of Denmark: returning to France and in poverty, he lived in Alsace on the retired list; it was there that the king's summons came to find him out. In his solitude M. de St. Germain had conceived a thousand projects of reform; he wanted to apply them all at once. He made no sort of case of the picked corps and suppressed the majority of them, thus irritating, likewise, all the privileged. " M. de St. Germain," wrote Frederick

II. to Voltaire, "had great and noble plans very advantageous
for your Welches; but everybody thwarted him, because the
reforms he proposed would have entailed a strictness which was
repugnant to them on ten thousand sluggards, well frogged, well
laced." The enthusiasm which had been excited by the new
minister of war had disappeared from amongst the officers; he lost
the hearts of the soldiers by wanting to establish in the army the
corporal punishments in use amongst the German armies in which
he had served. The feeling was so strong, that the attempt was
abandoned. "In the matter of sabres," said a grenadier, "I like
only the edge." Violent and weak both together, in spite of his
real merit and his genuine worth, often giving up wise resolutions
out of sheer embarrassment, he nearly always failed in what he
undertook; the outcries against the reformers were increased
thereby; the faults of M. de St. Germain were put down to M.
Turgot.

It was against the latter indeed, that the courtiers' anger and
M. de Maurepas' growing jealousy were directed. "Once upon a
time there was in France," said a pamphlet, entitled *Le Songe de
M. de Maurepas*, attributed to Monsieur, the king's brother, "there
was in France a certain man, clumsy, crass, heavy, born with more
of rudeness than of character, more of obstinacy than of firmness,
of impetuosity than of tact, a charlatan in administration as well
as in virtue, made to bring the one into disrepute and the other
into disgust, in other respects shy from self-conceit, timid from
pride, as unfamiliar with men, whom he had never known, as with
public affairs, which he had always seen askew; his name was
Turgot. He was one of those half-thinking brains which adopt
all visions, all manias of a gigantic sort. He was believed to be
deep, he was really shallow; night and day he was raving of
philosophy, liberty, equality, net product." "He is too much (*trop
fort*) for me," M. de Maurepas would often say. "A man must
be possessed (or inspired—*enragé*)" wrote Malesherbes, "to force,
at one and the same time, the hand of the king, of M. de Maurepas,
of the whole court and of the Parliament."

Perhaps the task was above human strength; it was certainly
beyond that of M. Turgot. Ever occupied with the public weal,

he turned his mind to every subject, issuing a multiplicity of decrees, sometimes with rather chimerical hopes. He had proposed to the king six edicts; two were extremely important; the first abolished jurorships (*jurandes*) and masterships (*maîtrises*) among the workmen: "The king," said the preamble, "wishes to secure to all his subjects and especially to the humblest, to those who have no property but their labour and their industry, the full and entire enjoyment of their rights, and to reform, consequently, the institutions which strike at those rights, and which, in spite of their antiquity, have failed to be legalized by time, opinion and even the acts of authority." The second substituted for forced labour on roads and highways an impost to which all proprietors were equally liable.

This was the first step towards equal redistribution of taxes; great was the explosion of disquietude and wrath on the part of the privileged; it showed itself first in the council, by the mouth of M. de Miromesnil; Turgot sprang up with animation. "The keeper of the seals," he said, "seems to adopt the principle that, by the constitution of the State, the noblesse ought to be exempt from all taxation. This idea will appear a paradox to the majority of the nation. The commoners (*roturiers*) are certainly the greatest number, and we are no longer in the days when their voices did not count." The king listened to the discussion in silence. "Come," he exclaimed abruptly, "I see that there are only M. Turgot and I here who love the people," and he signed the edicts.

The Parliament, like the noblesse, had taken up the cudgels; they made representation after representation; "The populace of France," said the court boldly, "is liable to talliage and forced labour at will, and that is a part of the constitution which the king cannot change." Louis XVI. summoned the Parliament to Versailles, and had the edicts enregistered at a bed of justice. "It is a bed of beneficence!" exclaimed Voltaire, a passionate admirer of Turgot.

The comptroller-general was triumphant; but his victory was but the prelude to his fall. Too many enemies were leagued against him, irritated both by the noblest qualities of his character

TURGOT'S DISMISSAL.

and at the same time by the natural defects of his manners. Possessed of love "for a beautiful ideal, of a rage for perfection," M. Turgot had wanted to attempt everything, undertake everything, reform everything at one blow. He fought single-handed. M. de Malesherbes, firm as a rock at the head of the Court of Aids, supported as he was by the traditions and corporate feeling of the magistracy, had shown weakness as a minister. " I could offer the king only uprightness and good-heartedness," he said himself, " two qualities insufficient to make a minister, even a mediocre one." The courtiers, in fact, called him " good-heart " (*bonhomme*). " M. de Malesherbes has doubts about everything," wrote Madame du Deffand, " M. Turgot has doubts about nothing." M. de Maurepas having, of set purpose, got up rather a serious quarrel with him, Malesherbes sent in his resignation to the king; the latter pressed him to withdraw it: the minister remained inflexible. " You are better off than I," said Louis XVI. at last, " you can abdicate."

For a long while the king had remained faithful to M. Turgot. "People may say what they like," he would repeat, with sincere conviction, " but he is an honest man!" Infamous means were employed, it is said, with the king; he was shown forged letters, purporting to come from M. Turgot, intercepted at the post and containing opinions calculated to wound his Majesty himself. To pacify the jealousy of M. de Maurepas, Turgot had given up his privilege of working alone with the king. Left to the adroit manœuvres of his old minister, Louis XVI. fell away by degrees from the troublesome reformer against whom were leagued all those who were about him. The queen had small liking for M. Turgot, whose strict economy had cut down the expenses of her household; contrary to their usual practice, her most trusted servants abetted the animosity of M. de Maurepas. " I confess that I am not sorry for these departures," wrote Marie Antoinette to her mother, after the fall of M. Turgot, " but I have had nothing to do with them." " Sir," M. Turgot had written to Louis XVI., " monarchs governed by courtiers have but to choose between the fate of Charles I. and that of Charles IX." The coolness went on increasing between the king and his minister. On the 12th of May, 1776, the comptroller-general entered the king's closet; he had come to speak to him about a new project for an edict; the exposition of reasons was, as usual, a choice morsel of political philosophy. "Another commentary!" said the king with temper. He listened however. When the comptroller-general had finished, "Is that all?" asked the king. "Yes, sir." "So much the better," and he showed the minister out. A few hours later, M. Turgot received his dismissal.

He was at his desk, drawing up an important decree; he laid down his pen, saying quietly, "My successor will finish;" and, when M. de Maurepas hypocritically expressed his regret: "I retire," said M. Turgot, "without having to reproach myself with feebleness, or falseness, or dissimulation." He wrote to the king: "I have done, sir, what I believed to be my duty in setting before you, with unreserved and unexampled frankness the difficulty of the position in which I stood and what I thought of your own. If I had not done so, I should have considered myself to have behaved culpably towards you. You, no doubt, have come to a different conclusion, since you have withdrawn your confidence from me; but, even if I were mistaken, you cannot, sir, but do justice to the feeling by which I was guided. All I desire, sir, is that you may always be able to believe that I was short-sighted and that I pointed out to you merely fanciful dangers. I hope that time may not justify me and that your reign may be as happy and as tranquil, for yourself and your people, as they flattered themselves it would be, in accordance with your principles of justice and beneficence."

Useless wishes, belied in advance by the previsions of M. Turgot himself. He had espied the danger and sounded some of the chasms just yawning beneath the feet of the nation as well as of the king; he committed the noble error of believing in the instant and supreme influence of justice and reason. "Sir," said he to Louis XVI., "you ought to govern, like God, by general laws." Had he been longer in power, M. Turgot would still have failed in his designs. The life of one man was too short and the hand of one man too weak to modify the course of

events, fruit slowly ripened during so many centuries. It was
to the honour of M. Turgot that he discerned the mischief
and would fain have applied the proper remedy. He was often
mistaken about the means, oftener still about the strength he had at
disposal. He had the good fortune to die early, still sad and anxious
about the fate of his country, without having been a witness
of the catastrophes he had foreseen and of the sufferings as well as
wreckage through which France must pass before touching at the
haven he would fain have opened to her.

The joy of the courtiers was great, at Versailles, when the
news arrived of M. Turgot's fall; the public regretted it but
little: the inflexible severity of his principles which he never
veiled by grace of manners, a certain disquietude occasioned by
the chimerical views which were attributed to him, had alienated
many people from him. His real friends were in consternation.
"I was but lately rejoicing," said Abbé Véry, "at the idea that
the work was going on of coolly repairing a fine edifice which time
had damaged. Henceforth, the most that will be done will be to
see after repairing a few of its cracks. I no longer indulge in
hopes of its restoration; I cannot but apprehend its downfall
sooner or later." "Oh! what news I hear!" writes Voltaire to
D'Alembert; "France would have been too fortunate. What will
become of us? I am quite upset. I see nothing but death for
me to look forward to, now that M. Turgot is out of office.
It is a thunderbolt fallen upon my brain and upon my heart."

A few months later M. de St. Germain retired in his turn, not
to Alsace again, but to the Arsenal with forty thousand livres for
pension. The first, the great attempt at reform had failed.
"M. de Malesherbes lacked will to remain in power," said
Abbé Véry, "M. Turgot conciliatoriness (conciliabilité), and M.
de Maurepas soul enough to follow his lights." "M. de Malesherbes," wrote Condorcet, "has, either from inclination or from
default of mental rectitude, a bias towards eccentric and para-
doxical ideas; he discovers in his mind numberless arguments for
and against, but never discovers a single one to decide him.
In his private capacity he had employed his eloquence in proving
to the king and the ministers that the good of the nation was the

one thing needful to be thought of; when he became minister, he employed it in proving that this good was impossible." " I understand two things in the matter of war," said M. de St. Germain just before he became minister, " to obey and to command; but, if it comes to advising, I don't know anything about it." He was, indeed, a bad adviser; and with the best intentions he had no idea either how to command or how to make himself obeyed. M. Turgot had correctly estimated the disorder of affairs, when he wrote to the king on the 30th of April, a fortnight before his disgrace, " Sir, the parliaments are already in better heart, more audacious, more implicated in the cabals of the court than they were in 1770, after twenty years of enterprise and success. Minds are a thousand times more excited upon all sorts of matters, and your ministry is almost as divided and as feeble as that of your predecessor. Consider, sir, that, in the course of nature, you have fifty years to reign, and reflect what progress may be made by a disorder which, in twenty years, has reached the pitch at which we see it."

Turgot and Malesherbes had fallen; they had vainly attempted to make the soundest as well as the most moderate principles of pure philosophy triumphant in the government; at home a new attempt, bolder and at the same time more practical, was soon about to resuscitate for a while the hopes of liberal minds; abroad and in a new world there was already a commencement of events which were about to bring to France a revival of glory and to shed on the reign of Louis XVI. a moment's legitimate and brilliant lustre.

CHAPTER LVII.

LOUIS XVI. — FRANCE ABROAD. — UNITED STATES' WAR OF
INDEPENDENCE. — 1775—1783.

"TWO things, great and difficult as they may be, are a man's duty and may establish his fame. To support misfortune and be sturdily resigned to it; to believe in the good and trust in it perseveringly" [M. Guizot, *Washington*].

"There is a sight as fine and not less salutary than that of a virtuous man at grips with adversity; it is the sight of a virtuous man at the head of a good cause and securing its triumph.

"If ever cause were just and had a right to success, it was that of the English colonies which rose in insurrection to become the United States of America.

"Opposition, in their case, preceded insurrection.

"Their opposition was founded on historic right and on facts, on rational right and on ideas.

"It is to the honour of England that she had deposited in the cradle of her colonies the germ of their liberty; almost all, at their foundation, received charters which conferred upon the colonists the franchises of the mother-country.

"At the same time with legal rights, the colonists had creeds. It was not only as Englishmen, but as Christians, that they wanted to be free, and they had their faith even more at heart than their charters. Their rights would not have disappeared, even had they lacked their charters. By the mere impulse of their souls, with the assistance of divine grace, they would have derived them from a sublimer source and one inaccessible to human power, for they cherished feelings that soared beyond even the institutions of which they showed themselves to be so jealous.

"Such, in the English colonies, was the happy condition of man and of society, when England, by an arrogant piece of aggression, attempted to dispose, without their consent, of their fortunes and their destiny."

The uneasiness in the relations between the mother-country and the colonies was of old date; and the danger which England ran of seeing her great settlements beyond the sea separating from her had for some time past struck the more clear-sighted. "Colonies are like fruits which remain on the tree only until they are ripe," said M. Turgot in 1750: "when they have become self-sufficing, they do as Carthage did, as America will one day do." It was in the war between England and France for the possession of Canada that the Americans made the first trial of their strength.

Alliance was concluded between the different colonies, Virginia marched in tune with Massachusetts; the pride of a new power, young and already victorious, animated the troops which marched to the conquest of Canada. "If we manage to remove from Canada these turbulent Gauls," exclaimed John Adams, "our territory, in a century, will be more populous than England herself. Then all Europe will be powerless to subjugate us." "I am astounded," said the duke of Choiseul to the English negotiator who arrived at Paris in 1761, "I am astounded that your great Pitt should attach so much importance to the acquisition of Canada, a territory too scantily peopled to ever become dangerous for you and one which, in our hands, would serve to keep your colonies in a state of dependence from which they will not fail to free themselves the moment Canada is ceded to you." A pamphlet attributed to Burke proposed to leave Canada to France with the avowed aim of maintaining on the border of the American provinces an object of anxiety and an ever-threatening enemy.

America protested its loyalty and rejected with indignation all idea of separation. "It is said that the development of the strength of the colonies may render them more dangerous and bring them to declare their independence," wrote Franklin in 1760 : "such fears are chimerical. So many causes are against their union, that I do not hesitate to declare it not only improbable but impossible ; I say impossible—without the most provoking tyranny and oppression. As long as the government is mild and just, as long as there is security for civil and religious interests, the Americans will be respectful and submissive subjects. The waves only rise when the wind blows."

In England, many distinguished minds doubted whether the government of the mother-country would manage to preserve the discretion and moderation claimed by Franklin. "Notwithstanding all you say of your loyalty, you Americans," observed Lord Camden to Franklin himself, " I know that some day you will shake off the ties which unite you to us and you will raise the standard of independence." "No such idea exists or will enter into the heads of the Americans," answered Franklin, "unless you maltreat them quite scandalously." "That is true," rejoined the other, "and it is exactly one of the causes which I foresee and which will bring on the event."

The Seven Years' War was ended, shamefully and sadly for France ; M. de Choiseul, who had concluded peace with regret and a bitter pang, was ardently pursuing every means of taking his revenge. To foment disturbances between England and her colonies appeared to him an efficacious and a natural way of gratifying his feelings. "There is great difficulty in governing States in the days in which we live," he wrote to M. Durand, at that time French minister in London ; "still greater difficulty in governing those of America ; and the difficulty approaches impossibility as regards those of Asia. I am very much astonished that England, which is but a very small spot in Europe, should hold dominion over more than a third of America and that her dominion should have no other object but that of trade. . . . As long as the vast American possessions contribute no subsidies for the support of the mother-country, private persons in England will still grow rich for some time on the trade with America, but the State will be undone for want of means to keep together a too extended power; if, on the contrary, England proposes to establish imposts in her American domains, when they are more extensive and perhaps more populous than the mother-country, when they have fishing, woods, navigation, corn, iron, they will easily part asunder from her, without any fear of chastisement, for England could not undertake a war against them to chastise them." He encouraged his agents to keep him informed as to the state of feeling in America, welcoming and studying all projects, even the most fantastic, that might be hostile to England.

When M. de Choiseul was thus writing to M. Durand, the English government had already justified the fears of its wisest and most sagacious friends. On the 7th of March, 1765, after a short and unimportant debate, Parliament, on the motion of Mr. George Grenville, then first lord of the treasury, had extended to the American colonies the stamp-tax everywhere in force in England. The proposal had been brought forward in the preceding year, but the protests of the colonists had for some time retarded its discussion. "The Americans are an ungrateful people," said Townshend: "they are children settled in life by our care and nurtured by our indulgence." Pitt was absent. Colonel Barré rose: "Settled by your care!" he exclaimed: "nay, it was your oppression which drove them to America; to escape from your tyranny, they exposed themselves in the desert to all the ills that human nature can endure! Nurtured by your indulgence! Nay, they have grown by reason of your indifference; and do not forget that these people, loyal as they are, are as jealous as they were at the first of their liberties and remain animated by the same spirit that caused the exile of their ancestors." This was the only protest. "Nobody voted on the other side in the House of Lords," said George Grenville at a later period.

In America the effect was terrible and the dismay profound. The Virginia House was in session; nobody dared to speak against a measure which struck at all the privileges of the colonies and went to the hearts of the loyal gentlemen still passionately attached to the mother-country. A young barrister, Patrick Henry, hardly known hitherto, rose at last and in an unsteady voice said: " I propose to the vote of the Assembly the following resolutions; ' Only the general Assembly of this colony has the right and power to impose taxes on the inhabitants of this colony; every attempt to invest with this power any person or body whatever other than the said general Assembly has a manifest tendency to destroy at one and the same time British and American liberties.' " Then becoming more and more animated and rising to eloquence by sheer force of passion: "Tarquin and Cæsar," he exclaimed, " had each their Brutus; Charles I. had his Cromwell, and George III. . . ." " Treason! treason! " was shouted on all sides . . . " will doubtless profit by their example," continued Patrick Henry proudly, without allowing himself to be moved by the wrath of the government's friends. His resolutions were voted by 20 to 19.

The excitement in America was communicated to England; it served the political purposes and passions of Mr. Pitt; he boldly proposed in the House of Commons the repeal of the stamp-tax: " The colonists," he said " are subjects of this realm, having, like yourselves, a title to the special privileges of Englishmen; they are bound by the English laws and, in the same measure as yourselves, have a right to the liberties of this country. The Americans are the sons and not the bastards of England. . . . When in this House we grant subsidies to his Majesty, we dispose of that which is our own; but the Americans are not represented here: when we impose a tax upon them, what is it we do? We, the Commons of England, give what to his Majesty? Our own personal property? No; we give away the property of the Commons of America. There is absurdity in the very terms."

The bill was repealed and agitation was calmed for a while in

America. But, ere long, Mr. Pitt resumed office under the title of Lord Chatham, and with office he adopted other views as to the taxes to be imposed; in vain he sought to disguise them under the form of custom-house duties: the taxes on tea, glass, paper, excited in America the same indignation as the stamp-tax. Resistance was everywhere organized.

"Between 1767 and 1774 patriotic leagues were everywhere formed against the consumption of English merchandize and the exportation of American produce; all exchange ceased between the mother-country and the colonies; to extinguish the source of England's riches in America and to force her to open her eyes to her madness the colonists shrank from no privation and no sacrifice: luxury had vanished, rich and poor welcomed ruin rather than give up their political rights" [M. Cornélis de Witt, *Histoire de Washington*]. "I expect nothing more from petitions to the king," said Washington, already one of the most steadfast champions of American liberties, "and I would oppose them if they were calculated to suspend the execution of the pact of non-importation. As sure as I live, there is no relief to be expected for us but from the straits of Great Britain. I believe, or at least I hope, that there is enough public virtue still remaining among us to make us deny ourselves everything but the bare necessaries of life in order to obtain justice. This we have a right to do and no power on earth can force us to a change of conduct short of being reduced to the most abject slavery. . . ." He added in a spirit of strict justice: "As to the pact of non-exportation, that is another thing; I confess that I have doubts of its being legitimate. We owe considerable sums to Great Britain; we can only pay them with our produce. To have a right to accuse others of injustice, we must be just ourselves; and how can we be so if we refuse to pay our debts to Great Britain? That is what I cannot make out."

The opposition was as yet within the law and the national effort was as orderly as it was impassioned. "There is agitation, there are meetings, there is mutual encouragement to the struggle, the provinces concert opposition together, the wrath against Great Britain grows and the abyss begins to yawn; but such are the habits of order amongst this people, that, in the midst of this immense ferment amongst the nation, it is scarcely possible to pick out even a few acts of violence here and there; up to the day when the uprising becomes general, the government of George III. can scarcely find, even in the great centres of opposition, such as Boston, any specious pretexts for its own violence " [M. Cornélis de Witt, *Histoire de Washington*]. The declaration of independence was by this time becoming inevitable when Washington and Jefferson were still writing in this strain :—

Washington to Capt. Mackenzie.

" You are taught to believe that the people of Massachusetts are a people of rebels in revolt for independence, and what not. Permit me to tell you, my good friend, that you are mistaken, grossly mistaken. . . . I can testify, as a fact, that independence is neither the wish nor the interest of this colony or of any other on the continent, separately or collectively. But at the same time you may rely upon it that none of them will ever submit to the loss of those privileges, of those precious rights which are essential to the happiness of every free State, and without which liberty, property, life itself, are devoid of any security."

Jefferson to Mr. Randolph.

" Believe me, my dear sir, there is not in the whole British empire a man who cherishes more cordially than I do the union with Great Britain. But, by the God who made me, I would cease to live rather than accept that union on the terms proposed by Parliament. We lack neither motives nor power to declare and maintain our separation. It is the will alone that we lack, and that is growing little by little under the hand of our king."

It was indeed growing: Lord Chatham had been but a short time in office; Lord North, on becoming prime minister, zealously promoted the desires of George III. in Parliament and throughout the country. The opposition, headed by Lord Chatham, protested in the name of the eternal principles of justice and liberty against the measures adopted towards the colonies. " Liberty," said Lord Chatham, " is pledged to liberty, they are indissolubly allied in this great cause, it is the alliance between God and nature, immutable, eternal, as the light in the firmament of heaven! Have a care; foreign war is suspended over your heads by a thin and fragile thread, Spain and France are watching over your conduct, waiting for the fruit of your blunders; they keep their eyes fixed on America, and are more concerned with the dispositions of your colonies than with their own affairs, whatever they may be. I repeat to you, my lords, if ministers persist in their fatal counsels, I do not say that they may alienate the affections of its subjects, but I affirm that they will destroy the greatness of the crown; I do not say that the king will be betrayed, I affirm that the country will be ruined!"

Franklin was present at this scene. Sent to England by his fellow-countrymen to support their petitions by his persuasive and dexterous eloquence, he watched with intelligent interest the disposition of the Continent towards his country. "All Europe seems to be on our side," he wrote, "but Europe has its own reasons. It considers itself threatened by the power of England, and it would like to see her divided against herself. Our prudence will retard for a long time yet, I hope, the satisfaction which our enemies expect from our dissensions. . . . . Prudence, patience, discretion; when the catastrophe arrives, it must be clear to all mankind that the fault is not on our side."

The catastrophe was becoming imminent. Already a riot at Boston had led to throwing into the sea a cargo of tea which had arrived on board two English vessels, and which the governor had refused to send away at once as the populace desired; already, on the summons of the Virginia Convention, a general Congress of all the provinces had met at Philadelphia; at the head of the legal resistance as well as of the later rebellion in arms marched the puritans of New England and the sons of the cavaliers settled in Virginia; the opposition tumultuous and popular in the North, parliamentary and political in the South, was everywhere animated by the same spirit and the same zeal. "I do not pretend to indicate precisely what line must be drawn between Great Britain and the colonies," wrote Washington to one of his friends, "but it is most decidedly my opinion that one must be drawn, and our rights definitively secured." He had but lately

GEORGE WASHINGTON.

said: "Nobody ought to hesitate a moment to employ arms in defence of interests so precious, so sacred, but arms ought to be our last resource."

The day had come when this was the only resource henceforth remaining to the Americans. Stubborn and irritated, George III. and his government heaped vexatious measures one upon another, feeling sure of crushing down the resistance of the colonists by the ruin of their commerce as well as of their liberties. "We must fight," exclaimed Patrick Henry at the Virginia Convention, "I repeat it, we must fight; an appeal to arms and to the God of Hosts, that is all we have left." Armed resistance was already being organized, in the teeth of many obstacles and notwithstanding active or tacit opposition on the part of a considerable portion of the people.

It was time to act. On the 18th of April, 1775, at night, a picked body of the English garrison of Boston left the town by order of General Gage, governor of Massachusetts. The soldiers were as yet in ignorance of their destination, but the American patriots had divined it. The governor had ordered the gates to be closed; some of the inhabitants, however, having found means of escaping, had spread the alarm in the country; already men were repairing in silence to posts assigned in anticipation; when the king's troops, on approaching Lexington, expected to lay hands upon two of the principal movers, Samuel Adams and John Hancock, they came into collision, in the night, with a corps of militia blocking the way; the Americans taking no notice of the order given them to retire, the English troops, at the instigation of their officers, fired; a few men fell; war was begun between England and America. That very evening, Colonel Smith, whilst proceeding to seize the ammunition-depôt at Concord, found himself successively attacked by detachments hastily formed in all the villages; he fell back in disorder beneath the guns of Boston.

Some few days later the town was besieged by an American army and the Congress, meeting at Philadelphia, appointed Washington " to be general-in-chief of all the forces of the united colonies, of all that had been or should be levied, and of all

others that should voluntarily offer their services or join the said
army to defend American liberty and to repulse every attack
directed against it."

George Washington was born on the 22nd of February, 1732,
on the banks of the Potomac, at Bridge's Creek, in the county of
Westmoreland in Virginia. He belonged to a family of consideration among the planters of Virginia, descended from that
race of country-gentlemen who had but lately effected the revolution in England. He lost his father early and was brought up by
a distinguished, firm and judicious mother, for whom he always
preserved equal affection and respect. Intended for the life of a
surveyor of the still uncleared lands of Western America, he had
led, from his youth up, a life of freedom and hardship; at nineteen, during the Canadian war, he had taken his place in the
militia of his country, and we have seen how he fought with
credit at the side of General Braddock. On returning home at
the end of the war and settling at Mount Vernon, which had been
bequeathed to him by his eldest brother, he had become a great
agriculturist and great hunter, esteemed by all, loved by those
who knew him, actively engaged in his own business as well as
that of his colony, and already an object of confidence as well as
hope to his fellow-citizens. In 1774, on the eve of the great
struggle, Patrick Henry, on leaving the first Congress formed to
prepare for it, replied to those who asked which was the foremost
man in the Congress: " If you speak of eloquence, Mr. Rutledge
of South Carolina is the greatest orator; but, if you speak of solid
knowledge of things and of sound judgment, Colonel Washington
is indisputably the greatest man in the Assembly." " Capable of
rising to the highest destinies, he could have ignored himself
without a struggle and found in the culture of his lands satisfaction for those powerful faculties which were to suffice for the
command of armies and for the foundation of a government. But
when the occasion offered, when the need came, without any effort
on his own part, without surprise on the part of others, the sagacious planter turned out a great man; he had in a superior degree
the two qualities which in active life render men capable of great
things; he could believe firmly in his own ideas and act resolutely

BUNKER'S HILL.

upon them, without fearing to take the responsibility " [M. Guizot, *Washington*].

He was, however, deeply moved and troubled at the commencement of a contest of which he foresaw the difficulties and the trials, without fathoming their full extent, and it was not without a struggle that he accepted the power confided to him by Congress. " Believe me, my dear Patsy," he wrote to his wife, " I have done all I could to screen myself from this high mark of honour, not only because it cost me much to separate myself from you and from my family, but also because I felt that this task was beyond my strength." When the new general arrived before Boston to take command of the confused and undisciplined masses which were hurrying up to the American camp, he heard that an engagement had taken place on the 16th of June on the heights of Bunker's Hill, which commanded the town ; the Americans who had seized the positions had defended them so bravely that the English had lost nearly a thousand men before they carried the batteries. A few months later, after unheard of efforts on the general's part to constitute and train his army, he had taken possession of all the environs of the place, and General Howe, who had superseded General Gage, evacuated Boston (March 17, 1776).

Every step was leading to the declaration of independence. " If everybody were of my opinion," wrote Washington in the month of February, 1776, " the English Ministers would learn in few words what we want to arrive at. I should set forth simply, and without periphrasis, our grievances and our resolution to have justice. I should tell them that we have long and ardently desired an honourable reconciliation, and that it has been refused. I should add that we have conducted ourselves as faithful subjects, that the feeling of liberty is too strong in our hearts to let us ever submit to slavery, and that we are quite determined to burst every bond with an unjust and unnatural government, if our enslavement alone will satisfy a tyrant and his diabolical ministry. And I should tell them all this not in covert terms, but in language as plain as the light of the sun at full noon."

Many people still hesitated, from timidity, from foreseeing the sufferings which war would inevitably entail on America, from hereditary, faithful attachment to the mother-country. "Gentle-men," had but lately been observed by Mr. Dickinson, deputy from Pennsylvania, at the reading of the scheme of a solemn declaration justifying the taking up of arms, "there is but one word in this paper of which I disapprove — *Congress.*" "And as for me, Mr. President," said Mr. Harrison, rising, "there is but one word in this paper of which I approve—*Congress.*"

Deeds had become bolder than words. "We have hitherto made war by halves," wrote John Adams to General Gates, "you will see in to-morrow's papers that for the future we shall probably venture to make it by three-quarters. The continental navy, the provincial navies, have been authorized to cruise against English property throughout the whole extent of the Ocean. Learn, for your governance, that this is not Independence. Far from it! If one of the next couriers should bring you word of unlimited freedom of commerce with all nations, take good care not to call that Independence. Nothing of the sort! Inde-pendence is a spectre of such awful mien that the mere sight of it might make a delicate person faint."

Independence was not yet declared, and already, at the end of their proclamations, instead of the time-honoured formula, *God save the king!* the Virginians had adopted the proudly significant phrase, *God save the liberties of America!*

The great day came, however, when the Congress resolved to give its true name to the war which the colonies had been for more than a year maintaining against the mother-country. After a discussion which lasted three days, the scheme drawn up by Jefferson, for the declaration of Independence, was adopted by a large majority. The solemn proclamation of it was determined upon on the 4th of July, and that day has remained the national festival of the United States of America. John Adams made no mistake when, in the transport of his patriotic joy, he wrote to his wife:—"I am inclined to believe that this day will be celebrated by generations to come as the great anniversary of the nation. It should be kept as the day of deliverance by solemn thanks-givings to the Almighty. It should be kept with pomp, to the sound of cannon and of bells, with games, with bonfires and illuminations from one end of the continent to the other, for ever. You will think me carried away by my enthusiasm ; but no, I take into account, perfectly, the pains, the blood, the treasure we shall have to expend to maintain this declaration, to uphold and defend these States, but through all these shadows I perceive rays of ravishing light and joy, I feel that the end is worth all the means and far more, and that posterity will rejoice over this event with songs of triumph, even though we should have cause to repent of it, which will not be, I trust in God."

The declaration of American independence was solemn and grave ; it began with an appeal to those natural rights which the eighteenth century had everywhere learnt to claim. " We hold as self-evident all these truths," said the Congress of united colonies : " All men are created equal, they are endowed by their Creator with certain inalienable rights ; among those rights are life, liberty, and the pursuit of happiness. Governments are established amongst men to guarantee those rights, and their just power emanates from the consent of the governed."

To this declaration of the inalienable right of people to choose their own government for the greatest security and greatest happiness of the governed, succeeded an enumeration of the grievances which made it for ever impossible for the American colonists to render obedience to the king of Great Britain ; the list was long and over-whelming ; it ended with this declaration : " Wherefore we, the representatives of the United States of America, met together in general Congress, calling the Supreme Judge of the universe to witness the uprightness of our intentions, do solemnly publish and declare in the name of the good people of these colonies, that the United-colonies are and have a right to be free and independent States, that they are released from all allegiance to the crown of Great Britain, and that every political tie between them and Great Britain is and ought to be entirely dissolved. . . . Full of firm confidence in the protection of Divine Providence, we pledge, mutually, to the maintenance of this declaration our lives, our fortunes, and our most sacred possession, our honour."

The die was cast, and retreat cut off for the timid and the malcontent ; through a course of alternate successes and reverses

Washington had kept up hostilities during the rough campaign of 1776. Many a time he had thought the game lost, and he had found himself under the necessity of abandoning posts he had mastered to fall back upon Philadelphia. "What will you do if Philadelphia is taken?" he was asked. "We will retire beyond the Susquehanna, and then, if necessary, beyond the Alleghanies," answered the general without hesitation. Unwavering in his patriotic faith and resolution, he relied upon the savage resources and the vast wildernesses of his native country to wear out at last the patience and courage of the English generals. At the end of the campaign, Washington, suddenly resuming the offensive, had beaten the king's troops at Trenton and at Princeton one after the other. This brilliant action had restored the affairs of the Americans and was a preparatory step to the formation of a new army. On the 30th of December, 1776, Washington was invested by Congress with the full powers of a dictator.

Europe, meanwhile, was following with increasing interest the vicissitudes of a struggle which at a distance had from the first appeared to the most experienced an unequal one. "Let us not anticipate events, but content ourselves with learning them when they occur," said a letter, in 1775, to M. de Guines, ambassador in London, from Louis XVI.'s minister for foreign affairs, M. de Vergennes: "I prefer to follow, as a quiet observer, the course of events rather than try to produce them." He had but lately said with prophetic anxiety: "Far from seeking to profit by the embarrassment in which England finds herself on account of affairs in America, we should rather desire to extricate her. The spirit of revolt, in whatever spot it breaks out, is always of dangerous precedent; it is with moral as with physical diseases, both may become contagious. This consideration should induce us to take care that the spirit of independence, which is causing so terrible an explosion in North America, have no power to communicate itself to points interesting to us in this hemisphere."

For a moment French diplomats had been seriously disconcerted; remembrance of the surprise in 1755, when England had commenced hostilities without declaring war, still troubled men's minds. Count de Guines wrote to M. de Vergennes: "Lord

Rochford confided to me yesterday that numbers of persons on both sides were perfectly convinced that the way to put a stop to this war in America was to declare it against France and that he saw with pain that opinion gaining ground. I assure you, sir, that all which is said *for* is very extraordinary and far from encouraging. The partisans of this plan argue that fear of a war, disastrous for England, which might end by putting France once more in possession of Canada would be the most certain bug-bear for America, where the propinquity of our religion and our government is excessively apprehended; they say, in fact, that the Americans, forced by a war to give up their project of liberty and to decide between us and them, would certainly give them the preference."

The question of Canada was always, indeed, an anxious one for the American colonists; Washington had detached in that direction a body of troops which had been repulsed with loss. M. de Vergennes had determined to keep in the United States a semi-official agent, M. de Bonvouloir, commissioned to furnish the ministry with information as to the state of affairs. On sending Count de Guines the necessary instructions, the minister wrote on the 7th of August, 1775: " One of the most essential objects is to reassure the Americans on the score of the dread which they are no doubt taught to feel of us. Canada is the point of jealousy for them; they must be made to understand that we have no thought at all about it and that, so far from grudging them the liberty and independence they are labouring to secure, we admire, on the contrary, the grandeur and nobleness of their efforts, and that, having no interest in injuring them, we should see with pleasure such a happy conjunction of circumstances as would set them at liberty to frequent our ports; the facilities they would find for their commerce would soon prove to them all the esteem we feel for them."

Independence was not yet proclaimed and already the committee charged by Congress " to correspond with friends in England, Ireland, and other parts of the world," had made inquiry of the French government, by roundabout ways, as to what were its intentions regarding the American colonies, and was soliciting the

aid of France. On the 3rd of March, 1776, an agent of the
committee, Mr. Silas Deane, started for France; he had orders
to put the same question point blank at Versailles and at
Paris.

The ministry was divided on the subject of American affairs;
M. Turgot inclined towards neutrality. "Let us leave the
insurgents," he said, "at full liberty to make their purchases in
our ports and to provide themselves by the way of trade with the
munitions, and even the money, of which they have need. A
refusal to sell to them would be a departure from neutrality.
But it would be a departure likewise to furnish them with secret
aid in money, and this step, which it would be difficult to conceal,
would excite just complaints on the part of the English."

This was, however, the conduct adopted on the advice of
M. de Vergennes; he had been powerfully supported by the
arguments presented in a memorandum drawn up by M. de
Rayneval, senior clerk in the foreign office; he was himself
urged and incited by the most intelligent, the most restless
and the most passionate amongst the partisans of the American
rebellion—Beaumarchais.

Peter Augustin Caron de Beaumarchais, born at Paris on
the 24th of January, 1732, son of a clockmaker, had already
acquired a certain celebrity by his lawsuit against Councillor
Goëzman before the parliament of Paris. Accused of having
defamed the wife of a judge, after having fruitlessly attempted
to seduce her, Beaumarchais succeeded by dint of courage,
talent and wit in holding his own against the whole magistracy
leagued against him. He boldly appealed to public opinion:
"I am a citizen," he said, "that is to say, I am not a courtier, or
an abbé, or a nobleman, or a financier, or a favourite, nor anything
connected with what is called influence (*puissance*) nowadays. I
am a citizen; that is to say, something quite new, unknown,
unheard of in France. I am a citizen; that is to say, what you
ought to have been for the last two hundred years, what you will
be, perhaps, in twenty!" All the spirit of the French Revolution
was here, in those most legitimate and at the same time most
daring aspirations of his.

French citizen as he proclaimed himself to be, Beaumarchais was quite smitten with the American citizens; he had for a long while been pleading their cause, sure, he said, of its ultimate triumph. On the 10th of January, 1776, three weeks before the declaration of independence, M. de Vergennes secretly remitted a million to M. de Beaumarchais; two months later the same sum was entrusted to him in the name of the king of Spain. Beaumarchais alone was to appear in the affair and to supply the insurgent Americans with arms and ammunition. "You will

E. ROUJAT.

BENJAMIN FRANKLIN.

found," he had been told, "a great commercial house, and you will try to draw into it the money of private individuals; the first outlay being now provided, we shall have no further hand in it, the affair would compromise the government too much in the eyes of the English." It was under the style and title of *Rodrigo Hortalez and Co.* that the first instalment of supplies, to the extent of more than three millions, was forwarded to the Americans; and, notwithstanding the hesitation of the ministry and the rage of the English, other instalments soon followed. Beaumarchais was henceforth personally interested in the enterprise; he had commenced it from zeal for the American cause and from that yearning for activity and initiative which characterized him even in old age. " I should never have succeeded in fulfilling my mission here without the indefatigable, intelligent and generous efforts of M. de Beaumarchais," wrote Silas Deane to the secret committee of Congress : " the United States are more indebted to him, on every account, than to any other person on this side of the Ocean."

Negotiations were proceeding at Paris; Franklin had joined Silas Deane there. His great scientific reputation, the diplomatic renown he had won in England, his able and prudent devotion to the cause of his country, had paved the way for the new negotiator's popularity in France : it was immense. Born at Boston on the 17th of January, 1706, a printer before he came out as a great physician, Franklin was seventy years old when he arrived in Paris. His sprightly goodnature, the bold subtlety of his mind cloaked beneath external simplicity, his moderation in religion and the breadth of his philosophical tolerance, won the world of fashion as well as the great public, and were a great help to the success of his diplomatic negotiations. Quartered at Passy, at Madame Helvétius', he had frequent interviews with the ministers under a veil of secrecy and precaution which was, before long, skilfully and discreetly removed; from roundabout aid accorded to the Americans, at Beaumarchais' solicitations, on pretext of commercial business, the French Government had come to remitting money straight to the agents of the United States; everything tended to recognition of the independence of the colonies. In England, people were irritated and disturbed; Lord Chatham exclaimed with the usual exaggeration of his powerful and impassioned genius :—" Yesterday England could still stand against the world, to-day there is none so poor as to do her reverence. I borrow the poet's words, my lords, but what his verse expresses is no fiction. France has insulted you, she has encouraged and supported America, and, be America right or wrong, the dignity of this nation requires that we should thrust aside with contempt the officious intervention of France; ministers and ambassadors from those whom we call rebels and enemies are received at Paris, there they treat of the mutual interests of France and America, their countrymen are aided, provided with military resources, and our ministers suffer it, they do not protest! Is this maintaining the honour of a great kingdom, of that England which but lately gave laws to the House of Bourbon?"

The hereditary sentiments of Louis XVI. and his monarchical principles, as well as the prudent moderation of M. Turgot, retarded at Paris the negotiations which caused so much ill-humour among the English; M. de Vergennes still preserved, in all diplomatic relations, an apparent neutrality. "It is *my* line (*métier*), you see, to be a royalist," the Emperor Joseph II. had said during a visit he had just paid to Paris, when he was pressed to declare in favour of the American insurgents; at the bottom of his heart the king of France was of the same opinion; he had refused the permission to serve in America which he had been asked for by many gentlemen: some had set off without waiting for it; the most important as well as the most illustrious of them all, the marquis of La Fayette, was not twenty years old when he slipped away from Paris, leaving behind his young wife close to her confinement, to go and embark upon a vessel which he had bought, and which, laden with arms, awaited him in a Spanish port; arrested by order of the court, he evaded the vigilance of his guards; in the month of July, 1777, he disembarked in America.

Washington did not like France, he did not share the hopes which some of his fellow-countrymen founded upon her aid; he made no case of the young volunteers who came to enrol themselves amongst the defenders of independence and whom Congress loaded with favours. "No bond but interest attaches these men to America," he would say, "and, as for France, she only lets us get our munitions from her because of the benefit her commerce derives from it." Prudent, reserved, and proud, Washington looked for America's salvation to only America herself; neither had he foreseen nor did he understand that enthusiasm, as generous as it is unreflecting, which easily takes possession of the French nation, and of which the United States were just then the object. M. de La Fayette was the first who managed to win the general's affection and esteem. A great yearning for excitement and renown, a great zeal for new ideas and a certain political perspicacity had impelled M. de La Fayette to America; he showed himself courageous, devoted, more judicious and more able than had been expected from his youth and character. Washington came to love him as a son.

It was with the title of major-general that M. de La Fayette made his first campaign; Congress had passed a decree conferring upon him this grade, rather an excess of honour in Washington's opinion; the latter was at that time covering Philadelphia, the point aimed at by the operations of General Howe. Beaten at Brandywine and at Germantown, the Americans were obliged to abandon the town to the enemy and fall back on Valleyforge, where the general pitched his camp for wintering. The English had been beaten on the frontiers of Canada by General Gates; General Burgoyne, invested on all sides by the insurgents, had found himself forced to capitulate at Saratoga. The humiliation and wrath of the public in England were great, but the resolution of the politicians was beginning to waver; on the 10th of February, 1778, Lord North had presented two bills whereby England was to renounce the right of levying taxes in the American colonies, and was to recognize the legal existence of Congress. Three commissioners were to be sent to America to treat for conditions of peace. After a hot discussion, the two bills had been voted.

This was a small matter in view of the growing anxiety and the political manœuvrings of parties; on the 7th of April, 1778, the duke of Richmond proposed in the House of Lords the recall of all the forces, land and sea, which were fighting in America. He relied upon the support of Lord Chatham, who was now at death's door, but who had always expressed himself forcibly against the conduct of the government towards the colonists. The great orator entered the House, supported by two of his friends, pale, wasted, swathed in flannel beneath his embroidered robe. He with difficulty dragged himself to his place. The peers, overcome at the sight of this supreme effort, waited in silence. Lord Chatham rose, leaning on his crutch and still supported by his friends. He raised one hand to heaven.

" I thank God," he said, " that I have been enabled to come hither
to-day to fulfil a duty and say what has been weighing so heavily
on my heart.   I have already one foot in the grave, I shall soon
descend into it, I have left my bed to sustain my country's cause
in this House, perhaps for the last time.   I think myself happy,
my lords, that the grave has not yet closed over me, and that I am
still alive to raise my voice against the dismemberment of this
ancient and noble monarchy !   My lords, His Majesty succeeded
to an empire as vast in extent as proud in reputation.   Shall we

LA FAYETTE.

tarnish its lustre by a shameful abandonment of its rights and
of its fairest possessions ?   Shall this great kingdom, which
survived in its entirety the descents of the Danes, the incur-
sions of the Scots, the conquest of the Normans, which stood
firm against the threatened invasion of the Spanish Armada, now
fall before the House of Bourbon ?   Surely, my lords, we are not
what we once were ! . . . In God's name, if it be absolutely
necessary to choose between peace and war, if peace cannot be
preserved with honour, why not declare war without hesitation ?

. . . My lords, anything is better than despair, let us at least make an effort, and, if we must fail, let us fail like men ! "

He dropped back into his seat, exhausted, gasping. Soon he strove to rise and reply to the duke of Richmond, but his strength was traitor to his courage, he fainted; a few days later he was dead (May 11th, 1778); the resolution of the duke of Richmond had been rejected.

When this news arrived in America, Washington was seriously uneasy. He had to keep up an incessant struggle against the delays and the jealousies of Congress; it was by dint of unheard-of efforts and of unwavering perseverance that he succeeded in obtaining the necessary supplies for his army. " To see men without clothes to cover their nakedness," he exclaimed, " without blankets to lie upon, without victuals and often without shoes (for you might follow their track by the blood that trickled from their feet), advancing through ice and snow, and taking up their winter-quarters, at Christmas, less than a day's march from the enemy, in a place where they have not to shelter them either houses or huts but such as they have thrown up themselves, to see these men doing all this without a murmur, is an exhibition of patience and obedience such as the world has rarely seen."

As a set-off against the impassioned devotion of the patriots, Washington knew that the loyalists were still numerous and powerful; the burthen of war was beginning to press heavily upon the whole country, he feared some act of weakness. " Let us accept nothing short of Independence," he wrote at once to his friends : " we can never forget the outrages to which Great Britain has made us submit; a peace on any other conditions would be a source of perpetual disputes. If Great Britain, urged on by her love for tyranny, were to seek once more to bend our necks beneath her iron yoke, and she would do so, you may be sure, for her pride and her ambition are indomitable, what nation would believe any more in our professions of faith and would lend us its support ? It is to be feared, however, that the proposals of England will produce a great effect in this country. Men are naturally friends of peace, and there is more than one symptom to lead me to believe that the American people are generally weary of the war. If it be so, nothing can be more politic than to inspire the country with confidence by putting the army on an imposing footing, and by showing greater energy in our negotiations with European powers. I think that by now France must have recognized our independence, and that she will immediately declare war against Great Britain, when she sees that we have made serious proposals of alliance to her. But if, influenced by a false policy, or by an exaggerated opinion of our power, she were to hesitate, we should either have to send able negotiators at once, or give fresh instructions to our chargés d'affaires to obtain a definitive answer from her."

It is the property of great men, even when they share the prejudices of their time and of their country, to know how to get free from them and how to rise superior to their natural habits of thought. It has been said that, as a matter of taste, Washington did not like France and had no confidence in her, but his great and strong common-sense had enlightened him as to the conditions of the contest he had entered upon. He knew it was a desperate one, he foresaw that it would be a long one ; better than anybody he knew the weaknesses as well as the merits of the instruments which he had at disposal, he had learned to desire the alliance and the aid of France. She did not belie his hopes; at the very moment when Congress was refusing to enter into negotiations with Great Britain as long as a single English soldier remained on American soil, rejoicings and thanksgivings were everywhere throughout the thirteen colonies greeting the news of the recognition by France of the Independence of the United States; the treaties of alliance, a triumph of diplomatic ability on the part of Franklin, had been signed at Paris on the 6th of February, 1778.

"Assure the English government of the king's pacific intentions," M. de Vergennes had written to the marquis of Noailles, then French ambassador in England. George III. replied to these mocking assurances by recalling his ambassador.

"Anticipate your enemies," Franklin had said to the ministers of Louis XVI., "act towards them as they did to you in 1755, let your ships put to sea before any declaration of war, it will be time to speak when a French squadron bars the passage of Admiral Howe who has ventured to ascend the Delaware." The king's natural straightforwardness and timidity were equally opposed to this bold project; he hesitated a long while; when Count d'Estaing at last, on the 13th of April, went out of Toulon harbour to sail for America with his squadron, it was too late, the English were on their guard.

When the French admiral arrived in America, hostilities had commenced between France and England, without declaration of war, by the natural pressure of circumstances and the state of feeling in the two countries. England fired the first shot on the 17th of June, 1778. The frigate *La Belle Poule*, commanded by M. Chaudeau de la Clochetterie, was cruising in the Channel; she was surprised by the squadron of Admiral Keppel, issuing from Portsmouth; the Frenchman saw the danger in time, he crowded sail; but an English frigate, the *Arethusa*, had dashed forward in pursuit. La Clochetterie waited for her and refused to make the visit demanded by the English captain: a cannon-shot was the reply to this refusal. *La Belle Poule* delivered her whole broadside; when the *Arethusa* rejoined Lord Keppel's squadron, she was dismasted and had lost many men. A sudden calm had prevented two English vessels from taking part in the engagement; La Clochetterie went on and landed a few leagues from Brest. The fight had cost the lives of forty of his crew, fifty-seven had been wounded. He was made post-captain (*capitaine de vaisseau*). The glory of this small affair appeared to be of good augury; the conscience of Louis XVI. was soothed; he at last yielded to the passionate feeling which was hurrying the nation into war, partly from sympathy towards the Americans, partly from hatred and rancour towards England. The treaty of 1763 still lay heavy on the military honour of France.

From the day when the duke of Choiseul had been forced to sign that humiliating peace, he had never relaxed in his efforts to improve the French navy. In the course of ministerial alternations, frequently unfortunate for the work in hand. it had nevertheless been continued by his successors. A numerous fleet was preparing at Brest; it left the port on the 3rd of July, under

THE BELLE POULE AND THE ARETHUSA.

the orders of Count d'Orvilliers. It numbered thirty-two men-of-war and some frigates. Admiral Keppel came to the encounter with thirty ships, mostly superior in strength to the French vessels. The engagement took place on the 27th at thirty leagues' distance from Wessant and about the same from the Sorlingues islands. The splendid order of the French astounded the enemy, who had not forgotten the deplorable *Journée de M. de Conflans.* The sky was murky, and the manœuvres were interfered with from the difficulty of making out the signals. Lord Keppel could not succeed in breaking the enemy's line; Count d'Orvilliers failed in a like attempt. The English admiral extinguished his fires and returned to Plymouth harbour, without being forced to do so from any serious reverse; Count d'Orvilliers fell back upon Brest under the same conditions. The English regarded this retreat as a humiliation to which they were unaccustomed. Lord Keppel had to appear before a court-martial; in France, after the first burst of enthusiasm, fault was found with the inactivity of the duke of Chartres, who commanded the rear-guard of the fleet, under the direction of M. de La Motte-Piquet; the prince was before long obliged to leave the navy, he became colonel-general of the hussars. A fresh sally on the part of the fleet did not suffice to protect the merchant-navy, the losses of which were considerable. The English vessels everywhere held the seas.

Count d'Estaing had at last arrived at the mouth of the Delaware on the 9th of July, 1778; Admiral Howe had not awaited him, he had sailed for the anchorage of Sandy-Hook. The heavy French ships could not cross the bar; Philadelphia had been evacuated by the English as soon as the approach of Count d'Estaing was signalled. " It is not General Howe who has taken Philadelphia," said Franklin; " it is Philadelphia that has taken General Howe." The English commander had foreseen the danger; on falling back upon New York he had been hotly pursued by Washington, who had, at Monmouth, gained a serious advantage over him. The victory of the Americans would have been complete but for the jealous disobedience of General Lee. Washington pitched his camp thirty miles from New York.

" After two years' marching and counter-marching," he wrote, " after vicissitudes so strange that never perhaps did any other war exhibit the like since the beginning of the world, what a subject of satisfaction and astonishment for us to see the two armies back again at the point from which they started, and the assailants reduced in self-defence to have recourse to the shovel and the axe ! "

The combined expedition of D'Estaing and General Sullivan against the little English corps which occupied Rhode Island had just failed; the fleet of Admiral Howe had suddenly appeared at the entrance of the roads, the French squadron had gone out to meet it, an unexpected tempest separated the combatants; Count d'Estaing, more concerned for the fate of his vessels than with the clamours of the Americans, set sail for Boston to repair damages. The campaign was lost, cries of treason were already heard. A riot was the welcome which awaited the French admiral at Boston. All Washington's personal efforts, seconded by the marquis of La Fayette, were scarcely sufficient to restore harmony. The English had just made a descent upon the coasts of Georgia and taken possession of Savannah. They threatened Carolina and even Virginia.

Scarcely were the French ships in trim to put to sea when Count d'Estaing made sail for the Antilles. Zealous and brave, but headstrong and passionate, like M. de Lally-Tollendal under whom he had served in India, the admiral could ill brook reverses and ardently sought for an occasion to repair them. The English had taken St. Pierre and Miquelon. M. de Bouillé, governor of Iles-du-Vent, had almost at the same time made himself master of La Dominique. Four thousand English had just landed at St. Lucie; M. d'Estaing, recently arrived at Martinique, headed thither immediately with his squadron, without success however : it was during the absence of the English admiral, Byron, that the French seamen succeeded in taking possession first of St. Vincent and soon afterwards of Grenada. The fort of this latter island was carried after a brilliant assault; the admiral had divided his men into three bodies; he commanded the first, the second marched under the orders of Viscount de Noailles, and Arthur

Dillon, at the head of the Irish in the service of France, led the third. The cannon on the ramparts were soon directed against the English who thought to arrive in time to relieve Grenada.

Count d'Estaing went out of port to meet the English admiral; as he was sailing towards the enemy, the admiral made out, under French colours, a splendid ship of war, *Le Fier-Rodrigue*, which belonged to Beaumarchais and was convoying ten merchant-men. " Seeing the wide berth kept by this fine ship which was going proudly before the wind," says the sprightly and sagacious biographer of Beaumarchais, M. de Loménie, " Admiral d'Estaing signalled to her to bear down; learning that she belonged to his majesty Caron de Beaumarchais, he felt that it would be a pity not to take advantage of it, and, seeing the exigency of the case, he appointed her her place of battle without asking her pro- prietor's permission, leaving to the mercy of the waves and of the English the unhappy merchant-ships which the man-of-war was convoying. *Le Fier-Rodrigue* resigned herself bravely to her fate, took a glorious part in the battle off Grenada, contributed in forcing Admiral Byron to retreat, but had her captain killed and was riddled with bullets." Admiral d'Estaing wrote the same evening to Beaumarchais; his letter reached the scholar-merchant through the medium of the minister of marine. To the latter Beaumarchais at once replied: " Sir, I have to thank you for having forwarded to me the letter from Count d'Estaing. It is very noble in him at the moment of his triumph to have thought how very agreeable it would be to me to have a word in his hand- writing. I take the liberty of sending you a copy of his short letter, by which I feel honoured as the good Frenchman I am, and at which I rejoice as a devoted adherent of my country against that proud England. The brave Montault appears to have thought that he could not better prove to me how worthy he was of the post with which he was honoured than by getting killed; whatever may be the result as regards my own affairs, my poor friend Montault has died on the bed of honour, and I feel a sort of childish joy in being certain that those English who have cut me up so much in their papers for the last four years will read therein that one of my ships has helped to take from them the most fertile of their possessions. And as for the enemies of M. d'Estaing and especially of yourself, sir, I see them biting their nails, and my heart leaps for joy!"

The joy of Beaumarchais as well as that of France was a little excessive, and smacked of unfamiliarity with the pleasure of victory. M. d'Estaing had just been recalled to France; before he left, he would fain have rendered to the Americans a service pressingly demanded of him: General Lincoln was about to besiege Savannah; the English general, Sir Henry Clinton, a more able man than his predecessor, had managed to profit by the internal disputes of the Union, he had rallied round him the loyalists in Georgia and the Carolinas, civil war prevailed there with all its horrors; D'Estaing bore down with his squadron for Savannah. Lincoln was already on the coast ready to facilitate his landing; the French admiral was under pressure of the orders from Paris, he had no time for a regular siege. The trenches had already been opened twenty days, and the bombardment, terrible as it was for the American town, had not yet damaged the works of the English. On the 9th of October, D'Estaing determined to deliver the assault. Americans and French vied with each other in courage. For a moment the flag of the Union floated upon the ramparts, some grenadiers made their way into the place, the admiral was wounded; meanwhile, the losses were great, and perseverance was evidently useless. The assault was repulsed. Count D'Estaing still remained nine days before the place in hopes of finding a favourable opportunity; he was obliged to make sail for France, and the fleet withdrew, leaving Savannah in the hands of the English. The only advantage from the admiral's expedition was the deliverance of Rhode Island, abandoned by General Clinton who, fearing an attack from the French, recalled the garrison to New York. Washington had lately made himself master of the fort at Stony-Point, which had up to that time enabled the English to command the navigation of the Hudson.

In England the commotion was great: France and America in arms against her had just been joined by Spain. A government essentially monarchical, faithful to ancient traditions, the Spaniards had for a long while resisted the entreaties of M. de Vergennes,

who availed himself of the stipulations of the *Family pact.*
Charles III. felt no sort of sympathy for a nascent republic, he
feared the contagion of the example it showed to the Spanish
colonies, he hesitated to plunge into the expenses of a war.   His
hereditary hatred against England prevailed at last over the dic-
tates of prudence.   He was promised, moreover, the assistance of
France to reconquer Gibraltar and Minorca. The king of Spain consented to take part in the war, without however recognizing the independence of the United States or entering into alliance with them.

The situation of England was becoming serious, she believed
herself to be threatened with a terrible invasion.   As in the days
of the Great Armada, " orders were given to all functionaries,
civil and military, in case of a descent of the enemy, to see to the
transportation into the interior and into a place of safety of all
horses, cattle and flocks that might happen to be on the coasts."
" Sixty-six allied ships of the line ploughed the Channel, fifty thousand men, mustered in Normandy, were preparing to burst upon
the southern counties.   A simple American corsair, Paul Jones,
ravaged with impunity the coasts of Scotland, The powers of the
North, united with Russia and Holland, threatened to maintain,
with arms in hand, the rights of neutrals, ignored by the English
admiralty-courts.   Ireland awaited only the signal to revolt;
religious quarrels were distracting Scotland and England; the
authority of Lord North's cabinet was shaken in Parliament
as well as throughout the country, the passions of the mob
held sway in London, and amongst the sights that might have
been witnessed was that of this great city given up for nearly a
week to the populace, without anything that could stay its excesses
save its own lassitude and its own feeling of shame " [M. Cornélis
de Witt, *Histoire de Washington*].

So many and such imposing preparations were destined to
produce but little fruit : the two fleets, the French and the
Spanish, had effected their junction off Corunna, under the orders
of Count d'Orvilliers ; they slowly entered the Channel on the 31st
of August, near the Sorlingues (Scilly) Islands ; they sighted the
English fleet, with a strength of only thirty-seven vessels ; Count de
Guichen, who commanded the van-guard, was already manœuvring

to cut off the enemy's retreat; Admiral Hardy had the speed of him and sought refuge in Plymouth Sound. Some engagements which took place between frigates were of little importance, but glorious for both sides; on the 6th of October, the *Surveillante*, commanded by Chevalier du Couëdic, had a tussle with the *Quebec;* the broadsides were incessant, a hail of lead fell upon both ships, the majority of the officers of the *Surveillante* were killed or wounded. Du Couëdic had been struck twice on the head. A fresh wound took him in the stomach; streaming with blood, he remained at his post and directed the fight. The three masts of the *Surveillante* had just fallen, knocked to pieces by balls, the whole rigging of the *Quebec* at the same moment came down with a run. The two ships could no longer manoeuvre, the decimated crews were preparing to board when a thick smoke shot up all at once from the between-decks of the *Quebec;* the fire spread with unheard of rapidity, the *Surveillante*, already hooked on to her enemy's side, was on the point of becoming, like her, a prey to the flames, but her commander, gasping as he was and scarcely alive, got her loose by a miracle of ability. The *Quebec* had hardly blown up when the crew of the *Surveillante* set to work picking up the glorious wreck of their adversaries; a few prisoners were brought into Brest on the victorious vessel, which was so blackened by the smoke and damaged by the fight that tugs had to be sent to her assistance. A few months afterwards Du Couëdic died of his wounds, carrying to the grave the supreme honour of having been the only one to render his name illustrious in the great display of the maritime forces of France and Spain. Count d'Orvilliers made no attempt, the inhabitants upon the English coasts ceased to tremble, sickness committed ravages amongst the crews. After a hundred and four days' useless cruising in the Channel, the huge fleet returned sorrowfully to Brest; Admiral d'Orvilliers had lost his son in a partial engagement, he left the navy and retired ere long to a convent. Count de Guichen sailed for the Antilles with a portion of the French fleet and maintained with glory the honour of his flag in a series of frequently successful affairs against Admiral Rodney. At the beginning of the war, the latter, a great scapegrace and overwhelmed with debt, happened to be at Paris, detained by the state of his finances. " If I were free," said he one day in the presence of Marshal Biron, " I would soon destroy all the Spanish and French fleets." The marshal at once paid his debts : " Go, sir," said he with a flourish of generosity to which the eighteenth century was a little prone, " the French have no desire to gain advantages over their enemies save by their bravery." Rodney's first exploit was to revictual Gibraltar, which the Spanish and French armaments had invested by land and sea.

Everywhere the strength of the belligerents was being exhausted without substantial result and without honour ; for more than four years now America had been keeping up the war, and her Southern provinces had been everywhere laid waste by the enemy ; in spite of the heroism which was displayed by the patriots and of which the women themselves set the example, General Lincoln had just been forced to capitulate at Charlestown ; Washington, still encamped before New York, saw his army decimated by hunger and cold, deprived of all resources, and reduced to subsist at the expense of the people in the neighbourhood. All eyes were turned towards France ; the marquis of La Fayette had succeeded in obtaining from the king and the French ministry the formation of an auxiliary corps ; the troops were already on their way under the orders of Count de Rochambeau.

Misfortune and disappointments are great destroyers of some barriers, prudent tact can overthrow others ; Washington and the American army would but lately have seen with suspicion the arrival of foreign auxiliaries ; in 1780, transports of joy greeted the news of their approach ; M. de La Fayette, moreover, had been careful to spare the American general all painful friction. Count de Rochambeau and the French officers were placed under the orders of Washington and the auxiliary corps entirely at his disposal. The delicate generosity and the disinterestedness of the French government had sometimes had the effect of making it neglect the national interests in its relations with the revolted colonies ; but it had derived therefrom a spirit of conduct invariably calculated to triumph over the prejudices as well as the jealous pride of the Americans.

"The history of the War of Independence is a history of hopes deceived," said Washington. He had conceived the idea of making himself master of New York with the aid of the French. The transport of the troops had been badly calculated; Rochambeau brought to Rhode Island only the first division of his army, five thousand men about, and Count de Guichen, whose squadron had been relied upon, had just been recalled to France. Washington was condemned to inaction. "Our position is not sufficiently brilliant," he wrote to M. de La Fayette, "to justify our putting pressure upon Count de Rochambeau; I shall continue our arrangements, however, in the hope of more fortunate circumstances." The American army was slow in getting organized, obliged as it had been to fight incessantly and make head against constantly recurring difficulties; it was getting organized, however; the example of the French, the discipline which prevailed in the auxiliary corps, the good understanding thenceforth established amongst the officers, helped Washington in his difficult task. From the first the superiority of the general was admitted by the French as well as by the Americans; naturally and by the mere fact of the gifts he had received from God, Washington was always and everywhere chief of the men placed within his range and under his influence.

This natural ascendancy, which usually triumphed over the base jealousies and criminal manœuvres into which the rivals of General Washington had sometimes allowed themselves to be drawn, had completely failed in the case of one of his most brilliant lieutenants; in spite of his inveterate and well-known vices, Benedict Arnold had covered himself with glory by daring deeds and striking bravery exhibited in a score of fights, from the day when, putting himself at the head of the first bands raised in Massachusetts he had won the grade of general during his expedition to Canada. Accused of malversation and lately condemned by a court-martial to be reprimanded by the general-in-chief, Arnold, through an excess of confidence on Washington's part, still held the command of the important fort of West Point: he abused the trust.

Washington, on returning from an interview with Count de Rochambeau, went out of his way to visit the garrison of West Point: the commandant was absent. Surprised and displeased, the general was impatiently waiting for his return, when his aide-de-camp and faithful friend, Colonel Hamilton, brought him important despatches. Washington's face remained impassible; but throughout the garrison and amongst the general's staff there had already spread a whisper of Arnold's treachery: he had promised, it was said, to deliver West Point to the enemy. An English officer, acting as a spy, had actually been arrested within the American lines.

It was true, and General Arnold, turning traitor to his country from jealousy, vengeance, and the shameful necessities entailed by a disorderly life, had sought refuge at New York with Sir Henry Clinton. Major André was in the hands of the Americans. Young, honourable, brave, endowed with talents, and of elegant and cultivated tastes, the English officer, brought up with a view to a different career but driven into the army from a disappointment in love, had accepted the dangerous mission of bearing to the perfidious commandant of West Point the English general's latest instructions. Sir Henry Clinton had recommended him not to quit his uniform; but, yielding to the insinuating Arnold, the unhappy young man had put on a disguise; he had been made prisoner. Recognized and treated as a spy, he was to die on the gallows. It was the ignominy alone of this punishment which perturbed his spirit. "Sir," he wrote to Washington, "sustained against fear of death by the reflection that no unworthy action has sullied a life devoted to honour, I feel confident that in this my extremity your Excellency will not be deaf to a prayer the granting of which will soothe my last moments. Out of sympathy for a soldier, your Excellency will, I am sure, consent to adapt the form of my punishment to the feelings of a man of honour. Permit me to hope that, if my character have inspired you with any respect, if I am in your eyes sacrificed to policy and not to vengeance, I shall have proof that those sentiments prevail in your heart by learning that I am not to die on the gallows."

With a harshness of which there is no other example in his life and of which he appeared to always preserve a painful recollection, Washington remained deaf to his prisoner's noble appeal: Major André underwent the fate of a spy. " You are a witness that I die like a man of honour," he said to an American officer whose duty it was to see the orders carried out. The general did him justice. " André," he said, " paid his penalty with the spirit to be expected from a man of such merit and so brave an officer. As to Arnold, he has no heart. . ·. . Every body is surprised to see that he is not yet swinging on a gibbet." The passionate endeavours of the Americans to inflict upon the traitor the chastisement he deserved remained without effect. Constantly engaged, as an English general, in the war, with all the violence bred of uneasy hate, Arnold managed to escape the just vengeance of his countrymen; he died twenty years later, in the English possessions, rich and despised. " What would you have done, if you had succeeded in catching me?" he asked an American prisoner one day. " We would have severed from your body the leg that had been wounded in the service of the country, and would have hanged the rest on a gibbet," answered the militiaman quietly.

The excitement caused by the treachery of Arnold had not yet subsided, when a fresh cup of bitterness was put to the lips of the general-in-chief and disturbed the hopes he had placed on the re-organization of his army. Successive revolts amongst the troops of Pennsylvania, which threatened to spread to those of New Jersey, had convinced him that America had come to the end of her sacrifices. " The country's own powers are exhausted," he wrote to Colonel Lawrence in a letter intended to be com- municated to Louis XVI., " single-handed we cannot restore public credit and supply the funds necessary for continuing the war. The patience of the army is at an end, the people are discontented; without money, we shall make but a feeble effort, and probably the last."

The insufficiency of the military results obtained by land and sea, in comparison with the expenses and the exhibition of force, and the slowness and bad management of the operations had been attributed, in France as well as in America, to the incapacity of the ministers of war and marine, the prince of Montbarrey and M. de Sartines. The finances had up to that time sufficed for the enormous charges which weighed upon the treasury; credit for the fact was most justly given to the consummate ability and inexhaustible resources of M. Necker, who was, first of all, made director of the treasury on October 22, 1776, and then director-general of finance on June 29, 1777. By his advice, backed by the favour of the queen, the two ministers were superseded by M. de Ségur and the marquis of Castries. A new and more energetic impulse before long restored the hopes of the Americans. On the 21st of March, 1780, a fleet left under the orders of Count de Grasse; after its arrival at Martinique, on the 28th of April, in spite of Admiral Hood's attempts to block his passage, Count de Grasse took from the English the island of Tobago, on the 1st of June; on the 3rd of September, he brought Washington a reinforcement of three thousand five hundred men and twelve hundred thousand livres in specie. In a few months King Louis XVI. had lent to the United States or procured for them on his security sums exceeding sixteen million livres. It was to Washington personally that the French government confided its troops as well as its subsidies. " The king's soldiers are to be placed exclusively under the orders of the general-in-chief," M. Girard, the French minister in America had said, on the arrival of the auxiliary corps.

After so many and such painful efforts, the day of triumph was at last dawning upon General Washington and his country. Alternations of success and reverse had signalized the commencement of the campaign of 1781. Lord Cornwallis, who commanded the English armies in the South, was occupying Virginia with a considerable force, when Washington, who had managed to conceal his designs from Sir Henry Clinton, shut up in New York, crossed Philadelphia on the 4th of September and advanced by forced marches against the enemy. The latter had been for some time past harassed by the little army of M. de La Fayette. The fleet of Admiral de Grasse cut off the retreat of the English. Lord Cornwallis threw himself into Yorktown; on the 30th of September the place was invested.

It was but slightly and badly fortified, the English troops were fatigued by a hard campaign, the besiegers were animated by a zeal further stimulated by emulation; French and Americans vied with one another in ardour. Batteries sprang up rapidly, the soldiers refused to take any rest, the trenches were open by the 6th of October. On the 10th, the cannon began to batter the town; on the 14th an American column, commanded by M. de La Fayette, Col. Hamilton and Col. Lawrence, attacked one of the redoubts which protected the approaches to the town, whilst the French dashed forward on their side to attack the second redoubt, under the orders of Baron de Vioménil, Viscount de Noailles and marquis de St. Simon, who, ill as he was, had insisted on being carried at the head of his regiment. The flag of the Union floated above both works at almost the same instant; when the attacking columns joined again on the other side of the outwork they had attacked, the French had made five hundred prisoners. All defence became impossible. Lord Cornwallis in vain attempted to escape; he was reduced, on the 17th of October, to signing a capitulation more humiliating than that of Saratoga: eight thousand men laid down their arms, the vessels which happened to be lying at Yorktown and Gloucester were given up to the victors. Lord Cornwallis was ill of grief and fatigue. General O'Hara, who took his place, tendered his sword to Count de Rochambeau; the latter stepped back and, pointing to General Washington, said aloud, "I am only an auxiliary." In receiving the English general's sword, Washington was receiving the pledge of his country's independence.

England felt this. "Lord North received the news of the capitulation like a bullet in his breast," said Lord George Germaine, secretary of state for the colonies, "he threw up his arms without being able to utter a word beyond 'My God, all's lost!'" To this growing conviction on the part of his ministers, as well as of the nation, George III. opposed an unwavering persistency: "None of the members of my cabinet," he wrote immediately, "will suppose, I am quite sure, that this event can in any way modify the principles which have guided me hitherto and which will continue to regulate my conduct during the rest of this struggle."

Whilst the United States were celebrating their victory with thanksgivings and public festivities, their allies were triumphing at all the different points, simultaneously, at which hostilities had been entered upon. Becoming embroiled with Holland, where the republican party had prevailed against the stadtholder, who was devoted to them, the English had waged war upon the Dutch colonies. Admiral Rodney had taken St. Eustache, the centre of an immense trade; he had pillaged the warehouses and laden his vessels with an enormous mass of merchandise; the convoy which was conveying a part of the spoil to England was captured by Admiral La Motte-Piquet; M. Bouillé surprised the English garrison remaining at St. Eustache and recovered possession of the island, which was restored to the Dutch. They had just maintained gloriously, at Dogger Bank, their old maritime renown: " Officers and men all fought like lions," said Admiral Zouttman. The firing had not commenced until the two fleets were within pistol-shot. The ships on both sides were dismasted, scarcely in a condition to keep afloat; the glory and the losses were equal, but the English admiral, Hyde Parker, was irritated and displeased. George III. went to see him on board his vessel: " I wish your Majesty younger seamen and better ships," said the old sailor, and he insisted on resigning. This was the only action fought by the Dutch during the war; they left to Admiral de Kersaint the job of recovering from the English their colonies of Demerara, Essequibo and Berbice on the coasts of Guiana.

A small Franco-Spanish army was at the same time besieging Minorca; the fleet was considerable, the English were ill-prepared; they were soon obliged to shut themselves up in Fort St. Philip. The ramparts were as solid, the position was as impregnable as in the time of Marshal Richelieu; the admirals were tardy in bringing up the fleet, their irresolution caused the failure of operations that had been ill-combined, the squadrons entered port again; the duke of Crillon, who commanded the besieging force, weary of investing the fortress, made a proposal to the commandant to give the place up to him: the offers were magnificent, but Colonel Murray answered indignantly: " Sir, when the king his master ordered your brave ancestor to assassinate the duke of

Guise, he replied to Henry III., *Honour forbids!* You ought to have made the same answer to the king of Spain when he ordered you to assassinate the honour of a man as well born as the duke of Guise or yourself. I desire to have no communication with you but by way of arms." And he kept up the defence of his fortress continually battered by the besiegers' cannon-balls. Assault succeeded assault : the duke of Crillon himself escaladed the ramparts to capture the English flag which floated on the top of a tower : he was slightly wounded. "How long have generals done grenadiers' work?" said the officers to one another. The general heard them : "I wanted to make my Spaniards thorough French," he said, "that nobody might any longer perceive that there are two nationalities here." Murray at last capitulated on the 4th of February, 1782 : the fortress contained but a handful of soldiers exhausted with fatigue and privation.

Great was the joy at Madrid as well as in France, and deep the dismay in London : the ministry of Lord North could not stand against this last blow. So many efforts and so many sacrifices ending in so many disasters were irritating and wearing out the nation : "Great God!" exclaimed Burke, "is it still a time to talk to us of the rights we are upholding in this war! Oh! excellent rights! Precious they should be, for they have cost us dear. Oh! precious rights, which have cost Great Britain thirteen provinces, four islands, a hundred thousand men, and more than ten millions sterling! Oh! wonderful rights, which have cost Great Britain her empire upon the Ocean and that boasted superiority which made all nations bend before her! Oh! inestimable rights, which have taken from us our rank amongst the nations, our importance abroad and our happiness at home, which have destroyed our commerce and our manufactures, which have reduced us from the most flourishing empire in the world to a kingdom circumscribed and grandeur-less! Precious rights, which will, no doubt, cost us all that we have left!" The debate was growing more and more bitter. Lord North entered the House with his usual serenity : "This discussion is a loss of valuable time to the House," said he : "His Majesty has just accepted the resignation of his ministers." The Whigs came into power; Lord Rockingham, the duke of

SUFFREN.

Richmond, Mr. Fox; the era of concessions was at hand.   An
unsuccessful battle delivered against Hood and Rodney by Admiral
de Grasse restored for a while the pride of the English.   A good
sailor, brave and for a long time successful in war, Count de Grasse
had many a time been out-manœuvred by the English.   He had suffered himself to be enticed away from St. Christopher, which he was
besieging, and which the marquis of Bouillé took a few days later;
embarrassed by two damaged vessels, he would not abandon them
to the English and retarded his movements to protect them.   The
English fleet was superior to the French in vessels and weight of
metal; the fight lasted ten hours, the French squadron was broken,
disorder ensued in the manœuvres, the captains got killed one after
another, nailing their colours to the mast or letting their vessels
sink rather than strike; the flag-ship, the *Ville de Paris*, was
attacked by seven of the enemies' ships at once, her consorts could
not get at her; Count de Grasse, maddened with grief and rage,
saw all his crew falling around him : " The admiral is six foot every
day," said the sailors, " on a fighting day he is six foot one."   So
much courage and desperation could not save the fleet, the count
was forced to strike; his ship had received such damage that it
sank before its arrival in England; the admiral was received in
London with great honours against which his vanity was not proof,
to the loss of his personal dignity and his reputation in Europe.   A
national subscription in France reinforced the fleet with new vessels;
a squadron, commanded by M. de Suffren, had just carried into the
East Indies the French flag, which had so long been humiliated,
and which his victorious hands were destined to hoist aloft again
for a moment.

As early as 1778, even before the maritime war had burst out in
Europe, France had lost all that remained of her possessions on the
Coromandel coast.   Pondicherry, scarcely risen from its ruins, was
besieged by the English, and had capitulated on the 17th of October,
after a heroic resistance of forty days' open trenches.   Since that
day a Mussulman, Hyder Ali, conqueror of the Carnatic, had
struggled alone in India against the power of England : it was
around him that a group had been formed by the old soldiers of
Bussy and by the French who had escaped from the disaster of

Pondicherry.   It was with their aid that the able robber-chief, the crafty politician, had defended and consolidated the empire he had founded against that foreign dominion which threatened the independence of his country.   He had just suffered a series of reverses, and he was on the point of being forced to evacuate the Carnatic and take refuge in his kingdom of Mysore when he heard, in the month of July, 1782, of the arrival of a French fleet commanded by M. de Suffren.   Hyder Ali had already been many times disappointed.   The preceding year Admiral d'Orves had appeared on the Coromandel coast with a squadron, the Sultan had sent to meet him, urging him to land and attack Madras, left defenceless; the admiral refused to risk a single vessel or land a single man, and he returned without striking a blow to Île-de-France.   Ever indomitable and enterprising, Hyder Ali hoped better things of the new comers: he was not deceived.

Born at St. Cannat in Provence on the 13th of July, 1726, of an old and a notable family amongst the noblesse of his province, Peter Andrew de Suffren, admitted before he was seventeen into the marine guards, had procured his reception into the order of Malta; he had already distinguished himself in many engagements, when M. de Castries gave him the command of the squadron commissioned to convey to the Cape of Good Hope a French garrison promised to the Dutch, whose colony was threatened.   The English had seized Negapatam and Trincomalee; they hoped to follow up this conquest by the capture of Batavia and Ceylon.   Suffren had accomplished his mission, not without a brush with the English squadron, commanded by Commodore Johnston.   Leaving the Cape free from attack, he had joined, off Île-de-France, Admiral d'Orves, who was ill and at death's door.   The vessels of the commander (of the Maltese order) were in a bad state, the crews were weak, the provisions were deficient; the inexhaustible zeal and the energetic ardour of the chief sufficed to animate both non-combatants and combatants.   When he put to sea on the 7th of December, Count d'Orves still commanded the squadron; on the 9th of February he expired out at sea, having handed over his command to M. de Suffren.   All feebleness and all hesitation disappeared from that moment in the management of the expedition; when the nabob sent a French officer in his service to compliment M. de Suffren and proffer alliance, the commander interrupted the envoy : " We will begin," said he, " by settling the conditions of this alliance," and not a soldier set foot on land before the independent position of the French force, the number of its auxiliaries and the payment for its services had been settled by a treaty. Hyder Ali consented to everything. M. de Suffren set sail to go in search of the English.

He sought them for three months without any decisive result ; it was only on the 4th of July in the morning, at the moment when Hyder Ali was to attack Negapatam, that a serious engagement began between the hostile fleets. The two squadrons had already suffered severely, a change of wind had caused disorder in the lines : the English had several vessels dismantled ; one single French vessel, the *Sévère*, had received serious damage ; her captain, with cowardly want of spirit, ordered the flag to be hauled down. His lieutenants protested ; the volunteers to whom he had appealed refused to execute his orders. By this time the report was spreading amongst the batteries that the captain was giving the order to cease firing, the sailors were as indignant as the officers : a cry arose, " The flag is down ! "   A complaisant subaltern had at last obeyed the captain's repeated orders. The officers jumped upon the quarter-deck : " You are master of your flag," fiercely cried an officer of the blue, Lieut. Dien, " but we are masters as to fighting, and the ship shall not surrender ! "   By this time a boat from the English ship, the *Sultan*, had put off to board the *Sévère*, which was supposed to have struck, when a fearful broadside from all the ship's port-holes struck the *Sultan*, which found herself obliged to sheer off. Night came ; without waiting for the admiral's orders, the English went and cast anchor under Negapatam.

M. de Suffren supposed that hostilities would be resumed ; but, when the English did not appear, he at last prepared to set sail for Gondelour to refit his vessels, when a small boat of the enemy's hove in sight : it bore a flag of truce. Admiral Hughes claimed the *Sévère*, which had for an instant hauled down her flag. M. de Suffren had not heard anything about her captain's poltroonery ; the flag had been immediately replaced ; he answered that none of

the French vessels had surrendered; "However," he added with
a smile, "as this vessel belongs to Sir Edward Hughes, beg him
from me to come for it himself." Suffren arrived without hindrance
at Gondelour (Kaddalore).

Scarcely was he there when Hyder Ali expressed a desire to see
him, and set out for that purpose without waiting for his answer.
On the 26th of July, M. de Suffren landed with certain officers of
his squadron; an escort of cavalry was in waiting to conduct him
to the camp of the nabob, who came out to meet him: "Heretofore I thought myself a great man and a great general," said
Hyder Ali to the admiral, "but now I know that you alone are
a great man." Suffren informed the nabob that M. de Bussy-
Castelnau, but lately the faithful lieutenant of Dupleix and the con-
tinuer of his victories, had just been sent to India with the title of
commander-in-chief; he was already at Île de France, and was
bringing some troops. "Provided that you remain with us, all
will go well," said the nabob, detaching from his turban an aigrette
of diamonds which he placed on M. de Suffren's hat. The nabob's
tent was reached; Suffren was fat, he had great difficulty in sitting
upon the carpets; Hyder Ali perceived this and ordered cushions
to be brought: "Sit as you please," said he to the commander,
"etiquette was not made for such as you." Next day, under the
nabob's tent, all the courses of the banquet offered to M. de Suffren
were prepared in European style. The admiral proposed that
Hyder Ali should go to the coast and see all the fleet dressed, but,
"I put myself out to see *you* only," said the nabob, "I will not go
any farther." The two great warriors were never to meet again.

The French vessels were ready, the commander had more than once
put his own hand to the work in order to encourage the workmen's
zeal. Carpentry-wood was wanted; he had ransacked Gondelour
(Kaddalore) for it, sometimes pulling down a house to get hold of a
beam which suited him. His officers urged him to go to Bourbon
or Île-de-France for the necessary supplies and for a good port to
shelter his damaged ships: "Until I have conquered one in India,
I will have no port but the sea," answered Suffren. He had retaken Trincomalee before the English could come to its defence.
The battle began. As had already happened more than once, a

part of the French force showed weakness in the thick of the action either from cowardice or treason; a cabal had formed against the commander; he was fighting single-handed against five or six assailants: the main-mast and the flag of the *Héros*, which he was on, fell beneath the enemies' cannon-balls. Suffren, standing on the quarter-deck, shouted beside himself: " Flags! Set white flags all round the *Héros!*" The vessel, all bristling with flags, replied so valiantly to the English attacks, that the rest of the squadron had time to re-form around it; the English went and anchored before Madras.

Bussy had arrived, but aged, a victim to gout, quite a stranger amidst those Indian intrigues with which he had but lately been so well acquainted. Hyder Ali had just died on the 7th of December, 1782, leaving to his son Tippoo Sahib affairs embroiled and allies enfeebled. At this news the Mahrattas, in revolt against England, hastened to make peace, and Tippoo Sahib who had just seized Tanjore was obliged to abandon his conquest and go to the protection of Malabar. Ten thousand men, only, remained in the Carnatic to back the little corps of French. Bussy allowed himself to be driven to bay by General Stuart beneath the walls of Gondelour; he had even been forced to shut himself up in the town. M. de Suffren went to his release. The action was hotly contested; when the victor landed, M. de Bussy was awaiting him on the shore. " Here is our saviour," said the general to his troops, and the soldiers taking up in their arms M. de Suffren, who had been lately promoted by the grand-master of the order of Malta to the rank of grand-cross (*bailli*), carried him in triumph into the town. " He pressed M. de Bussy every day to attack us," says Sir Thomas Munro, " offering to land the greater part of his crews and to lead them himself to deliver the assault upon our camp. Bussy had, in fact, resumed the offensive and was preparing to make fresh sallies, when it was known at Calcutta that the preliminaries of peace had been signed at Paris on the 9th of February. The English immediately proposed an armistice. The *Surveillante* shortly afterwards brought the same news, with orders for Suffren to return to France. India was definitively given up to the English, who restored to the French Pondicherry,

Chandernuggur, Mahé and Karikal, the last strips remaining of that French dominion which had for a while been triumphant throughout the Peninsula. The feebleness and the vices of Louis XV.'s government weighed heavily upon the government of Louis XVI. in India as well as in France, and at Paris itself.

It is to the honour of mankind and their consolation under great reverses that political checks and the inutility of their efforts do not obscure the glory of great men. M. de. Suffren had just arrived at Paris, he was in low spirits; M. de Castries took him to Versailles. There was a numerous and brilliant court. On entering the guards' hall, " Gentlemen," said the minister to the officers on duty, "this is M. de Suffren." Everybody rose, and the bodyguards, forming an escort for the admiral, accompanied him to the king's chamber. His career was over ; the last of the great sailors of the old regimen died on the 8th of December, 1788.

Whilst Hyder Ali and M. de Suffren were still disputing India with England, that power had just gained in Europe an important advantage in the eyes of public opinion as well as in respect of her supremacy at sea.

For close upon three years past a Spanish army had been investing by land the town and fortress of Gibraltar ; a strong squadron was cruising out of cannon-shot of the place, incessantly engaged in barring the passage against the English vessels. Twice already, in 1780 by Admiral Rodney and in 1781 by Admiral Darby, the vigilance of the cruisers had been eluded and reinforcements of troops, provisions and ammunition had been thrown into Gibraltar. In 1782 the town had been half destroyed by an incessantly renewed bombardment, the fortifications had not been touched. Every morning, when he awoke, Charles III. would ask anxiously, " Have we got Gibraltar ? " and when " No " was answered, " We soon shall," the monarch would rejoin imperturbably. The capture of Fort Philip had confirmed him in his hopes ; he considered his object gained, when the duke of Crillon with a corps of French troops came and joined the besiegers ; the count of Artois, brother to the king, as well as the duke of Bourbon had come with him ; the camp of St. Roch was the scene of continual festivities, sometimes interrupted by

SEA-FIGHT OFF GONDELOUR.

the sallies of the besieged; the fights did not interfere with mutual good offices: in his proud distress, General Eliot still kept up an interchange of refreshments with the French princes and the duke of Crillon; the count of Artois had handed over to the English garrison the letters and correspondence which had been captured on the enemy's ships and which he had found addressed to them on his way through Madrid.

Preparations were being made for a grand assault. A French engineer, Chevalier d'Arcon, had invented some enormous floating batteries, fire-proof, as he believed; a hundred and fifty pieces of cannon were to batter the place all at once, near enough to facilitate the assault. On the 13th of September, at 9 a.m., the Spaniards opened fire: all the artillery in the fort replied at once, the surrounding mountains repeated the cannonade, the whole army covered the shore awaiting with anxiety the result of the enterprise. Already the fortifications seemed to be beginning to totter; the batteries had been firing for five hours; all at once the prince of Nassau who commanded a detachment thought he perceived flames mastering his heavy vessel; the fire spread rapidly; one after another, the floating batteries found themselves disarmed. "At seven o'clock we had lost all hope," said an Italian officer who had taken part in the assault, "we fired no more and our signals of distress remained unnoticed. The red-hot shot of the besieged rained down upon us; the crews were threatened from every point." Timidly and by weak detachments, the boats of the two fleets crept up under cover of the batteries in hopes of saving some of the poor creatures that were like to perish; the flames which burst out on board the doomed ships served to guide the fire of the English as surely as in broad daylight. At the head of a small squadron of gunboats Captain Curtis barred the passage of the salvors; the conflagration became general, only the discharges from the fort replied to the hissing of the flames and to the Spaniards' cries of despair. The fire at last slackened; the English gun-boats changed their part; at the peril of their lives the brave seamen on board of them approached the burning ships, trying to save the unfortunate crews; four hundred men owed their preservation to those efforts. A month after this

disastrous affair, Lord Howe, favoured by the accidents of wind
and weather, revictualled for the third time, and almost without
any fighting, the fortress and the town under the very eyes of the
allied fleets.   Gibraltar remained impregnable.

Peace was at hand, however : all the belligerents were tired of
the strife, the marquis of Rockingham was dead; his ministry,
after being broken up, had re-formed with less lustre under
the leadership of Lord Shelburne ; William Pitt, Lord Chatham's
second son, at that time twenty-two years of age, had a seat in
the cabinet. Already negotiations for a general peace had begun
at Paris, but Washington, who eagerly desired the end of the war,
did not yet feel any confidence. "The old infatuation, the
political duplicity and perfidy of England render me, I confess,
very suspicious, very doubtful," he wrote, "and her position seems
to me to be perfectly summed up in the laconic saying of Dr.
Franklin : 'They are incapable of continuing the war and too
proud to make peace.'   The pacific overtures made to the
different belligerent nations have probably no other design than to
detach some one of them from the coalition. At any rate, whatever be the enemy's intentions, our watchfulness and our efforts,
so far from languishing, should become more vigorous than ever.
Too much trust and confidence would ruin everything."

America was the first to make peace, without however detaching
herself officially from the coalition which had been formed to maintain her quarrel and from which she had derived so many advantages.   On the 30th of November, 1782, in disregard of the treaties
but lately concluded between France and the revolted colonies, the
American negotiators signed with stealthy precipitation the preliminary articles of a special peace, " thus abandoning France to
the dangers of being isolated in negotiations or in arms." The
votes of Congress as well as the attitude of Washington did not
justify this disloyal and ungrateful eagerness. "The articles of
the treaty between Great Britain and America," wrote the general
to Chevalier de La Luzerne, French minister at Philadelphia, " are
so far from conclusive as regards a general pacification that we
must preserve a hostile attitude and remain ready for any contin-
gency, for war as well as peace."

On the 5th of December, at the opening of Parliament, George III. announced in the speech from the throne that he had offered to recognize the independence of the American colonies. " In thus admitting their separation from the crown of this kingdom, I have sacrificed all my desires to the wishes and opinion of my people," said the king. " I humbly pray Almighty God that Great Britain may not feel the evils which may flow from so important a dismemberment of its empire, and that America may be a stranger to the calamities which have before now proved to the mother-country that monarchy is inseparable from the benefits of constitutional liberty. Religion, language, interests, affections may still form a bond of union between the two countries, and I will spare no pains or attention to promote it." " I was the last man in England to consent to the independence of America," said the king to John Adams, who was the first to represent the new republic at the Court of St. James's; " I will now be the last in the world to sanction any violation of it." Honest and sincere in his concessions as he had been in his persistent obstinacy, the king supported his ministers against the violent attacks made upon them in Parliament. The preliminaries of general peace had been signed at Paris on the 20th of January, 1783.

To the exchange of conquests between France and England was added the cession to France of the island of Tobago and of the Senegal river with its dependencies. The territory of Pondicherry and Karikal received some augmentation. For the first time for more than a hundred years the English renounced the humiliating conditions so often demanded on the subject of the harbour of Dunkerque. Spain saw herself confirmed in her conquest of the Floridas and of the island of Minorca. Holland recovered all her possessions, except Negapatam.

Peace was made, a glorious and a sweet one for the United States, which, according to Washington's expression, " saw opening before them a career that might lead them to become a great people, equally happy and respected." Despite all the mistakes of the people and the defects every day more apparent in the form of its government, this noble and healthy ambition has always been present to the minds of the American nation as the ultimate aim of their hopes and their endeavours. More than eighty years after the war of independence the indomitable energy of the fathers re-appeared in the children, worthy of being called a great people even when the agonies of a civil war without example denied to them the happiness which had a while ago been hoped for by the glorious founder of their liberties as well as of their Constitution.

France came out exhausted from the struggle but relieved in her own eyes as well as those of Europe from the humiliation inflicted upon her by the disastrous Seven Years' War and by the treaty of 1763. She saw triumphant the cause she had upheld and her enemies sorrow-stricken at the dismemberment they had suffered. It was a triumph for her arms and for the generous impulse which had prompted her to support a legitimate but for a long while doubtful enterprise. A fresh element, however, had come to add itself to the germs of disturbance, already so fruitful, which were hatching within her. She had promoted the foundation of a Republic based upon principles of absolute right, the government had given way to the ardent sympathy of the nation for a people emancipated from a long yoke by its deliberate will and its indomitable energy. France felt her heart still palpitating from the efforts she had witnessed and shared on behalf of American freedom; the unreflecting hopes of a blind emulation were already agitating many a mind. "In all states," said Washington, "there are inflammable materials which a single spark may kindle." In 1783, on the morrow of the American war, the inflammable materials everywhere accumulated in France were already providing means for that immense conflagration in the midst of which the country well-nigh perished.

CHAPTER LVIII.

LOUIS XVI.—FRANCE AT HOME.—MINISTRY OF M. NECKER.—
1776—1781.

E have followed the course of good and bad fortune; we have exhibited France engaged abroad in a policy at the same time bold and generous, proceeding from rancour as well as from the sympathetic enthusiasm of the nation; we have seen the war, at first feebly waged, soon extending over every sea and into the most distant colonies of the belligerents, though the European continent was not attacked at any point save the barren rock of Gibraltar; we have seen the just cause of the United States triumphant and freedom established in the New World: it is time to inquire what new shocks had been undergone by France whilst she was supporting far away the quarrel of the revolted colonies and what new burthens had come to be added to the load of difficulties and deceptions which she had seemed to forget whilst she was fighting England at so many different points. It was not without great efforts that France had acquired the generous fame of securing to her allies blessings which she did not herself yet possess to their full extent; great hopes, and

powers fresh and young had been exhausted in the struggle; at
the close of the American war M. Necker was played out politically
as well as M. Turgot.

It was not to supersede the great minister who had fallen that
the Genevese banker had been called to office. M. de Maurepas
was still powerful, still up and doing; he loved power, in spite of
his real levity and his apparent neglectfulness. M. Turgot had
often galled him, had sometimes forced his hand; M. de Clugny
who took the place of the comptroller-general had no passion for
reform and cared for nothing but leading, at the treasury's
expense, a magnificently scandalous life; M. de Malesherbes had
been succeeded in the king's household by Marquis Amelot. "At
any rate," said M. de Maurepas, "nobody will accuse me of
having picked him out for his wits."

Profoundly shocked at the irreligious tendencies of the philosophers, the court was, nevertheless, aweary of the theoricians
and of their essays in reform; it welcomed the new ministers with
delight; without fuss and as if by a natural recurrence to ancient
usage, the edict relative to forced labour was suspended, the
anxieties of the noblesse and of the clergy subsided; the peasantry
knew nothing yet of M. Turgot's fall, but they soon found out
that the evils from which they had imagined they were delivered
continued to press upon them with all their weight. For their
only consolation Clugny opened to them the fatal and disgraceful
chances of the lottery, which became a royal institution. To
avoid the remonstrances of Parliament, the comptroller-general
established the new enterprise by a simple decree of the council:
"The entries being voluntary, the lottery is no tax and can
dispense with enregistration," it was said. It was only seventy-five
years later, in 1841, under the government of King Louis Philippe
and the ministry of M. Humann, that the lottery was abolished
and this scandalous source of revenue forbidden to the treasury.

So much moral weakness and political changeableness, so much
poltroonery or indulgence towards evil and blind passions disquieted serious minds, and profoundly shook the public credit.
The Dutch refused to carry out the loan for sixty millions which
they had negotiated with M. Turgot; the discount-fund (*caisse*

d'escompte) founded by him brought in very slowly but a moderate portion of the assets required to feed it; the king alone was ignorant of the prodigalities and irregularities of his minister. M. de Maurepas began to be uneasy at the public discontent, he thought of superseding the comptroller-general; the latter had been ill for some time, on the 22nd of October he died. By the advice of M. de Maurepas, the king sent for M. Necker.

James Necker was born at Geneva in 1732. Engaging in business without any personal taste for it and by his father's wish, he had been successful in his enterprises; at forty he was a rich man, and his banking-house enjoyed great credit when he retired from business, in 1772, in order to devote himself to occupations more in accordance with his natural inclinations. He was ambitious and disinterested. The great operations in which he had been concerned had made his name known. He had propped up the *Compagnie des Indes* nearly falling to pieces, and his financial resources had often ministered to the necessities of the State. "We entreat your assistance in the day of need," wrote Abbé Terray when he was comptroller-general, "deign to come to our assistance with a sum which is absolutely necessary." On ceasing to be a banker, Necker soon gave indications of the direction in which his thoughts turned; he wrote an indifferent *Éloge de Colbert*, crowned by the French Academy, in 1773. He believed that he was destined to wear the mantle of Louis XIV.'s great minister.

Society and public opinion exercised an ever-increasing influence in the eighteenth century; M. Necker managed to turn it to account. He had married, in 1764, Mdlle. Suzanne Curchod, a Swiss pastor's daughter, pretty, well informed and passionately devoted to her husband, his successes and his fame. The respectable talents, the liberality, the large scale of living of M. and Madame Necker attracted round them the literary and philosophical circle; the religious principles, the somewhat stiff propriety of Madame Necker maintained in her drawing-room an intelligent and becoming gravity which was in strong contrast with the licentious and irreligious frivolity of the conversations customary amongst the philosophers as well as the courtiers.

Madame Necker paid continuous and laborious attention to the duties of society. She was not a Frenchwoman, and she was uncomfortably conscious of it. " When I came to this country," she wrote to one of her fair friends, " I thought that literature was the key to everything, that a man cultivated his mind with books only and was great by knowledge only." Undeceived by the very fact of her admiration for her husband, who had not found leisure to give himself up to his natural taste for literature and who remained rather unfamiliar with it, she made it her whole desire to be of good service to him in the society in which she had been called upon to live with him. " I hadn't a word to say in society," she writes, " I didn't even know its language. Obliged, as a woman, to captivate people's minds, I was ignorant how many shades there are of self-love and I offended it when I thought I was flattering it. Always striking wrong notes and never hitting it off, I saw that my old ideas would never accord with those I was obliged to acquire; so I have hid my little capital away, never to see it again, and set about working for my living and getting together a little stock, if I can." Wit and knowledge thus painfully achieved are usually devoid of grace and charm. Madame du Deffand made this a reproach against M. Necker as well as his wife: " He wants one quality, that which is most conducive to agreeability, a certain readiness which, as it were, provides wits for those with whom one talks; he doesn't help to bring out what one thinks, and one is more stupid with him than one is all alone or with other folks." People of talent, nevertheless, thronged about M. and Madame Necker. Diderot often went to see them; Galiani, Raynal, Abbé Morellet, M. Suard, quite young yet, were frequenters of the house; Condorcet did not set foot in it, passionately enlisted as he was amongst the disciples of M. Turgot, who were hostile to his successor; Bernardin de St. Pierre never went thither again from the day when the reading of *Paul and Virginia* had sent the company to sleep. " At first everybody listens in silence," says M. Aimé Martin; " by degrees attention flags, people whisper, people yawn, nobody listens any more; M. de Buffon looks at his watch and asks for his carriage; the nearest to the door slips out, Thomas falls asleep, M. Necker

THE READING OF "PAUL AND VIRGINIA."

smiles to see the ladies crying, and the ladies ashamed of their tears dare not acknowledge that they have been interested." The persistent admiration of the general public and fifty imitations of *Paul and Virginia* published in a single year were soon to avenge Bernardin de St. Pierre for the disdainful yawns of the philosophers. It is pretty certain that Madame Necker's daughter, little Germaine, if she were present at the reading, did not fall asleep as M. Thomas did, and that she was not ashamed of her tears.

Next to M. Buffon, to whom Madame had vowed a sort of cult, and who was still writing to this faithful friend when he was near his last gasp, M. Thomas had more right than anybody to fall asleep at her house if he thought fit. Marmontel alone shared with him the really intimate friendship of M. and Madame Necker; the former had given up tragedies and moral tales; a pupil of Voltaire's, without the splendour and inexhaustible vigour of his master, he was less prone to licence, and his feelings were more serious; he was at that time correcting his *Éléments de Littérature,* but lately published in the *Encyclopédie,* and commencing the *Mémoires d'un père, pour servir à l'instruction de ses enfants.* Thomas was editing his *Éloges,* sometimes full of eloquence, often subtle and delicate, always long, unexceptionable and wearisome. His noble character had won him the sincere esteem and affection of Madame Necker. She, laboriously anxious about the duties politeness requires from the mistress of a house, went so far as to write down in her tablets: " *To recompliment* M. Thomas more strongly on the song of France in his poem of *Pierre le Grand.*" She paid him more precious homage when she wrote to him: "We were united in our youth in every honourable way; let us be more than ever united now when ripe age, which diminishes the vivacity of impressions, augments the force of habit, and let us be more than ever necessary to one another when we live no longer save in the past and in the future, for, as regards myself, I, in anticipation, lay no store by the approbation of the circles which will surround us in our old age, and I desire nothing amongst posterity but a tomb to which I may precede M. Necker and on which you will write the epitaph. Such resting-place will be dearer to me than that amongst the poplars which cover the ashes of Rousseau."

It was desirable to show what sort of society, cultivated and virtuous, lively and serious, all in one, the new minister whom Louis XVI. had just called to his side had managed to get about him. Though friendly with the philosophers, he did not belong to them, and his wife's piety frequently irked them. " The conversation was a little constrained through the strictness of Madame Necker," says Abbé Morellet, " many subjects could not be touched upon in her presence, and she was particularly hurt by freedom in religious opinions." Practical acquaintance with business had put M. Necker on his guard against the chimerical theories of the economists. Rousseau had exercised more influence over his mind; the philosopher's wrath against civilization seemed to have spread to the banker, when the latter wrote in his *Traité sur le commerce des grains:* " One would say that a small number of men, after dividing the land between them, had made laws of union and security against the multitude, just as they would have made for themselves shelters in the woods against the wild beasts. What concern of ours are your laws of property? the most numerous class of citizens might say : we possess nothing. Your laws of right and wrong? We have nothing to defend. Your laws of liberty ? If we do not work to-morrow, we shall die."

Public opinion was favourable to M. Necker, his promotion was well received ; it presented, however, great difficulties : he had been a banker, and hitherto the comptrollers-general had all belonged to the class of magistrates or superintendents ; he was a Protestant, and, as such, could not hold any office. The clergy were in commotion ; they tried certain remonstrances. " We will give him up to you," said M. de Maurepas, " if you undertake to pay the debts of the State." The opposition of the Church, however, closed to the new minister an important opening ; at first director of the treasury, then director-general of finance, M. Necker never received the title of comptroller-general, and was not admitted to the council. From the outset, with a disinterestedness not devoid of ostentation, he had declined the salary attached to his functions. The courtiers looked at one another in astonishment : " It is easy to see that he is a foreigner, a republican and a Protestant," people said.   M. de Maurepas laughed : " M. Necker," he declared, " is a maker of gold ; he has introduced the philosopher's stone into the kingdom."

This was for a while the feeling throughout France.   "No bankruptcies, no new imposts, no loans," M. Turgot had said, and had looked to economy alone for the resources necessary to restore the finances.   Bolder and less scrupulous, M. Necker, who had no idea of having recourse to either bankruptcy or imposts, made unreserved use of the system of loans.   During the five years that his ministry lasted, the successive loans he contracted amounted to nearly 500 million livres.   There was no security given to insure its repayment to the lenders.   The mere confidence felt in the minister's ability and honesty had caused the money to flow into the treasury.

M. Necker did not stop there : a foreigner by birth, he felt no respect for the great tradition of French administration ; practised in the handling of funds, he had conceived as to the internal government of the finances theories opposed to the old system ; the superintendents established a while ago by Richelieu had become powerful in the central administration as well as in the provinces and the comptroller-general was in the habit of accounting with them ; they nearly all belonged to old and notable families ; some of them had attracted the public regard and esteem.   The new minister suppressed several offices and diminished the importance of some others ; he had taken away from M. Trudaine, administrator of gabels and heavy revenues (*grosses fermes*), the right of doing business with the king ; M. Trudaine sent in his resignation ; he was much respected, and this reform was not approved of. " M. Necker," people said, " wants to be assisted by none but removeable slaves."   At the same time the treasurers-general, numbering forty-eight, were reduced to a dozen, and the twenty-seven treasurers of marine and war to two ; the farmings-general (of taxes) were renewed with an advantage to the treasury of fifteen millions.   The posts at court likewise underwent reform : the courtiers saw at one blow the improper sources of their revenues in the financial administration cut off, and obsolete and ridiculous appointments, to which numerous pensions were attached, reduced. "Acquisitions of posts, projects of marriage or education, unforeseen losses, abortive hopes, all such matters had become an occasion for having recourse to the sovereign's munificence," writes M. Necker. "One would have said that the royal treasury was bound to do all the wheedling, all the smoothing-down, all the reparation, and as the method of pensions, though pushed to the uttermost (the king was at that time disbursing in that way some twenty-eight millions of livres) could not satisfy all claims or sufficiently gratify shameful cupidity, other devices had been hit upon and would have gone on being hit upon every day; interests in the collection of taxes, in the customs, in army-supplies, in the stores, in many pay-offices, in markets of every kind, and even in the furnishing of hospitals, all was fair game, all was worthy of the attention of persons often, from their position, the most above any business of the kind."

The discontent of the great financiers and that of the courtiers were becoming every day more noisy, without as yet shaking the credit of M. Necker. "M. Necker wants to govern the kingdom of France like his little republic of Geneva," people said : "he is making a desert round the king; each loan is the recompense for something destroyed." "Just so," answered M. de Maurepas : "he gives us millions, provided that we allow him to suppress certain offices." "And if he were to ask permission to have the superintendents' heads cut off?" "Perhaps we should give it him," said the veteran minister laughing. "Find us the philosopher's stone, as he has done, and I promise you that his Majesty will have you into the ministry that very day."

M. Necker did not indulge in illusions, he owed to the embarrassments of the government and to the new burthens created by the American war a complaisance which his bold attempts would not have met with under other circumstances. "Nobody will ever know," he himself said, "the steadfastness I found necessary; I still recall that long and dark staircase of M. de Maurepas' which I mounted in fear and sadness, uncertain of succeeding with him as to some new idea which I had in my mind and which aimed most frequently at obtaining an increase of revenue

by some just but severe operation. I still recall that upstairs
closet, beneath the roof of Versailles but over the rooms, and,
from its smallness and its situation, seeming to be really a superfine extract and abstract of all vanities and ambitions; it was
there that reform and economy had to be discussed with a minister
grown old in the pomps and usages of the court. I remember all
the delicate management I had to employ to succeed, after many a
rebuff. At last I would obtain some indulgences for the commonwealth. I obtained them, I could easily see, as recompense for the
resources I had found during the war. I met with more courage
in dealing with the king. Young and virtuous, he could and
would hear all. The queen, too, lent me a favourable ear, but,
all around their Majesties, in court and city, to how much enmity
and hatred did I not expose myself? There were all kinds of
influence and power which I had to oppose with firmness, there
were all sorts of interested factions with which I had to fight in
this perpetual struggle."

"Alas!" Madame Necker would say, "my heart and my
regrets are ever yearning for a world in which beneficence should
be the first of virtues. What reflections do I not make on
our own particular case! I thought to see a golden age under so
pure an administration; I see only an age of iron. All resolves
itself into doing as little harm as possible."

O the grievous bitterness of past illusions! Madame Necker
consoled herself for the enmity of the court and for the impotence
of that beneficence which had been her dream by undertaking on
her own account a difficult reform, that of the hospitals of Paris,
scenes, as yet, of an almost savage disorderliness. The sight
of sick, dead, and dying huddled together in the same bed had
excited the horror and the pity of Madame Necker. She opened
a little hospital, supported at her expense and under her own
direction, which still bears the name of *Necker* Hospital and
which served as a model for the reforms attempted in the great
public establishments. M. Necker could not deny himself the
pleasure of rendering homage to his wife's efforts in a report to
the king; the ridicule thrown upon this honest but injudicious
gush of conjugal pride proved the truth of what Madame Necker

herself said : " I did not know the language of this country.
What was called frankness in Switzerland became egotism at Paris."

The active charity of Madame Necker had won her the esteem
of the archbishop of Paris, Christopher de Beaumont, a virtuous,
fanatical priest ; he had gained a great law-suit against the city of
Paris, which had to pay him a sum of three hundred thousand
livres. " It is our wish," said the archbishop, " that M. Necker
should dispose of these funds to the greatest advantage for the
State, trusting to his zeal, his love of good and his wisdom for the
most useful employment of the said funds and desiring further that
no account be required of him, as to such employment, by any
person whatsoever." The prelate's three hundred thousand livres
were devoted to the internal repairs of the Hôtel-Dieu. " How is
it," people asked, " that the archbishop thinks so highly of
M. Necker and even dines with him ? " " Oh ! " answered the
wicked wags : " it is because M. Necker is not a Jansenist, he is
only a Protestant."

Notwithstanding this unusual tolerance on the part of Christopher de Beaumont, his Protestantism often placed M. Necker in
an awkward position. " The title of liberator of your Protestant
brethren would be a flattering one for you," said one of the
pamphlets of the day, " and it would be yours for ever, if you could
manage to obtain for them a civil existence, to procure for them the
privileges of a citizen, liberty and tolerance. You are sure of a
diminution in the power of the clergy. Your vigorous edict
regarding hospitals will pave the way for the ruin of their credit
and their wealth ; you have opened the trenches against them, the
great blow has been struck. All else will not fail to succumb ; you
will put all the credit of the State and all the money of France in
the hands of Protestant bankers, Genevese, English, and Dutch.
Contempt will be the lot of the clergy, your brethren will be held
in consideration. These points of view are full of genius, you will
bring great address to bear upon them." M. Necker was at the same
time accused of being favourable to England. " M. Necker is our
best and our last friend on the Continent," Burke had said in the
House of Commons. Knowing better than anybody the burthens
which the war imposed upon the State and which he alone had

managed to find the means of supporting, M. Necker desired peace. It was for Catholics and philosophers that the honour was reserved of restoring to Protestants the first right of citizens, recognition of their marriages and a civil status for their children. The court, the parliaments, and the financiers were leagued against M. Necker. "Who, pray, is this adventurer," cried the fiery Eprémesnil, "who is this charlatan who dares to mete out the patriotism of the French magistracy, who dares to suppose them lukewarm in their attachments and to denounce them to a young king?" The assessment of the twentieths (tax) had raised great storms; the mass of citizens were taxed rigorously, but the privileged had preserved the right of themselves making a declaration of their possessions; a decree of the council ordered verification of the income from properties. The parliaments burst out into remonstrances: "Every owner of property has the right to grant subsidies by himself or by his representatives," said the Parliament of Paris; "if he do not exercise this right as a member of a national body, it must be reverted to indirectly, otherwise he is no longer master of his own, he is no longer undisturbed owner. Confidence in personal declarations, then, is the only indemnity for the right, which the nation has not exercised but has not lost, of itself granting and assessing the twentieths." A bold principle, even in a free State, and one on which the *income-tax* rests in England, but an untenable principle, without absolute equality on the part of all citizens and a common right to have their consent asked to the imposts laid upon them.

M. Necker did not belong to the court; he had never lived there, he did not set foot therein when he became minister; a while ago Colbert and Louvois had founded families and taken rank amongst the great lords who were jealous of their power and their wealth; under Louis XVI., the court itself was divided, and one of the queen's particular friends, Baron de Besenval, said without mincing the matter in his *Mémoires:* "I grant that the depredations of the great lords who are at the head of the king's household are enormous, revolting. . . . . Necker has on his side the depreciation into which the great lords have fallen; it is such that they are certainly not to be dreaded, and that their opinion does not deserve to be taken into consideration in any political speculation."

M. Necker had a regard for public opinion, indeed he attached great importance to it, but he took its influence to be more extensive and its authority to rest on a broader bottom than the court or the parliaments would allow. "The social spirit, the love of regard and of praise," said he, "have raised up in France a tribunal at which all men who draw its eyes upon them are obliged to appear: there public opinion, as from the height of a throne, decrees prizes and crowns, makes and unmakes reputations. A support is wanted against the vacillations of ministers, and this important support is only to be expected from progress in the enlightenment and resisting power of public opinion. Virtues are more than ever in want of a stage, and it becomes essential that public opinion should rouse the actors; it must be supported, then, this opinion, it must be enlightened, it must be summoned to the aid of ideas which concern the happiness of men."

M. Necker thought the moment had come for giving public opinion the summons of which he recognized the necessity; he felt himself shaken at court, weakened in the regard of M. de Maurepas, who was still puissant in spite of his great age and jealous of him as he had been of M. Turgot; he had made up his mind, he said, to let the nation know how its affairs had been managed, and in the early days of the year 1781 he published his *Compte rendu au roi*.

It was a bold innovation; hitherto the administration of the finances had been carefully concealed from the eyes of the public as the greatest secret in the affairs of State; for the first time the nation was called upon to take cognizance of the position of the public estate and, consequently, pass judgment upon its administration. "The principal cause of the financial prosperity of England, in the very midst of war," said the minister, "is to be found in the confidence with which the English regard their administration and the source of the government's credit." The annual publication of a financial report was, M. Necker thought, likely to inspire the same confidence in France. It was paying a great compliment to public opinion to attribute to it the power derived from free institutions and to expect from satisfied curiosity the serious results of a control as active as it was minute.

The Report to the king was, moreover, not of a nature to stand the investigation of a parliamentary committee. In publishing it M. Necker had a double end in view. He wanted, by an able exposition of the condition of the treasury, to steady the public credit which was beginning to totter, to bring in fresh subscribers for the loans which were so necessary to support the charges of the war; he wanted at the same time to call to mind the benefits and successes of his own administration, to restore the courage of his friends and reduce his enemies to silence. With this complication of intentions, he had drawn up a report on the *ordinary* state of expenditure and receipts, designedly omitting the immense sacrifices demanded by the land and sea armaments as well as the advances made to the United States. He thus arrived, by a process rather ingenious than honest, at the establishment of a budget showing a surplus of ten million livres. The maliciousness of M. de Maurepas found a field for its exercise in the calculations which he had officially overhauled in council. The Report was in a cover of blue marbled paper. " Have you read the *Conte bleu* (a lying story) ?" he asked everybody who went to see him; and, when he was told of the great effect which M. Necker's work was producing on the public : " I know, I know," said the veteran minister shrugging his shoulders, " we have fallen from Turgomancy into Necromancy."

M. Necker had boldly defied the malevolence of his enemies. " I have never," said he, " offered sacrifice to influence or power. I have disdained to indulge vanity. I have renounced the sweetest of private pleasures, that of serving my friends or winning the gratitude of those who are about me. If anybody owes to my mere favour a place, a post, let us have the name." He enumerated all the services he had rendered to the king, to the State, to the nation, with that somewhat pompous satisfaction which was afterwards discernible in his *Mémoires*. There it was that he wrote: " Perhaps he who contributed, by his energies, to keep off new imposts during five such expensive years; he who was able to devote to all useful works the funds which had been employed upon them in the most tranquil times; he who gratified the king's heart by providing him with the means of distributing amongst his provinces the same aids as during the war, and even greater; he who, at the same time, proffered to the monarch's amiable impatience the resources necessary in order to commence, in the midst of war, the improvement of the prisons and the hospitals; he who indulged his generous inclinations by inspiring him with the desire of extinguishing the remnants of serfage; he who, rendering homage to the monarch's character, seconded his disposition towards order and economy; he who pleaded for the establishment of paternal administrations in which the simplest dwellers in the country-places might have some share; he who, by manifold cares, by manifold details, caused the prince's name to be blest even in the hovels of the poor, perhaps such a servant has some right to dare, without blushing, to point out, as one of the first rules of administration, love and care for the people."

" On the whole," says M. Droz, with much justice, in his excellent *Histoire du règne de Louis XVI.*, " the Report was a very ingenious work, which appeared to prove a great deal and proved nothing." M. Necker, however, had made no mistake about the effect which might be produced by this confidence, apparently so bold, as to the condition of affairs: in a single year, 1781, the loans amounted to 236 millions, thus exceeding in a few months the figures reached in the four previous years. A chorus of praises arose even in England, reflected from the minister on to his sovereign: " It is in economy," said Mr. Burke, " that Louis XVI. has found resources sufficient to keep up the war. In the first two years of this war, he imposed no burthen on his people. The third year has arrived, there has as yet been no question of any impost, indeed I believe that those which are a matter of course in time of war have not yet been put on. I apprehend that in the long-run it will no doubt be necessary for France to have recourse to imposts, but these three years saved will scatter their beneficent influence over a whole century. The French people feel the blessing of having a master and minister devoted to economy; economy has induced this monarch to trench upon his own splendour rather than upon his people's subsistence. He has found in the suppression of a great number of places a resource for continuing the war without increasing his expenses. He has stripped himself of the magnificence and pomp of royalty, but he has manned a navy; he has reduced the number of persons in his private service, but he has increased that of his vessels. Louis XVI., like a patriotic king, has shown sufficient firmness to protect M. Necker, a foreigner, without support or connexion at court, who owes his elevation to nothing but his own merit and the discernment of the sovereign who had sagacity enough to discover him, and to his wisdom which can appreciate him. It is a noble example to follow : if we would conquer France, it is on this ground and with her own weapons that we must fight her : economy and reforms."

It was those reforms, for which the English orator gave credit to M. Necker and Louis XVI., that rendered the minister's fall more imminent every day. He had driven into coalition against him the powerful influences of the courtiers, of the old families whose hereditary destination was office in the administration, and of the Parliament everywhere irritated and anxious. He had lessened the fortunes and position of the two former classes, and his measures tended to strip the magistracy of the authority whereof they were so jealous. "When circumstances require it," M. Necker had said in the Report, "the augmentation of imposts is in the hands of the king, for it is the power to order them which constitutes sovereign greatness;" and, in a secret *Mémoire* which saw publicity by perfidious means: "The imposts are at their height and minds are more than ever turned towards administrative subjects. The result is a restless and confused criticism which adds constant fuel to the desire felt by the Parliaments to have a hand in the matter. This feeling on their part becomes more and more manifest and they set to work, like all those bodies that wish to acquire power, by speaking in the name of the people, calling themselves defenders of the nation's rights; there can be no doubt but that, though they are strong neither in knowledge nor in pure love for the well-being of the State, they will put themselves forward on all occasions as long as they believe that they are supported by public opinion. It is necessary,

therefore, either to take this support away from them or to prepare for repeated contests which will disturb the tranquillity of
your Majesty's reign and will lead successively either to a degrada-
tion of authority or to extreme measures of which one cannot
exactly estimate the consequences."

In order to apply a remedy to the evils he demonstrated as well
as to those which he foresaw, M. Necker had borrowed some
shreds from the great system of local assemblies devised by
M. Turgot; he had proposed to the king and already organized
in Berry the formation of provincial assemblies, recruited in every
district (*généralité*) from amongst the three orders of the noblesse,
the clergy and the third estate. A part of the members were to
be chosen by the king; these were commissioned to elect their
colleagues, and the assembly was afterwards to fill up its own
vacancies as they occurred. The provincial administration was
thus confided almost entirely to the assemblies. That of Berry
had already abolished forced labour and collected two hundred
thousand livres by voluntary contribution for objects of public
utility. The assembly of Haute-Guyenne was in course of formation. The districts (*généralités*) of Grenoble, Montauban and
Moulins claimed the same privilege. The Parliaments were wroth
to see this assault upon their power. Louis XVI. had hesitated
a long while before authorizing the attempt. "The presidents-
born, the councillors, the members of the states-districts (*pays
d'états*) do not add to the happiness of Frenchmen in the districts
which are under their administration," wrote the king in his
marginal notes to M. Necker's scheme. "Most certainly Brittany,
with its states, is not happier than Normandy which happens to
be without them. The most just and most natural amongst the
powers of the Parliaments is that of hanging robbers of the
finances. In the event of provincial administrations, it must not
be taken away. It concerns and appertains to the repose of my
people to preserve privileges."

The instinct of absolute power and the traditions of the kingship
struggled in the narrow mind and honest heart of Louis XVI.
against the sincere desire to ameliorate the position of his people
and against a vague impression of new requirements. It was to

the former of these motives that M. de Vergennes appealed in his Note to the king on the effect of the Report: " Your Majesty," he said, " is enjoying the tranquillity which you owe to the long experience of your ancestors and to the painful labours of the great ministers who succeeded in establishing subordination and general respect in France. There is no longer in France clergy, or noblesse or third estate; the distinction is factitious, merely representative and without real meaning; the monarch speaks, all else are people and all else obey.

" M. Necker does not appear content with this happy state of things. Our inevitable evils and the abuses flowing from such a position are in his eyes monstrosities; a foreigner, a republican and a protestant, instead of being struck with the majestic totality of this harmony, he sees only the discordants, and he makes out of them a totality which he desires to have the pleasure and the distinction of reforming in order to obtain for himself the fame of a Solon or a Lycurgus.

" Your Majesty, Sir, told me to open my heart to you: a contest has begun between the regimen of France and the regimen of M. Necker. If his ideas should triumph over those which have been consecrated by long experience, after the precedent of Law, of Mazarin, and of the Lorraine princes, M. Necker, with his Genevese and protestant plans, is quite prepared to set up in France a system in the finance, or a league in the State, or a " Fronde " against the established administration. He has conducted the king's affairs in a manner so contrary to that of his predecessors that he is at this moment suspected by the clergy, hateful to the grandees of the State, hounded to the death by the heads of finance (*la haute-finance*), dishonoured amongst the magistracy. His Report, on the whole, is a mere appeal to the people, the pernicious consequences whereof to this monarchy cannot as yet be felt or foreseen. M. Necker, it is true, has won golden opinions from the philosophy and the innovators of these days, but your Majesty has long ago appraised the character of such support. In his Report M. Necker lays it down that advantage has been taken of the veil drawn over the state of the finances in order to obtain, amidst the general confusion, a credit which the State would not otherwise be entitled to. It is a new position, and a remarkable one in our history is that of M. Necker teaching the party he calls public opinion that under a good king, under a monarch beloved of the people, the minister of finance has become the sole hope, the sole security, by his moral qualities, of the lenders and experts who watch the government. It will be long before your Majesty will close up the wound inflicted upon the dignity of the throne by the hand of the very person in the official position to preserve it and make it respected by the people."

The adroit malevolence of M. de Vergennes had managed to involve in one and the same condemnation the bold innovations of M. Necker and the faults he had committed from a self-conceit which was sensitive and frequently hurt. He had not mentioned M. de Maurepas in his long exposition of public administration, and it was upon the virtue of the finance-minister that he had rested all the fabric of public confidence. The contest was every day becoming fiercer and the parties warmer. The useful reforms, the generous concern for the woes and the wants of the people, the initiative of which belonged to M. Necker, but which the king always regarded with favour, were by turns exclusively attributed to the minister and to Louis XVI. in the pamphlets published every day. Madame Necker became anxious and heart-broken at the vexation which such attacks caused her husband. "The slightest cloud upon his character was the greatest suffering the affairs of life could cause him," writes Madame de Staël; "the worldly aim of all his actions, the land-breeze which sped his bark, was love of reputation." Madame Necker took it into her head to write, without her husband's knowledge, to M. de Maurepas to complain of the libels spread about against M. Necker and ask him to take the necessary measures against these anonymous publications: this was appealing to the very man who secretly encouraged them. Although Madame Necker had plenty of wits, she, bred in the mountains of Switzerland, had no conception of such an idiosyncrasy as that of M. de Maurepas, a man who saw in an outspoken expression of feeling only an opportunity of discovering the vulnerable point. As soon as he knew M. Necker's susceptibility he flattered himself that, by irritating it, he would drive him to give in his resignation " [*Considérations sur la Révolution française*, t. i. p. 105].

M. Necker had gained a victory over M. de Maurepas when he succeeded in getting M. de Sartines and the prince of Montbarrey superseded by MM. de Castries and de Ségur. Late lieutenant of police, with no knowledge of administration, M. de Sartines, by turns rash and hesitating, had failed in the difficult department of the ministry of marine during a distant war waged on every sea ; to him were attributed the unsatisfactory results obtained by the great armaments of France ; he was engaged in the intrigue against M. Necker. The latter relied upon the influence of the queen, who supported MM. de Castries and de Ségur, both friends of hers. M. de Sartines was disgraced ; he dragged down with him in his fall the prince of Montbarrey, the heretofore indifferent lieutenant of M. de Saint-Germain. M. de Maurepas was growing feeble, the friends of M. Necker declared that he drivelled, and the latter already aspired to the aged minister's place. As a first step, the director-general of finance boldly demanded to be henceforth admitted to the council.

Louis XVI. hesitated, perplexed and buffeted between- contrary influences and desires. He was grateful to M. Necker for the courageous suppressions he had accomplished, and for the useful reforms whereof the honour was to remain inseparable from his name ; it was at M. Necker's advice that he had abolished mortmain in his dominions. A remnant of feudal serfdom still deprived certain of the rural classes, subject to the *tenement* law, of the right to marry or bequeath what they possessed to their children without permission of their lord. If they left the land which made them liable to this tyranny, their heritage reverted of right to the proprietor of the fief. Perfectly admitting the iniquity of the practice, Louis XVI. did not want to strike a blow at the principle of property ; he confined himself to giving a precedent which the Parliament enregistered with this reservation : " Without there being anything in the present edict which can in any way interfere with the rights of lords." A considerable number of noblemen imitated the sovereign ; many held out, amongst others the chapter of St. Claude : the enfranchisement of the serfs of the Jura, in whose

favour Voltaire had but lately pleaded, would have cost the chapter
twenty-five thousand livres a year; the monks demanded an indem-
nification from Government.   The *body* serfs, who were in all places
persecuted by the signiorial rights, and who could not make wills
even on free soil, found themselves everywhere enfranchised from
this harsh law.   Louis XVI. abolished the *droit de suite (henchman-
law)*, as well as the use of the *preparatory question* or preliminary
torture applied to defendants.   The regimen of prisons was at the
same time ameliorated, the dark dungeons of old times restored to
daylight the wretches who were still confined in them.

So many useful and beneficent measures, in harmony with the
king's honest and generous desires, but opposed to the prejudices
still potent in many minds and against the interests of many people,
kept up about M. Necker, for all the esteem and confidence of the
general public, powerful hatreds, ably served: his admission to the
council was decidedly refused.   "You may be admitted," said M.
de Maurepas with his usual malice, "if you please to abjure the
errors of Calvin."   M. Necker did not deign to reply.   "You who,
being quite certain that I would not consent, proposed to me a
change of religion in order to smoothe away the obstacles you put
in my path," says M. Necker in his *Mémoires*, "what would you
not have thought me worthy of after such baseness?   It was rather
in respect of the vast finance-administration that this scruple should
have been raised.   Up to the moment when it was entrusted to me,
it was uncertain whether I was worth an exception to the general
rules.   What new obligation could be imposed upon him who
held the post before promising?"

"If I was passionately attached to the place I occupied," says
M. Necker again, "it is on grounds for which I have no reason to
blush.   I considered that the administrator of finance, who is
responsible on his honour for ways and means, ought, for the welfare
of the State and for his own reputation, to be invited, especially after
several years' ministry, to the deliberations touching peace and
war, and I looked upon it as very important that he should be able
to join his reflections to those of the king's other servants.   A
place in the council may, as a general rule, be a matter in which
self-love is interested; but I am going to say a proud thing: when

NECKER AT SAINT OUEN.

one has cherished another passion, when one has sought praise and glory, when one has followed after those triumphs which belong to oneself alone, one regards rather coolly such functions as are shared with others."

" Your Majesty saw that M. Necker, in his dangerous proposal, was sticking to his place with a tenacity which lacks neither reason nor method," said M. de Vergennes in a secret Note addressed to the king; " he aspires to new favours, calculated from their nature to scare and rouse that long array of enemies by whom his religion, his birth, his wife, the epochs and improvements of their fortune are, at every moment of his administration, exposed to the laughter or the scrutiny of the public.   Your Majesty finds yourself once more in the position in which you were with respect to M. Turgot, when you thought proper to accelerate his retirement; the same dangers and the same inconveniencies arise from the nature of their analogous systems."

It was paying M. Necker a great compliment to set his financial talents on a par with the grand views, noble schemes, and absolute disinterestedness of M. Turgot.   Nevertheless, when the latter fell, public opinion had become, if not hostile, at any rate indifferent to him; it still remained faithful to M. Necker.   Withdrawing his pretensions to admission into the council, the director-general of finance was very urgent to obtain other marks of the royal confidence, necessary, he said, to keep up the authority of his administration.   M. de Maurepas had no longer the pretext of religion, but he hit upon others which wounded M. Necker deeply; the latter wrote to the king on a small sheet of common paper, without heading or separate line, and as if he were suddenly resuming all the forms of republicanism : " The conversation I have had with M. de Maurepas permits me to no longer defer placing my resignation in the king's hands.   I feel my heart quite lacerated by it, and I dare to hope that his Majesty will deign to preserve some remembrance of five years successful but painful toil, and especially of the boundless zeal with which I devoted myself to his service."   [May 19, 1783.]

M. Necker had been treated less harshly than M. Turgot.   The king accepted his resignation without having provoked it.   The

queen made some efforts to retain him, but M. Necker remained
inflexible. "Reserved as he was," says his daughter, "he had
a proud disposition, a sensitive spirit; he was a man of energy
in his whole style of sentiments." The fallen minister retired to
his country-house at St. Ouen.

He was accompanied thither by the respect and regret of the
public, and the most touching proofs of their esteem. "You would
have said, to see the universal astonishment, that never was news
so unexpected as that of M. Necker's resignation," writes Grimm
in his *Correspondance littéraire;* "consternation was depicted on
every face; those who felt otherwise were in a very small minority;
they would have blushed to show it. The walks, the cafés, all the
public thoroughfares were full of people, but an extraordinary
silence prevailed. People looked at one another, and mournfully
wrung one another's hands as if in the presence, I would say, of a
public calamity, were it not that these first moments of distress resembled rather the grief of a disconsolate family which has just lost
the object and the mainstay of its hopes. The same evening they
gave, at the Comédie-Française, a performance of the *Partie de
Chasse de Henri IV.* I have often seen at the play in Paris allusions
to passing events caught up with great cleverness, but I never saw
any which were so with such palpable and general an interest.
Every piece of applause, when there was anything concerning Sully,
seemed, so to speak, to bear a special character, a shade appropriate
to the sentiment the audience felt; it was by turns that of sorrow
and sadness, of gratitude and respect; the applause often came so as
to interrupt the actor the moment it was foreseen that the sequel of
a speech might be applicable to the public feeling towards M. Necker.
The players have been to make their excuses to the lieutenant of
police, they established their innocence by proving that the piece
had been on the list for a week. They have been forgiven, and it was
thought enough to take this opportunity of warning the journalists
not to speak of M. Necker for the future—well or ill."

M. Necker derived some balm from these manifestations of public
feeling, but the love of power, the ambition that prompted the work
he had undertaken, the bitterness of hopes deceived still possessed
his soul. When he entered his study at St. Ouen and saw on his

desk the memoranda of his schemes, his plans for reforming the gabel, for suppressing custom-houses, for extending provincial assemblies, he threw himself back in his arm-chair, and, dropping the papers he held in his hand, burst into tears. Like him, M. Turgot had wept when he heard of the re-establishment of forced labour and jurands.

"I quitted office," says M. Necker, "leaving funds secured for a whole year; I quitted it when there were in the royal treasury

PUBLIC GRIEF AT NECKER'S FALL.

more ready money and more realizable effects than had ever been there within the memory of man, and at a moment when the public confidence, completely restored, had risen to the highest pitch.

"Under other circumstances I should have been more appreciated; but it is when one can be rejected and when one is no longer essentially necessary that one is permitted to fall back upon one's own reflections. Now there is a contemptible feeling which may be easily found lurking in the recesses of the human heart, that of preferring for one's retirement the moment at which one might enjoy the embarrassment of one's successor. I should have been for ever ashamed of such conduct ; I chose that which was alone becoming for him who, having clung to his place from honourable motives, cannot, on quitting it, sever himself for one instant from the commonwealth."

M. Necker fell with the fixed intention and firm hope of soon regaining power. He had not calculated either the strength or inveteracy of his enemies, or the changeableness of that public opinion on which he relied. Before the distresses of the State forced Louis XVI. to recall a minister whom he had deeply wounded, the evils which the latter had sought to palliate would have increased with frightful rapidity and the remedy would have slipped definitively out of hands too feeble for the immense burthen they were still ambitious to bear.

CHAPTER LIX.

LOUIS XVI.—M. DE CALONNE AND THE ASSEMBLY OF NOTABLES (1781—1787).

WE leave behind us the great and serious attempts at reform. The vast projects of M. Turgot, seriously meant and founded on reason, for all their somewhat imaginative range, had become, in M. Necker's hands, financial expedients or necessary remedies, honourably applied to the most salient evils; the future, however, occupied the mind of the minister just fallen; he did not content himself with the facile gratifications of a temporary and disputed power, he had wanted to reform, he had hoped to found; his successors did not raise so high their real desires and hopes. M. Turgot had believed in the eternal potency of abstract laws; he had relied upon justice and reason to stop the kingdom and the nation on the brink of the abyss; M. Necker had nursed the illusion that his courage and his intelligence, his probity and his reputation would suffice for all needs and exorcise all dangers; both of them had found themselves thwarted in their projects, deceived in their hopes, and finally abandoned by a monarch as weak and undecided as he was honest and good.

M. de Turgot had lately died (March 20, 1781), in bitter sorrow and anxiety; M. Necker was waiting, in his retirement at St. Ouen, for public opinion, bringing its weight to bear upon the king's will, to recall him to office. M. de Maurepas was laughing in that little closet at Versailles which he hardly quitted any more : " The man impossible to replace is still unborn," he would say to those who were alarmed at M. Necker's resignation. M. Joly de Fleury, councillor of State, was summoned to the finance-department; but so strong was the current of popular opinion that he did not take up his quarters in the residence of the comptroller-general and considered himself bound to pay M. Necker a visit at St. Ouen.

Before experience had been long enough to demonstrate the error committed by M. de Maurepas in depriving the king of M. Necker's able and honest services, the veteran minister was dead (November 21, 1784). In the teeth of all inclinations opposed to his influence, he had managed to the last to preserve his sway over the mind of Louis XVI. : prudent, moderate, imperturbable in the evenness of his easy and at the same time sarcastic temper, he had let slide, so far as he was concerned, the reformers and their projects, the foreign war, the wrath of the Parliaments, the remonstrances of the clergy, without troubling himself at any shock, without ever persisting to obstinacy in any course, ready to modify his policy according to circumstances and the quarter from which the wind blew, always master, at bottom, in the successive cabinets, and preserving over all the ministers, whoever they might be, an ascendancy more real than it appeared. The king regretted him sincerely. " Ah ! " said he, " I shall no more hear, every morning, my friend over my head." The influence of M. de Maurepas had often been fatal; he had remained, however, like a pilot still holding with feeble hand the rudder he had handled for so long. After him, all direction and all predominance of mind disappeared from the conduct of the government. " The loss is more than we can afford," said clear-sighted folks already.

For a moment, and almost without consideration, the king was tempted to expand his wings and take the government into his

own hands; he had a liking for and confidence in M. de
Vergennes; but the latter, a man of capacity in the affairs of his
own department and much esteemed in Europe, was timid, devoid
of ambition and always disposed to shift responsibility into the
hands of absolute power.   Notwithstanding some bolder attempts,
the death of M. de Maurepas did not seriously augment his
authority.   The financial difficulties went on getting worse; on
principle and from habit, the new comptroller-general, like M. de
Vergennes, was favourable to the traditional maxims and practices
of the old French administration; he was, however, dragged into
the system of loans by the necessities of the State as well as by
the ideas impressed upon men's minds by M. Necker.   To loans
succeeded imposts; the dues and taxes were increased uniformly,
without regard for privileges and the burthens of different
provinces; the Parliament of Paris, in the body of which the
comptroller-general counted many relatives and friends, had enregistered the new edicts without difficulty; the Parliament of
Besançon protested, and its resistance went so far as to place the
comptroller-general on his defence.   " All that is done in my
name is done by my orders," replied Louis XVI. to the deputation
from Franche-Comté.   The deputation required nothing less than
the convocation of the States-general.   On all sides the nation was
clamouring after this ancient remedy for their woes; the most
clearsighted had hardly a glimmering of the transformation which
had taken place in ideas as well as manners; none had guessed
what, in the reign of Louis XVI., those States-general would be
which had remained dumb since the regency of Mary de' Medici.

Still more vehement and more proud than the Parliamentarians,
the States of Brittany, cited to elect the deputies indicated by the
governor, had refused any subsidy.   " Obey," said the king to the
deputies; " my orders have nothing in them contrary to the
privileges which my predecessors were graciously pleased to grant
to my province of Brittany."   Scarcely had the Bretons returned
to the States, when M. Amelot, who had charge of the affairs of
Brittany, received a letter which he did not dare to place before
the king's eyes.   " Sir," said the States of Brittany, " we are
alarmed and troubled when we see our franchises and our liberties,

conditions essential to the contract which gives you Brittany, regarded as mere privileges, founded upon a special concession. We cannot hide from you, Sir, the direful consequences of expressions so opposed to the constant principles of our national code. You are the father of your people and exercise no sway but that of the laws; they rule by you and you by them. The conditions which secure to you our allegiance form a part of the positive laws of your realm." Contrary to all received usages during the session of the States, the royal troops marched into Rennes; the noblesse refused to deliberate, so long as the assembly had not recovered its independence. The governor applied to the petty nobles who preponderated in their order; ignorant and poor as they were, they allowed themselves to be bought, their votes carried the day, and the subsidies were at last voted, notwithstanding the opposition on the part of the most weighty of the noblesse; a hundred of them persistently stayed away.

Internal quarrels in the cabinet rendered the comptroller-general's situation daily more precarious; he gave in his resignation. The king sent for M. d'Ormesson, councillor of state, of a virtue and integrity which were traditional in his family, but without experience of affairs and without any great natural capacity. He was, besides, very young, and he excused himself from accepting such a post on the score of his age and his feeble lights. "I am only thirty-one, Sir," he said. "I am younger than you," replied the king, "and my post is more difficult than yours." A few months later, the honest magistrate, overwhelmed by a task beyond his strength, had made up his mind to resign; he did not want to have any hand in the growing disorder of the finances; the king's brothers kept pressing him to pay their debts; Louis XVI. himself, without any warning to the comptroller-general, had just purchased Rambouillet from the duke of Penthièvre, giving a bond for fourteen millions; but Madame d'Ormesson had taken a liking to grandeur; she begged her husband hard to remain, and he did. It was not long before the embarrassments of the Treasury upset his judgment: the tax-farming contract, so ably concluded by M. Necker, was all at once quashed; a *régie* was established; the Discount-fund (*Caisse*

MARIE ANTOINETTE.

d'Escompte) had lent the Treasury six millions : the secret of this loan was betrayed, and the holders of bills presented themselves in a mass demanding liquidation ; a decree of the council forbad payment in coin over a hundred livres and gave the bills a forced currency. The panic became general ; the king found himself obliged to dismiss M. d'Ormesson, who was persecuted for a long while by the witticisms of the court. His incapacity had brought his virtue into ridicule.

Marshal de Castries addressed to the king a private note. " I esteem M. d'Ormesson's probity," said the minister of marine frankly, " but if the financial affairs should fall into such discredit that your Majesty finds yourself forced at last to make a change, I dare entreat you to think of the valuable man who is now left unemployed ; I do beg you to reflect that, without Colbert, Louis XIV. would never perhaps have been called *Louis le Grand ;* that the wish of the nation, to be taken into account by a good king, is secretly demanding, Sir, that the enlightened, economical and incorruptible man whom Providence has given to your Majesty, should be re-called to his late functions. The errors of your other ministers, Sir, are nearly always reparable, and their places are easily filled. But the choice of him to whom is committed the happiness of twenty-four millions of souls and the duty of making your authority cherished is of frightful importance. With M. Necker, Sir, even in peace, the imposts would be accepted, whatever they might be, without a murmur. The conviction would be that inevitable necessity had laid down the law for them, and that a wise use of them would justify them . . ., whereas, if your Majesty puts to hazard an administration on which all the rest depend, it is to be feared that the difficulties will be multiplied with the selections you will be obliged to have recourse to ; you will find one day destroy what another set up, and at last there will arrive one when no way will be seen of serving the State but by failing to keep all your Majesty's engagements and thereby putting an end to all the confidence which the commencement of your reign inspired."

The honest zeal of Marshal de Castries for the welfare of the State had inspired him with prophetic views ; but royal weakness exhibits sometimes unexpected doggedness. " As regards M. Necker," answered Louis XVI., " I will tell you frankly that after the manner in which I treated him and that in which he left me, I couldn't think of employing him at all." After some court-intrigues which brought forward names that were not in good odour, that of Foulon, late superintendent of the forces, and of the archbishop of Toulouse, Loménie de Brienne, the king sent for M. de Calonne, superintendent of Lille, and entrusted him with the post of comptroller-general.

It was court-influence that carried the day and, in the court, that of the queen, prompted by her favourite, Madame de Polignac. Tenderly attached to his wife, who had at last given him a son, Louis XVI., delivered from the predominant influence of M. de Maurepas, was yielding, almost unconsciously, to a new power. Marie Antoinette, who had long held aloof from politics, hence-forth changed her part; at the instigation of the friends whom she honoured with a perhaps excessive intimacy, she began to take an important share in affairs, a share which was often exaggerated by public opinion, more and more hard upon her every day.

Received on her arrival in France with some mistrust, of which she had managed to get the better amongst the public, having been loved and admired as long as she was dauphiness, the young queen, after her long period of constraint in the royal family, had soon profited by her freedom; she had a horror of etiquette, to which the court of Austria had not made her accustomed, she gladly escaped from the grand palaces of Louis XIV., where the traditions of his reign seemed still to exercise a secret influence, in order to seek at her little manor-house of Trianon new amusements and rustic pleasures, innocent and simple, and attended with no other inconvenience but the air of cliquedom and almost of mystery in which the queen's guests enveloped themselves. Public rumour soon reached the ears of Maria Theresa. She, tenderly concerned for her daughter's happiness and conduct, wrote to her on this subject:

" I am always sure of success if you take anything in hand, the good God having endowed you with such a face and so many charms besides, added to your goodness, that hearts are yours if you try and exert yourself, but I cannot conceal from you, nevertheless, my apprehension; it reaches me from every quarter and only too often, that you have diminished your attentions and politenesses in the matter of saying something agreeable and becoming to everybody, and of making distinctions between persons. It is even asserted that you are beginning to indulge in ridicule, bursting out laughing in people's faces; this might do you infinite harm and very properly, and even raise doubts as to the goodness of your heart; in order to amuse five or six young ladies or gentlemen, you might lose all else. This defect, my dear child, is no light one in a princess; it leads to imitation, in order to pay their court, on the part of all the courtiers, folks ordinarily with nothing to do and the least estimable in the State, and it keeps away honest folks who do not like being turned into ridicule or exposed to the necessity of having their feelings hurt, and in the end you are left with none but bad company, which by degrees leads to all manner of vices. . . . . . Likings carried too far are baseness or weakness, one must learn to play one's part properly if one wishes to be esteemed; you can do it if you will but restrain yourself a little and follow the advice given you; if you are heedless, I foresee great troubles for you, nothing but squabbles and petty cabals which will render your days miserable. I wish to prevent this and to conjure you to take the advice of a mother who knows the world, who idolizes her children and whose only desire is to pass her sorrowful days in being of service to them."

Wise counsels of the most illustrious of mothers uselessly lavished upon her daughters! Already the queen of Naples was beginning to betray the fatal tendencies of her character, whilst, in France, frivolous pleasures, unreflecting friendships, and petty court-intrigues were day by day undermining the position of Marie Antoinette. "I am much affected at the situation of my daughter," wrote Maria Theresa, in 1776, to Abbé Vermond, whom she had herself not long ago placed with the dauphiness, then quite a child, and whose influence was often pernicious; "she is hurrying at a great pace to her ruin, surrounded as she is, by base flatterers who urge her on for their own interests."

Almost at the same moment she was writing to the queen: " I am very pleased to learn that you had nothing to do with the change that has been made in the cases of MM. Turgot and Malesherbes, who, however, have a great reputation amongst the public and whose only fault, in my opinion, is that they attempted too much at once. You say that you are not sorry; you must have your own good reasons, but the public, for some time past, has not spoken so well of you, and attributes to you point blank petty practices which would not be seemly in your place. The king loving you, his ministers must needs respect you; by asking nothing that is not right and proper, you make yourself respected and loved at the same time. I fear nothing in your case (as you are so young) but too much dissipation. You never did like reading, or any sort of application: this has often caused me anxieties. I was so pleased to see you devoted to music; that is why I have often plagued you with questions about your reading; for more than a year past there has no longer been any question of reading or of music, I hear of nothing but horse-racing, hunting too, and always without the king and with a number of young people not over-select, which disquiets me a great deal, loving you as I do so tenderly. I must say, all these pleasures in which the king takes no part, are not proper. You will tell me, 'he knows, he approves of them.' I will tell you, he is a good soul, and therefore you ought to be circumspect and combine your amusements with his; in the long-run you can only be happy through such tender and sincere union and affection."

The misfortune and cruel pangs of their joint lives were alone destined to establish between Marie Antoinette and her husband that union and that intimacy which their wise mother would have liked to create in the days of tranquillity. Affectionate and kind, sincerely devoted to his wife, Louis XVI. was abrupt and awkward; his occupations and his tastes were opposed to all the elegant or frivolous instincts of the young queen. He liked books and solid books, his cabinet was hung with geographical charts which he studied with care; he had likewise a passion for mechanical works and would shut himself up for hours together in a workshop in company with a blacksmith named Gamin. "The king used to hide from the queen and the court to forge and file with me," this man would remark in after days: "to carry about his anvil and mine, without anybody's knowing anything about it, required a thousand stratagems which it would take no end of time to tell of." "You will allow that I should make a sorry figure at a forge," writes the queen to her brother Joseph II.; "I should not be Vulcan and the part of Venus might displease the king more than those tastes of mine of which he does not disapprove."

Louis XVI. did not disapprove, but without approving. As he was weak in dealing with his ministers, from kindliness and habit, so he was towards the queen with much better reason. Whilst she was scampering to the Opera ball, and laughing at going thither in a hackney-coach one day when her carriage had met with an accident, the king went to bed every evening at the same hour, and the talk of the public began to mix up the name of Marie Antoinette with stories of adventure. In the hard winter of 1775, whilst the court amused themselves by going about in elegantly got-up sledges, the king sent presents of wood to the poor: "There are my sledges, sirs," said he as he pointed out to the gentlemen in attendance the heavy waggons laden with logs. The queen more gladly took part in the charities than in the smithy. She distributed alms bountifully; in a moment of gratitude the inhabitants of Rue St. Honoré had erected in her honour a snow pyramid bearing these verses:—

> Fair queen, whose goodness is thy chiefest grace,
> With our good king, here occupy thy place;
> Though this frail monument be ice or snow,
> Our warm hearts are not so.

Bursts of kindness and sympathy, sincere as they may be, do not suffice to win the respect and affection of a people. The reign of Louis XV. had used up the remnants of traditional veneration, the new right of the public to criticize sovereigns was being exercised malignantly upon the youthful thoughtlessnesses of Marie Antoinette.

In the home-circle of the royal family, the queen had not found
any intimate : the king's aunts had never taken to her; the crafty
ability of the count of Provence and the giddiness of the count of
Artois seemed in the prudent eye of Maria Theresa to be equally
dangerous; Madame Elizabeth, the heroic and pious companion of
the evil days, was still a mere child; already the duke of Chartres,
irreligious and debauched, displayed towards the queen who kept
him at a distance symptoms of a bitter rancour which was destined
to bear fruit; Marie Antoinette, accustomed to a numerous family,
affectionately united, sought friends who could "love her for
herself," as she used to say. An illusive hope, in one of her rank,
for which she was destined to pay dearly. She formed an attachment to the young princess of Lamballe, daughter-in-law of the
duke of Penthièvre, a widow at twenty years of age, affectionate
and gentle, for whom she revived the post of lady-superintendent,
abolished by Mary Leczinska. The court was in commotion, and
the public murmured; the queen paid no heed, absorbed as she
was in the new delights of friendship; the intimacy, in which
there was scarcely any inequality, with the princess of Lamballe,
was soon followed by a more perilous affection; the countess
Jules de Polignac, who was generally detained in the country by
the narrowness of her means, appeared at court on the occasion of
a festival; the queen was pleased with her, made her remain and
loaded her, her and her family, not only with favours but with
unbounded and excessive familiarity. Finding the court-circles a
constraint and an annoyance, Marie Antoinette became accustomed
to seek in the drawing-room of Madame de Polignac amusements
and a freedom which led before long to sinister gossip. Those
who were admitted to this royal intimacy were not always prudent
or discreet, they abused the confidence as well as the generous
kindness of the queen; their ambition and their cupidity were
equally concerned in urging Marie Antoinette to take in the
government a part for which she was not naturally inclined.
M. de Calonne was intimate with Madame de Polignac; she, created
a duchess and appointed governess to the children of France (the
royal children), was all-powerful with her friend the queen; she
dwelt upon the talents of M. de Calonne, the extent and fertility

of his resources; M. de Vergennes was won over, and the office of comptroller-general, which had but lately been still discharged with lustre by M. Turgot and M. Necker, fell on the 30th of October, 1784, into the hands of M. de Calonne.

Born in 1734 at Douai, Charles Alexander de Calonne belonged to a family of magistrates of repute and influence in their province; he commenced his hereditary career by the perfidious manœuvres which contributed to the ruin of M. de la Chalotais. Discredited

CALONNE.

from the very first by a dishonourable action, he had invariably managed to get his vices forgotten, thanks to the charms of a brilliant and fertile wit. Prodigal and irregular as superintendent of Lille, he imported into the comptroller-generalship habits and ideas opposed to all the principles of Louis XVI. "The peace would have given hope a new run," says M. Necker in his Mémoires, "if the king had not confided the important functions of administering the finances to a man more worthy of being the hero of courtiers than the minister of a king. The reputation of M. de Calonne was a contrast to the morality of Louis XVI., and

I know not by what argumentation, by what ascendancy such a prince was induced to give a place in his council to a magistrate who was certainly found agreeable in the most elegant society of Paris but whose levity and principles were dreaded by the whole of France. Money was lavished, largesses were multiplied, there was no declining to be goodnatured or complaisant, economy was made the object of ridicule, it was daringly asserted that immensity of expenditure, animating circulation, was the true principle of credit."

M. de Calonne had just been sworn in at the Court of Aids, pompously attended by a great number of magistrates and financiers; he was for the first time transacting business with the king: "Sir," said he, "the comptrollers-general have many means of paying their debts, I have at this moment two hundred and twenty thousand livres' worth payable on demand, I thought it right to tell your Majesty and leave everything to your goodness." Louis XVI., astounded at such language, stared a moment at his minister, and then, without any answer, walked up to a desk: "There are your two hundred and twenty thousand livres," he said at last," handing M. de Calonne a packet of shares in the Water Company. The comptroller-general pocketed the shares and found elsewhere the resources necessary for paying his debts. "If my own affairs had not been in such a bad state, I should not have undertaken those of France," said Calonne gaily to M. de Machault, at that time advanced in age and still the centre of public esteem. The king, it was said, had but lately thought of sending for him as minister in the room of M. de Maurepas, he had been dissuaded by the advice of his aunts; the late comptroller-general listened gravely to his frivolous successor; the latter told the story of his conversation with the king: "I had certainly done nothing to deserve a confidence so extraordinary," said M. de Machault to his friends. He set out again for his estate at Arnonville, more anxious than ever about the future.

If the first steps of M. de Calonne dismayed men of foresight and of experience in affairs, the public was charmed with them, no less than the courtiers. The *bail des fermes* was re-established, the *Caisse d'escompte* had resumed payment, the stock-holders (*rentiers*) received their quarters' arrears, the loan whereby the comptroller-general met all expenses had reached 11 per cent. "A man who wants to borrow," M. de Calonne would say, "must appear rich, and to appear rich he must dazzle by his expenditure. Act we thus in the public administration. Economy is good for nothing, it warns those who have money not to lend it to an indebted Treasury, and it causes decay amongst the arts which prodigality vivifies." New works, on a gigantic scale, were undertaken everywhere. "Money abounds in the kingdom," the comptroller-general would remark to the king, "the people never had more openings for work, lavishness rejoices their eyes, because it sets their hands going. Continue these splendid undertakings which are an ornament to Paris, Bordeaux, Lyons, Nantes, Marseilles and Nîmes, and which are almost entirely paid for by those flourishing cities. Look to your ports, fortify Havre, and create a Cherbourg, braving the jealousy of the English. None of those measures which reveal and do not relieve the straits of the Treasury! The people, whom declaiming jurisconsults so vehemently but vainly incite to speak evil of lavishness, would be grieved if they saw any interruption in the expenditure which a silly parsimony calls superfluous."

The comptroller-general's practice tallied with his theories, the courtiers had recovered the golden age; it was scarcely necessary to solicit the royal favour. "When I saw everybody holding out hands, I held out my hat," said a prince. The offices abolished by M. Turgot and M. Necker were re-established, the abuses which they had removed came back, the acceptances (*acquits de comptant*) rose in 1785 to more than a hundred and thirty-six millions of livres. The debts of the king's brothers were paid; advantageous exchanges of royal lands were effected to their profit; the queen bought St. Cloud, which belonged to the duke of Orleans; all the great lords who were ruined, all the courtiers who were embarrassed, resumed the pleasant habit of counting upon the royal treasury to relieve their wants. The polite alacrity of the comptroller-general had subdued the most rebellious; he obtained for Brittany the right of freely electing its deputies; the states-hall at Rennes, which had but lately resounded with curses upon him, was now repeating a new cry of "Hurrah! for Calonne!" A vote of the assembly doubled the gratuitous gift which the province ordinarily offered the king. "If it is possible, it is done," the comptroller-general would say to applicants; "if it is impossible, it will get done."

The captivation was general, the blindness seemed to be so likewise; a feverish impulse carried people away into all new-fangled ways, serious or frivolous. Mesmer brought from Germany his mysterious revelations in respect of problems as yet unsolved by science, and pretended to cure all diseases around the magnetic battery; the adventurer Cagliostro, embellished with the title of count and lavishing gold by handfuls, bewitched court and city and induced Councillor d'Éprémesnil to say, "The friendship of M. de Cagliostro does me honour." At the same time splendid works in the most diverse directions maintained at the topmost place in the world that scientific genius of France which the great minds of the seventeenth century had revealed to Europe. "Special men sometimes testify great disdain as regards the interest which men of the world may take in their labours, and, certainly, if it were merely a question of appraising their scientific merit, they would be perfectly right. But the esteem, the inclination of the public for science, and the frequent lively expression of that sentiment, are of high importance to it and play a great part in its history. The times for that sympathy, somewhat ostentatious and frivolous as it may be, have always been, as regards sciences, times of impulse and progress, and, regarding things in their totality, natural history and chemistry profited by the social existence of M. de Buffon and of M. Lavoisier as much as by their discoveries" [M. Guizot, *Mélanges biographiques*, Madame de Rumford].

It was this movement in the public mind, ignorant but sympathetic, which, on the eve of the Revolution, supported, without understanding them, the efforts of the great scholars whose peaceful conquests survived the upheaval of society. Farmer-general (of taxes) before he became a chemist, Lavoisier sought to apply the discoveries of science to common and practical wants. " Devoted to the public instruction, I will seek to enlighten the people," he said to the king who proposed office to him. The people were to send him to the scaffold. The ladies of fashion crowded to the brilliant lectures of Fourcroy. The princes of pure science, M. de Lagrange, M. de Laplace, M. Monge, did not disdain to wrench themselves from their learned calculations in order to second the useful labours of Lavoisier. Bold voyagers were scouring the world, pioneers of those enterprises

LAVOISIER.

of discovery which had appeared for a while abandoned during the seventeenth century. M. de Bougainville had just completed the round of the world, and the English captain, Cook, during the war which covered all seas with hostile ships, had been protected by generous sympathy. On the 19th of March, 1779, M. de Sartines, at that time minister of marine, wrote by the king's order, at the suggestion of M. Turgot : " Captain Cook, who left Plymouth in the month of July, 1776, on board the frigate *Discovery*, to make explorations on the coasts, islands, and seas of Japan and California, must be on the point of returning to Europe. As such enterprises are for the general advantage of all nations, it is the king's will that Captain Cook be treated as the commander

of a neutral and allied power, and that all navigators who meet
this celebrated sailor do inform him of His Majesty's orders
regarding him."

Captain Cook was dead, massacred by the savages, but the
ardour which had animated him was not extinct; on the 10th of
August, 1785, a French sailor, M. de La Peyrouse, left Brest with
two frigates for the purpose of completing the discoveries of the
English explorer. The king had been pleased to himself draw up
his instructions, bearing the impress of an affectionate and over-
strained humanity. "His Majesty would regard it as one of the
happiest successes of the expedition," said the instructions, "if it
were terminated without having cost the life of a single man."
La Peyrouse and his shipmates never came back. Louis XV. was
often saddened by it: "I see what it is quite well," the poor
king would repeat, "I am not lucky."

M. de La Peyrouse had scarcely commenced the preparations
for his fatal voyage, when, on the 5th of June, 1783, the States
of the Vivarais, assembled in the little town of Annonay,
were invited by MM. de Montgolfier, proprietors of a large paper-
manufactory, to be witnesses of an experiment in physics. The
crowd thronged the thoroughfare. An enormous bag, formed of
a light canvas lined with paper, began to swell slowly before the
curious eyes of the public; all at once the cords which held it
were cut and the first balloon rose majestically into the air.
Successive improvements made in the Montgolfiers' original
invention permitted bold physicists ere long to risk themselves
in a vessel attached to the air-machine. There sailed across
the Channel a balloon bearing a Frenchman, M. Blanchard, and
an Englishman, Dr. Jefferies; the latter lost his flag. Blanchard
had set the French flag floating over the shores of England;
public enthusiasm welcomed him on his return. The queen was
playing cards at Versailles: "What I win this game shall go to
Blanchard," she said. The same feat, attempted a few days later
by a professor of physics, M. Pilâtre de Rozier, was destined to
cost him his life.

So many scientific explorations, so many new discoveries of
nature's secrets were seconded and celebrated by an analogous

movement in literature. Rousseau had led the way to impassioned admiration of the beauties of nature ; Bernardin de St. Pierre had just published his *Études de la Nature;* he had in the press his *Paul et Virginie;* Abbé Delille was reading his *Jardin,* and M. de St. Lambert his *Saisons.* In their different phases and according to their special instincts, all minds, scholarly or political, literary or philosophical, were tending to the same end and pursuing the · same attempt. It was nature which men wanted to discover or recover : scientific laws and natural rights divided men's souls between them. Buffon was still alive and the great sailors were every day enriching with their discoveries the Jardin du Roi ; the physicists and the chemists, in the wake of Lavoisier, were giving to science a language intelligible to common folks ; the jurisconsults were attempting to reform the rigours of criminal legislation at the same time with the abuses they had entailed, aud Beaumarchais was bringing on the boards his *Mariage de Figaro.*

The piece had been finished and accepted at the Théâtre Français since the end of 1781, but the police-censors had refused permission to bring it out. Beaumarchais gave readings of it, the Court itself was amused to see itself attacked, caricatured, turned into ridicule ; the friends of Madame de Polignac reckoned amongst the most ardent admirers of the *Mariage de Figaro.* The king desired to become acquainted with the piece. He had it read by Madame de Campan, lady of the chamber to the queen, and very much in her confidence. The taste and the principles of Louis XVI. were equally shocked : " Perpetually Italian *concetti!* " he exclaimed. When the reading was over : " It is detestable," said the king ; " it shall never be played ; the Bastille would have to be destroyed to make the production of this play anything but a dangerous inconsistency. This fellow jeers at all that should be respected in a Government."

Louis XVI. had correctly criticized the tendencies as well as the effects of a production sparkling with wit, biting, insolent, licentious ; but he had relied too much upon his persistency in his opinions and his personal resolves. Beaumarchais was more headstrong than the king ; the readings continued. The hereditary grand duke of Russia, afterwards Paul I., happening to be at Paris in 1782, under the name of Count North, no better diversion could be thought of for him than a reading of the *Mariage de Figaro*. Grimm undertook to obtain Beaumarchais' consent. "As," says Madame de Oberkirsch, who was present at the reading, "as the mangy (*chafouin*) looks of M. de la Harpe had disappointed me, so the fine face, open, clever, somewhat bold, perhaps, of M. de Beaumarchais bewitched me. I was found fault with for it. I was told that he was a good-for-naught. I do not deny it, it is possible; but he has prodigious wit, courage enough for anything, a strong will which nothing can stop, and these are great qualities."

Beaumarchais took advantage of the success of the reading to boldly ask the keeper of the seals for permission to play the piece; he was supported by public curiosity and by the unreflecting enthusiasm of a court anxious to amuse itself; the game appeared to have been won, the day for its representation, at the Menus-Plaisirs Theatre, was fixed, an interdiction on the part of the king only excited the ill-humour and intensified the desires of the public. "This prohibition appeared to be an attack upon liberty in general," says Madame Campan. "The disappointment of all hopes excited discontent to such a degree that the words *oppression* and *tyranny* were never uttered, in the days preceding the fall of the throne, with more passion and vehemence." Two months later, the whole court was present at the representation of the *Mariage de Figaro*, given at the house of M. de Vandreuil, an intimate friend of the Duchess of Polignac's, on his stage at Gennevilliers. "You will see that Beaumarchais will have more influence than the keeper of the seals," Louis XVI. had said, himself foreseeing his own defeat. The *Mariage de Figaro* was played at the Théâtre Français on the 27th of April, 1784.

"The picture of this representation is in all the collections of the period," says M. de Loménie. "It is one of the best known reminiscences of the eighteenth century: all Paris hurrying early in the morning to the doors of the Théâtre Français, the greatest ladies dining in the actresses' dressing-rooms in order to secure places." "The blue ribands," says Bachaumont, "huddled up in the crowd and elbowing Savoyards; the guard dispersed, the doors burst, the iron gratings broken beneath the efforts of the assailants." "Three persons stifled," says La Harpe, " one more than for *Scudéry*, and on the stage, after the rising of the curtain, the finest collection of talent that had probably ever had possession of the Théâtre Français, all employed to do honour to a comedy scintillating with wit, irresistibly lively and audacious, which, if it shocks and scares a few of the boxes, enchants, rouses and fires an electrified pit." A hundred representations succeeding the first

BEAUMARCHAIS.

uninterruptedly and the public still eager to applaud, such was the twofold result of the audacities of the piece and the timid hesitations of its censors. The *Mariage de Figaro* bore a sub-title, *la Folle Journée*. "There is something madder than my piece," said Beaumarchais, " and that is its success."

Figaro ridiculed everything with a dangerously pungent vigour; the days were coming when the pleasantry was to change into insults. Already public opinion was becoming hostile to the queen: she was accused of having remained devoted to the interests of her German family; the people were beginning to call her *the Austrian*. During the American war, M. de Vergennes had managed to prevail upon the king to remain neutral in the difficulties that arose in 1778 between Austria and Prussia on the subject of the succession to the elector palatine; the young queen had not wanted or had not been able to influence the behaviour of France, as her mother had conjured her to do: "My dear lady-daughter," wrote Maria Theresa, "Mercy is charged to inform you of my cruel position, as sovereign and as mother. Wishing to save my dominions from the most cruel devastation, I must, cost what it may, seek to wrest myself from this war, and, as a mother, I have three sons who are not only running the greatest danger but are sure to succumb to the terrible fatigues, not being accustomed to that sort of life. By making peace at this juncture, I not only incur the blame of great pusillanimity, but I render the king of Prussia still greater, and the remedy must be prompt. I declare to you, my head whirls and my heart has for a long time been entirely numb." France had refused to engage in the war, but she had contributed to the peace of Teschen, signed on the 13th of May, 1779. On the 29th of November, 1780, Maria Theresa died at the age of sixty-three, weary of life and of that glory to which she "was fain to march by all roads," said the Great Frederick, who added: "It was thus that a woman executed designs worthy of a great man."

In 1784, Joseph II. reigned alone. Less prudent and less sensible than his illustrious mother, restless, daring, nourishing useful or fanciful projects, bred of humanity or disdain, severe and affectionate at the same time towards his sister the queen of France, whose extravagance he found fault with during the trip he made to Paris in 1777, he was now pressing her to act on his behalf in the fresh embarrassments which his restless ambition had just excited in Europe. The mediation of King Louis XVI. between the emperor and the Dutch, as to the navigation of the Scheldt, had just terminated the incident pacifically: the king had concluded a treaty of defensive alliance with Holland. The minister of war, M. de Ségur, communicated to the queen the note he had drawn up on this important question: "I regret," he said to Marie Antoinette, "to be obliged to give the king advice opposed to the desire of the emperor." "I am the emperor's sister, and I do not forget it," answered the queen, "but I remember above all that I am queen of France and mother of the dauphin." Louis XVI. had undertaken to pay part of the indemnity imposed upon Joseph II.; this created discontent in France: "Let the emperor pay for his own follies," people said: and the ill-humour of the public openly and unjustly accused the queen.

This direful malevolence on the part of public opinion, springing from a few acts of imprudence and fomented by a long series of calumnies, was about to burst forth on the occasion of a scandalous and grievous occurrence. On the 15th of August, 1785, at mass-time, Cardinal Rohan, grand almoner of France, already in full pontificals, was arrested in the palace of Versailles and taken to the Bastille. The king had sent for him into his cabinet: "Cardinal," said Louis XVI. abruptly, "you bought some diamonds of Bœhmer?" "Yes, Sir." "What have you done with them?" "I thought they had been sent to the queen." "Who gave you the commission?" (The cardinal began to be uneasy.) "A lady, the countess de la Motte Valois, . . . she gave me a letter from the queen, I thought I was obliging her Majesty. . . ." The queen interrupted. She had never forgiven M. de Rohan for some malevolent letters written about her when she was dauphiness. On the accession of Louis XVI., this intercepted correspondence had cost the prince his embassy to Vienna. "How, sir," said the queen, "could you think, you to whom I have never spoken for eight years, that I should choose you for conducting this nego-tiation and by the medium of such a woman?" "I was mistaken, I see; the desire I felt to please your Majesty misled me, . . ." and he drew from his pocket the pretended letter from the queen to Madame de la Motte. The king took it, and, casting his eye over the signature: "How could a prince of your house and my grand almoner suppose that the queen would sign *Marie Antoinette de France?* Queens sign their names quite short. It is not even the queen's writing. And what is the meaning of all these doings with jewellers, and these notes shown to bankers?"

The cardinal could scarcely stand, he leaned against the table. "Sir," he stammered, "I am too much overcome to be able to reply." " Walk into this room, cardinal," rejoined the king kindly; " write what you have to say to me." The written explanations of M. de Rohan were no clearer than his words; an officer of the body-guard took him off to the Bastille; he had just time to order his grand-vicar to burn all his papers.

The correspondence as well as the life of M. de Rohan was not worthy of a prince of the Church: the vices and the credulity of the cardinal had given him over, bound hand and foot, to an intriguing woman as adroit as she was daring. Descended from a bastard of Henry II.'s, brought up by charity and married to a ruined nobleman, Madame de La Motte Valois had bewitched, duped and robbed Cardinal Rohan. Accustomed to an insensate prodigality, asserting everywhere that a man of gallantry could not live on twelve hundred thousand livres a year, he had considered it very natural that the queen should have a fancy for possessing a diamond necklace worth sixteen hundred thousand livres. The jewellers had, in fact, offered this jewellery to Marie Antoinette; it was during the American war: " That is the price of two frigates," the king had said. " We want ships and not diamonds," said the queen, and dismissed her jeweller. A few months afterwards he told anybody who would listen that he had sold the famous collar in Constantinople for the favourite sultana. " This was a real pleasure to the queen," says Madame Campan; " she, however, expressed some astonishment that a necklace made for the adornment of French women should be worn in the seraglio, and, thereupon, she talked to me a long while about the total change which took place in the tastes and desires of women in the period between twenty and thirty years of age. She told me that when she was ten years younger she loved diamonds madly, but that she had no longer any taste for anything but private society, the country, the work and the attentions required by the education of her children. From that moment until the fatal crisis, there was nothing more said about the necklace."

The crisis would naturally come from the want of money felt by the jewellers. Madame de La Motte had paid them some instalments on account of the stones, which her husband had sold in England: they grew impatient and applied to the queen. For

CARDINAL ROHAN'S DISCOMPITURE.

a long while she did not understand their applications; when the complaints of the purveyors at last made her apprehend an intrigue, she sent for Abbé de Vermond and Baron de Breteuil, minister of the king's household : both detested the cardinal, both fanned the queen's wrath; she decided at last to tell the king everything. " I saw the queen after the departure of the baron and the abbé," says Madame Campan; " she made me tremble at her indignation." The cardinal renounced the privileges of his rank and condition; he boldly accepted the jurisdiction of the Parliament.

The trial revealed a gross intrigue, a disgraceful comedy, a prince of the Church and a merchant equally befooled by a shameless woman, with the aid of the adventurer Cagliostro, and the name, the favours and even the personality of the queen impudently dragged in. The public feeling was at its height, constantly over-excited by the rumours circulated during the sessions of the court. Opinion was hostile to the queen. " It was for her and by her orders that the necklace was bought," people said. The houses of Condé and Rohan were not afraid to take sides with the cardinal : these illustrious personages were to be seen, dressed in mourning, waiting for the magistrates on their way, in order to canvass them on their relative's behalf. On the 31st of May, 1786, the Court condemned Madame de la Motte to be whipped, branded and imprisoned; they purely and simply acquitted Cardinal Rohan. In its long and continual tussle with the crown, the Parliament had at last found the day of its revenge : political passions and the vagaries of public opinion had blinded the magistrates.

" As soon as I knew the cardinal's sentence, I went to the queen," says Madame Campan. " She heard my voice in the room leading to her closet; she called to me. I found her very sad. She said to me in a broken voice : ' Condole with me; the intriguer who wanted to ruin me, or procure money by using my name and forging my signature, has just been fully acquitted. But,' she added vehemently, ' as a Frenchwoman, accept my condolence. A people is very unfortunate to have for its supreme tribunal a lot of men who consult nothing but their passions, and

of whom some are capable of bribery and others of an audacity
which they have always displayed towards authority and of which
they have just given a striking example against those who are
clothed therewith.' The king entered at this moment. 'You
find the queen in great affliction,' he said to me: 'she has great
reason to be. But what then! They would not see in this
business anything save a prince of the Church and the prince
of Rohan, whereas it is only the case of a man in want of money
and a mere dodge for raising the wind, wherein the cardinal has
been swindled in his turn. Nothing can be easier to understand,
and it needs no Alexander to cut this Gordian knot.'"

Guilty in the king's eyes, a dupe according to the judgment of
history, Cardinal Rohan was exiled to his abbey of Chaise-Dieu, less
to be pitied than the unhappy queen abruptly wrenched from the
sweet dreams of a romantic friendship and confidence, as well as
from the nascent joys of maternal happiness, to find herself henceforth confronting a deluded people and an ever-increasing hostility
which was destined to unjustly persecute her even to the block.

M. de Calonne had taken little part in the excitement which the
trial of Cardinal Rohan caused in court and city: he was absorbed
by the incessantly recurring difficulties presented by the condition
of the Treasury; speculation had extended to all classes of
society; loans succeeded loans, everywhere there were formed
financial companies, without any resources to speak of, speculating
on credit. Parliament began to be alarmed, and enregistered no
more credits save with repugnance. Just as he was setting out on
a trip to Normandy, which afforded him one of the last happy
days of his life and as it were a dying flicker of his past popularity,
the king scratched out on the registers of the Parliament the
restrictions introduced by the court into the new loan of 80
millions presented by M. de Calonne. "I wish it to be known
that I am satisfied with my comptroller-general," said Louis XVI.
with that easy confidence which he did not always place wisely.
When he returned from Cherbourg at the end of June, 1786,
M. de Calonne had at last arrived at the extremity of his financial
expedients. He set his views and his ideas higher. Speculation
was succeeded by policy.

" Sir," said the note handed to the king by the comptroller-general, " I will not go back to the fearful position in which the finances were when your Majesty deigned to entrust them to me. It is impossible to recall without a shudder that there was at that time neither money nor credit, that the pressing debts were immense, the revenues exhausted in anticipation, the resources annihilated, the public securities valueless, the coinage impoverished and without circulation, the discount-fund bankrupt, the general tax-exchequer (*ferme général*) on the point of failing to meet its bills, and the royal treasury reduced to two bags of 1200 livres.   I am far from claiming credit for the success of the operations which, owing to the continuous support given by your Majesty, promptly established abundance of coin, punctuality in the payments, public confidence proved by the rise in all securities and by the highest degree of credit, abroad as well as at home : what I must forcibly call your Majesty's attention to is the importance of the present moment, the terrible embarrassment concealed beneath the appearance of the happiest tranquillity, the necessity of soon taking some measure for deciding the lot of the State.   It must be confessed, Sir, that France at this moment is only kept up by a species of artifice ; if the illusion which stands for reality were destroyed, if the confidence at present inseparable from the working staff were to fail, what would become of us with a deficit of a hundred millions every year ?   Without a doubt no time must be lost in filling up a void so enormous ; and that can be done only by great measures.   The plan I have formed appears to me the only one that can solve so difficult a problem.   Solely occupied with this great object, which demands enormous labour, and for the accomplishment of which I would willingly sacrifice my existence, I only beg your Majesty to accord to me, until I have carried it out, so much support and appearance of favour as I need to give me strength to attain it.   It will perhaps be an affair of six months or a year at most.   After that your Majesty may do as you please with me ; I shall have followed the promptings of the heartiest zeal for your service, I shall be able to say,—

'Nunc dimittis servum tuum, Domine.'"

This mysterious plan, which was to produce results as desirable as rare, and which M. de Calonne had hit upon to strengthen his shaky position, was the same which, in 1628, had occurred to Cardinal Richelieu, when he wanted to cover his responsibility in regard to the court of Rome. In view of the stress at the Treasury, of growing discontent, of vanished illusions, the comptroller-general meditated convoking the Assembly of Notables, the feeble resource of the old French kingship before the days of pure monarchy, an expedient more insufficient and more dangerous than the most far-seeing divined after the lessons of the philosophers and the continuous abasement of the kingly Majesty.

The convocation of the Notables was the means upon which M. de Calonne relied; the object was the sanctioning of a financial system new in practice but old in theory. When the comptroller-general proposed to the king to abolish privileges, and assess the impost equally, renouncing the twentieths, diminishing the gabel, suppressing custom-houses in the interior and establishing provincial assemblies, Louis XVI. recognized an echo of his illustrious ministers: "This is sheer Necker!" he exclaimed. "In the condition in which things are, Sir, it is the best that can be done," replied M. de Calonne. He had explained his reasons to the king in an intelligent and able note.

"Such a plan," said the comptroller-general, after having unfolded his projects, "demands undoubtedly the most solemn examination and the most authentic sanction. It must be presented in the form most calculated to place it beyond reach of any retardation and to acquire for it unassailable strength by uniting all the suffrages of the nation. Now, there is nothing but an Assembly of Notables that can fulfil this aim. It is the only means of preventing all parliamentary resistance, imposing silence on the clergy, and so clinching public opinion that no special interest dare raise a voice against the overwhelming evidence of the general interest. Assemblies of Notables were held in 1558, in 1583, in 1596, in 1617 and in 1626; none was convoked for objects so important as those in question now, and never were circumstances more favourable to success; as the situation requires strong measures, so it permits of the employment of strong means."

The king hesitated, from instinctive repugnance and the

traditions of absolutism, at anything that resembled an appeal
to the people. He was won, however, by the precedent of
Henry IV. and by the frank honesty of the project. The secret
was strictly kept. The general peace was threatened afresh by
the restless ambition of Joseph II. and by the constant encroachments of the Empress Catherine. The Great Frederick was now
dead. After being for a long while the selfish disturber of
Europe, he had ended by becoming its moderator, and his
powerful influence was habitually exerted on behalf of peace. The
future was veiled and charged with clouds. M. de Vergennes,
still possessing Louis XVI.'s confidence, regarded with dread the
bold reforms proposed by M. de Calonne; he had yielded to the
comptroller-general's representations, but he made all haste to
secure for France some support in Europe: he concluded with
England the treaty of commerce promised at the moment of
signing the peace. There was a lively debate upon it in the
English Parliament: Mr. Fox, then in opposition, violently
attacked the provisions of the treaty; Mr. Pitt, quite young as yet,
but already established in that foremost rank amongst orators and
statesmen which he was to occupy to his last hour, maintained the
great principles of European policy. " It is a very false maxim,"
said he, " to assert that France and England are not to cease to
be hostile because they have been so heretofore. My mind revolts
at so monstrous a principle, which is an outrage upon the constitution of societies as well as upon the two nations. Situated as
we are in respect of France, it is expedient, it is a matter of
urgency for the welfare of the two countries, to terminate this
constant enmity which has been falsely said to be the basis of the
true sentiments felt by the two nations towards each other. This
treaty tends to augment the means of making war and to retard
its coming."

Generous and sound maxims, only too often destined to be
strikingly belied by human passions ! When he supported in the
House of Commons, in 1786, an alliance with monarchical France,
Mr. Pitt did not foresee the terrible struggle he would one day
maintain, in the name of England and of Europe, against revolutionary, anarchical, or absolutist France.

The treaty had just been signed (September 26, 1786). M. de Vergennes was not long to survive his latest work : he died on the 13th of February, 1787, just before the opening of the Assembly of notables, as if he would fain escape the struggle and the crisis he dreaded. Capable and farsighted in his foreign policy, ever conciliatory and sometimes daring, M. de Vergennes, timid and weak as he was in home affairs, was nevertheless esteemed : he had often served as a connecting link between the different elements of the government. The king gave his place to M. de Montmorin, an honest but insignificant man, without influence in France as well as in Europe.

On the 29th of December, 1786, at the close of the despatch-council, the king at last broke the silence he had so long kept even as regarded the queen herself: "Gentlemen," he said, " I shall convoke for the 29th of January an Assembly composed of persons of different conditions and the best qualified in the State, in order to communicate to them my views for the relief of my people, the ordering of the finances and the reformation of several abuses." Louis XVI.'s hesitations had disappeared : he was full of hope. "I have not slept a wink all night," he wrote on the morning of the 30th of December to M. de Calonne, " but it was for joy."

The sentiments of the public were very diverse : the court was in consternation. "What penalty would King Louis XIV. have inflicted upon a minister who spoke of convoking an Assembly of notables ?" asked old Marshal Richelieu, ever witty, frivolous and corrupt. "The king sends in his resignation," said the young Viscount de Ségur. At Paris curiosity was the prevalent feeling ; but the jokes were bitter. "The comptroller-general has raised a new troop of comedians ; the first performance will take place on Monday the 20th instant," said a sham play-bill : " they will give as the principal piece *False Confidences*, followed by *Forced Consent* and an allegorical ballet, composed by M. de Calonne, entitled *The Tub of the Danaids*."

The convocation of the notables was better received in the provinces : it was the first time for a hundred and sixty years that the nation had been called upon to take a part, even nominally, in

the government of its affairs; it already began to feel powerful
and proud. A note had been sent to the *Journal de Paris* to
announce the convocation of the Assembly: "The nation," it
said, "will see with transport that the king deigns to draw near
to her." The day of excessive humiliation was no more,
even in forms; M. de Calonne modified the expression thus:
"The nation will see with transport that the king draws near
to her."

Indisposition on the part of the comptroller-general had retarded
the preparatory labours; the session opened on the 22nd of
February, 1787. The Assembly numbered 144 members, all
nominated by the king: to wit, 7 princes of the blood; 14 arch-
bishops and bishops; 36 dukes and peers, marshals of France and
noblemen; 12 councillors of State and Masters of requests; 38
magistrates of sovereign courts; 12 deputies of States-districts,
the only ones allowed to present to the king memorials of
grievances; and 25 municipal officers of the large towns. In this
Assembly, intended to sanction the abolition of privileges, a few
municipal officers alone represented the third estate and the
classes intended to profit by the abolition. The old marquis of
Mirabeau said facetiously: "This Calonne assembles a troop of
Guillots, which he calls the nation, to present them with the
cow by the horns and say to them: 'Gentlemen, we take all
the milk and what not, we devour all the meat and what not,
and we are going to try and get that what not out of the
rich, whose money has no connexion with the poor, and we give
you notice that the rich means you. Now, give us your opinion
as to the manner of proceeding.'"

The king's speech was short and unimportant. Though honestly
impressed with reminiscences of Henry IV., he could not manage,
like him, to say to the notables he had just convoked: "I have
had you assembled to take your counsels, to trust in them, to
follow them, in short, to place myself under tutelage in your hands,
a feeling which is scarcely natural to kings, greybeards and
conquerors; but the violent love I bear my subjects, the extreme
desire I have to add the title of liberator and restorer of this
realm to that of king, make me find everything easy and honour-

able." M. de Calonne had reserved to himself the duty of explaining the great projects he had suggested to the king. "Gentlemen," said he in his exordium, "the orders I am under at present do me the more honour in that the views of which the king has charged me to set before you the sum and the motives have been entirely adopted by him personally." Henry IV. might have said to the notables assembled by his successor, as he had said regarding his predecessors: "You were summoned hither not long ago to approve of the king's wishes."

The State was prosperous, at any rate in appearance; the comptroller-general assumed the credit for it: "The economy of a minister of finance," he said, "may exist under two forms so different that one might say they were two sorts of economy: one, which strikes the eye by its external strictness, which proclaims itself by startling and harshly uttered refusals, which flaunts its severity in the smallest matters in order to discourage the throng of applicants. It has an imposing appearance which really proves nothing, but which does a great deal as regards opinion; it has the double advantage of keeping importunate cupidity at arm's length and of quieting anxious ignorance. The other, which considers duty rather than force of character, can do more, whilst showing less strictness and reserve, as regards whatever is of any importance; it affects no austerity as regards that which is of none; it lets the talk be of what it grants and does not talk about what it saves. Because it is seen to be accessible to requests, people will not believe that it refuses the majority of them; because it has not the useful and vulgar character of inflexibility, people refuse it that of wise discretion, and often, whilst by assiduous application to all the details of an immense department, it preserves the finances from the most fatal abuses and the most ruinously unskilful handling, it seems to calumniate itself by an easy-going appearance which the desire to injure transforms very soon into lavishness."

So much easy grace and adroitness succeeding the austere stiffness of M. Necker had been powerless to relieve the disorder of the finances; it was great and of ancient date. "A deficit has been existing in France for centuries," the comptroller-general asserted.   It at last touched the figure of a hundred millions a year.   "What is left for filling up so frightful a void and for reaching the desired level?" exclaimed M. de Calonne : " abuses! Yes, gentlemen, it is in abuses themselves that there is to be found a mine of wealth which the State has a right to reclaim and which must serve to restore order.   Abuses have for their defenders interests, influence, fortune and some antiquated prejudices which time seems to have respected.   But of what force is such a vain confederation against the public welfare and the necessity of the State ?   Let others recall this maxim of our monarchy : '*As willeth the king, so willeth the law ;*' his Majesty's maxim is : '*As willeth the happiness of the people, so willeth the king.*' "

Audaciously certain of the success of his project, M. de Calonne had not taken the trouble to disguise the vast consequences of it ; he had not thought any the more about pre-securing a majority in the assembly.   The members were divided into seven committees presided over by the princes ; each committee disposed of one single vote ; the comptroller-general had not taken exception to the selections designated by his adversaries.   " I have made it a point of conscience," he said, " to give suitable nominations according to the morality, and talent and importance of individuals."   He had burnt his ships and, without a care for the defective composition of the assembly, he set forth one after the other projects calculated to alarm the privileged orders.   "More will be paid," he said in the preamble printed at the head of his notes and circulated in profusion over the whole of France, "undoubtedly more will be paid, but by whom? . . . By those only who do not pay enough; they will pay what they ought according to a just proportionment, and nobody will be aggrieved.   Privileges will be sacrificed!   Yes! Justice wills it, necessity requires it !   Would it be better to surcharge the non-privileged, the people ?"

The struggle was about to begin, with all the ardour of personal interest ; the principle of provincial assemblies had been favourably received by the notables ; the committees (*bureaux*) had even granted to the third estate a representation therein equal to that of the two upper orders, on condition that the presidents of the delegates should be chosen from the nobility or the clergy.

The recognition of a civil status for Protestants did not seem likely to encounter any difficulty. For more than twenty years past the parliaments, especially the parliament of Toulouse, had established the ruling of the inadmissibility of any one who disputed the legitimacy of children issue of protestant marriages. In 1778, the Parliament of Paris had deliberated as to presenting to the king a resolution in favour of authentic verification of non-catholic marriages, births and deaths; after a long interval, on the 2nd of February, 1787, this resolution had been formally promulgated.

It was M. de La Fayette who had the honour of supporting in the Assembly of notables the royal project announced by M. de Calonne and advised by the Parliament. In the ministry, MM. de Castries and De Breteuil had supported the equitable measure so long demanded by Protestants. M. de Rulhières had drawn up for the king a note entitled *Historic.evidences as to the causes of the revocation of the edict of Nantes*, and M. de Malesherbes had himself presented to Louis XVI. a scheme for a law. " It is absolutely necessary," said he, " that I should render the Protestants some kind offices; my great-uncle De Bâville did them so much injury !" The Assembly of notables appealed to the king's benevolence on behalf of " that considerable portion of his subjects which groans under a regimen of proscription equally opposed to the general interests of religion, to good morals, to population, to national industry and to all the principles of morality and policy." " In the splendid reign of Louis XIV.," M. de Calonne had said, " the State was impoverished by victories, and the kingdom dispeopled through intolerance." " Are assemblies of non-Catholics dangerous ?" asked M. Turgot: " yes, as long as they are forbidden ; no, when they are authorized."

The preliminary discussions had been calm, the great question was coming on ; in theory, the notables were forced to admit the principle of equal assessment of the impost; in practice, they were, for the most part, resolved to restrict its application. They carried the war into the enemy's camp, and asked to examine the financial accounts. The king gave notice to the committees that his desire was to have the deliberations directed not to the basis

of the question but to the form of collection of taxes. The archbishop of Narbonne (Dillon) raised his voice against the king's
exclusive right to decide upon imposts. "Your Royal Highness
will allow me to tell you," was the reply made to the count of
Artois, president of his committee, by an attorney-general of the
Parliament of Aix, M. de Castillon, "that there exists no authority
which can pass a territorial impost such as that proposed, nor
this assembly, august as it may be, nor the Parliaments, nor the
several States, nor the king himself; the States-general alone
would have that power."

Thus was proposed, in the very midst of the Assembly intended
to keep it out, that great question of the convocation of the States-
general which had been so long uppermost in all minds. "It is
the States-general you demand!" said the count of Artois to
M. de La Fayette. "Yes, my lord," replied the latter, "and
something better still if possible!" The comptroller-general
continued to elude inquiry into the state of the Treasury. M.
Necker, offended by the statements of his successor, who questioned the truthfulness of the Report, addressed explanatory notes
to the several committees of the Assembly. He had already, in
1784, published an important work in explanation and support of
his financial system; the success of the book had been immense;
in spite of the prohibition issued, at first, against the sale, but soon
tacitly withdrawn, the three volumes had sold, it was said, to the
extent of eighty thousand copies. In 1787, the late director-general
asked leave to appear before the Assembly of notables to refute
the statements of M. de Calonne; permission was refused. "I
am satisfied with your services," the king sent word to him, "and
I command you to keep silence." A pamphlet, without any title,
was however sent to the notables: "I served the king for five
years," said M. Necker, "with a zeal which knew no limits; the
duties I had taken upon myself were the only object of my solicitude. The interests of the State had become my passion and
occupied all my faculties of heart and mind. Forced to retire
through a combination of singular circumstances, I devoted my
powers to the composition of a laborious work, the utility of which
appears to me to have been recognized. I heard it said that a

portion of those ideas about administration which had been so dear to me formed the basis of the projects which were to be submitted to the Assembly of notables. I rendered homage to the beneficent views of his Majesty. Content with the contributions I had offered to the common weal, I was living happily and in peace, when all at once I found myself attacked or rather assailed in the most unjust and the strangest manner. M. de Calonne, finding it advisable to trace to a very remote period the causes of the present condition of the finances, was not afraid, in pursuance of this end, to have recourse to means with which he will, probably, sooner or later reproach himself; he declared in a speech, now circulated throughout Europe, that the Report to his Majesty, in 1781, was so extraordinarily erroneous that, instead of the surplus published in that Report, there was, at that very time, an enormous deficit."

At the moment when M. Necker was publishing, as regarded the statements of M. de Calonne, an able rectification which did not go to the bottom of things any more than the Report had previously gone, the comptroller-general was succumbing beneath his enemies' attacks and his own errors. Justly irritated at the perfidious manœuvres practised against him by the keeper of the seals in secretly heading at the Assembly of notables the opposition of the magistracy, Calonne had demanded and obtained from the king the recall of M. Miromesnil. He was immediately superseded by M. de Lamoignon, president of the Parliament of Paris and a relative of M. de Malesherbes. The comptroller-general had the imprudence to push his demands further, he required the dismissal of M. de Breteuil. "I consent," said Louis XVI. after some hesitation, "but leave me time to forewarn the queen, she is much attached to M. de Breteuil." When the king quitted Marie Antoinette, the situation had changed face; the disgrace of M. de Calonne was resolved upon.

The queen had represented the dissatisfaction and opposition of the notables, which "proceeded solely," she said, "from the mistrust inspired by the comptroller-general;" she had dwelt upon the merits and resources of the archbishop of Toulouse. "I don't like priests who haven't the virtues of their cloth," Louis XVI. had answered drily. He called to the ministry M. Fourqueux, councillor of State, an old man, highly esteemed, but incapable of sustaining the crushing weight of affairs. The king himself presented M. de Calonne's last projects to the Assembly of notables; the rumour ran that the comptroller-general was about to re-enter the cabinet. Louis XVI. was informed of the illicit manœuvres which M. de Calonne had authorized in operations on 'Change: he exiled him to his estate in Berry and a few days afterwards to Lorraine. M. Necker had just published without permission his reply to the attacks of M. de Calonne; the king was put out at it. "The eye of the public annoys those who manage affairs with carelessness," M. Necker had but lately said in his work on financial administration, "but those who are animated by a different spirit would be glad to multiply lights from every quarter." "I do not want to turn my kingdom into a republic screeching over State-affairs as the city of Geneva is and as happened during the administration of M. Necker," said Louis XVI. He banished his late minister to a distance of twenty leagues from Paris: Madame Necker was ill, and the execution of the king's order was delayed for a few days.

Meanwhile the notables were in possession of the financial accounts, but the satisfaction caused them by the disgrace of M. de Calonne was of short duration; they were awaiting a new comptroller-general, calculated to enlighten them as to the position of affairs. M. de Montmorin and M. de Lamoignon were urgent for the recall of M. Necker. The king's ill-feeling against his late minister still continued. "As long as M. Necker exists," said M. de Montmorin, "it is impossible that there should be any other minister of finance, because the public will always be annoyed to see that post occupied by any but by him." "I did not know M. Necker personally," adds M. de Montmorin in his notes left to Marmontel, "I had nothing but doubts to oppose to what the king told me about his character, his haughtiness and his domineering spirit." Louis XVI. yielded, however: "Well!" he said snappishly, "if it must be, recall him." M. de Breteuil was present: "Your Majesty," said he, "has but just banished M. Necker; he has scarcely arrived at Montargis: to recall him now would have a deplorable effect." He once more mentioned the name of Loménie de Brienne, and the king again yielded. Ambitious, intriguing, debauched, unbelieving, the new minister, like his predecessor, was agreeable, brilliant, capable even, and accustomed in his diocese to important affairs. He was received without disfavour by public opinion. The notables and the chief of the council of finance undertook in concert the disentanglement of the accounts submitted to them.

In this labyrinth of contradictory figures and statements, the deficit alone came out clearly. M. de Brienne promised important economies, the Assembly voted a loan : they were not willing to accept the responsibility of the important reforms demanded by the king. The speeches were long and vague, the objections endless. All the schemes of imposts were censured one after the other. " We leave it to the king's wisdom," said the notables at last ; " he shall himself decide what taxes will offer the least inconveniences, if the requirements of the State make it necessary to impose new sacrifices upon the people." " The notables have seen with dismay the depth of the evil caused by an administration whereof your parliament had more than once foreseen the consequence," said the premier president of the Parliament of Paris. " The different plans proposed to your Majesty deserve careful deliberation. The most respectful silence is at this moment our only course."

The notables had themselves recognized their own impotence and given in their resignation. A formal closing session took place on the 25th of May, 1787. The keeper of the seals, enumerating the results of the labours of the Assembly, enregistered the royal promises as accomplished facts : " All will be set right without any shock, without any ruin of fortunes, without any alteration in the principles of government, without any of those breaches of faith which should never be so much as mentioned in the presence of the monarch of France.

" The resolved or projected reform of various abuses and the permanent good for which the way is being paved by new laws concerted with you, gentlemen, are about to co-operate successfully for the present relief of the people.

" Forced labour is proscribed, the gabel (or salt-tax) is revised (*jugée*), the obstacles which hamper home-trade are destroyed, and agriculture, encouraged by the free exportation of grain, will become day by day more flourishing.

" The king has solemnly promised that disorder shall not appear

THE MONTGOLFIER BALLOON.

again in his finances, and his Majesty is about to take the most effective measures for fulfilling this sacred engagement, of which you are the depositaries.

" The administration of the State will approach nearer and nearer to the government and vigilance of a private family, and a more equitable assessment, which personal interest will incessantly watch over, will lighten the burthen of impositions."

Only the provincial administrations were constituted; the hopes which had been conceived of the Assembly of notables remained more vague than before its convocation: it had failed, like all the attempts at reform made in succession by Louis XVI.'s advisers, whether earnest or frivolous, whether proved patriots or ambitious intriguers. It had, however, revealed to the whole country the deplorable disorder of the finances; it had taught the third estate and even the populace how deep was the repugnance amongst the privileged classes towards reforms which touched their interests. Whilst spreading, as a letter written to America by M. de La Fayette put it, "the salutary habit of thinking about public affairs," it had at the same time betrayed the impotence of the government and the feebleness of its means of action. It was a stride, and an immense stride, towards the Revolution.

CHAPTER LX.

LOUIS XVI.—CONVOCATION OF THE STATES-GENERAL.
1787—1789.

THIRTEEN years had rolled by since King Louis XV. had descended to a dishonoured grave, and on the mighty current which was bearing France towards reform, whilst dragging her into the Revolution, King Louis XVI., honest and sincere, was still blindly seeking to clutch the helm which was slipping from his feeble hands. Every day his efforts were becoming weaker and more inconsistent, every day the pilot placed at the tiller was less and less deserving of public confidence. From M. Turgot to M. Necker, from Calonne to Loménie de Brienne, the fall had been rapid and deep. Amongst the two parties which unequally divided the nation, between those who defended the past in its entirety, its abuses as well as its grandeurs, and those who were marching on bewildered towards a reform of which they did not foresee the scope, the struggle underwent certain moments of stoppage and of abrupt reaction towards the old state of things. In 1781, the day after M. Necker's fall, an ordinance of the minister of war, published against the will of that minister himself, had restored to the *verified and qualified* noblesse (who could show four quarterings) the exclusive privilege of military grades. Without any ordinance, the same regulation had been applied to the clergy. In 1787, the Assembly of notables and its opposition to the king's projects presented by M. de Calonne were the last triumph of the enthusiastic partisans of the past. The privileged classes had still too much influence to be attacked with success by M. de Calonne, who appeared to be in himself an assemblage of all the abuses whereof he desired to be the reformer. A plan so vast, however ably conceived, was sure to go to pieces in the hands of a man who did not enjoy public esteem and confidence, but the triumph of the notables in their own cause was a fresh warning to the people that they would have to defend theirs with more vigour" [*Mémoires de Malouet,* t. i. p. 253]. We have seen how monarchy, in concert with the nation, fought feudality, to reign thenceforth as sovereign mistress over the great lords and over the nation; we have seen how it slowly fell in public respect and veneration, and how it attempted unsuccessfully to respond to the confused wishes of a people that did not yet know its own desires or its own strength; we shall henceforth see it, panting and without sure guidance, painfully striving to govern and then to live. "I saw," says M. Malouet in his *Mémoires,* " under the ministry of the archbishop (of Toulouse, and afterwards of Sens), all the avant-couriers of a revolution in the government. Three parties were already pronounced: the first wanted to take to itself all the influence of which it despoiled the king, whilst withstanding the pretensions of the third estate; the second proclaimed open war against the two upper orders, and already laid down the bases of a democratic government; the third, which was at that time the most numerous, although it was that of the wisest men, dreaded the ebullience of the other two, wanted compromises, reforms, and not revolution." By their conflicts the two extreme parties were to stifle for a while the party of the wise men, the true exponent of the national aspirations and hopes, which was destined, through a course of cruel vicissitudes and long trials, to yet save and govern the country.

The Assembly of notables had abdicated; contenting itself with a negative triumph, it had left to the royal wisdom and responsibility the burthen of decisions which Louis XVI. had hoped to get sanctioned by an old and respected authority. The public were expecting to see all the edicts, successively presented to the notables as integral portions of a vast system, forthwith assume force of law by simultaneous registration of Parliament. The feebleness and inconsistency of governors often stultify the most sensible foresight. M. de Brienne had come into office as a support to the king's desires and intentions, for the purpose of obtaining from the notables what was refused through their aversion for M. de Calonne; as soon as he was free of the notables as well as of M. de Calonne, he hesitated, drew back, waited, leaving time for a fresh opposition to form and take its measures. " He had nothing but bad moves to make," says M. Mignet. Three edicts touching the trade in grain, forced labour and the provincial assemblies were first sent up to the Parliament and enregistered without any difficulty; the two edicts touching the stamp-tax and equal assessment of the impost were to meet with more hindrance; the latter at any rate united the sympathies of all the partisans of genuine reforms; the edict touching the stamp-tax was by itself and first submitted for the approval of the magistrates: they rejected it, asking, like the notables, for a communication as to the state of finance. " It is not states of finance we want," exclaimed a councillor, Sabatier de Cabre, " it is States-general." This bold sally became a theme for deliberation in the Parliament. " The nation represented by the States-general," the court declared, " is alone entitled to grant the king subsidies of which the need is clearly demonstrated." At the same time the Parliament demanded the impeachment of M. de Calonne; he took fright and sought refuge in England. The mob rose in Paris, imputing to the court the prodigalities with which the Parliament reproached the late comptroller-general. Sad symptom of the fatal progress of public opinion! The cries heretofore raised against the queen under the name of *Austrian* were now uttered against *Madame Deficit*, pending the time when the fearful title of *Madame Veto* would give place in its turn to the sad name of *the woman Capet* given to the victim of October 16, 1793.

The king summoned the Parliament to Versailles, and on the 6th of August, 1787, the edicts touching the stamp-tax and territorial subvention were enregistered in bed of justice. The Parliament had protested in advance against this act of royal authority, which it called "a phantom of deliberation." On the 13th of August, the court declared "the registration of the edicts null and without effect, incompetent to authorize the collection of imposts opposed to all principles;" this resolution was sent to all the seneschalties and bailiwicks in the district. It was in the name of the privilege of the two upper orders that the Parliament of Paris contested the royal edicts and made appeal to the supreme jurisdiction of the States-general; the people did not see it, they took out the horses of M. d'Esprémesnil, whose fiery eloquence had won over a great number of his colleagues, and he was carried in triumph. On the 15th of August, the Parliament was sent away to Troyes.

Banishment far away from the capital, from the ferment of spirits and from the noisy centre of their admirers had more than once brought down the pride of the members of parliament; they were now sustained by the sympathy ardently manifested by nearly all the sovereign courts. "Incessantly repeated stretches of authority," said the Parliament of Besançon, "forced registrations, banishments, constraint and severity instead of justice, are astounding in an enlightened age, wound a nation that idolizes its kings, but is free and proud, freeze the heart and might break the ties which unite sovereign to subjects and subjects to sovereign." The Parliament of Paris declared that it needed no authority for its sittings, considering that it rendered justice wherever it happened to be assembled. "The monarchy would be transfigured into a despotic form," said the decree, "if ministers could dispose of persons by sealed letters (*lettres de cachet*), property by beds of justice, criminal matters by change of venue (*évocation*) or cassation, and suspend the course of justice by special banishments or arbitrary removals."

Negotiations were going on, however; the government agreed to withdraw the new imposts which it had declared to be indispensable; the Parliament, which had declared itself incompetent as to the establishment of taxes, prorogued for two years the second twentieth. "We left Paris with glory upon us, we shall return with mud," protested M. d'Esprémesnil in vain; more moderate, but not less resolute, Duport, Robert de St. Vincent and Fréteau sought to sustain by their speeches the wavering resolution of their colleagues. The Parliament was recalled to Paris on the 19th of September, 1787.

The state of Europe inclined men's minds to reciprocal concessions; a disquieting good understanding appeared to be growing up between Russia and Austria. The emperor Joseph II. had just paid a visit to the Crimea with the czarina. "I fancy I am still dreaming," wrote the prince of Ligne, who had the honour of being in the trip, "when in a carriage with six places which is a real triumphal car adorned with cyphers in precious stones I find myself seated between two persons on whose shoulders the heat often sets me dozing, and I hear, as I wake up, one of my comrades say to the other: 'I have thirty millions of subjects, they say, counting males only.' 'And I twenty-two,' replies the other, 'all included.' 'I require,' adds the former, 'an army of at least six hundred thousand men, between Kamtchatka and Riga.' 'With half that,' replied the other, 'I have just what I require.' God knows how we settle all the States and great personages. 'Rather than sign the separation of thirteen provinces, like my brother George,' says Catherine II. sweetly, 'I would have put a bullet through my head.' 'And rather than give in my resignation like my brother and brother-in-law, by convoking and assembling the nation to talk treason, I don't know what I wouldn't have done,' says Joseph II." Before the two allies could carry out their designs against Turkey, that ancient power, enfeebled as it was, had taken the offensive at the instigation of England; the king of Sweden, on his side, invaded Russia; war burst out in all directions. The traditional influence of France remained powerless in the East to maintain peace; the long weakness of the government was everywhere bearing fruit.

Nowhere was this grievous impotence more painfully striking than in Holland. Supported by England, whose slavish instrument he had been for so long, the stadtholder William V. was struggling, with the help of the mob, against the patriotic, independent and proud patricians. For the last sixty years the position of Holland had been constantly declining in Europe. "She is afraid of everything," said Count de Broglie in 1773, "she puts up with everything, grumbles at everything and secures herself against nothing." "Holland might pay all the armies of Europe," people said in 1787, "she couldn't manage to hold her own against any one of them." The civil war imminent in her midst and fomented by England had aroused the solicitude of M. de Calonne; he had prepared the resources necessary for forming a camp near Givet; his successor diverted the funds to another object; when the Prussians entered Dutch territory, being summoned to the stadtholder's aid by his wife, sister of the young king Frederick William II., the French government afforded no assistance to its ally; it confined itself to offering an asylum to the Dutch patriots, long encouraged by its diplomats, and now vanquished in their own country, which was henceforth under the yoke of England. "France has fallen, I doubt whether she will get up again," said the emperor Joseph II. "We have been caught napping," wrote M. de La Fayette to Washington, "the king of Prussia has been ill advised, the Dutch are ruined, and England finds herself the only power which has gained in the bargain."

The echo of humiliations abroad came to swell the dull murmur of public discontent. Disturbance was arising every where. "From stagnant chaos France has passed to tumultuous chaos," wrote Mirabeau, already an influential publicist, despite the irregularity of his morals and the small esteem excited by his life, "there may, there should come a creation out of it." The Parliament had soon resumed its defiant attitude; like M. de La Fayette at the Assembly of notables, it demanded the convocation of the States-general at a fixed epoch, in 1792; it was the date fixed by M. de Brienne in a vast financial scheme which he had boldly proposed for registration by the court. By means of a series of loans which were to reach the enormous total of 420 millions, the States-general, assembled on the conclusion of this vast operation and relieved from all pecuniary embarrassment, would be able to concentrate their thoughts on the important

LOMÉNIE DE BRIENNE.

interests of the future.   At the same time with the loan-edict, Brienne presented to the Parliament the law-scheme, for a long time past under discussion, on behalf of Protestants.

The king had repaired in person to the palace in royal session; the keeper of the seals, Lamoignon, expounded the necessity of the edicts.   " To the monarch alone," he repeated, " belongs the legislative power, without dependence and without partition." This was throwing down the gauntlet to the whole assembly as well as to public opinion.   Abbé Sabatier and Councillor Fréteau had already spoken, when Robert de St. Vincent rose, an old Jansenist and an old member of parliament, accustomed to express his thoughts roughly: " Who, without dismay, can hear loans still talked of?" he exclaimed: " and for what sum? 420 millions!   A plan is being formed for five years?   But, since your Majesty's reign began, have the same views ever directed the administration of finance for five years in succession?   Can you be ignorant, sir (here he addressed himself to the comptroller-general), that each minister, as he steps into his place, rejects the system of his predecessor in order to substitute that which he has devised?   Within only eight months, you are the fourth minister of finance, and yet you are forming a plan which cannot be accomplished in less than five years!   The remedy, sir, for the wounds of the State has been pointed out by your Parliament, it is the convocation of the States-general.   Their convocation, to be salutary, must be prompt.   Your ministers would like to avoid this assembly whose surveillance they dread.   Their hope is vain. Before two years are over, the necessities of the State will force you to convoke the States-general."

M. d'Esprémesnil was overcome; less violent than usual, he had appealed to the king's heart; for a moment Louis XVI. appeared to be moved, and so was the assembly with him; the edicts were about to be enregistered despite the efforts of the opposition; already the premier president was collecting the votes; the keeper of the seals would not, at this grave moment, renounce any kingly prerogative.   " When the king is at the Parliament, there is no deliberation, his will makes law," said the legal rule and the custom of the magistracy.   Lamoignon went

up to the throne, he said a few words in a low voice : " Mr. Keeper
of the seals, have the edicts enregistered," said Louis XVI.; the
minister immediately repeated the formula used at beds of justice.
A murmur ran through the assembly ; the duke of Orleans rose ;
he had recently become the head of his house through his father's
death, and found himself more than ever involved in intrigues
hostile to the court: " Sir," said he in a broken voice, " this
registration appears to me illegal . . . . It should be distinctly stated
that the registration is done by the express command of your
Majesty." The king was as much moved as the prince : " It is
all the same to me," he replied : " You are master, of course. . .
Well, then,—it is legal, because I so will." The edict relative to
non-Catholics was read, and Louis XVI. withdrew.

There was violent commotion in the assembly, the protest of
the duke of Orleans was drawn up in a more explicit form. " The
difference between a bed of justice and a royal session is that one
exhibits the frankness of despotism and the other its duplicity,"
cried d'Esprémesnil. Notwithstanding the efforts of M. de
Malesherbes and the duke of Nivernais, the Parliament inscribed
on the registers that it was not to be understood to take any part
in the transcription here ordered of gradual and progressive loans
for the years 1788, 1789, 1790, 1791 and 1792. In reply, the
duke of Orleans was banished to Villers-Cotterets, whilst Councillors Fréteau and Sabatier were arrested and taken to a state-
prison.

By the scandalousness of his life as well as by his obstructive
buildings in the Palais-Royal, the duke of Orleans had lost favour
with the public ; his protest and his banishment restored him at
once to his popularity. The Parliament piled remonstrance upon
remonstrance, every day more and more haughty in form as well
as in substance. Dipping into the archives in search of antiquated
laws, the magistrates appealed to the liberties of olden France,
mingling therewith the novel principles of the modern philosophy.
" Several pretty well known facts," they said, " prove that the
nation, more enlightened as to its true interests, even in the least
elevated classes, is disposed to accept from the hands of your
Majesty the greatest blessing a king can bestow upon his subjects

—liberty. It is this blessing, Sir, which your Parliament come to ask you to restore, in the name of a generous and faithful people. It is no longer a prince of your blood, it is no longer two magistrates whom your Parliament ask you to restore in the name of the laws and of reason, but three Frenchmen, three men."

To peremptory demands were added perfidious insinuations: "Such ways, Sir," said one of these remonstrances, "have no place in your heart, such samples of proceeding are not the principles of your Majesty, they come from another source." For the first time the queen was thus held up to public odium by the Parliament which had dealt her a fatal blow by acquitting Cardinal Rohan; she was often present at the king's conferences with his ministers, reluctantly and by the advice of M. de Brienne, for and in whom Louis XVI. never felt any liking or confidence. "There is no more happiness for me since they have made me an intriguer," she said sadly to Madame Campan. And when the latter objected: "Yes," replied the queen, "it is the proper word: every woman who meddles in matters above her lights and beyond the limits of her duty, is nothing but an intriguer; you will remember, however, that I do not spare myself, and that it is with regret I give myself such a title. The other day, as I was crossing the Bull's Eye (Œil de Bœuf), to go to a private committee at the king's, I heard one of the chapel-band say out loud, 'A queen who does her duty remains in her rooms at her needlework.' 'I said to myself: 'Thou'rt quite right, wretch; but thou know'st not my position, I yield to necessity and my evil destiny.'" A true daughter of Maria Theresa in her imprisonment and on the scaffold, Marie Antoinette had neither the indomitable perseverance nor the simple grandeur in political views which had restored the imperial throne in the case of her illustrious mother. She weakened beneath a burthen too heavy for a mind so long accustomed to the facile pleasures of youth. "The queen certainly has wits and firmness which might suffice for great things," wrote her friend, the count of La Marck, to M. de Mercy Argenteau, her mother's faithful agent in France, "but it must be confessed that, whether in business or in mere conversation, she does not always exhibit that

degree of attention and that persistence which are indispensable
for getting at the bottom of what one ought to know, in order to
prevent errors and to insure success."

The same want of purpose and persistence of which the count
of La Marck complained, was strikingly apparent everywhere and
in all matters; the duke of Orleans was soon tired of banishment:
he wrote to the queen who obtained his recall. The ministers
were making mysterious preparations for a grand stroke. The
Parliament, still agitated and anxious, had at last enregistered the
edict relating to non-Catholics. Public opinion, like the government, supported it eagerly; the principles of tolerance which had
prompted it were henceforth accepted by all; certain bishops and
certain bigots were still trying to hinder this first step towards a
legal status for a long while refused to Protestants. M. d'Esprémesnil, an earnest disciple of the *philosophe inconnu*, the mystic
St. Martin, just as he had been the dupe of Mesmer and of
Cagliostro, was almost single-handed in the Parliament in his
opposition to the registration of the edict. Extending his hand
towards the crucifix, he exclaimed with violence: "Would you
crucify him a second time?" The court was a better judge of
Christian principles, and Protestants were permitted to be born, to
marry and to die on French territory. The edict did not as yet
concede to them any other right.

The contest extended as it grew hotter; everywhere the Parliaments took up the quarrel of the court of Paris; the formation of
the provincial assemblies furnished new centres of opposition; the
petty noblesse made alliance with the magistracy, the antagonism
of principles became every day more evident; after the five months
elapsed since the royal session, the Parliament was still protesting
against the violence done to it. "I had no need to take or count
the votes," said the king's reply; "being present at the deliberation,
I judged for myself without taking any account of plurality. If
plurality in my courts were to force my will, the monarchy would
be nothing but an aristocracy of magistrates." "No, Sir, no aristocracy in France, but no despotism either," replied the members
of parliament.

The indiscretion of a printer made M. d'Esprémesnil acquainted with the great designs which were in preparation; at his instigation the Parliament issued a declaration as to the reciprocal rights and duties of the monarch and the nation. "France," said the resolution, "is a monarchy hereditary from male to male, governed by the king following the laws; it has for fundamental laws the nation's right to freely grant subsidies by means of the States-general convoked and composed according to regulation, the customs and capitulations of the provinces, the irremoveability of the magistrates, the right of the courts to enregister edicts, and that of each citizen to be judged only by his natural judges, without liability ever to be arrested arbitrarily." "The magistrates must cease to exist before the nation ceases to be free," said a second protest.

Bold and defiant in its grotesque mixture of the ancient principles of the magistracy with the novel theories of philosophy, the resolution of the Parliament was quashed by the king. Orders were given to arrest M. d'Esprémesnil and a young councillor, Goislard de Montsabert, who had proposed an inquiry into the conduct of the comptrollers commissioned to collect the second twentieth. The police of the Parliament was perfect and vigilant; the two magistrates were warned and took refuge in the Palace of Justice; all the chambers were assembled and the peers convoked. Ten or a dozen appeared, notwithstanding the king's express prohibition.

The Parliament had placed the two threatened members "under the protection of the king and of the law;" the premier president, at the head of a deputation, had set out for Versailles to demand immunity for the accused; the court was in session awaiting his return.

The mob thronged the precincts of the Palace, some persons had even penetrated into the grand chamber; no deliberations went on. Towards midnight, several companies of the French guards entered the hall of the Pas-Perdus, all the exits were guarded. The court was in commotion, the young councillors demanded that the deliberations should go on publicly. "Gentlemen," said President de Gourgues, "would you derogate from the ancient forms?" The spectators withdrew. The marquis d'Agoult, aide-major of the French guards, demanded admission; he had orders from the king. The ushers opened the doors; at sight of the magistrates in scarlet robes, motionless upon their seats, the officer was for a moment abashed; he cast his eye from bench to bench, his voice faltered when he read the order signed by the king to arrest "MM. d'Esprémesnil and de Montsabert, in the grand chamber or elsewhere." "The court will proceed to deliberate thereon, sir," replied the president. "Your forms are to deliberate," hotly replied M. d'Agoult, who had recovered himself; "I know nothing of those forms, the king's orders must be executed without delay, point out to me those whom I have to arrest." Silence reigned throughout the hall; not a word, not a gesture indicated the accused. Only the dukes and peers made merry aloud over the nobleman charged with so disagreeable a mission: he repeated his demand: "We are all d'Esprémesnil and Montsabert," exclaimed the magistrates. M. d'Agoult left the room.

He soon returned, accompanied by an exon of the short robe, named Larchier: "Show me whom I have to arrest," was the officer's order. The exon looked all round the room, he knew every one of the magistrates, the accused were sitting right in front of him: "I do not see MM. d'Esprémesnil and Montsabert anywhere," he at last said tremulously. M. d'Agoult's threats could not get any other answer out of him.

The officer had gone to ask for fresh orders; the deputation sent to Versailles had returned, without having been received by Louis XVI., of whom an audience had not been requested. The court wanted to send some of the king's people at once to notify a fresh request; the troops guarded all the doors, nobody could leave the Palace.

"Gentlemen," said d'Esprémesnil at last, "it would be contrary to our honour as well as to the dignity of the Parliament to prolong this scene any further; and besides we cannot be the ruin of Larchier; let M. d'Agoult be shown in again." The officer was recalled, the magistrates were seated and covered. "Sir," said M. d'Esprémesnil, "I am one of those you are in search of. The law forbids me to obey orders irregularly obtained (*surpris*) of the

ARREST OF THE MEMBERS.

sovereign, and it is to be faithful to him that I have not mentioned who I am until this moment. I call upon you to state whether, in case I should not go with you voluntarily, you have orders to drag me from this building." "Certainly, sir." D'Agoult was already striding towards the door to order in his troops. "Enough," said M. d'Esprémesnil, "I yield to force," and, turning to his colleagues, "Gentlemen," he said, "to you I protest against the violence of which I am the object, forget me and think henceforth of nothing but the common weal; I commend to you my family; whatever may be my fate, I shall never cease to glory in professing to the last hour the principles which do honour to this court." He made a deep obeisance, and followed the major, going out by the secret staircases in order to avoid the crowd whose shouts could be heard even within the Palace buildings. Goislard de Montsabert followed his colleague's example: he was confined at Pierre-Encise; M. d'Esprémesnil had been taken to the isle of St. Marguerite.

Useless and ill-judged violence which excited the passions of the public without intimidating opponents! The day after the scene of May 6th, at the moment when the whole magistracy of France was growing hot over the thrilling account of the arrest of the two councillors, the Parliament of Paris was sent for to Versailles (May 8, 1788).

The magistrates knew beforehand what fate awaited them. The king uttered a few severe words. After a pompous preamble, the keeper of the seals read out six fresh edicts intended to ruin for ever the power of the sovereign courts. Forty-seven great baillie-courts, as a necessary intermediary between the Parliaments and the inferior tribunals, were henceforth charged with all civil cases not involving sums of more than 20,000 livres, as well as all criminal cases of the third order (estate). The representations of the provincial assembly of Dauphiny severely criticized the impropriety of this measure. "The ministers," they said, "have not been afraid to flout the third estate, whose life, honour and property no longer appear to be objects worthy of the sovereign courts, for which are reserved only the causes of the rich and the crimes of the privileged." The number of members of the Parliament of Paris was reduced to sixty-nine. The registration of edicts, the only real political power left in the hands of the magistrates, was transferred to a plenary court, an old title without stability and without tradition, composed, under the king's presidency, of the great functionaries of State, assisted by a small number of councillors. The absolute power was thus preparing a rampart against encroachments of authority on the part of the sovereign courts ; it had fortified itself beforehand against the pretensions of the States-general, "which cannot pretend to be anything but a more extended council on behalf of the sovereign, the latter still remaining supreme arbiter of their representations and their grievances."

Certain useful ameliorations in the criminal legislation, amongst others total abolition of torture, completed the sum of edicts. A decree of the council declared all the Parliaments prorogued until the formation of the great baillie-courts. The plenary court was to assemble forthwith at Versailles. It only sat once; in presence of the opposition amongst the majority of the men summoned to compose it, the ministers, unforeseeing and fickle even with all their ability and their boldness, found themselves obliged to adjourn the sittings indefinitely. All the members of the Parliament of Paris had bound themselves by a solemn oath not to take a place in any other assembly. "In case of dispersal of the magistracy," said the resolution entered upon the registers of the court, "the Parliament places the present act as a deposit in the hands of the king, of his august family, of the peers of the realm, of the States-general and of each of the orders, united or separate, representing the nation."

At sight of this imitation, less absolute and less cleverly calculated, of the attempts made by Chancellor Maupeou, after seventeen years' rapid marching towards a state of things so novel and unheard of, the commotion was great in Paris; the disturbance, however, did not reach to the masses, and the disorder in the streets was owing less to the Parisian populace than to mendicants, rascals of sinister mien, flocking in, none knew why, from the four points of the compass. The provinces were more seriously disturbed. All the sovereign courts rose up with one accord; the Parliament of Rouen declared "traitors to the king, to the nation, to the province, perjured and branded with infamy, all officers and judges" who should proceed in virtue of the ordinances of May 8. "The authority of the king is unlimited for doing good to his subjects," said one of the presidents, "but everybody should put limits to it when it turns towards oppression." It was the very commandant of the royal troops whom the magistrates thus reproached with their passive obedience.

Normandy confined herself to declarations and speeches; other provinces went beyond those bounds: Brittany claimed performance "of the marriage contract between Louis XII. and the Duchess Anne." Notwithstanding the king's prohibition, the Parliament met at Rennes. A detachment of soldiers having been ordered to disperse the magistrates, a band of gentlemen supported by an armed mob went to protect the deliberations of the court. Fifteen officers fought duels with fifteen gentlemen. The court issued a decree of arrest against the holders of the king's commission. The youth of Nantes hurried to the aid of the youth of Rennes. The intermediary commission of the states ordered the bishops to have the prayers said which were customary in times of public calamity and a hundred and thirty gentlemen carried to the governor a declaration signed by the noblesse of almost the whole province. "We, members of the noblesse of Brittany, do declare infamous those who may accept any place, whether in the new administration of justice or in the administration of the states, which is not recognized by the laws and constitutions of the province." A dozen of them set off for Versailles to go and denounce the ministers to Louis XVI. Being put in the Bastille, eighteen of their friends went to demand them back; they were followed by fifty others. The officers of the Bassigny regiment had taken sides with the opposition and discussed the orders sent to them. Amongst the great lords of the province, attached to the king's own person, MM. de La Trémoille, de Rieux, and de Guichen left the court to join their protests to those of their friends; the superintendent, Bertrand de Molleville, was hanged in effigy and had to fly.

In Béarn, the peasantry had descended from the mountains;

hereditary proprietors of their little holdings, they joined the
noblesse to march out and meet the duke of Guiche, sent by the
king to restore order.   Already the commandant of the province
had been obliged to authorize the meeting of the Parliament.
The Bearnese bore in front of their ranks the cradle of Henry IV.,
carefully preserved in the castle of Pau.   " We are no rebels,"
they said : " we claim our contract and fidelity to the oaths of a
king whom we love.   The Bearnese is free-born, he will not die a
slave.   Let the king have all from us in love and not by force ;
our blood is his and our country's.   Let none come to take our
lives when we are defending our liberty."

Legal in Normandy, violent in Brittany, tumultuous in Béarn,
the parliamentary protests took a politic and methodical form in
Dauphiny.   An insurrection amongst the populace of Grenoble,
soon supported by the villagers from the mountains, had at first
flown to arms at the sound of the tocsin.   The members of the
Parliament, on the point of leaving the city, had been detained by
force and their carriages had been smashed.   The troops offered
little resistance ; an entry was effected into the house of the
governor, the duke of Clermont-Tonnerre, and, with an axe above
his head, the insurgents threatened to hang him to the chandelier
in his drawing-room if he did not convoke the Parliament.
Ragged ruffians ran to the magistrates, and compelled them to
meet in the sessions-hall.   The members of parliament succeeded
with great difficulty in pacifying the mob.   As soon as they found
themselves free, they hastened away into exile.   Other hands had
taken up their quarrel.   A certain number of members of the
three orders met at the town hall, and, on their private authority,
convoked for the 21st of July the special states of Dauphiny,
suppressed a while before by Cardinal Richelieu.

The duke of Clermont-Tonnerre had been superseded by old
Marshal Vaux, rough and ready.   He had at his disposal twenty
thousand men.   Scarcely had he arrived at Grenoble when he
wrote to Versailles, " It is too late," he said.   The prerogatives of
royal authority were maintained, however.   The marshal granted
a meeting of the states-provincial, but he required permission to
be asked of him.   He forbade the assembly to be held at Grenoble.

It was in the castle of Vizille, a former residence of the dauphins, that the three orders of Dauphiny met, closely united together in wise and patriotic accord. The archbishop of Vienne, Lefranc de Pompignan, brother of the poet, lately the inveterate foe of Voltaire, an ardently and sincerely pious man, led his clergy along the most liberal path ; the noblesse of the sword, mingled with the noblesse of the robe, voted blindly all the resolutions of the third estate ; these were suggested by the real head of the assembly, M. Mounier, judge-royal of Grenoble, a friend of M. Necker's, an enlightened, loyal, honourable man, destined ere long to make his name known over the whole of France by his courageous resistance to the outbursts of the National Assembly. Unanimously the three orders presented to the king their claims to the olden liberties of the province; they loudly declared, however, that they were prepared for all sacrifices and aspired to nothing but the common rights of all Frenchmen. The double representation of the third in the estates of Dauphiny was voted without contest, as well as equal asessment of the impost intended to replace forced labour. Throughout the whole province the most perfect order had succeeded the first manifestations of popular irritation.

It was now more than a year since Brienne had become chief minister. MM. de Ségur and de Castries had retired, refusing to serve under a man whom they did not esteem. Alone, shut up in his closet, the archbishop listened without emotion to the low murmur of legal protests, the noisy tumult of insurrections : " I have foreseen all, even civil war. The king shall be obeyed, the king knows how to make himself obeyed," he kept repeating in the assured tones of an oracle. Resolved not to share the responsibility of the reverse he foresaw, Baron de Breteuil sent in his resignation.

Meanwhile the Treasury was found to be empty : Brienne appealed to the clergy, hoping to obtain from ecclesiastical wealth one of those gratuitous gifts which had often come in aid of the State's necessities. The Church herself was feeling the influence of the times. Without relaxing in her pretensions to the maintenance of privileges, the ecclesiastical assembly thought itself bound to plead the cause of that magistracy which it had so often fought. "Our silence," said the remonstrances, "would be a crime, of which the nation and posterity would never absolve us. Your Majesty has just effected at the bed of justice of May 8 a great movement as regards things and persons. Such ought to be a consequence rather than a preliminary of the States-general; the will of a prince which has not been enlightened by his courts may be regarded as a momentary will. Your Majesty has issued an edict carrying the restoration of the plenary court, but that court has recalled an ancient reign without recalling ancient ideas. Even if it had been once the supreme tribunal of our kings, it now presents no longer that numerous assemblage of prelates, barons and lieges united together. The nation sees in it nothing but a court-tribunal whose complaisance it would be afraid of and whose movements and intrigues it would dread in times of minority and regency. . . . Our functions are sacred when, from the height of the altars, we pray heaven to send down blessings on kings and on their subjects; they are still so, when, after teaching people their duties, we represent their rights and make solicitations on behalf of the afflicted, on behalf of the absent despoiled of their position and their liberty. The clergy of France, Sir, stretch forth to you their suppliant hands; it is so beautiful to see might and puissance yielding to prayer! The glory of your Majesty is not in being king of France, but in being king of the French, and the heart of your subjects in the fairest of your domains." The assembly of the clergy granted to the Treasury only a poor gift of eighteen hundred thousand livres.

All the resources were exhausted, disgraceful tricks had despoiled the hospitals and the poor; credit was used up, the payments of the State were backward; the discount-bank (*caisse d'escompte*) was authorized to refuse to give coin. To divert the public mind from this painful situation, Brienne proposed to the king to yield to the requests of the members of Parliament, of the clergy, and of the noblesse themselves. A decree of August 8, 1788, announced that the States-General would be convoked May 1, 1789; the re-establishment of the plenary court was suspended to that date. Concessions wrested from the weakness and irresolution of governments do not strengthen their failing powers. Brienne had exhausted his boldness as well as his basenesses; he succumbed beneath the outcry of public wrath and mistrust. He offered the comptroller-general-ship to M. Necker, who refused. "He told M. de Mercy," is the expression in Brienne's own account, "that under a minister who, like me, had lost the favour of the public, he could not do any good." A court-intrigue at last decided the minister's fall. The count of Artois, egged on by Madame de Polignac, made urgent entreaties to the queen; she was attached to Brienne; she, however, resigned herself to giving him up, but with so many favours and such an exhibition of kindness towards all his family that the public did not feel at all grateful to Marie Antoinette. Already Brienne had ex-changed the archbishopric of Toulouse for that of Sens, a much richer one. "The queen offered me the hat and anything I might desire," writes the prelate, "telling me that she parted from me with regret, weeping at being obliged to do so, and permitting me to kiss her (*l'embrasser*) in token of her sorrow and her interest." "After having made the mistake of bringing him into the ministry," says Madame Campan [*Mémoires*, t. i. p. 33], "the queen unfortunately made an equally grave one in supporting him at the time of a disgrace brought upon him by the despair of the whole nation. She considered it only consistent with her dignity to give him, at his departure, ostensible proofs of her esteem, and, her very sensibility misleading her, she sent him her portrait adorned with precious stones and the patent of lady of the palace for his niece, Madame de Courcy, saying that it was necessary to indemnify a minister sacrificed by the trickery of courts and the factious spirit of the nation. I have since seen the queen shed bitter tears over the errors she committed at this period."

On the 25th of August, 1788, the king sent for M. Necker.

A burst of public joy greeted the fall of the detested minister and the return of the popular minister. There were illuminations in the provinces as well as at Paris, at the Bastille as well as the houses of members of Parliament; but joy intermingled with hate is a brutal and a dangerous one: the crowd thronged every evening on the Pont-Neuf, forcing carriages as well as foot-passengers to halt in front of Henry IV.'s statue. "Hurrah! for Henry IV.! To the devil with Lamoignon and Brienne!" howled the people,

requiring all passers to repeat the same cry.   It was remarked that
the Duke of Orleans took pleasure in crossing over the Pont-Neuf
to come in for the cheers of the populace.   " He was more crafty
than ambitious, more depraved than naturally wicked," says M.
Malouet : " resentment towards the court had hurried him into
intrigue ; he wanted to become formidable to the queen.   His personal aim was vengeance rather than ambition, that of his petty
council was to effect an upheaval in order to set the prince at the
head of affairs as lieutenant-general and share the profits."

The tumult in the streets went on increasing : the keeper of the
seals, Lamoignon, had tried to remain in power.   M. Necker, supported by the queen, demanded his dismissal.   His departure, like
that of Brienne, had to be bought ; he was promised an embassy
for his son ; he claimed a sum of four hundred thousand livres ; the
Treasury was exhausted, and there was no finding more than half.
The greedy keeper of the seals was succeeded by Barentin, premier-
president of the Court of Aids.   Two dummies, one dressed in a
simarre (gown) and the other in pontifical vestments, were burned on
the Pont-Neuf : the soldiers, having been ordered to disperse the
crowds, some persons were wounded and others killed ; the mob had
felt sure that they would not be fired upon, whatever disorder they
showed ; the wrath and indignation were great ; there were threats
of setting fire to the houses of MM. de Brienne and de Lamoignon ;
the quarters of the commandant of the watch were surrounded.
The number of folks of no avocation, of mendicants and of vaga-
bonds was increasing every day in Paris.

Meanwhile the Parliament had gained its point, the great baillie-
courts were abolished ; the same difficulty had been found in con-
stituting them as in forming the plenary court ; all the magistrates
of the inferior tribunals refused to sit in them ; the Breton deputies
were let out of the Bastille ; everywhere the sovereign courts were
recalled.   The return of the exiles to Paris was the occasion for a
veritable triumph and the pretext for new disorders amongst the
populace.   It was the Parliament's first duty to see to the extraordinary police (*haute police*) in its district ; it performed the duty
badly and weakly.   The populace had applauded its return and had
supported its cause during its exile ; the first resolution of the

court was directed against the excesses committed by the military in repressing the disorders. When it came to trying the men seized with arms in their hands and the incendiaries who had threatened private houses, all had their cases dismissed; by way of example, one was detained a few days in prison. Having often been served in its enterprises by the passions of the mob, the Parliament had not foreseen the day when those same outbursts would sweep it away like chaff before the wind with all that regimen of tradition and respect to which it still clung even in its most audacious acts of daring.

For an instant the return of M. Necker to power had the effect of restoring some hope to the most far-sighted. On his coming into office, the Treasury was empty, there was no scraping together as much as five thousand livres. The need was pressing, the harvests were bad; the credit and the able resources of the great financier sufficed for all; the funds went up thirty per cent. in one day, certain capitalists made advances, the chamber of the notaries of Paris paid six millions into the Treasury, M. Necker lent two millions out of his private fortune. Economy had already found its way into the royal household; Louis XVI. had faithfully kept his promises; despite the wrath of courtiers, he had reduced his establishment. The duke of Coigny, premier equerry, had found his office abolished. " We were truly grieved, Coigny and I," said the king kindly, " but I believe he would have beaten me had I let him." " It is fearful to live in a country where one is not sure of possessing to-morrow what one had the day before," said the great lords who were dispossessed, " it's the sort of thing seen only in Turkey." Other sacrifices and more cruel lessons in the instability of human affairs were already in preparation for the French noblesse.

The great financial talents of M. Necker, his probity, his courage had caused illusions as to his political talents; useful in his day and in his degree, the new minister was no longer equal to the task. The distresses of the Treasury had powerfully contributed to bring about, to develope the political crisis; the public cry for the States-general had arisen in a great degree from the deficit; but henceforth financial resources did not suffice to conjure away the danger;

the Discount-bank had resumed payment, the State honoured its engagements, the phantom of bankruptcy disappeared from before the frightened eyes of stockholders; nevertheless the agitation did not subside, minds were full of higher and more tenacious concernments. Every gaze was turned towards the States-general. Scarcely was M. Necker in power, when a royal proclamation, sent to the Parliament returning to Paris, announced the convocation of the Assembly for the month of January, 1789.

The States-general themselves had become a topic of the most lively discussion. Amidst the embarrassment of his Government and in order to throw a sop to the activity of the Opposition, Brienne had declared his doubts and his deficiency of enlightenment as to the form to be given to the deliberations of that ancient assembly, always convoked at the most critical junctures of the national history, and abandoned for 175 years past. "The researches ordered by the king," said a decree of the Council, "have not brought to light any positive information as to the number and quality of the electors and those eligible, any more than as to the form of the elections; the king will always try to be as close as possible to the old usages, and, when they are unknown, his Majesty will not supply the hiatus till after consulting the wish of his subjects, in order that the most entire confidence may hedge a truly national assembly. Consequently the king requests all the municipalities and all the tribunals to make researches in their archives; he likewise invites all scholars and well-informed persons, and especially those who are members of the Academy of inscriptions and literature, to study the question and give their opinion." In the wake of this appeal, a flood of tracts and pamphlets had inundated Paris and the provinces: some devoted to the defence of ancient usages; the most part intended to prove that the Constitution of the olden monarchy of France contained in principle all the political liberties which were but asking permission to soar; some finally, bolder and the most applauded of all, like that of Count d'Entraigues, *Note on the States-general, their rights and the manner of convoking them,* and that of Abbé Sièyes, *What is the third estate?* Count d'Entraigues' pamphlet began thus: "It was doubtless in order to give the most heroic virtues a home worthy of them that heaven willed the existence of republics, and, perhaps to punish the ambition of men, it permitted great empires, kings and masters to arise." Sièyes' pamphlet had already sold to the extent of thirty thousand copies; the development of his ideas was an audacious commentary upon his modest title. "What is the third estate?" said that able revolutionist: "Nothing. What ought it to be? Everything?" It was hoisting the flag against the two upper orders. "The deputies of the clergy and of the noblesse have nothing in common with national representation," he said,

ABBÉ SIÈYES.

"and no alliance is possible between the three orders in the States-general."

It may be permissible to quote here a page or so from the second volume of this history. "At the moment when France was electing the constituent Assembly, a man, whose mind was more powerful than accurate, Abbé Sièyes, could say: 'What is the third estate? Everything. What has it been hitherto in the body politic? Nothing. What does it demand? To be something.' There were in these words three grave errors. In the **course of** the regimen anterior to 1789, so far was the third estate from being nothing that it had every day become greater and stronger. What was demanded for it in 1789 by M. Sièyes and his friends was not that it should become something but that it should be everything. It was to desire what was beyond its right and its might; the Revolution, which was its victory, itself proved this. Whatever may have been the weaknesses and the faults of its adversaries, the third estate had to struggle terribly to vanquish them, and the struggle was so violent and so obstinate that the third estate was shattered to pieces in it and paid right dearly for its triumph. It first of all found despotism instead of liberty; and when the liberty returned, the third estate found itself face to face with a two-fold hostility: that of its adversaries of the old regimen and that of absolute democracy, which, in its turn, claimed to be everything. Excessive pretension entails unmanageable opposition and excites unbridled ambition. What there was in the words of Abbé Sièyes, in 1789, was not the truth as it is in history; it was a lying programme of revolution. Taking the history of France in its totality and in all its phases, the third estate has been the most active and most decisive element in French civilization. If we follow it in its relations with the general government of the country, we see it first of all allied during six centuries with the kingship, struggling pauselessly against the feudal aristocracy, and giving the prevalence in place of that to a central and unique power, pure monarchy to wit, closely approximating, though with certain often repeated but vain reservations, to absolute monarchy. But, so soon as it has gained this victory and accomplished this revolution, the third estate pursues another; it attacks this unique power which it had contributed so much to establish, and it undertakes the task of changing pure monarchy into constitutional monarchy. Under whatever aspect we consider it in its two great and so very different enterprises, whether we study the progressive formation of French society itself or that of its government, the third estate is the most powerful and the most persistent of the forces which have had influence over French civilization. Not only is this fact novel, but it has for France quite a special interest, for, to make use of an expression which is much abused in our day, it is a fact eminently French, essentially national. Nowhere has burgessdom had a destiny so vast, so fertile as that which has fallen to it in France. There have been commons all over Europe, in Italy, in Spain, in Germany, in England, as well as in France. Not only have there been commons everywhere, but the commons in France are not those which, *quà* commons, under that name and in the middle ages, have played the greatest part and held the highest place in history. The Italian commons begot glorious republics. The German commons became free towns, sovereign towns, which have their own special history, and exercised throughout the general history of Germany a great deal of influence. The commons of England allied themselves with a portion of the English feudal aristocracy, formed, with it, the preponderating house in the British government, and thus played, full early, a powerful part in the history of their country. The French commons, under that name and in their season of special activity, were certainly far from rising to that importance in politics and that rank in history. And yet it is in France that the people of the commons, the burgessdom, became most completely, most powerfully developed, and ended by acquiring, in the general social body, the most decided preponderance. There have been commons throughout the whole of Europe; there has been in truth no third estate victorious save in France; it is in the French Revolution of 1789, assuredly the greatest, that the French third estate reached its ultimatum, and France is the only country where, in an access of burgess-pride, a man of great mind could say: 'What is the third estate? Everything.' "

So much excitement in men's minds and so much commotion amongst the masses reasonably disquieted prudent folks. In spite of its natural frivolity, the court was at bottom sad and anxious. The time had passed for the sweet life at the manor-house of Trianon, for rustic amusements and the charity of youth and romance. Marie Antoinette felt it deeply and bitterly; in the preceding year, at the moment when M. de Calonne was disputing with the Assembly of notables, she wrote to the duchess of Polignac, who had gone to take the waters in England: " Where you are you can at least enjoy the pleasure of not hearing affairs talked about.

Though in the country of upper and lower houses, of opposi-
tions and motions, you can shut your ears and let the talk glide;
but here there is a deafening noise, notwithstanding all I can do;
those words opposition and motion are as firmly established here
as in the Parliament of England, with this difference that, when
you go over to the opposition in London, you commence by relin-
quishing the king's graces, whereas here many oppose all the wise
and beneficent views of the most virtuous of masters and keep his
benefits all the same; that perhaps is more clever but it is not so
noble.   The time of illusions is over, and we are having some
cruel experiences.   Happily all the means are still in the king's
hands, and he will arrest all the mischief which the imprudent
want to make."   The queen preserved some confidence : she only
half-perceived the abyss beginning to yawn beneath her feet, she
had not yet criticized the weakness and insufficiency of the king
her husband; she did not as yet write : " The personage over me
is not fit, and as for me, whatever may be said and come what
may, I am never anything but secondary, and, in spite of the confidence reposed by the first, he often makes me feel it ; " she was
troubled, nevertheless, and others more sagacious were more so than
she.   " When I arrived at Paris, where I had not been for more than
three years," says M. Malouet, for a long while the king's com-
missioner in the colonies, and latterly superintendent of Toulon,
" observing the heat of political discussions as well as of the
pamphlets in circulation, M. d'Entraigues' work and Abbé Sièyes',
the troubles in Brittany and those in Dauphiny, my illusions
vanished; I was seized with all the terrors confided to me by
Abbé Raynal on my way to Marseilles.   I found M. Necker
beginning to be afraid, but still flattering himself that he would
have means of continuing, directing and bringing everything
right."   The Parliament was still more affrighted than M. Malouet
and M. Necker.   Summoned, on the 28th of September, to
enregister the king's proclamation relative to the convocation of
the States-general, it added this clause : " According to the forms
observed in 1614."   It was a reply in the negative on the part of
the magistracy to all the new aspirations, to the vote by polling
(*vote par tête*) as well as to the *doubling* of the third already gained

THE MANOR-HOUSE OF TRIANON.

in principle amongst the provincial assemblies; the popularity of the Parliament at once vanished. M. d'Esprémesnil, hardly returned from the isles of St. Marguerite and all puffed up with his glory, found himself abandoned by those who had been loudest in vaunting his patriotic zeal. An old councillor had but lately said to him, when he was calling for the States-general with all his might, " Providence will punish your fatal counsels by granting your wishes." After the triumph of his return to Paris, amidst the desert which was forming around the Parliament, "the martyr, the hero of liberty," as his enthusiastic admirers had been wont to call him, had to realize that instability of human affairs and that fragility of popularity to which he had shut his eyes even in his prison, when Mirabeau, ever biting and cynical, wrote to one of his friends : "Neighbourhood will doubtless procure you a visit from that immense D'Esprémesnil, the sage commentator upon Mesmer, who, from the isles of St. Marguerite even unto this place, has made everybody laugh at the ostentation with which he shook his fetters to make them clank."

The troubles amongst the populace had subsided, but agitation amongst the thoughtful went on increasing and the embarrassments of M. Necker increased with the agitation amongst the thoughtful. Naturally a stranger to politics properly so called, constantly engaged as he was in finance or administration, the minister's constitutional ideas were borrowed from England; he himself saw how inapplicable they were to the situation of France. " I was never called upon," he says in his Memoirs, " to examine closely into what I could make, at the time of my return to office, of my profound and particular esteem for the government of England, for, if at a very early period my reflections and my conversation could not but show symptoms of the opinions I held, at a very early period, also, I perceived how averse the king was from anything that might resemble the political practices and institutions of England." " M. Necker," says M. Malouet, " showed rare sagacity in espying in the greatest detail and on the furthest horizon the defects, the inconveniences of every measure, and it was this faculty of extending his observations to infinity which made him so often undecided." What with these doubts existing in his own mind and what with the antagonistic efforts of parties as well as individual wills, the minister conceived the hope of releasing himself from the crushing burthen of his personal responsibility; he convoked for the second time the Assembly of notables.

Impotent as it was in 1787, this assembly was sure to be and was even more so in 1788. Mirabeau had said with audacious intuition: "It is no longer a question of what has been, but of what has to be." The notables clung to the past like shipwrecked mariners who find themselves invaded by raging waters. Meeting on the 6th of November at Versailles, they opposed in mass the doubling of the third (estate); the committee presided over by *Monsieur*, the king's brother, alone voted for the double representation, and that by a majority of only one voice. The Assembly likewise refused to take into account the population of the circumscriptions (outlying districts) in fixing the number of its representatives; the seneschalty of Poitiers which numbered seven hundred thousand inhabitants was not to have more deputies than the bailiwick of Dourdan which had but eight thousand. The liberality on which the notables plumed themselves as regarded the qualifications required in respect of the electors and the eligible was at bottom as interested as it was injudicious. The fact of domicile and payment of taxes did not secure to the electors the guarantee given by property; the vote granted to all nobles whether enfeoffed or not and to all members of the clergy for the elections of their orders was intended to increase the weight of those elected by the number of suffrages; the high noblesse and the bishops reckoned wrongly upon the influence they would be able to exercise over their inferiors. Already, on many points, the petty nobles and the parish-priests were engaged and were to be still more deeply engaged on the popular side.

At the very moment when the public were making merry over the Assembly of notables and were getting irritated at the delay caused by their useless discussions in the convocation of the States-general, the Parliament, in one of those sudden fits of reaction with which they were sometimes seized from their love of popularity, issued a decree explanatory of their decision on the 24th of September. "The real intentions of the court," said the decree, "have been distorted in spite of their plainness. The number of deputies of each order is not determined by any law, by any invariable usage, and it depends upon the King's wisdom to adjudge what reason, liberty, justice and the general wish may indicate." The Parliament followed up this strange retractation with a series of wise and farsighted requests touching the totality of the public administration. Its part was henceforth finished, wisdom in words could not efface the effect of imprudent or weak acts; when the decree was presented to the king, he gave the deputation a cold reception. "I have no answer to make to the prayers of the Parliament," he replied, "it is with the States-general that I shall examine into the interests of my people."

Whilst all the constituted bodies of the third estate, municipalities, corporations, commissions of provincial assemblies were overwhelming the king with their addresses in favour of the people's rights, the prince of Conti, whose character always bore him into reaction against the current of public opinion, had put himself at the head of the opposition of the courtiers. Already at one of the committees of the Assembly of notables he had addressed *Monsieur*, the most favourable of all the princes to the liberal movement. "The very existence of the monarchy is threatened," he said, "its annihilation is desired and we are close upon that fatal moment. It is impossible that the king should not at last open his eyes and that the princes his brothers should not co-operate with him; be pleased, therefore, to represent to the king how important it is for the stability of his throne, for the laws and for good order, that the new systems be for ever put away and that the constitution and ancient forms be maintained in their integrity." Louis XVI. having shown some ill-humour at the prince of Conti's remarks, the latter sent him a letter signed by all the princes of the royal family except *Monsieur* and the duke of Orleans. The perils with which the State was threatened were evident and even greater than the prince's letter made out; the remedies they indicated were as insufficient in substance as they were contemptuous in form. "Let the third estate," they said, "cease to attack the rights of the two upper orders, rights which, not less ancient than the monarchy, ought to be as unalterable as

the Constitution; but let it confine itself to asking for diminution of
the imposts with which it may be surcharged; then the two upper
orders might, in the generosity of their feelings, give up prerogatives which have pecuniary interests for their object." . . . . Whilst
demanding on the part of the third estate this modest attitude, the
princes let fall threatening expressions, the use of which had been a
lost practice to the royal house since the days of the Fronde. "In
a kingdom in which for so long a time there have been no civil
dissensions, the word schism cannot be uttered without regret,"
they said; "such an event, however, would have to be expected if
the rights of the two upper orders suffered any alteration, and
what confidence would not be felt in the mind of the people
in protests which tended to release them from payment of imposts
agreed upon in the States?"

Thirty dukes and peers had beforehand proposed to the king the
renunciation of all their pecuniary privileges, assuring him that the
whole French noblesse would follow the example if they were consulted. Passions were too violently excited and the disorder of
ideas was too general to admit of the proper sense being given to
this generous and fruitless proceeding. The third estate looked
upon it as a manœuvre against double representation; the mass of
the two orders protested against the forced liberality which it was
attempted to thrust upon them. People made merry over the
signataries: "Have you read the letter of the *dupes* and peers?"
they said.

The Assembly of Notables had broken up on the 12th of
December; the convocation of the States-general was at hand,
and the government of King Louis XVI. still fluctuated unde-
cidedly between the various parties which were so violently disputing together over public opinion left to itself. The dismay
of wise men went on increasing, they were already conscious
of the fruitlessness of their attempts to direct those popular
passions of which they had but lately been reckoning upon availing
themselves in order to attain an end as laudable as it was moderate.
One of the most virtuous as well as the most enlightened and the
most courageous, M. Malouet, has related in his *Mémoires* the conversations he held at this very juncture with the ministers, M.

Necker and M. de Montmorin especially.   It is worth while to give
the complete summary, as sensible as it is firm, a truthful echo of
the thoughts in the minds of the cream of the men who had
ardently desired reforms and who attempted in vain to rein up the
Revolution in that fatal course which was to cost the lives of many
amongst them, and the happiness and peace of nearly all.

"It is the first Assembly of notables," said M. Malouet, "which
has apprised the nation that the government was henceforth
subordinated to public opinion.

MALOUET.

"This is a false and dangerous position, if it is not strong
enough to enlighten that opinion, direct it and restrain it.

"The wish of France has summoned the States-general, there
was no way but to obey it.   The doubling of the third (estate) is
likewise proclaimed in an irresistible manner, but as yet there is
nothing but your own mistakes to imperil the kingly authority.

"Your shiftings, your weaknesses, your inconsistencies no
longer leave you the resource of absolute power.   From the
moment that, exhibiting your embarrassments, you are obliged to
invoke the counsels and aid of the nation, you can no longer walk
without it; from its strength you must recruit your own; but

your wisdom must control its strength; if you leave it bridleless
and guideless, you will be crushed by it.

"You must not wait, then, for the States-general to make
demands upon you or issue orders to you; you must hasten to
offer all that sound minds can desire, within reasonable limits,
whether of authority or of national rights.

"Everything ought to be foreseen and calculated in the king's
council before the opening of the States-general. You ought to
determine what can be given up without danger in ancient usages,
forms, maxims, institutions, obsolete or full of abuses. All that
the public experience and reason denounce to you as proscribed,
take heed that you do not defend; but do not be so imprudent as
to commit to the risks of a tumultuous deliberation the fundamental
basis and the essential springs of the kingly authority. Commence
by liberally granting the requirements and wishes of the public,
and prepare yourselves to defend, even by force, all that violent,
factious and extravagant systems would assail. In the state of
uncertainty, embarrassment and denudation in which you have
placed yourselves, you have no strength, I can feel, I can see. Get
out, then, of this state; put fresh energy into your concessions,
into your plans; in a word, take up a decided attitude, for you
have it not.

"The revolution which is at this instant being effected and
which we may regard as accomplished is the elevation of the commons to an influence equal to that of the two other orders. Another
revolution must follow that, and it is for you to carry it out: that
is the destruction of privileges fraught with abuse and onerous to
the people. When I say that it is for you to carry it out, I mean
that you must take your measures in such wise as to prevent anything from being done without you, and otherwise than by your
direction.

"Thus, then, you should have a fixed plan of concessions, of
reforms, which, instead of upsetting everything, will consolidate
the basis of legitimate authority. This plan should become, by
your influence, the text of all the bailiwick memorials. God forbid
that I should propose to you to bribe, to seduce, to obtain influence
by iniquitous means over the elections! You need, on the con-

trary, the most honest, the most enlightened, the most energetic men. Such are those who must be brought to the front, and on whom the choice should be made to fall."

Admirable counsels on the part of the most honest and most far-sighted of minds; difficult, however, if not impossible, to be put into practice by feeble ministers, themselves still undecided on the very brink of the abyss, having to face the repugnance and the passions of the two privileged orders on which it was a question of imposing painful sacrifices, however legitimate and indispensable they might be.

M. Malouet and those who thought with him, more in number than anybody could tell, demanded instructions as to the elections in the bailiwicks. "Can you have allowed this great crisis to come on without any preparations for defence, without any combination?" they said to the ministers: "you have, through the police, the superintendents, the king's proctors in the tribunals, means of knowing men and choosing them, or, at any rate, of directing choice; these means, have you employed them?"

M. Necker could not give his instructions, he had not yet made up his mind on the question which was engaging everybody's thoughts; he hesitated to advise the king to consent to the doubling of the third. "He had a timid pride which was based on his means, on his celebrity, and which made him incessantly afraid of compromising himself with public opinion, which he could no longer manage to to control when he found himself opposed by it," said Malouet. Marmontel, who knew the minister well, added, "That solitary mind, abstracted, self-concentred, naturally enthusiastic, had little communication with men in general, and few men were tempted to have communication with him; he knew them only by glimpses too isolated or too vague, and hence his illusions as to the character of the people at whose mercy he was placing the State and the king."

M. Necker's illusions as to himself never disappeared; he had a vague presentiment of the weakening of his influence over public opinion, and he was pained thereat. He resolved at last to follow it. "It is a great mistake," he wrote at a later period in his *Mémoires*, "to pretend to struggle, with only antiquated notions on your side, against all the vigour of the principles of natural justice, when that justice renews its impulse and finds itself seconded by the natural desire of a nation.   The great test of ability in affairs is to obtain the merit of the sacrifice before the moment when that same sacrifice will appear a matter of necessity."

This favourable moment, which M. Necker still thought of seizing, had already slipped by him.   The royal resolution, proclaimed under this strange title, *Result of the king's council held on the 27th of December*, 1788, caused neither great astonishment nor lively satisfaction amongst the public.   M. Necker was believed to be more favourable to the doubling of the third (estate) than he really was; the king was known to be weak and resigned to following the counsels of the minister who had been thrust upon him.   "The cause of the third estate," said the report to the king, "will always have public opinion for it; the wishes of the third estate, when unanimous, when in conformity with the principles of equity, will always be only another name for the wishes of the nation; the judgment of Europe will encourage it.   I will say, then, upon my soul and conscience, and as a faithful servant of his Majesty, I do decidedly think that he may and ought to call to the States-general a number of deputies of the third estate equal to that of the deputies of the two other orders together, not in order to force on decisions by poll (*déliberation par tête*), as appears to be feared, but in order to satisfy the general wishes of the commons of his kingdom."   "The king," said the edict, "having heard the report made in his council by the minister of finance relative to the approaching convocation of the States-general, his Majesty has adopted its principles and views and has ordained what follows : 1° That the deputies shall be at least one thousand in number; 2° That the number shall be formed as nearly as possible in the compound ratio of the population and taxes of each bailiwick; 3° That the number of deputies of the third estate shall be equal to that of the two other orders together, and that this proportion shall be established by the letters of convocation."   The die was cast, the victory remained with the third (estate), legitimate in principle, and still possible perhaps to be directed and regulated, but dangerous and already menacing.   "It is not resistance from the two upper orders that I fear," said M. Malouet to the ministers, "it is the excess of the commons; you have done too much or let too much be done to prevent now the propositions I submitted to you from being realized; the point is not to go any further, for beyond lies anarchy. But if, in the very decided and very impetuous course taken by public opinion, the king should hesitate and the clergy and noblesse resist, woe to us, for all is lost! Do you expect the least appearance of order and reason in a gathering of twelve hundred legislators, drawn from all classes, without any practice in discussion and meditation over the important subjects they are about to handle, carried away by party-spirit, by the impetuous force of so many diverging interests and opinions? If you do not begin by giving them fixed ideas, by hedging them, through their constituents, with instructions and impediments which they cannot break through, look out for all sorts of vagaries, for irremediable disorders."

In his sad forecast of the confusion which threatened the new Assembly, M. Malouet counted too much upon the authority of mandates and upon the influence of the constituents; he was destined to look on, impotent and despairing, at that great outburst of popular passions which split asunder all ties and broke through all engagements as so many useless impediments. "When the Assembly in the first paroxysms of its delirium dared to annul its oaths and declared itself freed from the yoke of the instructions which we received from our constituents, the king had a right, what do I say? he was bound, to send us back to our bailiwicks," says M. Malouet. The States-general were convoked for the 27th of April, 1789, and not a soul had yet received instructions from the government. "Those that we did at last receive were as honest as they were insufficient. They told us in substance to get adopted, if we could, the proposal to present candidates for the departments and to admit into the list of candidates none but men whose morality, means and fair reputation were established, to prevent wrangles, schism between the orders, and to carry, as far as in us lay, the most moderate notions as regarded reforms and innovations. It was no longer the king speaking, it was the consulting counsel for the crown, asking advice of everybody and appearing to say to everybody: ' What's to be done? What can

I do? How much do they want to lop from my authority? How much of it will they leave me'?" [*Mémoires de M. Malouet*, t. i. p. 249.] It was a tacit abdication of the kingship at the juncture when its traditional authority, if not its very existence, was brought to book.

The party of honest men, still very numerous and recruited amongst all classes of society, went confidently to the general elections and preparatory assemblies which had to precede them. "Hardly conscious were they of the dark clouds which had gathered around us; the clouds shrouded a tempest which was not slow to burst" [*Ibidem*, p. 260].

The whole of France was fever-stricken. The agitation was contradictory and confused, a medley of confidence and fear, joy and rage, everywhere violent and contagious. This time again Dauphiny showed an example of politic and wise behaviour. The special states of the province had met on the 1st of December, 1788, authorized by the government, according to a new system proposed by the delegates of the three orders. Certain members of the noblesse and of the clergy had alone protested against the mode of election. Mounier constantly directed the decisions of the third (estate); he restrained and enlightened young Barnave, advocate in the court, who, for lack of his counsels, was destined to frequently go astray hereafter. The deliberations were invariably grave, courteous; a majority, as decided as it was tolerant, carried the day on all the votes. "When I reflect upon all we gained in Dauphiny by the sole force of justice and reason," wrote Mounier afterwards, in his exile, "I see how I came to believe that Frenchmen deserved to be free." M. Mounier published a work on the convocation of the States-general demanding the formation of two chambers. That was likewise the proposition of M. de La Luzerne, Bishop of Langres, an enlightened, a zealous and a farsighted prelate: "This plan had probably no approbation but mine," says M. Malouet. The opposition and the objections were diverse and contradictory, but they were general. Constitutional notions were as yet novel and full of confusion in all minds. The most sagacious and most prudent were groping their way towards a future enveloped in mist.

The useful example of Dauphiny had no imitators : Bourbonness and Hainault had accepted the system proposed by M. Necker for the formation of preparatory assemblies ; Normandy, faithful to its spirit of conservative independence, claimed its ancient privileges and refused the granted liberties. In Burgundy the noblesse declared that they would give up their pecuniary privileges, but that, on all other points, they would defend to the last gasp the ancient usages of the province. The clergy and noblesse of Languedoc held pretty much the same language. In Franche-Comté, where the states-provincial had not sat since Louis XIV.'s conquest, the strife was so hot on the subject of the administrative regimen, that the minister declared the assembly dissolved and referred the decision to the States-general. The Parliament of Besançon protested, declaring that the constitution of the province could not be modified save by the nationality of Franche-Comté, and that deputies to the States-general could not be elected save by the estates of the country assembled according to the olden rule. This pretension of the magistrates excluded the people from the elections ; they rose and drove the court from the sessions-hall.

Everywhere the preparatory assembles were disturbed, they were tumultuous in many spots : in Provence as well as in Brittany they became violent. In his province, Mirabeau was the cause or pretext for the troubles. Born at Bignon, near Nemours, on the 9th of March, 1749, well known already for his talent as a writer and orator as well as for the startling irregularities of his life, he was passionately desirous of being elected to the States-general. " I don't think I shall be useless there," he wrote to his friend Cerruti. Nowhere, however, was his character worse than in Provence : there people had witnessed his dissensions with his father as well as with his wife. Public contempt, a just punishment for his vices, caused his admission into the states-provincial to be unjustly opposed. The assembly was composed exclusively of nobles in possession of fiefs, of ecclesiastical dignitaries and of a small number of municipal officers. It claimed to elect the deputies to the States-general according to the ancient usages. Mirabeau's common sense, as well as his great and puissant genius, revolted against the absurd theories of the privileged; he overwhelmed them with his terrible eloquence, whilst adjuring them to renounce their abuseful and obsolete rights; he scared them by his forceful and striking hideousness: "Generous friends of peace," said he, addressing the two upper orders, "I hereby appeal to your honour! Nobles of Provence, the eyes of Europe are upon you, weigh well your answer! Ye men of God, have a care; God hears you! But, if you keep silence or if you intrench yourselves in the vague utterances of a piqued self-love, allow me to add a word. In all ages, in all countries, aristocrats have persecuted the friends of the people, and if, by I know not what combination of chances, there have arisen one in their own midst, he it is whom they have struck above all, thirsting as they were to inspire terror by their choice of a victim. Thus perished the last of the Gracchi, by the hand of the patricians; but, wounded to the death, he flung dust towards heaven, calling to witness the gods of vengeance, and from that dust sprang Marius, Marius less great for having exterminated the Cimbri than for having struck down at Rome the aristocracy of the noblesse."

Mirabeau was shut out from the states-provincial and soon adopted eagerly by the third estate. Elected at Marseilles as well as at Aix for the States-general, he quieted in these two cities successively riots occasioned by the dearness of bread. The people, in their enthusiasm, thronged upon him, accepting his will without a murmur when he restored to their proper figure provisions lowered in price through the terror of the authorities. The petty noblesse and the lower provincial clergy had everywhere taken the side of the third estate. Mirabeau was triumphant: "I have been, am, and shall be to the last," he exclaimed, "the man for public liberty, the man for the constitution. Woe to the privileged orders, if that means better be the man of the people than the man of the nobles, for privileges will come to an end, but the people is eternal!"

Brittany possessed neither a Mounier nor a Mirabeau; the noblesse there were numerous, bellicose and haughty, the burgess-dom rich and independent. Discord was manifested at the commencement of the states-provincial assembled at Rennes in the

latter part of December, 1788.   The governor wanted to suspend
the sessions, the two upper orders persisted in meeting; there was
fighting in the streets.   The young men flocked in from the neighbouring towns; the states-room was blockaded.   For three days
the members who had assembled there endured a siege; when they
cut their way through, sword in hand, several persons were killed:
the enthusiasm spread to the environs.   At Angers, the women
published a resolution declaring that " the mothers, sisters, wives,
and sweethearts of the young citizens of Angers would join them
if they had to march to the aid of Brittany and would perish
rather than desert the nationality."   When election-time arrived,
and notwithstanding the concessions which had been made to them
by the government, the Breton nobles refused to proceed to the
nominations of their order if the choice of deputies were not
entrusted to the states-provincial; they persisted in staying away,
thus weakening by thirty voices their party in the States-general.

The great days were at hand.   The whole of France was
absorbed in the drawing-up of the *memorials* (*cahiers*) demanded by
the government from each order, in each bailiwick.   The weather
was severe, the harvest had been bad, the suffering was extreme.
" Famine and fear of insurrection overthrew M. Necker, the
means of providing against them absorbed all his days and nights
and the greater part of the money he had at his disposal."
Agitators availed themselves ably of the misery as a means of
exciting popular passion.   The alms-giving was enormous, charity
and fear together opened both hearts and purses.   The gifts of the
duke of Orleans to the poor of Paris appeared to many people
suspicious; but the archbishop of Paris, M. de Juigné, without
any other motive but his pastoral devotion, distributed all he
possessed and got into debt four hundred thousand livres in order
to relieve his flock.   The doors of the finest houses were opened
to wretches dying of cold, anybody might go in and get warmed
in the vast halls.   The regulations for the elections had just been
published (24th of January, 1789).   The number of deputies was
set at twelve hundred.   The electoral conditions varied according
to order and dignity, as well as according to the extent of the bailiwicks; in accordance with the opinion of the Assembly of notables,

the simple fact of nationality and of inscription upon the register of taxes constituted electoral rights. No rating (*cens*) was required.

The preparatory labours had been conducted without combination, the elections could not be simultaneous; no powerful and dominant mind directed that bewildered mass of ignorant electors, exercising for the first time, under such critical circumstances, a right of which they did not know the extent and did not foresee the purport. "The people has more need to be governed and subjected to a protective authority than it has fitness to govern," M. Malouet had said in his speech to the assembly of the three orders in the bailiwick of Riom. The day, however, was coming when the conviction was to be forced upon this people, so impotent and incompetent in the opinion of its most trusty friends, that the sovereign authority rested in its hands, without direction and without control.

"The elective assembly of Riom was not the most stormy," says M. Malouet who, like M. Mounier at Grenoble, had been elected by acclamation head of the deputies of his own order at Riom, "but it was sufficiently so to verify all my conjectures and cause me to truly regret that I had come to it and had obtained the deputyship. I was on the point of giving in my resignation, when I found some petty burgesses, lawyers, advocates without any information about public affairs, quoting the *Contrat social*, declaiming vehemently against tyranny, abuses, and proposing a constitution apiece. I pictured to myself all the disastrous consequences which might be produced upon a larger stage by such outrageousness, and I arrived at Paris very dissatisfied with myself, with my fellow-citizens, and with the ministers who were hurrying us into this abyss."

The king had received all the memorials; on some few points the three orders had commingled their wishes in one single *memorial*. M. Malouet had failed to get this done in Auvergne. "The clergy insist upon putting theology into their memorials," he wrote to M. de Montmorin, on the 24th of March, 1789, "and the noblesse compensations for pecuniary sacrifice. I have exhausted my lungs and have no hope that we shall succeed completely on all points, but the differences of opinion between the noblesse and the third estate are not embarrassing. There is rather more pigheadedness amongst the clergy as to their debt, which they decline to pay, and as to some points of discipline which, after all, are matters of indifference to us; we shall have, all told, three memorials of which the essential articles are pretty similar to those of the third estate. We shall end as we began, peaceably."

"The memorials of 1789," says M. de Tocqueville [*L'ancien régime et la Révolution*, p. 211], "will remain as it were the will and testament of the old French social system, the last expression of its desires, the authentic manifesto of its latest wishes. In its totality and on many points it likewise contained in the germ the principles of new France. I read attentively the memorials drawn up by the three orders before meeting in 1789, I say the three orders, those of the noblesse and clergy as well as those of the third estate, and when I come to put together all these several wishes, I perceive with a sort of terror that what is demanded is the simultaneous and systematic abolition of all the laws and all the usages having currency in the country, and I see at a glance that there is about to be enacted one of the most vast and most dangerous revolutions ever seen in the world. Those who will to-morrow be its victims have no idea of it, they believe that the total and sudden transformation of so complicated and so old a social system can take effect without any shock by the help of reason and its power alone. Poor souls! They have forgotten even that maxim which their fathers expressed four hundred years before in the simple and forcible language of those times: 'By quest of too great franchise and liberties, getteth one into too great serfage.'"

However terrible and radical it may have been in its principles and its results, the French Revolution did not destroy the past and its usages, it did not break with tradition so completely as was demanded, in 1789, by the memorials of the three orders, those of the noblesse and the clergy, as well as those of the third estate.

One institution, however, was nowhere attacked or discussed. "It is not true," says M. Malouet, "that we were sent to constitute the kingship, but undoubtedly to regulate the exercise of powers conformably with our instructions. Was not the kingship constituted in law and in fact? Were we not charged to respect it, to maintain it on all its bases?" Less than a year after the Revolution had begun, Mirabeau wrote privately to the king: "Compare the new state of things with the old regimen, there is the source of consolations and hopes. A portion of the acts of the National Assembly, and the most considerable too, is clearly favourable to monarchical government. Is it nothing, pray, to be without parliaments, without states-districts, without bodies of clergy, of privileged, of noblesse? The idea of forming but one single class of citizens would have delighted Richelieu. This even surface facilitates the exercise of power. Many years of absolute government could not have done so much as this single year of revolution for the kingly authority."

Genius has lights which cannot be obscured by either mental bias or irregularities of life. Rejected by the noblesse, dreaded by the third estate, even when it was under his influence, Mirabeau constantly sought alliance between the kingship and liberty. "What is most true and nobody can believe," he wrote to the duke of Lauzun on the 24th of December, 1788, "is that, in the National Assembly, I shall be a most zealous monarchist, because I feel most deeply how much need we have to slay ministerial despotism and resuscitate the kingly authority." The States-general were scarcely assembled when the fiery orator went to call upon M. Malouet. The latter was already supposed to be hostile to the revolution. "Sir," said Mirabeau, "I come to you because of your reputation; and your opinions, which are nearer my own than you suppose, determine this step on my part. You are, I know, one of liberty's discreet friends, and so am I; you are scared by the tempests gathering, and I no less; there are amongst us more than one hot head, more than one dangerous man; in the two upper orders all that have brains have not common sense, and amongst the fools I know several capable of setting fire to the magazine. The question, then, is to know whether the monarchy and the monarch shall survive the storm which is a-brewing, or whether the faults committed and those which will not fail to be still committed shall engulf us all."

M. Malouet listened, not clearly seeing the speaker's drift.

Mirabeau resumed : " What I have to add is very simple : I know that you are a friend of M. Necker's and of M. de Montmorin's, who form pretty nearly all the king's council ; I don't like either of them, and I don't suppose that they have much liking for me. But it matters little whether we like one another, if we can come to an understanding. I desire, then, to know their intentions. I apply to you to get me a conference. They would be very culpable or very narrow-minded, the king himself would be inexcusable, if he aspired to reduce the States-general to the same limits and the same results as all the others have had. That will not do, they must have a plan of adhesion or opposition to certain principles. If that plan is reasonable under the monarchical system, I pledge myself to support it and employ all my means, all my influence to prevent that invasion of the democracy which is coming upon us."

This was M. Malouet's advice, incessantly repeated to the ministers for months past ; he reported to them what Mirabeau had said ; both had a bad opinion of the man and some experience of his want of scruple. " M. Necker looked at the ceiling after his fashion, he was persuaded that Mirabeau had not and could not have any influence." He was in want of money, it was said. M. Necker at last consented to the interview. Malouet was not present, as he should have been. Deprived of this sensible and well-disposed intermediary, the Genevese stiffness and the Provençal ardour were not likely to hit it off. Mirabeau entered. They saluted one another silently and remained for a moment looking at one another. " Sir," said Mirabeau, " M. de Malouet has assured me that you understood and approved of the grounds for the explanation I desire to have with you." " Sir," replied M. Necker, " M. Malouet has told me that you had proposals to make to me, what are they ?" Mirabeau, hurt at the cold, interrogative tone of the minister and the sense he attached to the word *proposals*, jumps up in a rage and says, " My proposal is to wish you good day." Then, running all the way and fuming all the while, Mirabeau arrives at the sessions-hall. " He crossed all scarlet with rage over to my side," says M. Malouet, " and, as he put his leg over one of our benches, he said to me, ' Your man is a fool, he shall hear of me.' "

When the expiring kingship recalled Mirabeau to its aid, it was too late for him and for it. He had already struck fatal blows at the cause which he should have served, and already death was threatening himself with its finishing stroke. " He was on the point of rendering great services to the State," said Malouet: " shall I tell you how ? By confessing to you his faults and pointing out your own, by preserving to you all that was pure in the Revolution and by energetically pointing out to you all its excesses and the danger of those excesses, by making the people affrighted at their blindness and the factious at their intrigues. He died ere this great work was accomplished ; he had hardly given an inkling of it."

Timidity and maladdress do not retard perils by ignoring them. The day of meeting of the States-general was at hand. Almost everywhere the elections had been quiet and the electors less numerous than had been anticipated. We know what indifference and lassitude may attach to the exercise of rights which would not be willingly renounced ; ignorance and inexperience kept away from the primary assemblies many working-men and peasants ; the middle class alone proceeded in mass to the elections. The irregular slowness of the preparatory operations had retarded the convocations ; for three months, the agitation attendant upon successive assemblies kept France in suspense. Paris was still voting on the 28th of April, 1789, the mob thronged the streets ; all at once the rumour ran that an attack was being made on the house of an ornamental-paper maker in the faubourg St. Antoine, named Réveillon. Starting as a simple journeyman, this man had honestly made his fortune; he was kind to those who worked in his shops : he was accused, nevertheless, amongst the populace, of having declared that a journeyman could live on fifteen sous a day. The day before, threats had been levelled at him ; he had asked for protection from the police, thirty men had been sent to him. The madmen who were swarming against his house and stores soon got the better of so weak a guard, everything was destroyed ; the rioters rushed to the archbishop's, there was voting going on there ; they expected to find Réveillon there, whom they wanted to murder. They were repulsed by the battalions of the French and Swiss guards. More than two hundred were killed. Money was found in their pockets. The Parliament suspended its prosecutions against the ringleaders of so many crimes. The Government, impotent and disarmed, as timid in presence of this riot as in presence of opposing parties, at last came before the States-general, but blown about by the contrary winds of excited passions, without any guide and without fixed resolves, without any firm and compact nucleus in the midst of a new and unknown Assembly, without confidence in the troops, who were looked upon, however, as a possible and last resort.

The States-general were presented to the king on the 2nd of May, 1789. It seemed as if the two upper orders, by a prophetic instinct of their ruin, wanted, for the last time, to make a parade of their privileges. Introduced without delay to the king, they left, in front of the palace, the deputies of the third estate to wait in the rain. The latter were getting angry and already beginning to clamour, when the gates were opened to them. In the magnificent procession on the 4th, when the three orders accompanied the king to the church of St. Louis at Versailles, the laced coats and decorations of the nobles, the superb vestments of the prelates easily eclipsed the modest cassocks of the country-priests as well as the sombre costume imposed by ceremonial upon the deputies of the third estate; the bishop of Nancy, M. de la Fare, maintained the traditional distinctions even in the sermon he delivered before the king: " Sir," said he, " accept the homage of the clergy, the respects of the noblesse and the most humble supplications of the third estate." The untimely applause which greeted the bishop's words was excited by the picture he drew of the misery in the country-places exhausted by the rapacity of the fiscal agents. At this striking solemnity, set off with all the pomp of the past, animated with all the hopes of the future, the eyes of the public sought out, amidst the sombre mass of deputies of the third (estate), those whom their deeds, good or evil, had already made celebrated: Malouet, Mounier, Mirabeau, the last greeted with a murmur which was for a long while yet to accompany his name. " When the summons by name per bailiwick took place," writes an eye-witness, " there were cheers for certain deputies who

were known, but at the name of Mirabeau there was a noise of
a very different sort. He had wanted to speak on two or three
occasions, but a general murmur had prevented him from making
himself heard. I could easily see how grieved he was, and I
observed some tears of vexation standing in his bloodshot eyes"
[*Souvenirs de Dumont*, p. 47].

Three great questions were already propounded before the
Assembly entered into session; those of verification of powers, of
deliberation by the three orders in common and of vote by poll.
The wise men had desired that the king should himself see to the
verification of the powers of the deputies and that they should
come to the Assembly confirmed in their mandates. People likewise expected to find, in the speech from the throne or in the
minister's report, an expression of the royal opinions on the two
other points in dispute. In a letter drawn up by M. Mounier and
addressed to the king, the estates of Dauphiny had referred, the
year before, to the ancient custom of the States-general. "Before
the States held at Orleans in 1569," said this document, "the
orders deliberated most frequently together, and, when they broke
up, they afterwards met to concert their deliberations; they
usually chose only one president, only one speaker for all the
orders, generally amongst the members of the clergy. The States
of Orleans had the imprudence not to follow the forms previously
observed and the orders broke up. The clergy in vain invited
them to have but one common memorial and to choose one single
speaker, but they were careful to protest that this innovation
would not interfere with the unity and integrity of the body of the
States. The clergy's speaker said in his address that the three
estates, as heretofore, had but one mouth, one heart and one spirit.
In spite of these protests, the fatal example set by the States of
Orleans was followed by those of Blois and those of 1614. Should
it be again imitated, we fear that the States-general will be powerless to do anything for the happiness of the kingdom and the glory
of the throne, and that Europe will hear with surprise that the
French know neither how to bear servitude nor how to deserve
freedom."

An honest but useless appeal to the memories of the far past!

Times were changed ; whereas the municipal officers representing the third estate used to find themselves powerless in presence of the upper orders combined, the third (estate), now equal to the privileged by extension of its representation, counted numerous adherents amongst the clergy, amongst the country-parsons and even in the ranks of the noblesse. Deliberation in common and vote by poll delivered the two upper orders into its hands ; this was easily forgotten by the partisans of a re-union which was desirable and even necessary, but which could not be forced upon the clergy or noblesse, and which they could only effect with a view to the public good and in the wise hope of preserving their influence by giving up their power. All that preparatory labour characteristic of the free, prudent and bold, frank and discreet government, had been neglected by the feebleness or inexperience of the ministers. " This poor government was at grips with all kinds of perils, and the man who had shown his superiority under other difficult circumstances flinched beneath the weight of these. His talents were distempered, his lights danced about, he was sustained only by the rectitude of his intentions and by vanity born of his hopes, for he had ever in reserve that perspective of confidence and esteem with which he believed the third estate to be impressed towards him ; but the promoters of the revolution, those who wanted it complete and subversive of the old government, those men who were so small a matter at the outset, either in weight or in number, had too much interest in annihilating M. Necker not to represent as pieces of perfidy his hesitations, his tenderness towards the two upper orders and his air of restraint towards the commons " [*Mémoires de M. Malouet*, t. i. p. 236].

It was in this state of feeble indecision as regarded the great questions and with this minuteness of detail in secondary matters that M. Necker presented himself on the 5th of May before the three orders at the opening of the session in the palace of Versailles by King Louis XVI. The royal procession had been saluted by the crowd with repeated and organized shouts of " Hurrah ! for the duke of Orleans !" which had disturbed and agitated the queen. " The king," says Marmontel, " appeared with simple dignity, without pride, without timidity, wearing on

his features the impress of the goodness which he had in his
heart, a little affected by the spectacle and by the feelings
which the deputies of a faithful nation ought to inspire in
its king." His speech was short, dignified, affectionate, and
without political purport. With more of pomp and detail, the
minister confined himself within the same limits. "Aid his
Majesty," said he, "to establish the prosperity of the kingdom on
solid bases, seek for them, point them out to your sovereign, and
you will find on his part the most generous assistance." The mode
of action corresponded with this insufficient language. Crushed
beneath the burthen of past defaults and errors, the government
tendered its abdication, in advance, into the hands of that mightily
bewildered Assembly it had just convoked. The king had left the
verification of powers to the States-general themselves. M. Necker
confined himself to pointing out the possibility of common action
between the three orders, recommending the deputies to examine
those questions discreetly. "The king is anxious about your first
deliberations," said the minister, throwing away at hap-hazard upon
leaders as yet unknown the direction of those discussions which he
with good reason dreaded. "Never did political assembly combine so great a number of remarkable men," says M. Malouet,
"without there being a single one whose superiority was decided
and could command the respect of the others. Such abundance of
stars rendered this assembly unmanageable, as they will always be
in France when there is no man conspicuous in authority and in
force of character to seize the helm of affairs or to have the direction
spontaneously surrendered to him. Fancy then the state of a
meeting of impassioned men, without rule or bridle, equally
dangerous from their bad and their good qualities, because they
nearly all lacked experience and a just appreciation of the gravity
of the circumstances under which they were placed; insomuch
that the good could do no good and the bad, from levity, from
violence, did nearly always more harm than they intended."

It was amidst such a chaos of passions, wills, and desires, legitimate or culpable, patriotic or selfish, that there was, first of all,
propounded the question of verification of powers. Prompt and
peremptory on the part of the noblesse, hesitating and cautious on

MIRABEAU AND DREUX-BRÉZÉ.

the part of the clergy, the opposition of the two upper orders to any common action irritated the third estate; its appeals had ended in nothing but conferences broken off, then resumed at the king's desire, and evidently and painfully to no purpose. "By an inconceivable oversight on the part of M. Necker in the local apportionment of the building appointed for the Assembly of the States-general, there was the throne-room or room of the three orders, a room for the noblesse, one for the clergy, and none for the commons, who remained, quite naturally, established in the states-room, the largest, the most ornate, and all fitted up with tribunes for the spectators who took possession of the public boxes (*loges communes*) in the room. When it was perceived that this crowd of strangers and their plaudits only excited the audacity of the more violent speakers, all the consequences of this installation were felt. Would anybody believe," continues M. Malouet, "that M. Necker had an idea of inventing a ground-slip, a falling-in of the cellars of the Menus, and of throwing down, during the night, the carpentry of the grand room, in order to remove and install the three orders separately? It was to me myself that he spoke of it, and I had great difficulty in dissuading him from the notion, by pointing out to him all the danger of it." The want of foresight and the nervous hesitation of the ministers had placed the third estate in a novel and a strong situation. Installed officially in the states-room, it seemed to be at once master of the position, waiting for the two upper orders to come to it. Mirabeau saw this with that rapid insight into effects and consequences which constitutes, to a considerable extent, the orator's genius. The third estate had taken possession, none could henceforth dispute with it its privileges, and it was the defence of a right that had been won which was to inspire the fiery orator with his mighty audacity, when on the 23rd of June, towards evening, after the miserable affair of the royal session, the marquis of Dreux-Brézé came back into the room to beg the deputies of the third estate to withdraw. The king's order was express, but already certain nobles and a large number of ecclesiastics had joined the deputies of the commons; their definitive victory on the 27th of June and the fusion of the three orders were foreshadowed; Mirabeau rose at the entrance of the grand-master of the ceremonies : " Go," he shouted, " and tell those who send you, that we are here by the will of the people, and that we shall not budge save at the point of the bayonet." This was the beginning of revolutionary violence.

On the 12th of June the battle began ; the calling over of the bailiwicks took place in the States-room. The third estate sat alone. At each province, each chief-place, each roll (*procès-verbal*), the secretaries repeated in a loud voice, " Gentlemen of the clergy? None present. Gentlemen of the noblesse? None present." Certain parish-priests alone had the courage to separate from their order and submit their powers for verification. All the deputies of the third (estate) at once gave them precedence. The day of persecution was not yet come.

Legality still stood, the third estate maintained a proud moderation, the border was easily passed, a name was sufficient.

The title of States-general was oppressive to the new Assembly, it recalled the distinction between the orders as well as the humble posture of the third estate heretofore. " This is the only true name," exclaimed Abbé Siéyes : " Assembly of acknowledged and verified representatives of the nation." This was a contemptuous repudiation of the two upper orders. Mounier replied with another definition : " Legitimate Assembly of the majority amongst the deputies of the nation, deliberating in the absence of the duly invited minority." The subtleties of metaphysics and politics are powerless to take the popular fancy. Mirabeau felt it : " Let us call ourselves *representatives of the people !* " he shouted. For this ever fatal name he claimed the kingly sanction : " I hold the king's *veto* so necessary," said the great orator, " that, if he had it not, I would rather live at Constantinople than in France. Yes, I protest, I know of nothing more terrible than a sovereign aristocracy of six hundred persons who, having the power to declare themselves to-morrow irremoveable and the next day hereditary, would end, like the aristocracies of all countries in the world, by swooping down upon everything."

An obscure deputy here suggested during the discussion the name of *National Assembly*, often heretofore employed to designate the States-general ; Siéyes took it up, rejecting the subtle and carefully prepared definitions: "I am for the amendment of M. Legrand," said he, "and I propose the title of *National Assembly.*" Four hundred and ninety-one voices against ninety adopted this simple and superb title. In contempt of the two upper orders of the State, the national assembly was constituted. The decisive step was taken towards the French Revolution.

During the early days, in the heat of a violent discussion, Barrère had exclaimed, "You are summoned to recommence history." It was an arrogant mistake. For more than eighty years modern France has been prosecuting laboriously and in open day the work which had been slowly forming within the dark womb of olden France. In the almighty hands of eternal God a people's history is interrupted and recommenced never.

INDEX.

———◆———

The Roman Numerals refer to the Volumes, and the Arabic to the Pages.

END OF THE FIFTH VOLUME.